M. and Mme de La Tour du Pin.

Their children

Humbert

Aymar

Charlotte

Cécile

ESCAPE FROM THE TERROR

The Journal of Madame de la Tour du Pin

EDITED AND TRANSLATED BY
FELICE HARCOURT

London
The Folio Society
1979

PRINTED IN GREAT BRITAIN
by W & J Mackay Limited, Chatham

CONTENTS

INTRODUCTION   7

PART ONE

I   My uncle, the archbishop. Life at Hautefontaine   13
II My mother and grandmother. My mother's last illness. A
    journey to Montpellier   18
III The problems of travel. My father's diplomatic career.
    Mme Dillon's family   27
IV The Maréchal de Biron. My future is to be decided   39
V   I see my future husband. The Assembly of Notables. I am
    received by the queen   45
VI My wedding day. I am presented at Court. A month's
    leave at Montfermeil   52
VII Dissension in the Netherlands. My aunt's house in Paris.
    Mme De Bouillon. The Court at Versailles   62
VIII Discontent in my husband's regiment. Musical gatherings 73
IX My new acquaintance, Mme de Genlis. The opening
    of the States-General. The capture of the Bastille. I am
    mistaken for the queen   80
X   Feudal rights abolished. Mme de Staël. The regimental
    dinner. The women march to Versailles. Order is restored.
    The mob attacks. A sad procession to Paris   92
XI 'Bastille Day.' The queen's hatred for M. de La Fayette.
    Questioned by the Commune. We arrive in Lausanne   111
XII We prepare to leave for Holland. The king accepts the
    Constitution. Fêtes, balls, suppers and amusements. The flight
    of the émigrés. Antwerp falls to the French. A hazardous
    journey   124
XIII Life at Passy. An arrest and some decisions. The revolu-
    tionary army enters Bordeaux. A visit from the Citizen
    Guard. My husband's escape. Le Bouilh is seized   140
XIV A surfeit of taxes. 'Citizeness Thérèsia Cabarrus.' My
    meeting with Tallien. My husband in hiding. The climax of
    the Terror   153
XV Escape plans. A dangerous journey. Obtaining a passport 165
XVI We are ready to leave. Aboard the *Diana*. 'No passengers,
    no cargo.' Privations on board ship   171

PART TWO

XVII   A familiar bark. A month in Boston. The Renslaer family   183

XVIII   The Van Buren's Farm. A log house at Troy. The end of the Terror. A day with the Renslaers. Adding to our negro staff   192

XIX   Colonists on the road to prosperity. 'Old Squaw.' I catch a fever. The Quaker settlement. The Duc de Liancourt   206

XX   The treason of General Arnold. A family tragedy. News of our properties in France   217

XXI   A passage to Cadiz. A birth on the journey. Arrival in Madrid   227

XXII   The Escurial. Return to France. Marguérite's story. A magnificent luncheon   238

XXIII   We decide to go to England. Settling in Bolton Row. A day's racing at Newmarket. Mme Dillon's debts   248

XXIV   Mme de Bouillon's visit. Émigré life in Richmond. An unhappy marriage   260

XXV   The fall of the Directorate. Cécile is born. Mme Bonaparte, a rising star. A visit to Malmaison   268

XXVI   Educating Mlle de Lally. Mme de Duras at Le Bouilh. My husband returns from Paris   280

XXVII   Napoleon comes to Cubzac. I am presented to the emperor. The Queen of Spain   287

XXVIII   My half-sister, Fanny. My sister agrees to marry. Napoleon's interest in the marriage   297

XXIX   Napoleon marries Marie-Louise. Dining with the emperor. An official visit of inspection   306

XXX   My husband is dismissed. My audience with the emperor. Expressions of regret and goodwill   315

XXXI   The Prefecture of Amiens. 'Your emperor is finished.' Louis XVIII returns to France   324

XXXII   André Dumont's pamphlet. Aymar's illness. Rumours of Napoleon's return. I prepare to leave France. Napoleon lands at Cannes   335

FAMILY TREES   347

ILLUSTRATIONS

M. and Mme de La Tour du Pin and their children, Humbert, Charlotte, Cécile and Aymar. (*Comte Christian de Liedekerke-Beaufort*) *frontispiece*

Comte Arthur Dillon (1750–1794), father of Mme de La Tour du Pin
Comte de La Tour du Pin de Gouvernet (1727–1794), father of M. de La Tour du Pin.
(*Comte Christian de Liedekerke-Beaufort*) *facing page* 32

Louis XVI (1754–1793). Painting by Duplessis, at Versailles
Marie-Antoinette (1755–1793). Painting by Drouais
(*Radio Times Hulton Picture Library*) 65

The opening of the States-General, 5 May 1789. Engraving by Monet.
The Regimental Banquet, held in the Opera House at Versailles, 1789.
(*Mansell Collection*) 96

The women of Les Halles set out for Versailles, 5 October 1789.
The return from Versailles, 5 October 1789.
(*Mansell Collection*) 105

The General Federation of 14 July 1790, held in the Champ de Mars. (*Mansell Collection*)
The Arrest of Louis XVI at Varennes, 22 June 1791. (*Mary Evans Picture Library*) 120

Three Revolutionary Figures:
M. Tallien, leader of the Revolution in Bordeaux. Engraving, 1794. (*Mansell Collection*)
Honoré Gabriel Riquetti, Comte de Mirabeau, 1749–1791. Lithograph. (*Radio Times Hulton Picture Library*)
Robespierre. Painting by Greuze. (*Mansell Collection*) 161

The *Diane*, 1794. The ship in which the family escaped to America. (*Comte Christian de Liedekerke-Beaufort*)
Albany, from Van Renslaer's Island. (*Mary Evans Picture Library*) 192

Mme de La Tour du Pin on her farm, near Albany. (*Comte Christian de Liedekerke-Beaufort*)
West Point, New York. Engraving by James D. Smillie. (*Mary Evans Picture Library*)   225

Mme de Staël, by Mlle E de Godefroy at Versailles, from a painting by Gerard. (*Radio Times Hulton Picture Library*)
Mme d'Hénin (1749–1826), Mme de La Tour du Pin's aunt. (*Comte Christian de Liedekerke-Beaufort*)   256

Napoleon, Emperor of the French (1769–1821). By Delaroche. (*Radio Times Hulton Picture Library*)
Louis XVIII. (*Mansell Collection*)   289

Château du Bouilh, near St André-de-Cubzac, Gironde. (From a photograph)
Comte Auguste de Liedekerke-Beaufort (1789–1855). (*Comte Christian de Liedekerke-Beaufort*)   320

INTRODUCTION

The Marquise de La Tour du Pin was born Henrietta-Lucy Dillon, descendent of Irish and English Jacobites exiled after the defeat of James II in 1691. She was born in 1770, when France had been the home of her family, and many of its connections, for some four generations. They were prominent in Jacobite circles and also at Versailles, Catholic in religion, French by upbringing and in their loyalties, but closely in touch with those members of their families who had remained in England or Ireland.

In 1688, when Louis XIV encouraged James II to invade Ireland in order to regain his English throne, Theobald, 7th Viscount Dillon, had raised on his Irish estates a regiment of two battalions for the Stuart cause. In April 1690, it was sent to France under the command of a younger son, eighteen-year-old Colonel Arthur Dillon, as part of the Mountcashel Brigade, a force of 6,000 Irish troops demanded by Louis in return for the 6,000 trained French soldiers James had asked for. After James' defeat in 1691, the Dillon Regiment remained in France with the exiled king and the many supporters who had accompanied him. It continued to serve France, part of what became known as the Irish Brigade, and its young Colonel proprietor earned both distinction and ennoblement.

The Comte Dillon, as he became, married Miss Christine Sheldon and, of their five sons, four commanded the regiment in turn. In 1743, when England took the field against France in support of Austria, the Colonel proprietor was their second son, Henry. He had by then succeeded to the Dillon peerage and, in order to preserve both the peerage and the Irish family properties, he gave the Dillon Regiment to his younger brother, James, a Knight of Malta. Colonel James Dillon led the Regiment at Dettingen (1743) and at Fontenoy (1745), where he was killed. Louis XV appointed the fourth brother, Edward, to be colonel of the Regiment, but he was killed two years later at Lawfeld (1747). Since the fifth brother, Arthur, had entered the Church – as Archbishop of Narbonne he is prominent in the Journal of his great-great niece, the Marquise de La Tour du Pin – there remained no one of the family to take over the command. However, Louis XV refused to allow it to be disposed of, pointing out that the eldest of the brothers, Henry, 11th Viscount Dillon, had recently married, so the king felt he 'could not consent to this family losing a possession so closely theirs by virtue of the blood they had shed and the excellent service they had given, so long as there was any hope at all of seeing the connection revived'. Interim commanders were appointed until, in 1767, Viscount Dillon's second son, Arthur – father of the writer – was given command. He was seventeen and the last Colonel proprietor of the Regiment. He led it in the service of France until 1792 when, after reaffirming his own oath of loyalty to the deposed king and recommending his troops to do likewise, he was removed from command and ordered to return to Paris. There he was guillotined in 1794. In 1793, the 1st Battalion of the Dillon Regiment became the 87ᵉ Régiment d'Infantérie which it remained until disbandment in 1920. The 2nd Battalion, commanded by General Dillon's younger brother, Henry, was sent to San Domingo. There, it had to capitulate to the English and transferred its allegiance to George III whom it served until 1798. Mme de La Tour du Pin writes that it was by then so decimated by disease that it had to be released from service. Its colour was returned to Charles, 12th Viscount Dillon.

Throughout her long life, Henrietta-Lucy Dillon was to show the same practical courage and resourcefulness as her military forebears. Her French husband, too, was a soldier. It was stories of his courage and accomplishments that first attracted her attention and when they met, it was his soldierly dress and bearing that evoked her warmest praise. But the military tradition of her family was very closely linked with that of service at Court. Members of her family had held high office at the Court of James II in London and some of them served him in exile at Saint-Germain, where her family had a grace-and-favour apartment. Later, they held appointments at the French Court and were held in esteem by a succession of monarchs. Her mother was a lady-in-waiting to Marie-Antoinette and it was intended that she herself should one day hold the same appointment.

Her background and the circles in which she moved gave her a breadth of vision, an independence of mind and a directness that enabled her to write of her times with unusual perspicacity and a sympathy which had its roots in understanding. She was interested in all people, regardless of their degree or occupation.

From comments in the text, it is likely that the Journal was written for two main reasons. First, to ensure that her only surviving son, Aymar, and her daughter's two small children should have some idea of their family story before successive revolutions had swept its world away and reduced the remaining members of the family to poverty-stricken exile. The second reason was probably a hope that such knowledge would help them avoid the faults she saw in the younger generation, many of whom she found aimless, superficial, frivolous. This she blamed on the twenty-five years of revolution and war which had destroyed that continuity of tradition so essential to stability. She herself had known the France of Louis XVI, of the Revolution, the Directorate, the Empire, the Restoration. She had spent three years farming most successfully in the United States and a further two years more idly and less happily in England. When her husband retired from the army and turned to foreign affairs and administration, she accompanied him wherever he was sent, whether before the Revolution, under the Empire or during the Restoration. Despite her independence of mind, she was a devoted wife. Together, they knew great happiness and deep sorrow, considerable wealth and dire poverty.

Madame de La Tour du Pin was fifty when she began her Journal and probably wrote it over a period of years, possibly at long intervals. It was never completed and ends with the return of Napoleon from Elba. It is in two parts, the first being dated 1 January 1820, a few months before her husband was created Marquis de La Tour du Pin and appointed ambassador in Turin. He held this appointment for ten years and it is possible that the patient detail and serenity of style in this part of the Journal owe much to this long period in a relatively quiet post. By 1820, only two of the seven children she had borne remained to her: her daughter, Alix, Comtesse Auguste de Liedekerke-Beaufort, and her youngest son, Aymar. Two years later, her daughter died.

In 1830, M. de La Tour du Pin decided to retire. He was seventy-one, tired and very unhappy at the style of government under Charles X. He took a house at Versailles but, shortly afterwards, when the king was deposed, returned with his wife and son to live at Le Bouilh, their family house near Bordeaux. A year later, Aymar de La Tour du Pin joined the insurrection in the Vendée led by the Duchesse de Berry on behalf of her exiled son, heir to Charles X. Aymar was captured and condemned to four months in prison, where his father joined him voluntarily. After his release, Aymar again went off to join Mme de Berry, but when she was arrested, fled to Jersey. He was condemned to death in his absence and his father was imprisoned for three months and fined for defending him. Mme de La Tour du Pin joined her husband in prison. Since their only remaining child could no longer return to France, they decided to share his exile. In 1833, their last, sad, odyssey began: Nice, Turin, Pignerol and, finally, Lausanne. They reached Lausanne in 1835 and there, two years later, M. de La Tour du Pin died. He was seventy-eight.

Aymar, now the Marquis de La Tour du Pin, was still proscribed and Mme de La Tour du Pin set out with him to live in Italy. There, the second part of the Journal was written. The first four chapters are dated from Lucca in February 1843, the remainder from Pisa, three months later. Mme de La Tour du Pin was seventy-three.

The second part of the Journal is less serene than the first but the account is still amazing in its vivid detail and the writer's admiration and enthusiasm for the powerful figure of Napoleon glow with youthful vigour. Comments on people are apt to become less tolerant as the chapters go by and the pride so often shown by the elderly in their own achievements becomes more pronounced, but this merely adds to the humanity of the whole document. It is intensely personal and sometimes criticised for being too self-centred. It is the more important to remember that Mme de La Tour du Pin's entire married life was linked to her husband's career and on several occasions she fought fiercely for his interests. She firmly enjoins her children to remember that, although their father was not very successful in managing the family's finances, everything he did was intended for their benefit. She shared her husband's foreign postings and, in later life, his self-imposed exile. Readers of eighteenth and nineteenth century French social history know that such wifely devotion was by no means general. When she died, those who knew her said it was rare to find such strength combined with so much charm, such serenity with so much conscientiousness, such steadfast devotion to duty with so much kindliness. Her husband paid his own tribute: 'During a marriage that has lasted nearly fifty years, she has brought happiness and consolation to a life so frequently and so painfully troubled. My sole purpose [in writing just before his death a short account of his life] is to enable my wife to recall the endlessly recurring vicissitudes which her courage always overcame with unshakeable and unfailing calm. It is a great comfort to me that, in reminding her of myself, I have some small means of enabling her to see herself to such very great advantage. Complete abnegation of self is her dominant quality. It is quite impossible to conceive of any sacrifice too great for the devotion of which she is capable.'

The manuscript was given to a grandson, Hadelin, Comte de Liedekerke-Beaufort who, shortly before his own death in 1890, entrusted it to one of his sons, Colonel Comte Aymar de Liedekerke-Beaufort, to whom we owe its original publication in 1906.

FELICE HARCOURT

PART ONE

⚜⚜⚜⚜⚜⚜⚜⚜⚜⚜⚜⚜⚜ I ⚜⚜⚜⚜⚜⚜⚜⚜⚜⚜⚜⚜⚜

1st of January, 1820. I am not writing a book, simply a journal of my life. I do not intend it to be a confession but, distasteful as I would find it to reveal my faults, I do nonetheless wish to give a faithful picture of myself as I am and as I have been. Never before have I written anything except letters to those I love. My thoughts ramble, I am not methodical, my memory is already much dimmed. At heart, I still feel so young that it is only by looking into the mirror that I can convince myself that I am no longer twenty years of age. Let me take advantage, then, of the warmth that is still in me and which may at any moment be chilled by the infirmities of age, to tell something of a troubled and restless life.

In my earliest years, I saw things and heard conversations which might have been expected to warp my mind, pervert my affections, deprave my character and destroy in me every notion of religion and morality. Brought up, as I was, in the house of an archbishop* where every rule of religion was broken daily, I was fully aware that my lessons in dogma and doctrine were given no more importance than those in history and geography.

My mother had married Arthur Dillon, her first cousin once removed. They had been brought up together and her affection for him was entirely sisterly. She was as beautiful as an angel and the equally angelic sweetness of her nature made her generally beloved. Although innocent of coquetry, she was not perhaps sufficiently distant in her relations with the men she liked and whom the world considered in love with her.

There was one in particular who spent all his time at the house where my mother lived with my grandmother† and my uncle, the

* Arthur Richard Dillon, 1721–1806. He became Archbishop of Narbonne in 1763 and Primate of the Gauls. He was virtually Viceroy of Languedoc, the province which enjoyed the largest measure of self-government, and he actively promoted roads, bridges, canals, harbours and other improvements. In 1788, he became President of the Assembly of the Clergy. He emigrated in 1790 to Coblentz and then to London, refused to recognise Napoleon's Concordat, and died in London. He is buried in St Pancras churchyard. (Tr. – Source: Dictionary of National Biography.)

† The Comtesse Edward de Rothe, born Lucy Cary, daughter of Laura Dillon and the 5th Viscount Falkland. She married General de Rothe, a Jacobite of Irish origin, whose regiment formed part of the Irish Brigade serving with the French army. (Tr.)

archbishop, and he also came with us to the country. He was the Prince de Guéménée* whom the world accounted my mother's lover. But I do not think he was, for the Duc de Lauzun, the Duc de Liancourt and the Comte de Saint-Blancard were all equally assiduous in their attentions to her.† The Comte de Fersen, said to be the lover of Queen Marie-Antoinette, also came to see us every day. The queen liked my mother. She was always ready to be captivated by sparkle and Madame Dillon was very much the rage. It was to this alone that she owed her entry into the Queen's Household and her appointment as lady-in-waiting. I was seven or eight years old at the time.

My mother loved my grandmother, despite the latter's overbearing nature and the outrageous malice which sometimes mounted to veritable furies of rage. Indeed, my mother was completely in her power, living, as it were, in thrall to her. She was entirely dependent on her financially and had never dared to point out that, as the only daughter of her father, who had been dead for ten years, she had a right to control at least her own fortune.

My grandmother, daughter of an impecunious English peer, had had scarcely a penny from her own parents and had taken possession of the Hautefontaine property which her husband had bought with his own money. But my mother, married at seventeen to a boy of eighteen, who owned nothing in the world except his Regiment,‡ would never have had the courage to talk to my grandmother of money matters. The queen explained her entitlement and encouraged her to ask for accounts. My grandmother flew into a passion and maternal affection was transformed into one of those incredible hatreds so beloved of writers of romance and tragedy.

My first thoughts and earliest memories are connected with this hatred. I was a continual witness of the appalling scenes which my mother had to face and, although obliged to appear unaware, understood nonetheless, as I played with my doll or studied my lessons, that my situation was a difficult one. Reserve and discretion became essential. I learned to hide my feelings and judge for myself the actions of my parents. I remember being shocked that my mother should complain of my grandmother to her friends and thought they fanned the flames instead of helping to dampen them down. My

* Son of the Duc de Rohan and one of the most extravagant and fashionable younger nobles at Court. (Tr.)
† This may not be filial prejudice for the Duc de Lauzun, who found it necessary to flee her mother's charm, gives a strikingly similar account of her. (Tr.)
‡ The Dillon Regiment. See Introduction.

father took my mother's part, which seemed to me entirely proper. Yet I already realised that, financially, he was greatly in my uncle's debt so he seemed to me to be in a false position. Indeed, since my uncle took my grandmother's part, I thought my father must have felt torn between his duty towards him and his affection for my mother, brotherly though it was.

There was perhaps only one being who sheltered me from contamination, who helped me see evil wherever it existed and who encouraged me in virtue. It was someone who could neither read nor write: Marguérite was a good countrywoman from the neighbourhood of Compiègne who had been found to serve me. She was young and my constant companion. She was deeply attached to me and had the heaven-sent gift of healthy judgement, fairness of mind and strength of soul. Princes and dukes, the great of the earth, stood arraigned, therefore, before a girl of twelve and a peasant woman of twenty-five.

Customs and society itself have so changed since the Revolution that I want to describe in detail what I can remember of my family's manner of life.

My uncle, the Archbishop of Narbonne, went but rarely to his diocese. By virtue of his See, he was President of the States of Languedoc* but he never visited Languedoc except to preside over the meeting of the States. These lasted six weeks during November and December. No sooner were they over than my uncle returned to Paris on the pretext that the interests of the Province urgently required his presence at Court, but really in order to resume his life as a *grand seigneur* in Paris and a courtier at Versailles.

As Archbishop of Narbonne and the holder of various other rich benefices, he had an income of at least 500,000 francs. With such a fortune, he might reasonably have been expected to live honourably and free from anxiety, but it was not so. He was always having to resort to expedients. It was certainly not because he lived in any great luxury. In Paris, he kept noble state, but of a simple kind. Food was plentiful, but not extravagant.

In those days it was not customary to give great dinner parties, for people dined early: at half-past two or three o'clock at the latest. The ladies would sometimes have had their hair dressed by then, but would still be in *déshabille*. Gentlemen, on the other hand, were nearly always formally dressed, never in a plain town coat or in

* Each Province had its own assembly – the States – in which the three orders: nobles, clergy and commons, were represented. (Tr.)

uniform, but in a dress coat, embroidered or plain, according to their age and taste. The master of the house or those who did not intend going into company later in the evening, would wear a town coat or informal dress, for the need to wear a hat disturbed the fragile edifice of the curled wig, which was always snow-white with powder. After dinner, there was conversation, sometimes a game of back-gammon. Then the ladies would go off to dress and the gentlemen would wait to accompany them to the theatre, if they were to be in the same box. If one stayed at home after dinner, there was a con-tinuous stream of visitors.

Supper guests did not arrive until half-past nine. Socially, that was the really important hour of the day. There were two kinds of suppers, those given by people whose supper table was open to guests on every day of the week, thus allowing a certain number of people to come when they wished, and those to which one was invited, which were fairly numerous and brilliant. I am speaking of the days when I was a child, that is to say, between 1778 and 1784. All the toilettes, all the elegance, everything that the beautiful, fashionable society of Paris could offer in refinement and charm was to be found at these suppers. In those good old days, before anyone had begun to think of national representation, a list of supper guests was a most important and carefully considered item. There were so many interests to foster, so many people to bring together, so many tiresome ones to keep away. And what a social disaster for a husband to consider himself invited to a house simply because his wife was asked! What a detailed knowledge of protocol and current intrigues was needed!

There were fewer balls than in later years, for the ladies' fashions of that day made dancing a form of torture: narrow heels, three inches high, which held the foot in a similar position to when stand-ing on tiptoe to reach a book on the highest shelf in the library; a panier of stiff, heavy whalebone, spreading out on either side; hair dressed at least a foot high, sprinkled with a pound of powder and pomade, which the slightest movement shook down on to the shoulders, and crowned by a bonnet known as a 'pouf' on which feathers, flowers and diamonds were piled pell-mell – an erection which quite spoiled the pleasure of dancing. A supper-party, on the other hand, where people only talked or made music, did not disturb this edifice.

To return to my family. We used to leave for the country early in the spring and spend the whole summer there. In the château of

Hautefontaine there were twenty-five apartments for guests, and often they were all occupied. But the best visits of all were in October. By then, the colonels were back from the four months they had spent with their regiments and had scattered to the various country houses to join their families and friends.

At Hautefontaine, there was a pack of staghounds whose upkeep was shared between my uncle, the Prince de Guéménée and the Duc de Lauzun. I have heard it said that its upkeep amounted to no more than 30,000 francs but this did not include the saddle-horses of members of the hunt, only the hounds, the wages of the hunt servants, who were English, their horses and all the food. This pack hunted in the forests of Compiègne and Villers-Cotterets throughout the summer and autumn. It was so well run that poor Louis XVI was really jealous and, much as he loved to talk hunting, nothing annoyed him more than to hear about the exploits of the Hautefontaine pack.

At the age of seven, I was already allowed to ride with the hunt once or twice a week and when I was ten, I broke my leg on the feast of St Hubert. They say I was very brave. I was carried five leagues on a stretcher made from branches and did not even murmur. The time spent in bed with that broken leg is my happiest childhood memory. My mother's friends flocked to Hautefontaine, where we stayed six weeks longer than usual. People read to me all day and every evening a small puppet theatre was wheeled to the foot of my bed and the marionettes performed some comedy or tragedy, the parts being spoken from the wings by the people present. If it were a comic opera, they sang instead. The ladies amused themselves making clothes for the marionettes. I can still remember the cloak and tiara of Ahasuerus and the linen coat of Joash. These amusements were not unprofitable for they acquainted me with all the good plays of the French theatre. The Arabian Nights was read to me from cover to cover and it was perhaps at this time that I acquired my liking for fiction and all works of the imagination.

I first stayed at Versailles in 1781, when the first Dauphin was born.* How often, when listening to tales of Queen Marie-Antoinette's sufferings and shame, have I not cast my mind back to those days of her triumph. I went to watch the ball given for her by the Gardes du Corps in the Grande Salle de Spectacle at Versailles. Wearing a blue dress strewn with sapphires and diamonds, she opened the ball with an unknown young guardsman. She was young, beautiful and adored by all. She had just given France a Dauphin and it would have been inconceivable to her that the brilliant career

* Louis-Joseph-Xavier-François, 1781–1789.

on which she was launched could ever suffer a reverse. Yet she was already close to the abyss.

I shall make no attempt to trace the Court intrigues which I was too young to judge or even understand. I had already heard of Madame de Polignac, for whom the queen had a growing liking. She was very pretty, but not very clever. It was her sister-in-law, the Comtesse Diane de Polignac, an older woman much given to intrigue, who guided her along the path to favour. Their friend, the Comte de Vaudreuil,* whose pleasant nature led the queen to cultivate his company, also worked to further her fortunes, which later became so great. I remember that M. de Guéménée tried to make my mother see the danger of the queen's growing friendship with Mme de Polignac, but my mother was serenely content to enjoy the queen's affection and had no thought of profiting from it, either to increase her own fortune or the fortunes of her friends. She was already suffering the first symptoms of the illness which was to cause her death less than two years later. As for my father, he was in America, fighting at the head of the first battalion of his Regiment.

⚜⚜⚜⚜⚜⚜⚜⚜⚜⚜⚜⚜ II ⚜⚜⚜⚜⚜⚜⚜⚜⚜⚜⚜⚜

I had no real childhood. By the time I was twelve, my education was already very advanced. I had read voraciously, but indiscriminately. Since the age of seven, I had had a tutor, an organist from Béziers named Combes. He came to teach me to play the harpsichord for there were as yet no pianos – or, at least, very few. My mother had one to accompany her singing but I was not allowed to use it. M. Combes was well educated and still studying. He has admitted to me since that he purposely slowed down my own studies for fear I might outstrip him in the subjects he was himself still studying.

I have always been remarkably eager to learn. I wanted to know about everything, from cookery to the experiments in chemistry which I used to watch in the laboratory of a small apothecary at Hautefontaine. The gardener was English and my nurse, Marguérite, took me every day to visit his wife who taught me to read in their language. Usually, the book was *Robinson Crusoe*, to which I was

* One of the closest companions of the Comte d'Artois, youngest brother of Louis XVI, a patron of the arts and the lover of Mme de Polignac. (Tr.)

most attached. From my earliest days I had a feeling that adventures lay in store for me. My imagination was continuously inventing changes of fortune and I wanted to know everything that might be useful in any conceivable circumstance.

The continual warring in the house meant that I was always on the defensive. If my mother wanted me to do something, my grandmother would forbid it. Each would have liked me to spy for her but my inborn honesty revolted at the very idea. My silence led to accusations of indifference and taciturnity, I was a butt for the moods of all and sundry and for many an unjust accusation as well. I was beaten or locked in as a punishment for the merest trifles. When I showed emotion at some noble deed in history, I was ridiculed. Every day I would hear tell of some ribald incident or some horrid intrigue. I saw every vice and heard much talk of it. No attempt was made to keep anything from me. I would seek out my nurse and her simple good sense would help me to judge, to differentiate, to see everything at its true value.

When I was eleven, my mother decided that I was speaking English less well and gave me a smart maid who had been especially brought over from England. Her arrival caused me the deepest grief. I was separated from my good Marguérite and although she remained in the house, she hardly ever came to my room. My affection for her increased. I used to escape whenever I could and try to find her, which became a new source of scoldings and punishments. How careful one should be when bringing up children not to wound their affections, not to be deceived by the apparent shallowness of their natures. Even now, at the age of fifty-five, as I write of the humiliations to which my maid was subjected, my heart is filled again with indignation. Yet the Englishwoman was pleasant. I liked her only too well. She was a Protestant, her past had been anything but moral and she had never read anything but novels. She did me much harm.

To return to my story. My mother had had a son who died when he was two and his birth had left her delicate. Eventually, a violent fever attacked her lungs. She made no attempt to live quietly. She rode, hunted and sang with the famous Piccini,* who was enchanted with her voice. But by the spring of 1782, when she was thirty-one, she was beginning to spit blood violently. Unfortunately, the very fashionable doctor she consulted said that the blood came from her

* One of the two leading musicians in Paris. The other was Gluck. Their rival merits roused heated controversy between their supporters – society was split between the Piccinistes and the Gluckists. The queen had been taught by Gluck and was, naturally, his leading supporter. (Tr.)

stomach and ordered her to Spa. It would be difficult to convey the depth of my grandmother's fury at the idea that her daughter should take the waters. She could not have been unaware that her daughter was seriously ill, but she suspected her of trying to take advantage of it to escape from her authority. She refused to accompany her and gave her no money for the journey. I think it was the queen who came to my mother's rescue on this occasion and we left Haute-fontaine for Brussels, where we stayed a month with my aunt, Mrs Charles Dillon. She was in the last stages of consumption but it had in no way affected her quite ethereal charm and beauty. She had two delightful children: a boy of four – the present Lord Dillon – and a daughter. I found them very amusing and it was a great joy to occupy myself with them. I had a presentiment that they were soon to lose their mother, but little realised that I was myself so close to the same tragedy.

My mother took me to call on the Archduchess Marie-Christine* who, with her husband, the Duke Albert of Saxe-Teschen, governed the Low Countries. At Spa, I tasted for the first time the heady poison of praise and success. My mother took me to the *ridotto* on the days when there was dancing and it was not long before the whole town was talking of the little French girl who danced so well. The Comte and Comtesse du Nord† had just arrived from the depths of Russia and had never seen girls of twelve dancing the gavotte, the minuet and so forth. They were shown the prodigy.

All this time, everything was combining to corrupt my mind and my heart. My English maid talked to me only of frivolities, of clothes and success. She told me of her own conquests and spoke of those I would myself be making in a few years' time. She gave me English novels, but I knew there were books a young lady should not read and that if I did read them and later hear them spoken of in my presence, nothing would be able to prevent my blushes. So it was simpler not to read them. In any case, I had no taste for sentimental novels. I have always hated false sentiment and exaggeration. I do, however, remember a romance written by the Abbé Prévost which made a great impression on me – it was *Cleveland*. The book describes acts of great devotion, the quality which appeals to me above all others. I was so anxious to practise it that I longed to give my mother

* Sister of Queen Marie-Antoinette. The Low Countries were ruled by Austria from 1713 until 1790. (Tr.)
† The incognito used by the Grand-Duke Paul of Russia, son and heir of Cather-ine the Great, and his second wife, Princess Marie of Wurtemburg, during a tour of Europe. (Tr.)

daily proofs of my own devotion to her. Often did I weep bitter tears because she would not allow me to nurse her, to watch beside her, to give her all the care I so longed to offer. But she rebuffed my efforts, kept me at a distance and I was puzzled by this strange aversion from her only daughter. Years later, M. Combes told me he thought it might have been the fault of M. de Guéménée, who had joined us at Spa. He lost no opportunity of belittling me to my mother and, looking back, my tutor thought the prince might have feared I knew of his financial difficulties and would speak of them to my mother, who was unaware of them.*

Meantime, the waters of Spa were shortening my mother's life. She was very unwilling to return to Hautefontaine, being quite sure that, there, my grandmother would greet her, as she always did, with scenes and furious rages. But her health was worsening with every minute that passed and she began to long, as do all who are attacked by this cruel illness of the chest, for a change of air. She wanted to go to Italy, and asked to return to Paris first. My grandmother consented and it was only then that she began to realise the true state of her unfortunate daughter's health. Certainly, it was from that moment that she spoke of her state as hopeless, which indeed it was.

When we reached Paris, my grandmother gave up her own apartment to my mother, since it was larger, and lavished on her every possible care. This was in such marked contrast to the outrageous manner in which I had seen her treat my mother only a few months earlier that I could not but believe in the sincerity of her feelings. Years afterwards, when I was older and more experienced, I realised that in a passionate character, such extremes are not unnatural.

During her last days, my mother was surrounded with care. The queen came to see her and every day a groom or a page was sent from Versailles for news of her. She grew hourly weaker but no one mentioned the Sacraments or spoke of calling a priest. As I write these pages forty-five years later, I regret that it should have been so but, at the time, had scarcely finished learning my catechism. There was no chaplain in that archbishop's house. The maids, though some

* It was during this year – 1782 – that the Prince de Guéménée was declared bankrupt. His debts were tremendous and particularly scandalous since the borrowings were largely from people of modest means. The Princesse de Guéménée had to resign her post as Governess to the Children of France and was succeeded by Madame de Polignac. The financial help given by Louis XVI to the former Governess to help the great family of Rohan to clear their name and to the latter to help them sustain their new position, were major weapons in the armoury of the revolutionaries. (Tr.)

of them were unquestionably devout, feared my grandmother too much to dare to speak out. My mother did not realise that her last hours had come. She died of suffocation in my nurse's arms on 7 September 1782.

I was told the sad news the following morning by Madame Nagle, a good old friend of my mother's, whom I found beside my bed when I awoke. She said that my grandmother had left the house, that I was to get up and go to her and beg her protection and care. She told me that my future lay now in my grandmother's hands, that she was on very unfriendly terms with my father – who was in America – and that she would certainly disinherit me if she took a dislike to me, which seemed only too probable. My grieving young heart revolted against the deception which this good lady was imposing on me and she had the greatest difficulty in persuading me to allow myself to be taken to my grandmother. The memory of all the tears I had seen my mother shed, of the terrible scenes she had had to endure in my presence and the thought that such treatment had shortened her life, made it utterly repugnant to me to submit to her authority. But my old friend assured me that if I made the slightest difficulty, a strict convent would be my lot, that my father would doubtless re-marry in order to beget a son and would not take me back to live with him, that I might be forced to take the veil and be sent to the same convent as my aunt,* a nun in the Benedictine house at Montargis, who had not left it since she was seven.

Mme Nagle ended by carrying me off to my grandmother who put on an act of such despair that it froze me with fear and left a most painful memory. I was thought cold and heartless and it was implied that I felt no sorrow at my mother's death. This charge, so very far from the truth, wrung my heart with indignation. I had a sudden glimpse of all the long years of deceit into which I was being forced. But I would remind you that I was only twelve.

A month later, in October, my grandmother and my uncle went to Hautefontaine, taking me and my tutor with them. I dearly loved that house, which I knew would one day belong to me. It stood in a fine estate between Villers-Cotteret and Soissons, about twenty-two leagues from Paris. The house had been built at the beginning of the previous century and stood on a sharply-rising hill, dominating a delightfully green valley or, to be more exact, a gorge opening on to the Forest of Compiègne. Meadows, woods, clear lakes stocked with fish lay beyond a magnificent kitchen garden set directly under the windows of the house. The courtyard was a sort of platform which,

* The Honourable Catherine Dillon.

in earlier centuries, had undoubtedly been fortified. Architecturally, the house was not at all beautiful, but it was comfortable, roomy, perfectly furnished and careful thought had been given to every detail.

In 1779, when my father had left to fight with his Regiment in the West Indies, my uncle, my grandmother and my mother had travelled with him as far as Brest. On the way back, at Lorient, my uncle bought the entire cargo of a ship just returned from the East Indies. There were porcelains from China and Japan, brightly-coloured glazed chintzes from Persia for hangings, silks, damasks, coloured pekins* and much else beside. To my great joy, all these beautiful things had been unpacked and arranged in great store-rooms where the old watchman allowed me to wander with my maid when the weather was too bad for us to go walking. He often said to me: 'It will all be yours.' But some presentiment, of which I said nothing, kept me from dwelling too much on future splendours. My young imagination was more inclined to dwell on thoughts of ruin and poverty, a fore-shadowing of the future which never left me, which made me want to learn all the handicrafts necessary to a poor girl. It drew me away from the usual occupations of a young lady known to be an heiress.

During my mother's lifetime, Hautefontaine had radiated gaiety and brilliance. After her death, all was utterly changed. My father being abroad, it was my grandmother who took possession of all my mother's papers and the letters she had kept. Just as they had not allowed her to see a priest, so they had not allowed her to concern herself with her worldly affairs. My grandmother had far too great an interest in them to permit any man of business to know how they stood. She had spent my grandfather's fortune and everything we owned had been changed during my mother's childhood. My mother was only twelve when her father, General de Rothe, died suddenly at Hautefontaine. He had bought it not long before in the name of his wife, stating that it was paid for entirely from the dowry of £10,000 given to my grandmother by her father, Lord Falkland. But the house in the Rue du Bac and 4,000 francs in bonds, all left him by his family, were given to my mother.

My uncle, the archbishop, had lived in the house in the Rue du Bac for twenty years without paying my mother a farthing in rent. On the excuse that she lived there herself, he had not even paid for repairs. Yet he already had more than 300,000 francs a year from Church benefices. It is true that he paid some gambling debts of my

* Coloured silk material, originally from China. Similar to taffetas. (Tr.)

father's, for he, like his two brothers, Lord Dillon and Henry Dillon, was afflicted with that wretched passion. I have never known how much my uncle paid, but have heard it said that the debts were considerable. However that may be, after my mother's death, all that remained to me was the house in the Rue du Bac – rented for 10,000 francs a year to the Baron de Staël, who later married the famous Mlle Necker – and the 4,000 francs in bonds. From my father I could expect nothing. He had already run through his own inheritance of £10,000 given to him at seventeen with the Dillon Regiment.

I therefore had to humour my grandmother and her tyranny affected my entire life. Never have I seen anyone with such a fierce urge to dominate, to impose authority. She began by separating me entirely from my childhood friends and she herself broke with all her daughter's friends. By a refinement of cruelty, she made the break with my young friends appear to come from me. I heard that I was accused of ingratitude, fickleness and lack of feeling and was not allowed to explain.

My good tutor, who knew my grandmother even better than I did, was the only being to whom I could talk of my sorrows. But he pointed out to me most forcefully that it would be best to humour her, that my future life depended on her, that if I crossed her and were put into a convent, she would still be clever enough to make it appear that the decision had been mine; that, separated from my father – of whom I might at any moment be deprived by the fortunes of war – I would be entirely alone if my grandmother and my uncle should withdraw their protection. So I had to resolve to endure the inevitable daily trials and can truthfully say that, for five years, not one day passed without my shedding bitter tears.

But, as I grew older, I suffered less, either because I had become used to ill-treatment or because my mind, which was mature beyond my years, my strength of character, the calm with which I endured my grandmother's passions and the imperturbable silence with which I met the slanders she told about everyone, especially the queen, forced her to feel a certain respect for me. Perhaps, also, she feared that when I did enter society, I would talk of all I had had to endure. Whatever the reason, by the time I was sixteen and she had noticed that I was taller than she, my grandmother was exercising a measure of restraint in her rages. But she certainly made up for it in other ways, as you will see later.

Towards the end of the autumn of 1782, my uncle set out for Montpellier to preside over the States of Languedoc, a prerogative of the Archbishops of Narbonne which he had exercised for the past twenty-eight years. I remained at Hautefontaine with my grand-mother who soon grew very bored. Her bad temper became frighten-ing in its intensity. She realised that, in losing my mother, she had also lost the friends who, until then, had surrounded and humoured her. They had done so in an attempt to secure peace for my mother and, by giving my grandmother the impression that she as well as my mother was the centre of their attentions, had perhaps effectively lessened my mother's sufferings. But after her death, when my grandmother found the letters of these supposed friends, she learned the true state of their feelings towards her and in her heart were lit such hatreds as only she could generate.

And so, when she grew lonely at Hautefontaine, in that great house which had been the scene of such activity and so many bril-liant gatherings, when she saw the stables empty and no longer heard the voices of the hounds nor the horns of the huntsmen, when she saw from the windows the long rides stretching away in vistas of unbroken emptiness, she realised it would be necessary to change her way of life and persuade the archbishop, until then concerned exclusively with his own pleasures and with upholding the dignity of his rank in society, to cultivate ambition and occupy himself with the affairs of his province and those of the clergy. The office of President of the Clergy* was in the king's gift and my uncle decided to apply for it. Doubtless, he promised to smoothe the passage of the 'don gratuit' at each Assembly to a greater extent than did the existing incumbent, the strictly honourable Cardinal de la Rochefoucauld.

To achieve her purpose, my grandmother determined to persuade my uncle, whom she dominated completely, to change his manner of life and his place of residence. When he returned from Montpellier, we went to see him in Paris. I think that, in the absence of my father, who had been Governor of St Kitts since its capture – his Regiment having contributed gloriously to the success of the French troops on that expedition – my guardians had pointed out to him that he could not continue to live in my house without paying rent or undertaking repairs. He, therefore, decided to move and most iniquitously borrowed 40,000 francs to pay for the most urgent of the repairs, without which it would have been impossible to find a tenant for the house. He borrowed this money by mortgaging the very house where he had lived for twenty years without once loosening his own purse strings. It was not until he left France at the time of the Revolution

* The Assembly of the Clergy met annually and, at the request of the king, imposed on themselves a 'voluntary' tax – the *don gratuit* – assessed by them-selves. The Provincial States voted a similar tax. (Tr.)

that his debt was discovered and it was I who had to repay it when
I sold the house in 1797. Until then, he had paid only the interest on
the loan, which was not mentioned in my marriage contract.

My uncle bought on a life-lease, in his own name, the house at the
corner of the Rue St Dominique and the Rue de Bourgogne. His
architect, M. Raimond, always mindful of my interests, strongly
advised him to buy it outright in my name, my uncle to have the use
of it for his lifetime. But this arrangement, which would have
increased my fortune without depriving him of any part of his, did not
appeal to him and, despite his age – he was seventy-seven – he persisted in buying it in his own name. Raimond then suggested that he
should buy, this time for me, a pretty little house in the square of the
Palais Bourbon, which was just being built. This he also refused to
do. The commendatory abbey of Cigny, worth 100,000 francs a year
in revenue, had recently been added to his benefices and he gave this
addition to his income as a reason for indulging his taste for building
and furnishing, an interest which took the place of his earlier recreation – horses and hunting – which he could no longer enjoy. He
spent large sums on the arrangement of his new house, which was
very dilapidated when he took it over.

At the same time, my grandmother, who had taken a dislike to
Hautefontaine after spending two such boring months there, bought
a house at Montfermeil, near Livry, five leagues from Paris. It cost
52,000 francs, a modest price for there were ninety acres of grounds.
The house, known as the Folie Joyeuse, was charmingly situated. It
had been built by a M. de Joyeuse who had begun its construction at
what is normally the final stage. After marking out a fine courtyard
and enclosing it with palings, he built two wings, each terminating in
a pretty, square pavilion. By then, he had no money left for the main
part of the house, so that the only link between the pavilions was a
corridor at least one hundred feet long. The creditors took possession
and sold the property. The park was enchanting, enclosed by a wall
and at the end of each walk was a gate opening into the Forest of
Bondy which, at that point, is very beautiful.

Cart-loads of furniture were brought from Hautefontaine and by
the spring of 1783 we were more or less comfortably settled in.
During the first year, my uncle and grandmother limited their
activities to planting and putting the garden in order. The summer
was spent drawing up plans with architects and draughtsmen, which
I found extremely interesting. My uncle enjoyed telling me all his
plans. He spoke to me of buildings, gardens, furniture, every kind of
improvement. He had confidence in my intelligence and set me to

calculate and measure, with his gardeners, the slopes and other surfaces. He wanted me to go through every detail of the estimates, checking the measurements.

I was very tall for my age, enjoyed excellent health and was very active, both in mind and body. I wanted to see everything, to know everything; to learn all the handicrafts, from embroidery and the making of flowers to laundering and the smallest kitchen tasks. I found time for everything, never wasting a moment, storing in my memory all I was taught and never forgetting it. I set myself to learn from the specialised knowledge of all who came to Montfermeil and it was thus, with the aid of a good memory, that I acquired the vast range of knowledge which has been so extremely useful throughout my life.

III

In November 1783, or thereabouts, I learned that my grandmother intended in future to accompany my uncle to the States of Languedoc. In those days the annual session of the States was a very brilliant occasion and I was overjoyed at her decision. A treaty of peace had recently been concluded* and the English, who for three years had been unable to visit the Continent, were arriving in large numbers, as they were to do again a few years later, in 1814. Visits to Italy were less common then than they are now. The fine roads through the Mont Cenis and Simplon passes had not been built, there were no steamships and the road along the Mediterranean coast was almost impassable. The climate of the south of France, especially of Languedoc and of Montpellier above all, was still exceedingly fashionable.

I will tell you here about just one of our journeys to Montpellier. It is typical of them all, for until 1786, when I went for the last time, they all followed much the same pattern.

The preparations for the journey, the shopping and packing were an occupation and a pleasure, but one of which I was to weary during the course of a frequently uprooted existence. We travelled in a large berline with six horses: my uncle and my grandmother in

* The Articles of Peace between England and France after the American War of Secession were signed on 20 January 1783. (Tr.)

the back, myself on the seat in front of them, next to a secretary or one of the priests on my uncle's staff, and two servants on the front seat. At the end of the journey, these servants were usually far more tired than those who had ridden all the way, for the seats of those days were not set on springs. They rested on two wooden posts which were themselves set on the transom and therefore as hard as any waggon. A second berline, also drawn by six horses, carried my grandmother's maid and mine, Miss Beck, two footmen and, seated on the cross-bench, two servants. The butler and the chef travelled in a postchaise.

There were also three couriers, one riding half-an-hour ahead of us and the other two with the carriages. M. Combes, my tutor, used to set out several days before us, travelling either in the diligence, known then as the 'Turgotine',* or in the mail-coach which carried only one passenger and was rather like an elongated waggon on shafts.

Every year, the ministers detained my uncle so long at Versailles that he had scarcely time to reach Montpellier for the opening of the States, which took place on a set date. This meant that he had to travel with the greatest possible speed, a very trying necessity so late in the year.

We travelled with eighteen horses and an order would be sent through the Administration of Posts several days ahead of us to ensure that fresh horses were ready at each stage. We drove for long hours every day, leaving at four o'clock in the morning and stopping only for dinner. The postchaise and the first courier would arrive an hour ahead of us to ensure that the table was ready, the fire lit and some good dishes prepared, or given at least a finishing touch by our own chef. He would have brought with him from Paris bottles of meat jelly and sauces prepared in advance, as well as everything else needful to make the bad inn meals palatable. The postchaise and the first courier would leave again as soon as we arrived and, when we stopped for the night, we would find, as in the morning, everything in readiness for us.

When travelling, I had to share my grandmother's room, which I did not like at all for she always took the best bed and a good part of mine as well. She took up most of the fire, too, and all her toilet articles left no room for mine. I was scolded on the slightest pretext and never allowed to go to bed on arrival despite the fact that each evening I was wearied to exhaustion, for she would not allow me to

* The first diligences were established in 1775, during the ministry of the economist and reformer, Turgot. (Tr.)

sleep in the carriage, nor even to lean back. Once, I think it was in 1785, I was so ill at Nîmes from over-tiredness that she was obliged to stay there with me for two days as I had not the strength to go on to Montpellier.

We used to spend a few days at Lyons when the archbishop was there but my uncle did not think very highly of him. He was not in favour at Court and went seldom to Paris. I do not remember ever seeing him there, not even during the Assemblies of the Clergy. He had once had an affair with the famous Duchesse de Mazarin, but that would have been no reason for disgrace in those dissolute days when virtuous living was the exception among the higher clergy. I, myself, think that it was, on the contrary, a good action which caused his fall from favour, an action prompted perhaps by ostentation but nonetheless useful for that: the city of Lyons had asked that the hospitals should be provided with iron bedsteads. The ministers refused, or were unwilling to authorise the expenditure so the archbishop, M. de Montazet, gave 200,000 francs from his own purse for the purpose. The ministers disliked the example they had been set but the king by no means disapproved. That excellent prince was always well disposed towards all good works but, from weakness or timidity, was too often led to reject ideas of which he had at first approved. It was this excessive modesty and diffidence which was so fatal to us.

The generosity of the Archbishop of Lyons made him very popular in the city and this aroused the jealousy of his peers. They preferred to use their revenues to build palaces or fine country houses rather than to found charitable institutions. But it was often in such dioceses as theirs that many parish priests were forced to live on straitened incomes, in presbyteries which were not even weatherproof.

To return to our journey to Languedoc. At that time, the road which followed the Rhône to Pont-Saint-Esprit was so bad that there was continual danger of overturning. Postilions demanded extra fees at each stage, claiming they had not brought us by the main highway but by small roads that waggoners could not use. We would spend a night at Montélimar, where there was a very well-kept inn with a high reputation among English travellers to the south of France. They all put up there for the night. The walls of the corridors and the staircase were entirely covered with medallions bearing the names of persons of note who had stayed there. It was a favourite pastime of mine to read them, especially those of the most recent arrivals, whom we hoped to meet at Montpellier.

There were occasions when the torrent which flows through this little town and which has to be crossed at a ford, would be so swollen by rain or, in spring, by the melting of the snows, that it would mean waiting several days for the waters to subside. One year, we were in great peril when we crossed. The water was high enough to float the carriage, so the doors were opened to allow it to pass through. My grandmother and I climbed on the cushions and tucked up our skirts. The men were on the cross benches. To the springs had been fastened small pieces of wood on which stood men with long, pointed sticks to prevent the carriage from turning over. All this was amusing to a young, adventurous person like myself but my poor grandmother, a terrible coward, suffered cruelly. Unfortunately, her fear expressed itself in bad temper, inevitably directed at me.

At La Palud stage, the traveller entered the Comtat Venaissin, which was Papal territory. Here, my uncle stopped to change into country clothes of purple cloth, adding, when it was cold, a quilted redingote lined with silk of the same colour, stockings of purple silk, gold buckled shoes, his insignia of the Order of the Holy Ghost, and a clerical tricorne with gold acorns. I liked to see the boundary signs painted with the tiara and the keys, I felt as if I were arriving in Italy.

It was at this point that we left the highway to Marseilles and took the excellent road which the Papal government had allowed the States of Languedoc to build, the most direct route to Pont-Saint-Esprit. There, after journeying 160 leagues over wretched, bumpy roads, crossing swift rivers without bridges and in real danger of his life, the traveller came at last to the passage of the Rhône and on the far bank lay a road as fine as any path in a well-kept garden. He crossed superb bridges, perfectly built; he drove through towns where industries flourished and a countryside cultivated with the greatest care. The contrast was striking, even to a fifteen-year-old.

As soon as the carriage had passed the last arch of the bridge at Saint-Esprit, the cannon of the small citadel which still stood at the the head of the bridge, fired a 21-gun salute. There would be a ruffle of drums and the garrison would turn out, the officers in full dress. All the civil and religious authorities would be waiting and come to the door of the berline to pay their respects to my uncle. If the weather was fine, he would climb down from his carriage while eight horses were harnessed to it.

He listened to the addresses and replied with the utmost affability and grace. My uncle was a stately figure, tall, with a fine voice and an air of elegant assurance. He would enquire about local matters, say a few words in reply to the petitions presented to him and never forgot any detail of the petitions which had been addressed to him the previous year. All this took nearly a quarter of an hour and when it was over, we would set off like the wind, for not only had the postilions' traces been doubled, but the honour of driving the coach of so great a personage was a source of considerable pride. In the minds of the people of Languedoc, the President of the States was a far more important personage than the king. My uncle was extremely popular, despite his very haughty manner. In fact, this manner was evident only when he was dealing with those who were, or thought they were, his superiors. That is why, when my uncle was Arch-bishop of Toulouse, the Cardinal de la Roche-Aymon who was then Archbishop of Narbonne, resigned his presidency of the States. He said that since it was impossible to be superior to Monsieur Dillon, one had perforce to make way for him.

We used to spend a night at Nîmes, where my uncle always had business to attend to. One year we stayed several days with the bishop and I had time to visit in detail the ancient monuments and the factories. Although the monuments were not so well cared for as they are today, they had already begun to clear the Arena and had pulled down recent buildings to free the *Maison Carrée*.* They had also found the inscription: 'To Caius and Lucius Agrippa, the princes of youth.'† It was M. Seguier, a distinguished archaeologist, to whom Nîmes is much indebted, who found this inscription. He traced it from the marks of the nails which had originally held the bronze letters in place.

My uncle timed his journey so that he would arrive in Montpellier after sunset. By so doing, he avoided receiving a salute of guns and spared the susceptibilities of the Comte de Périgord, Commander of the Province and the King's Commissioner at the opening of the States, who was not entitled to this privilege. It was deplorable that so great a gentleman should display such pettiness over a matter of ceremonial protocol quite without personal significance. It so happened that the Archbishop of Narbonne was, by birth, the equal of M. de Périgord, but had he been only a peasant, this privilege would still have been his due.

* A small temple dating from 16 BC, one of the most perfect of the Augustan period.
† C. CAESARI AUGUSTI F.L. CAESARI AUGUSTI F. COS DESIGNATO PRINCIPIBUS JUVENTUTIS (To Caius Caesar, son of Augustus, to Lucius Caesar, son of Augustus and Consul-designate, Princes of Youth). Caius and Lucius were the sons of Agrippa and the grandsons of Augustus, who adopted them as his heirs.

The business before the States amounted, in essence, to deciding what financial contributions could be levied and the Court always hoped for an increase in the *don gratuit*, which it lay within the power of the States to withhold entirely if any of its privileges had been infringed. The King's Commissioners would discuss the interests of the Province with the Syndics of the States, of whom there were two. They took it in turn to go to Paris each year, accompanied by a delegation from the States, to deliver to the king the *don gratuit* voted by their Province. The Archbishop of Narbonne presented the delegation to the king and everyone received at Court who was in Paris at that time – it was always during the summer – would join the delegation. After a dinner given by the First Gentleman of the Bedchamber, they were all taken for a walk in the gardens of Trianon or Marley and the fountains would be set in play. On one occasion, I accompanied the deputation and my grandmother and I were taken round the grounds in armchairs on wheels drawn by *suisses* (footmen). Those very same chairs had served the Court of Louis XIV. After being taken through the fine groves at Marly, and having admired the magnificence of the fountains and the waterfalls, we found an excellent collation prepared for us in one of the principal salons. I think this was in 1786. It was the only time I ever saw Marly in all its splendour, though I have been there many times since. That fine château no longer exists.* It has vanished without trace and the speed of its disappearance makes it easier to understand how it came to be that Rome is today surrounded by a wilderness.

The house in which we lived at Montpellier was very fine and very large, but terribly gloomy for it stood in a dark, narrow street. My uncle rented it furnished and it was excellently fitted out in red damask. He occupied the first-floor apartment which had very fine Turkish carpets everywhere. They were common in Languedoc in those days. The apartment enclosed a square courtyard. Along one of its four sides was a dining-room for fifty covers and along another side, an equally large drawing-room with six windows. In this room the furniture and hangings were of beautiful crimson damask and there was an immense fireplace in a very ancient style which would be much admired today.

My grandmother and I occupied the ground floor, where it was always dark by three o'clock in the afternoon. We never saw my

* The château of Marly was built by Mansart for Louis XIV as a retreat where he could escape from ceremonial. It was sold and destroyed during the Revolution. Only a few traces remain.

Comte Arthur Dillon, father of
Mme de La Tour du Pin.

Comte de La Tour du Pin de Gouvernet, father of M. de La Tour du Pin.

uncle during the morning. We breakfasted at nine o'clock and afterwards I would go for a walk with my English maid. For the three last years, I went three times a week to the fine applied physics laboratory run by the States. The professor in charge, the Abbé Bertholon, was kind enough to give me private lessons. This meant that I could study the apparatus, help him with his experiments, make some of my own and put as many questions as I liked, learning thus far more than would have been possible at public lectures. Physics interested me tremendously. I studied it most diligently and the Abbé Bertholon expressed himself satisfied with my ability. My maid came with me and as she understood hardly a word of French, busied herself cleaning and drying the apparatus, to the great delight of the professor.

We had to be formally dressed, even wearing jewels, by exactly three o'clock, in time for dinner. We would go up to the drawing-room where, except on Fridays, we always found fifty guests. On Saturdays, my uncle dined out, either with the bishop or with some important member of the States. There were never any ladies present except my grandmother and me and the most important of the guests would be placed between us. When there were foreigners, especially Englishmen, they were put next to me. It was training for me in the art of conversation and behaviour, in learning to decide which subjects would most interest my neighbour, often a person of note and sometimes of learning, too.

In those days, everyone with a decently dressed servant was waited on by him at table. There were no decanters or wine glasses on the table itself but, at big dinners, silver buckets were set on a sideboard with wines for the various courses. There were also stands of a dozen glasses and anyone wishing for a glass of one of the wines sent his servant to fetch it. This servant always stood behind his master's chair, holding a plate and cutlery ready for the next course. I had a servant of my own who also dressed my hair. He wore my livery which, since our braidings were exactly the same as those of the Bourbon liveries, had to be in red. The dark blue used by my family in England would have made our livery resemble that of the king, which was not allowed.

After dinner, which did not last more than an hour, we returned to the drawing-room where there would be a gathering of members of the States come to drink coffee with us. Everyone remained standing and, after half-an-hour, my grandmother and I would go downstairs to our own apartments. Afterwards, we often went visiting, carried in sedan chairs, which were the only means of transportation used in Montpellier.

Montpellier society centred around the wives of the presidents and councillors of the *Cours des Comptes** and those of the nobles who lived all the year on their estates and for whom the session of the States was the main diversion of the year. There were also visitors of note, relatives of the bishops who were attending the States and officers from the garrisons of the province who had been given leave to come and join in the festivities. There was a theatre, to which my grandmother took me once or twice, and balls – one given by the Comte de Périgord, another at the Intendance† and others in private houses, but not at my uncle's nor at the houses of any of the bishops.

When we returned to Paris at the beginning of 1784, we found that my father was back from America. After the signing of the peace treaty and the returning of St Kitts to the English, he had remained for a time in Martinique where he had become much attached to the Comtesse de La Touche, the thirty-year-old widow of a naval officer who had left her with two children, a son and a daughter. She was very pleasant and exceedingly rich. Her cousin‡ had recently married the Vicomte de Beauharnais who had brought her to France with him. Mme de La Touche also left for France with her two children. My father followed her and at once the possibility of a marriage between them became much talked of. My grandmother was furiously angry at the idea. Yet it was very natural that my father should wish to marry again in the hope of begetting a son. He was thirty-three and colonel of one of the finest regiments in the army. Unlike the other regiments of the Irish Brigade, it had kept its name and a proud warrant giving it the right to leave France with drums beating and colours flying whenever its owner wished. So, of course, my father wanted a son. It would doubtless have been preferable for him to choose his wife among the titled Catholic families of England but he did not like Englishwomen and he did like Mme de La Touche. She was amiable and good, though weak, with the careless good nature of all Creoles.

The marriage took place in spite of my grandmother. My father wished me to be presented to my stepmother but so bitter was my grandmother's opposition that the possibility had to be abandoned. The only visit I managed to pay her was in 1786 when my father was leaving to take up his appointment as Governor of

* The Audit Office. (Tr.)
† The seat of the administration of a Province. (Tr.)
‡ This first cousin was Josephine who, after the death under the guillotine of her first husband, married General Napoleon Bonaparte, later the Emperor Napoleon. (Tr.)

Tobago. He was very upset at not having been made Governor of Martinique or San Domingo, as he had earned a right to one of these two posts. He had served throughout the war with the greatest distinction. His regiment had won the first successful battle of the campaign, taking the island of Grenada by assault and capturing the governor, Lord Macartney. His intervention had contributed greatly to the capture of the islands of St Eustace and St Kitts. He had governed St Kitts for two years and when it was returned to the English by the Peace Treaty of 1783, the people of the island had showered on him tokens of their esteem and gratitude. Echoes of all this had found their way even to England, as my father discovered when he visited that country on his return to Europe. He was given a most flattering welcome there.

But our uncle, the archbishop, was so dominated by my grandmother that, at her instigation, he refused to support his nephew's candidature for the governorship of Martinique or San Domingo. However, although he did not support it, he put no obstacle in his way. My father had to accept the governorship of Tobago and he lived there until he was appointed to represent Martinique in the States-General.* He left France with his wife, my small sister, Fanny, and my tutor, M. Combes, whom he was taking out as registrar of the island. This was a great grief to me. Mlle de La Touche entered the Convent of the Assumption with a governess and her brother was sent to school with a tutor.

Before he left, my father spoke to my grandmother of a marriage he very much wished for me. During the war, he had met in Martinique a young man, aide-de-camp to the Marquis de Bouillé,† much liked by the latter and held by my father in high esteem. My grandmother refused even to consider him, although he was highly born and an eldest son. She declared he was a bad lot, that he was in debt and that he was short and ugly. I was so young that my father did not insist. He gave my uncle a power of proxy to marry me as he saw fit. But I myself often thought of the man whom my father had suggested. I asked about him. My cousin, Dominic Sheldon, who had been brought up by my grandmother and who lived with us, knew him and often spoke to me about him. I learned that he had, indeed, been wild in his youth and resolved to think no more about him.

* The assembly of the three estates of the realm: clergy, nobility and commons. It met only at the summons of the king to deal with matters affecting the kingdom as a whole, e.g., war, finance. It was very rarely summoned. The session referred to was that of 1789, the last ever held. (Tr.)
† The Commander-in-Chief.

In 1785, we stayed in Languedoc much longer than usual. After the States, we went to Alais to spend a month with kindly Bishop de Bausset, who later became a cardinal. I found it a very interesting journey. My uncle was very well liked in the Cevennes, where he had done much to encourage the development of industry. He took me to the coal and copper sulphate mines and, thanks to my studies in chemistry and experimental physics, I was able to understand something of the processes used. I often talked with the engineers who frequently dined with my uncle and the knowledge I gained in this way helped me to understand the plans being discussed in the drawing-room.

It is to my stay in Alais that I attribute my love of mountains. This small town is deep in the Cevennes, set in a charming valley surrounded by cool meadows, shaded by chestnut trees that must be centuries old. Every day there were delightful excursions. The young men of the district formed themselves into a guard of honour for my uncle and wore the English uniform of the Dillon Regiment – red with yellow facings. They all belonged to the best families in the region. Every day the bishop invited some of them to dinner. In the evening, their wives or sisters came, we made music together or danced. It was a very happy visit.

I was sad when we had to leave to spend two months in Narbonne. From there, we went to Toulouse, travelling by way of Saint-Papoul. My uncle went to visit the beautiful Benedictine college at Sorèze. It was there that I met the Vaudreuil family, who lived nearby. They had three daughters and one son. The latter was then seventeen or eighteen and would have been well pleased to marry the elegant niece of the powerful metropolitan archbishop. On that journey, Providence seemed to have strewn my path with suitors but my moment had not yet come and if it were permissible to believe in presentiment or predestination, then I would say that I did have a very marked presentiment at Bordeaux.

I do not know why Bordeaux should have interested me more than the other towns through which we passed. The fine theatre had just been opened and I went several times with my grandmother, sitting in the Jurats' box. The Jurats of Bordeaux held the same position in the town as the mayor does today. There were evening parties in various houses, a splendid luncheon on board a ship of six hundred tons belonging to a Mr MacHarty, an Irish merchant. This superb vessel, which was about to leave for India, was named after me: the *Henrietta-Lucy*.

In Bordeaux, I also saw Mme Dillon, the mother of all those

Dillons who have always claimed, though mistakenly, to be related to me. This lady, who was of a good English family, had married an Irish merchant named Dillon whose forefathers had probably come from that part of Ireland known, until the days of Queen Elizabeth, as Dillon's Country where, as in Scotland, many of the people took their lord's name. However that may be, the affairs of this particular Dillon went badly. He raised a certain amount of money and came to settle in Bordeaux, where he went into business. He bought a property at Blanquefort and established his wife there. She was a superbly handsome woman and her extraordinary beauty soon became famous throughout the province. She spent the winters in Bordeaux. Since she had polished manners, was intelligent, very well-bred and had a baby every year, she interested everyone. Her husband died, leaving her pregnant with her twelfth child, with very little money but all her charms and great courage.

The Maréchal de Richelieu took her under his protection and recommended her to my uncle who was to visit Bordeaux at about that time. My uncle promised to see that the children were given a good start in life and kept his word. The three eldest were girls. Thanks to their beauty, they made good marriages* and the two younger ones greatly furthered the fortunes of their brothers. My uncle and my grandmother fell completely under their spell and were induced to promote their interests by means which I have often heard described as questionable. For instance, my uncle's brother, Edward Dillon, had been a Knight of Malta. Means were found to use the patents of nobility he had had to produce in order to be admitted to the Order of Malta, to further the fortunes of three of these Dillon boys, Robert, William and Frank, the third, fourth and fifth sons.

Theobald, the eldest, went into the Dillon Regiment after finishing his service as a page and married in Belgium. I met him there, very well established in a picturesque château near Mons. Edward, the second son, owed his fortune to his handsome face. It is he who was nicknamed 'Beau Dillon'. His patrons were the queen and the Duchesse de Polignac and he was given a place in the household of the Comte d'Artois. He remained in favour until his death. His only daughter, a charming girl, was married in Germany to M. de Karoly and died very young.

Two other sons became priests and would doubtless have become

* The youngest of the three married the Marquis d'Osmond and their daughter, the Comtesse de Boigne, published memoirs in which references to Madame de La Tour du Pin are less than amiable. (Tr.)

bishops if it had not been for the Revolution. All these Dillons, without exception, were very steady and it was as rare as it was honourable that, of the nine brothers holding some form of employment in France, not one should have fallen into the errors and excesses which were the curse of so many families during that troubled period.

To return to my presentiment: I must tell you that a few days before leaving Bordeaux, perhaps only the day before, my servant asked me, as he dressed my hair, if he might go that same evening to a château not far off the highway. He had once been in service there and wanted to meet some of his old friends. He said he could rejoin the carriages at the halt nearest to the château, namely at Cubzac, where our road crossed the Dordogne. I asked him the name of the château, and he told me it was 'Le Bouilh' and belonged to the Comte de La Tour du Pin who lived there. His son was the young man my father had wanted me to marry and whom my grandmother had refused. I was far more troubled by my servant's reply than seemed reasonable. It was, after all, only a reminder of someone to whom I had until then been indifferent and whom I had never seen. I enquired the whereabouts of the house and was annoyed to learn that it could not be seen from the road. However, I made a note of the point along our route when we would be nearest to it and of the appearance of the countryside nearby.

I was deep in my own thoughts as we crossed the stream at Cubzac, a crossing which I knew belonged to M. de La Tour du Pin. As we stepped ashore, and all the way to Saint-André, I told myself again and again that I might have been châtelaine of all that beautiful countryside. But I was very careful to keep such thoughts hidden from my grandmother, who would have been far from pleased with them. Nonetheless, they remained in my mind and I often spoke to my cousin, M. Sheldon, of M. de Gouvernet, whom he used to meet out hunting with the Duc d'Orléans – Philippe Égalité.

IV

By the time we returned to Paris, I was sixteen and my grandmother told me that negotiations were in progress for my marriage to the Marquis Adrien de Laval. Through the death of his elder brother, he had recently become heir to the family honours. His mother, the Duchesse de Laval, had been my mother's great friend. She favoured the marriage and it was equally pleasing to me. The name of Laval-Montmorency rang pleasantly in my aristocratic ears. The younger Laval had left his seminary when his brother died and entered the army. Our fathers were closely connected but, to me, the greatest attraction of the proposed marriage was that I would leave my grandmother's house. I was no longer a child. My education had begun so early that, at sixteen, I was as mature as others are at twenty-five. Life with my grandmother was miserably unhappy; but I had thought much about my future and had firmly resolved not to be led by resentment into accepting a marriage out of keeping with my station.

It was known that I was my grandmother's sole heir and she herself did everything possible to foster the idea that she was devoted to my interests, that they were her sole preoccupation. There were two diametrically opposed qualities in her character: violence and duplicity. She was considered wealthy and so indeed she was. It was certain that I would inherit it all, for when I was sixteen, my grandmother was already sixty.

Who would have suspected that my uncle, with an income of 400,000 francs, was having to resort to expedients and had persuaded my grandmother to borrow in order to come to his aid? Everyone who wanted to marry me was dazzled by my apparently fine expectations. It was known that when I married, I would be appointed a Lady of the Queen's Household and in those days that was a weighty factor among the highly-born when considering possible alliances. 'To be at Court' was a magic phrase. There were only twelve Ladies of the Household. My mother had been one because the queen had a tender personal affection for her, because she was the daughter-in-law of one English peer and the grand-daughter of another and also because my father, a distinguished soldier, was one of the very few men likely to become a Marshal of France.

From every point of view I was, therefore, what might be called a good match and since this chapter is concerned with my personal attributes, this would seem to be the right place to describe myself. On paper, the portrait will not be flattering, for my reputation for beauty rested entirely on my figure and my bearing, not at all on my features. My greatest attribute was my thick, ash-blond hair. I had small grey eyes and my eyelashes were very thin, partly destroyed by a bad attack of smallpox when I was four. I had sparse, fair eyebrows, a high forehead and a nose described as Grecian, but long and too heavy at the tip. My best feature was my mouth, for my lips were well shaped and had a fresh bloom. I also had very good teeth. Even today, at the age of seventy-one, I still have them all. I was said to have a pleasant face and an attractive smile, yet in spite of this, my appearance as a whole might have been considered ugly. I am afraid a number of people must have thought so, for I myself considered hideous certain women said to resemble me. But my height and good figure, my dazzlingly clear and transparent complexion made me outstanding in any gathering, particularly by day, and I certainly overshadowed other women endowed with far better looks than mine.

I have never expected to be thought beautiful and therefore have never suffered that demeaning jealousy which I have seen tormenting so many women. It was, therefore, in all sincerity that I praised the looks, the wit or the talents of others and advised them concerning their dress. I will not say that I was indifferent to my own advantages or unaware of them but in my earliest youth I set myself a sort of code and have never departed from it. It came about like this: as my uncle was President of the Assembly of the Clergy, we often spent the summer in Paris and at the big dinners he gave during the session, I sometimes met the Maréchal de Biron, the last great gentleman of the period of Louis XIV, or at least, the last to preserve the traditions of that day. He was eighty-five when I was only fifteen. He took a liking to me and said that I resembled some lady of his own time. He sat me beside him at table and was kind enough to talk to me. One day he told me that from his earliest youth he had given much thought to the various difficulties of old age in society and that, having himself at my age been extremely bored and badgered by certain of his elders, had resolved that if he should himself live to a great age, he would avoid inflicting the same suffering. He advised me to do the same. I have never forgotten that piece of advice. I have followed it also in matters of dress and have often congratulated myself on having done so, for there is nothing so

ridiculous or so ugly as an elderly woman wearing flowers or
ornaments which do but emphasise the ravages of the years.

The Maréchal de Biron was colonel of the Gardes Françaises and
they adored him. There was nothing military about them except
their uniforms. I had seen him, when I was a child, parading before
the king at the head of his men in the review held every year on the
little plain of Sablons near the bridge at Neuilly.

He owned a magnificent and very beautiful house in Paris – it
belongs nowadays to the Order of the Sacred Heart* – adjoining a
splendid garden of three or four acres, with hot-houses filled with
rarest plants. The Maréchal lived in magnificent style and did the
honours of Paris in the grand manner. He owned boxes in all the
principal theatres and although he never went himself, his boxes were
always occupied by foreigners of distinction, particularly the English,
whom he preferred above all the others, and among whom he
selected the most notable. It was considered a very great honour to
be received at his house.

He never gave balls, but there would be a concert at his house
whenever any foreign singer or great musician visited Paris. He
gathered about him everyone of distinction, always with the greatest
courtesy and in the grand manner, but with unsurpassable ease amid
all the splendour, for that was his natural setting. One day, speaking
to my uncle and rolling his r's as was the fashion when Louis XV was
young, he said: 'Monsieur l'Archévêque' – for Marshals of France
did not accord bishops the customary 'Monseigneur' – 'if I should
have the misfortune to lose Madame la Maréchale de Biron, I should
beg Mlle Dillon to take my name and allow me to place my fortune
at her feet.' But this misfortune, for which he would have been so
easily comforted, did not befall him. His wife, from whom he had
been living separately for fifty years on account of some mis-
demeanour of which I know nothing, survived him and died on the
scaffold with her niece, the Duchesse de Biron.

The Maréchal de Biron died in 1787 or 1788 and his funeral was
the last splendour of the monarchy. Never had there been anything
so magnificent.

The Maréchal was not succeeded in the Regiment by his nephew,
the Duc de Biron,† as the Regiment had hoped, but by the Duc du

---

* Today, the Musée Rodin. (Tr.)
† Known until then as the Duc de Lauzun, whose great ambition had been to
command the Regiment. Despite his reputation for frivolity, he was a well-tried,
courageous and excellent soldier and a successful diplomat. He died on the
scaffold in 1793. (Tr.)

Châtelet. He made himself unpopular the moment he took up his appointment by setting immediately about the task of restoring military discipline which had been sadly neglected in that particular corps. Many of the soldiers did not even live in quarters and appeared in barracks only when they were on duty. As a result, they had mixed a great deal with the middle and lower classes and so fell an easy prey to the revolutionaries. M. du Châtelet, a hard and difficult man, looked on the Régiment des Gardes Françasies as an ordinary regiment in need of reform. He started by making himself odious and the revolutionaries turned it to their own account.

The plan to marry me to Adrien de Laval came to nothing because his grandfather decided he should marry his cousin, Mlle de Luxembourg. I was sorry, for I should have liked to bear his name. My grandmother suggested that I should marry the Vicomte de Fleury, but I did not wish to do so. His reputation was bad, he was neither intelligent nor distinguished and he belonged to the cadet branch of a not very illustrious family. I refused him.

The next suitor for my hand was Espérance de l'Aigle, of whom I had seen a great deal when we were children. I did not consider his name sufficiently illustrious. It was not, perhaps, a very sensible decision as he was indeed an excellent young man, with a very pleasant home. He was connected with the Rochechouart family, whom I was to meet again when I entered society, for we moved in the same circles. Tracy, his father's estate, was six or seven leagues from Hautefontaine. My grandmother did not want to continue her visits to Hautefontaine and would no doubt have agreed to partly hand over this property to me, to allow me at least to live there. This marriage seemed to have everything to commend it and I heard nothing but good of it, yet I refused.

Marriages are decided in heaven. My thoughts still turned to M. de Gouvernet. I was told unfavourable things about him. I had never seen him. I knew that he was short and ugly, that he had contracted debts, that he had gambled and so on, all those things which in any other man would instantly have repelled me. But my mind was made up. I told Sheldon he was the only man I would marry. He tried endlessly to argue me out of what he called my obsession, but I refused to be convinced.

One morning in November 1786, when we were preparing to leave for Languedoc, my grandmother told me: 'This M. de Gouvernet is back again with his offer of marriage. Mme de Monconseil, his grandmother, is hemming us in on all sides. His father is commander of a Province and will eventually be a Marshal of France. He is held in the highest esteem in military circles. His cousin, the Archbishop of Auch, is bringing to bear on your uncle all the influence he can muster. Another cousin sees that her nephew, the Abbé de Chauvigny, speaks to us of him every day. The queen herself wishes it, for Mme de Monconseil's daughter, the Princesse d'Hénin, has spoken to her about it. Think it over and make your decision.' I replied without any hesitation: 'My mind is already made up. There is nothing I should like better.'

My grandmother was astounded. I think she had hoped I would refuse him. She could not understand how I could prefer him to M. de l'Aigle. Frankly, I could not have explained it myself. It was an instinct, a guidance from above. God had destined me for him! And since that decision, which my sixteen-year-old lips uttered almost despite myself, I have felt that I belonged to him, that my life was his. As I write these lines at the age of seventy-one, after fifty years as his companion, I bless Heaven for my decision. Not once, in all the ups and downs of our fortunes, did I ever feel that I might have been happier with another man. I have thanked God every day for the husband he gave me and now that I mourn him every moment of every day, I pray for one last grace: to rejoin him in that place where we shall never more be parted.

We left for Montpellier without any further mention of this marriage. That year, Sheldon came with us and when we were alone, I questioned him endlessly about M. de Gouvernet. No formal request had yet been made. My grandmother never mentioned it to me.

The Abbé de Chauvigny acted as intermediary between Mme de Monconseil and my uncle. As was proper, he never spoke to me of this matter, no more did I to him in the conversations we had together. But I spoke with him whenever I could, for he had a pretty wit. One evening in the drawing-room, he was twisting in his fingers the envelope of a letter I had just seen him pass to my uncle. He looked at the seal, admiring the design, but when I unthinkingly held out my hand to see it, he kept hold of it and, looking hard at me, said 'No, not yet'. I realised at once that the letter was from Mme de Monconseil, or at least from someone who was writing about my marriage. The abbé was maliciously amused at my blushes and confusion and we did not speak to one another again that evening.

The next morning, my grandmother told me that my uncle had received a charming letter from Mme de Monconseil; that she was extremely anxious for me to marry her grandson, of whom she was very fond; that she would do all in her power to bring it about but that she did not possess any great influence with her son-in-law, the Comte de La Tour du Pin, with whom she had had some very unpleasant differences of opinion. It was then I learned that Mme de Monconseil's daughter, Mme de La Tour du Pin, had behaved very badly and for twenty years had been shut away in a convent, which she seldom left. Her husband made her a small allowance, but refused to see her. They were not legally separated. Every effort had been made to avoid the scandal of legal proceedings, partly in order not to embarrass her sister who, shortly before, had married the Prince d'Hénin, younger brother of the Prince de Chimay, and partly out of consideration for her own daughter.*

At that time, Mme la Marquise de Monconseil was eighty-five years of age and I have often been told that even at that great age, she was still beautiful. M. de Monconseil had married her when she was very young. He was a soldier, like most gentlemen of that period, and had spent a very gay and dissipated youth. He had been a page to Louis XIV and used to tell how, when lighting the way for the king one evening as he left Mme de Maintenon's house, carrying two torches in one hand, as was then the custom, he had set fire to the king's wig. Telling the story to his daughter, seventy years later, he trembled again at the memory of the fear he had felt at that moment.

M. de Monconseil fought in all the wars of the later years of the reign of Louis XIV and in all those of the reign of Louis XV. His wife, who was beautiful, witty and a mistress of intrigue, had greatly furthered his fortunes. I think they forgave each other many faults. They often lived far apart. M. de Monconseil commanded the forces in Upper Alsace, lived always in Colmar and came rarely to Paris, where his wife spent most of her time and where she was assiduous in fostering his interest. I have heard it said that she never let a mail leave without sending him a letter, very short, but full of interesting news. As there were no news sheets in those days, personal letters were highly prized. What a pity that collections of such letters should have been destroyed!

When he was forty, for some reason which I greatly regret not knowing, M. de Monconseil left the king's service and retired to his estate of Tesson in Saintonge. He settled there and did not leave it until he died at the age of ninety. He led a most edifying life and when he died his bequests to charity were far larger than might have

---

* Claire-Suzanne de La Tour du Pin de Gouvernet, sister of the writer's future husband. She married the Marquis de Lameth. (Tr.)

been expected from the size of his fortune which, though comfortable, was not immense. He had a fine house at Saintes and spent three months there every winter. The rest of the year, he lived at Tesson which he had built himself and whose park and gardens he had planted. He seldom went to Paris to see his wife, who lived there in a good, pleasant house. It was at his request that his son-in-law, M. de La Tour du Pin, sometimes allowed his wife to leave her convent to spend a few days with her father at Tesson. But, in forty-five years, this had happened on only two or three occasions. Mme de Monconseil went only once, I believe, to visit her husband. She found the journey so long that she felt no inclination to repeat it.

M. de Monconseil was deeply attached to his grandson who went often to Tesson and always came away with his purse well filled. But these visits to his grandfather gave him something far more precious than money: from them he learned the principles of chivalry proper to a young man of gentle birth and the rules of honour that were graven then on his young heart have never been effaced.

And so it happened that the journey I made to Montpellier between 1786 and 1787 was to be my last.

⚜⚜⚜⚜⚜⚜⚜⚜⚜⚜⚜⚜⚜ V ⚜⚜⚜⚜⚜⚜⚜⚜⚜⚜⚜⚜⚜

It will not be difficult to imagine my great eagerness to return to Paris where my future was to be decided. We set out even sooner than I had expected for news arrived that the first Assembly of Notables* had been summoned. My uncle was a member so we had to leave for Paris the day after the closing of the States. I myself date the Revolution from then.

My uncle decided that, as he was not too well, we would stop for a night at Fontainebleau. This would avoid his being overtired when we reached Paris and he would be able to go the following morning to Versailles. We always found the house looking as if we had never left it. Whether tired or not, the servants had to be in their places, dressed, powdered and trim as ever. I had to do the same. We arrived

* An extraordinary Council composed of leading citizens chosen by the king from the three estates. By convening it, the king could avoid summoning the powerful States-General. It was summoned in 1787 to deal with the financial confusion and to reform abuses. (Tr.)

at two o'clock, and at three, my grandmother and I were in the drawing-room ready to dine, taking no account at all of the 210 leagues we had just covered.

In the evening, people came to call. The first visitor was an elderly Comte de Bentheim, a stout German whose wife, always referred to as 'The Sovereign', was one of my grandmother's friends. After the usual opening remarks about the bad weather, weariness and the state of the roads, my uncle asked the Comte what news there was in Paris. 'Oh', replied the stout German, 'there's one piece of news that will interest everyone: Mme de Monconseil has died.' It would be impossible to describe my feelings on hearing those few words. I became pale and my uncle, fearing my agitation would betray me, said that I was tired and it would be better for me to retire, which I did immediately. But when I took his hand to kiss it, as I did every evening, he told me in English that it would not change our plans.

For a few days, the only topic of conversation was the death of Mme de Monconseil, the grief of her daughter, Mme d'Hénin, who had lived with her, and the admirable care given her by M. de Gouvernet.* It all concerned me closely but I had to appear indifferent. Fortunately, I was able to talk about it to my cousin, Charlotte Jerningham, who had just left the Ursuline Convent in the rue Saint-Jacques, where she had spent three years without once going out. Her mother had come to Paris to fetch her, but they stayed until after my marriage.

Since his father was not in Paris at the time, M. de Gouvernet quickly made it known to my uncle that his grandmother's death in no way changed his own wish for an alliance with my great-uncle's family and he asked permission to call on him privately. He came one evening and my uncle was very favourably impressed with him. M. de Gouvernet insisted he should be allowed to go and tell his father personally that the request he intended to make for the hand of Mlle Dillon would be accepted by her and by her grandmother. My uncle agreed and M. de Gouvernet took his leave. I tell you this in such detail so that you may see the ways of good society in a period so far removed from that in which I am writing. My uncle went up to see my grandmother and, finding me alone with her, embraced me, saying: 'Goodnight, Madame de Gouvernet.'

Several days passed, but before the week was over, my uncle was told one day that M. de Gouvernet was waiting in his study. 'But that is impossible,' he exclaimed. It was, however, true. He had been to Le Bouilh, spoken to his father, persuaded him to write the formal

* Grandson of Mme de Monconseil and future husband of the writer.

request for my hand, asked his wishes concerning all the arrangements and then, climbing back into his carriage, had returned to
Paris. This haste seemed to me in the best of taste. It was agreed that
he would wait on my grandmother the following morning, but that
he would not see me until the marriage contract had been signed.
Such was the custom in those days, unless there should happen to be
some chance meeting. In my case, that was very unlikely, for I never
went out on foot, never walked in any public place and never went
to the theatre.

The following day, such a memorable one for me, I hid behind a
curtain and saw M. de Gouvernet alight from a very pretty cabriolet
drawn by a fine, spirited grey. If you remember that I was not yet
seventeen, you will understand why such an arrival pleased me far
more than if he had come in a fine coach, escorted by a groom who
would have offered him an arm as he climbed out. In two bounds, he
was at the top of the steps. He was wearing very elegant morning
dress: a town coat – either black or very dark grey, for he was still in
deep mourning – a military collar and a military hat, the latter worn
almost exclusively by colonels for it was thought very dashing to
proclaim this high rank above a youthful countenance. I had been
told that he was ugly, but did not find him so. His assurance and
decisive air pleased me immediately. I had stationed myself where
I could see him when he went in to see my grandmother. She offered
him her hand, which he kissed with the greatest deference. I could
not hear their conversation, so I tried to imagine it. He stayed a
quarter of an hour and it was agreed that the contract would be
signed as soon as it had been drawn up by the lawyers. Then, M. de
Gouvernet would be able to come daily to my uncle's house.

It took eight days to prepare the contract, but before it was
complete, Mme d'Hénin called on my grandmother. She asked for
me, as I had thought she might do. The elegance and assurance of
this beautiful woman who would, I knew, examine me from head to
toe, so frightened me that my legs would hardly bear me forward into
the room and I literally could not see where I was going. She stood
up, took my hand and embraced me. Then, with the outspokenness
of ladies of her day, stood me at arms' length and cried: 'Ah, what a
pretty figure. She is charming. My nephew is very lucky.' It was
torture for me. She sat down again and asked me a lot of questions to
which I am sure I must have made the most stupid replies. As she
left, she embraced me again and made me a number of pretty compliments on the pleasure it would give her to take me into society.

This visit took place, if I remember rightly, on the day before the signing of the contract. It was not customary for the young lady to be present at the reading of this preliminary document which was signed only by members of the families and the lawyers. But once the lawyers had gone, I was sent for. My grandmother came to the door to take my hand and I crossed the salon in a state bordering on unconsciousness. I felt everyone's gaze upon me, especially that of M. de Gouvernet, at whom I was very careful not to look. I was put beside Mme d'Hénin and my aunt, Lady Jerningham, who took pity on my embarrassment.

I was very simply dressed. I had begged my grandmother to leave the choice to me. At that time we wore very straight gowns laced at the back and drawn in very tightly at the waist. They were known as 'sheaths'. Mine was of plain white muslin with a dark blue belt of good ribbon fringed at the ends with brilliantly-coloured silk. It came from England. They said I was as pretty as a picture. They looked at my hair, which was really very beautiful. Such scrutiny in the presence of the 'high and mighty lord, the future husband', as he had been named twenty times during the reading of the contract, was quite unbearable.

From then on, M. de Gouvernet came every day to dine or to spend the afternoon or to take supper with us, either in Paris or at Versailles, where my uncle had been living since the opening of the Assembly of Notables.

My grandmother and I had remained in Paris and set out every day of the week, at half-past one, for Versailles. We would arrive in time for dinner at three o'clock. My uncle was almost always still closeted with the committee of which he was a member, presided over, if I remember rightly, by Monsieur, the king's brother and later Louis XVIII. He would appear just as we were about to sit down to table, always bringing with him several guests. M. de Gouvernet, as I have said, came out from Paris every day to dine with us. He always wore formal dress and a sword, for it had not yet become the custom, especially at Versailles, to wear town dress and a round hat to dinner. No well-bred man would have allowed himself to be seen there dressed otherwise than formally, wearing a sword, unless he were about to ride to Paris or drive there in his cabriolet. And in that case, he would be careful to reach the courtyard by way of the back stairs, avoiding the apartments, galleries and guard rooms. Regard was still paid to the proprieties. Failure to observe, I do not say the etiquette, but even the slightest nuance in the courtesies so strictly observed in society, would have been in the worst possible taste.

During this Assembly of Notables, which I found unbearably

boring, politics were the sole topic of every conversation. Everyone coming into the salon was ready with some infallible remedy for the treasury deficit as well as for the abuses which had been allowed to take root in the state. My uncle wanted the entire country governed by States, as in Languedoc. M. de Gouvernet often joined in these conversations. His remarks were intelligent and forceful, and I enjoyed listening to him.

He had presented to my uncle the Marquis de Lameth, his brother-in-law, and two of the latter's brothers, Charles and Alexander. Alexander was a Knight of Malta and a great friend of M. de Gouvernet. The Marquis de Lameth was a handsome man of thirty, tall, well-built, serious, even solemn in manner. He nearly always lived either in the country, at his lovely château of Hénéncourt, near Amiens, or with his regiment, the Régiment de la Couronne. He was a good soldier, of the kind known at the time as 'faiseurs'* because of their concern for the strict observance of discipline and their insistence that orders should be carried out with scrupulous promptitude. They did not mix with their subordinates and had a very clear-cut conception of their duties. M. de Gouvernet was of the same school. In those days, he was still only second-in-command of the Royal-Comtois. It was not until his marriage that he was given command of the Royal-Vaisseaux, the regiment which was to give him such trouble.

I seem to remember that this Assembly of Notables ended its session towards the middle of April. I had found it tiring from every point of view and so had M. de Gouvernet, who came daily to Versailles, driven by gallantry, or perhaps by a more tender feeling. We found ways to talk a great deal together and to become increasingly certain that we were made for one another. We have often recalled with pleasure the charm of those first conversations in which we were both seeking to understand and know one another, in which we each studied the opinions and tastes of the other and from which we both always emerged so satisfied. What pleasant plans we made for our future, and not one of them has come true! We were too happy in the present to foresee the storms we would have to face, yet we were aware of a deep conviction that, however heavy the reverses we might have to endure, we would find in our mutual affection the strength to withstand them unfalteringly.

M. de Gouvernet had not yet fully understood my grandmother's character. He had accepted Mme d'Hénin's impression, which was based entirely on hearsay for she had not entered the queen's

* People who exaggerate their own importance. (Tr.)

Household until after my mother's death. Sadness is so quickly forgotten at Court! The queen mourned my mother for twenty-four hours and the very next day was expressing a wish to visit the Comédie Française. The Duchesse de Duras, who was in waiting that day, told her: 'It would perhaps be better for Your Majesty to go to the Opera, otherwise, as you pass Saint-Sulpice, Your Majesty will meet Mme Dillon's funeral procession.' The queen accepted the rebuke and remained at Versailles. The Duchesse de Duras was a woman of the greatest virtue and the queen stood in awe of her. She had dearly loved my mother and later extended this affection to me.

I first met my future father-in-law a few days before the signing of the contract. He was a short man, of upright carriage, very well built, who had been handsome in his youth. He still had the finest teeth one could wish for, fine eyes, an air of assurance and a charming smile which showed all his essential goodness and kindliness. He made no attempt to overawe me and I did my utmost to appear pleasing to him. He was a man of simple ways, scrupulously attentive to his duties as Commander of the Provinces of Saintonge and Poitou and of the district of Aunis. He devoted every minute he could spare to the building and planting he had undertaken at Le Bouilh, his favourite residence. As he was separated from his wife and came to Paris only on short visits, either to wait upon the king or to consult ministers on public matters, he kept no establishment there. He was not ambitious, his son thought he should have been more so and that a man of his ability should not have remained so much in the background. He belonged to an earlier age, to the days of St Louis. He had served in the Seven Years' War as colonel of a regiment composed of the cream of all the other regiments and known as the Grenadiers de France. He had greatly distinguished himself, and all his promotions, including that to the rank he then held, had been given without any seeking on his part. His intrigue-loving mother-in-law, Mme de Monconseil, could not understand such detachment. She did not like him. She found him unnecessarily severe towards his wife, whose misbehaviour had been so public that, although the gentlest of men, he had thought it necessary to treat her with the utmost strictness. He was very just and very good, rightly considering it his duty to remove her from a world in which she had set such a scandalous example. He permitted her to appear sometimes at her father's house and wished her to be present at his son's marriage. M. de Gouvernet and Mme de Lameth treated her with great deference and respect.

The queen, who approved of my marriage, expressed a wish to

see me. She openly declared her kind intention to take me under her protection and asked my uncle to bring me to call on her, together with Mme d'Hénin, of whom I already stood in such great awe. I was very shy and when this shyness, which makes one so awkward, came over me it made me almost incapable of movement: my legs would not bear me up, every limb seemed paralysed. In vain did I reason with myself and try to conquer it. Each attempt ended in failure. In addition to this form of cowardice, probably very similar to that which paralyses a soldier who disgraces himself in battle, there was another quirk in my character which has remained with me throughout my life: an unconquerable horror of insincerity and false professions of sentiment. I knew instinctively that the queen would make a show of emotional pity and I knew also that she had mourned my mother for barely one day. My whole heart rebelled at the thought of being obliged, in my own interest, to help her play this part. As I walked through the apartments on my way to that bed-chamber which I have since entered so often, Mme d'Hénin was tactlessly telling me all over again that I had to be very amiable to the queen, that I must not be unresponsive, that the queen would be very emotional and so on, advice which only served to increase my embarrassment.

I found myself in the queen's presence, but without any recollection of how I arrived there. She embraced me and I kissed her hand. She told me to sit beside her and asked me a thousand questions about my education, my accomplishments and so on, but despite the prodigious effort I was making, I could find no voice to reply. Eventually, seeing the large tears welling from my eyes, she took pity on my embarrassment and talked to my uncle and Mme d'Hénin. My shyness left her with a bad impression which she perhaps never quite forgot. I have since had reason to regret very deeply that, having doubtless judged me wrongly then, she never thought to put my devotion to the test on an occasion when my youth and, let me say it, my courage might perhaps have changed the destinies of France.

We went to Montfermeil on about 8 or 10 May 1787. As it was contrary to custom for a future husband to sleep under the same roof as his bride, M. de Gouvernet came from Paris every day to dine with us and stayed until after supper. On the evening of 21 May, he slept at the château of Montfermeil, which the kind owners had put at the disposal of my family. A number of the gentlemen were lodged there and the ladies stayed in my grandmother's charming house.* I myself was given a delightful apartment, furnished in perfect style.

* La Folie Joyeuse.

The hangings were of Indian cloth or calico, patterned with trees, flower-laden branches, fruits and birds against a buff-coloured ground, and lined throughout with fine green silk.

In the enormous wall closets was the beautiful trousseau my grandmother had given me. It consisted entirely of household linen, lace and gowns of muslin and had cost 45,000 francs. There was not a single silk gown. M. de Gouvernet's wedding presents to me included jewels, lengths of ribbon, flowers, feathers, gloves, blonde lace, lengths of cloth – shawls were not then in fashion – a number of hats and elegant bonnets, as well as mantles of black or white muslin trimmed with blonde lace.

Mme d'Hénin had given me a charming tea table and tea service. The teapot, sugar bowl and other pieces were in silver gilt and the porcelain was of Sèvres. Her gift was the one which gave me the greatest pleasure. I believe it cost 6,000 francs. The Abbé de Gouvernet, an uncle of M. de Gouvernet, gave me a fine dressing-case which had its own special place in my travelling coach. My grandfather* gave me a fine pair of ear-rings worth 10,000 francs.

When I entered this pretty apartment, I found a charming plant stand in the middle of my bedroom, filled with rare plants and vases of flowers. In the small room next door, where I usually sat, had been placed a small book-case filled with English books, including a pretty collection of English poets in seventy volumes and also some Italian books. On the walls were beautiful English prints in good frames. All these were from M. de Gouvernet and I thanked him very warmly.

I tell you of all this splendour and elegance only in order to show the contrast with the remainder of my story.

⚜⚜⚜⚜⚜⚜⚜⚜⚜⚜⚜ VI ⚜⚜⚜⚜⚜⚜⚜⚜⚜⚜⚜

On my wedding day, everyone gathered in the salon at noon. On my side, the company included my grandmother, my uncle; my aunt, Lady Jerningham, with her husband, Sir William, her daughter, Charlotte, and her eldest son, the present Lord Stafford; the Sheldons and their elder brother, Mr Constable, who was my first witness; Sir Charles Jerningham, Sir William's brother, who had

* Henry, 11th Viscount Dillon.

been my mother's friend and was mine also, and who acted as my second witness. All these were members of my family. The guests included all the ministers of the Government, the Archbishops of Paris and Toulouse, some bishops from Languedoc who were in Paris, M. de Lally-Tollendal, of whom I will tell you later, and many others whose names I do not remember.

M. de Gouvernet's family was represented by his father and mother; his uncle, the Abbé de Gouvernet; his sister, the Marquise de Lameth, with her husband and his brothers; his aunt, Mme d'Hénin; the Chevalier de Coigny and the Comte de Valence who were his witnesses, the Comtesse de Blot and a number of other distinguished persons, about fifty or sixty in all.

We went in procession across the courtyard to the chapel. I walked first, giving my hand to my cousin, the younger Jerningham. Then came my grandmother with M. de Gouvernet. The others followed, I do not know in what order. At the altar stood my uncle and M. de Juigné, the Archbishop of Paris. The Curé of Montfermeil celebrated a Low Mass and my uncle, with the permission of the Archbishop of Paris who assisted him, gave us the nuptial blessing. But first he preached a charming sermon in that fine, vibrant voice of his which never failed to touch the heart. The marriage canopy was held by young Alfred de Lameth, who was seven, and my sixteen-year-old cousin Jerningham to whom I gave a fine sword when we returned to the salon.

All the ladies embraced me, in order of kinship and age. Then a footman brought in a large basket of green and gold sword knots, favours, fans and cords for the bishops' hats, to be distributed among the guests. This was a very costly custom. Sword favours of the finest ribbon cost between twenty-five and thirty francs each. Military sword knots in gold and the tasselled cords for the bishops' hats cost fifty francs and the fans for the ladies varied in cost between twenty-five and one hundred francs each.

Nor must the bride's dress be forgotten. It was very simple: a gown of white crêpe and fine Brussels lace, with pinners,* for in those days brides wore a bonnet, not a veil. There was a cluster of orange blosson in my hair and another at my waist. For the dinner, I wore a fine turban trimmed with white feathers to which was added the posy of orange blossom.

We talked and felt a little bored until the dinner, which was at

* Two long streamers of material pinned to either side of a lady's coif or bonnet. They were worn especially by ladies of rank in the seventeenth and eighteenth centuries. (Tr.)

four o'clock. Afterwards, we made the round of the tables set up in the courtyard for the servants and farm workers. There was one of a hundred places for the livery servants whose variously coloured coats and trimmings looked very picturesque, and another for the country people and workmen. They drank my health with a will for I was greatly liked by them and they trusted me. Many of them had known me all my life and I had often looked after their interests and needs. Many times I had forgiven their faults or softened my grandmother's displeasure, which was frequent and often unfair. They wished me happiness in the union into which I had just entered and their goodwill touched me more than all the compliments I had been offered in the salon. In the evening, a delightful concert brought the occasion to an end.

Next day, most of the guests took their leave. I wore elegant half-mourning, as there was still a month of mourning for Mme de Monconseil. Mme d'Hénin told us of the queen's wish that I should be presented the following Sunday. I had been married on Monday and it was on Tuesday that my aunt told my grandmother, who had not been consulted. Mme d'Hénin added that I would have to go with her to Paris on the morning of Thursday so that my dancing master could give me two lessons in the curtsey. There was also my presentation dress to be fitted and a visit to be paid to Mme de La Tour du Pin* who, since my mother-in-law no longer went to Court, was the only member of my new family eligible to present me.

My grandmother did not hide her fury at the arrangement, but there could be no question of disputing it. She realised that her rule over me was at an end, that I had escaped her for ever. She shook with rage at the realisation that the queen would henceforth have me at her disposal and that Mme d'Hénin, who was to introduce me into society, would in the future determine my conduct. She did not, however, dare to show her displeasure and controlled herself in the presence of my new family, though I myself could clearly see the storms gathering over my head. I took care not to be alone with her that day.

The following day I left for Paris with Mme d'Hénin and spent the next two mornings with M. Huart, my dancing master. It is impossible to conceive of anything more ridiculous than those

* Louise-Charlotte de Béthune, wife of a cousin, Philippe-Antoine-Gabriel-Victor-Charles de La Tour du Pin de La Charce-Gouvernet, Marquis de Montmorin (1723–1794) who used the title Marquis de La Tour du Pin until 1775, when he succeeded to the title of Marquis de Gouvernet.

rehearsals of the presentation. M. Huart, a large man, his hair very well arranged and white with powder, wore a billowing underskirt and stood at the far end of the room to represent the queen. He told me what I had to do, sometimes taking the part of the lady who was to present me, sometimes returning to the position of the queen to indicate the moment when, removing my glove and stooping to kiss the hem of her gown, she would make the gesture to prevent my doing so. Nothing was forgotten or neglected in these rehearsals, which went on without a break for three or four hours. I wore a train and the wide paniers of Court dress but above and below was my ordinary morning dress and my hair was very simply pinned up. It was all very funny.

I was presented on Sunday morning, after Mass. I was 'en grand corps', that is to say, wearing a special, shoulderless bodice, laced at the back, but narrow enough for the lacings, four inches wide at the bottom, to show a chemise of the finest lawn through which it could easily be seen if the wearer's skin were not white. This chemise had sleeves but they were only three inches deep and the shoulders were uncovered. From the top of the arm to the elbow fell three or four flounces of blonde lace. The bodice was cut very low in front, my bosom being partly covered by the seven or eight rows of large diamonds which the queen had kindly lent me. The front of the bodice was, as it were, laced with rows of diamonds and on my head were many more, some in clusters and some in aigrets. The gown itself was very lovely. On account of my half-mourning, it was all in white with some fine pieces of jet among the diamonds lent me by the queen, and the entire skirt was embroidered with pearls and silver.

Thanks to M. Huart's good coaching, I made my three curtseys very well. I removed my glove and put it on again not too awkwardly. Then I went to receive the accolade from the king and his brothers, the princes,* from the Duc de Penthièvre,† the Princes of Condé, Bourbon and Enghien.‡ By a fortunate chance, for which I have often thanked Heaven, the Duc d'Orléans was not at Versailles that day, and so I avoided being embraced by that monster. However, I have often seen him since, even in his own house, at the famous suppers he gave in the Palais Royal.

* The Comte de Provence, later Louis XVIII, and the Comte d'Artois, later Charles X.
† Son of the Comte de Toulouse, son of Louis XIV and Mme de Montespan.
‡ The Prince de Condé, his son, the Duc de Bourbon and his grandson, the Duc d'Enghien.

The day of one's presentation was very embarrassing and exceedingly tiring. It meant being stared at by the whole Court and being torn to shreds by every critical tongue. On that day, one became the topic of every conversation and on returning to the 'jeu'* in the evening – I cannot remember if it was at seven or at nine o'clock – every eye was upon you.

The following Sunday, I returned to Versailles, still wearing mourning, and from then on I went nearly every week with my aunt. The queen had decided that I should not take my place as a Lady of her Household for another two years, but I was considered as such from the beginning and on Sundays I entered her bedchamber with the ladies in attendance. Since the ceremonial is no longer the same, it would perhaps be of interest to describe the Sunday Courts over which that unfortunate queen presided so brilliantly. Such details have now acquired an historical value.

A few minutes before midday, the ladies entered the salon next to the queen's bedchamber. Everyone remained standing except the elderly, who in those days were treated with great deference, and those of the younger ladies believed to be pregnant. There were always at least forty people present, often more. Sometimes, we were very closely packed, for our paniers took up a great deal of room. Ordinarily, when the Princesse de Lamballe, Mistress of the Household, arrived, she went straight into the bedchamber where the queen was dressing. She usually arrived before the queen had begun her toilette. The Princesse de Chimay, a sister-in-law of my aunt d'Hénin, and the Comtesse d'Ossun, the first a lady-in-waiting and the second the Mistress of the Robes, also went in. A few minutes later, a footman would come to the door of the bedchamber and call in a loud voice for 'Le Service'.† The four ladies in attendance that week and all those who had come, as was the custom, to wait on the queen between their periods on duty, would then enter the bedchamber, together with younger ladies like the Comtesse de Maillé (née Fitz-James), the Comtesse Mathieu de Montmorency and myself, who were eventually to be appointed to the Household.

As soon as the queen had greeted each of us in her charming, kindly way, the door was opened and everyone admitted. We stood to the right and left of the room in such a manner as to leave a clear space in the centre of the room and at the door. Often when there

* Games of cards, chess, backgammon and so on were played at Court every evening.
† Those in waiting.

were many ladies in attendance, we stood in rows two or three deep. But the first arrivals would withdraw skilfully towards the door leading to the card-room, through which the queen had to pass on her way to Mass. To this salon a few privileged gentlemen who had either been received earlier in private audience or who were to present visitors from abroad were often admitted.

Thus it happened one day that the queen, stopping unexpectedly to say a word to someone, saw me in the corner of the doorway shaking hands with the English Ambassador, the Duke of Dorset. She had never seen this English form of greeting before and found it very amusing. As jokes do not die easily at Court, she never failed to ask the duke on the many occasions when we were both present, 'Have you shaken hands with Mme de Gouvernet?'

This tragic queen still betrayed a few trifling and very feminine jealousies. She combined a very lovely complexion with a radiant personality and showed herself a little jealous of those young ladies who could bring to the hard light of noon a seventeen-year-old complexion more dazzling than her own. Mine was one of them and once, when she was passing through the door, the Duchesse de Duras, who was always very kind and helpful to me, whispered in my ear: 'Do not stand facing the windows.' I understood what she meant and always followed her advice. But this did not prevent the queen from sometimes directing at me comments which were almost cutting about my liking for bright colours and for the poppies and brown scabious that I often wore. However, she was usually very kind to me, sometimes paying me those forthright compliments which princes have a habit of casting at young women down the whole length of a room, making the unhappy recipients blush to the very roots of their hair.

These Sunday morning audiences lasted until forty minutes past noon. Then the door opened and the footman announced: 'The king!' The queen, who always wore Court dress, would go to meet him with a charming air of pleasure and deference. The king would incline his head to right and left and speak to a few ladies whom he knew, though never to the young ones. He was so short-sighted that he could not recognise anyone at more than three paces. He was stout, about five feet six or seven inches tall, square-shouldered and with the worst possible bearing. He looked like some peasant shambling along behind his plough; there was nothing proud or regal in his appearance. His sword was a continual embarrassment to him and he never knew what to do with his hat, yet in Court dress he looked really magnificent. He took no interest in his clothes, putting on without a glance whatever was handed to him. His formal coats were made of cloths suited to the various seasons, all very heavily embroidered, and on them he wore the diamond star of the Order of the Holy Ghost. It was only on his feast day, or on days of gala or great ceremonial that he wore the ribbon over his coat.

Preparations for attending Mass began at a quarter to one o'clock. The First Gentleman of the Bedchamber for the year led the procession and behind him came the Captain of the Guard on duty and many other officers, either of the Guard or holding high office. The Captain of the Guard walked immediately in front of the king. The king and queen walked together, slowly enough to be able to say a word as they passed to the large numbers of courtiers who lined the gallery. Often, the queen would speak to the foreign ladies who had been presented to her in private, to artists and to writers. An inclination of the head or a gracious smile was noted and carefully stored against future need. Behind them came the ladies, in order of rank. The young ones tried to be on the outside, for we walked four or five abreast, and those who were considered to be in fashion – among whom I had the honour to be included – took great care to walk close enough to the line of courtiers to be able to catch the pretty things whispered to them as they passed.

It took great skill to walk the length of that vast room without treading on the long train of the lady in front. Feet were never raised from the ground, they glided over the gleaming parquet until the Salon of Hercules was safely crossed. Then, each lady threw her train over one of her paniers and, making sure she had been seen by her servant who would be waiting with a large, gold-fringed, red velvet bag, rushed to one of the side galleries of the chapel, seeking a place as close as possible to the gallery occupied by the king and queen and the princesses who would have joined them either in the card-room or in the chapel. Mme Elisabeth* was always there and sometimes Madame† as well. Your servant put the red velvet bag on the floor in front of you, you took out a missal but never read it for, by the time you had found a place, arranged your train and searched through the immense bag, the priest would already have reached the Gospel.

At the end of Mass, the queen curtseyed deeply to the king and we left again in the same order in which we had arrived. The

---

* Sister of Louis XVI.

† Marie-Josephine-Louise of Savoy, wife of the Comte de Provence.

only difference was that the king and queen would stop longer to speak to people. We returned to the queen's room, the ladies who were at Court remaining in the card-room until it was time to attend the queen to dinner. Before dining, the king and queen always spent a quarter of an hour talking to the ladies who had come out from Paris. We of the younger set irreverently called them the 'traineuses'* because their Court robes had longer skirts and their ankles were hidden.

Dinner was in the first salon, where a small rectangular table was laid with two places, and two large green armchairs were placed side by side, so closely that they touched. The backs of these chairs were high enough to screen completely the persons seated in them. The table-cloth reached the ground. The queen sat on the king's left. Their backs were to the fireplace and in front of them, at a distance of about ten feet, was arranged a semi-circle of stools for the duchesses, princesses and other ladies whose office entitled them to this privilege. Behind them stood all the other ladies, facing the king and queen. The king ate heartily, but the queen neither removed her gloves nor unfolded her napkin, which was a very big mistake. As soon as the king had drunk his wine, everyone curtseyed and left. The ladies who had come to pay their court did not need to remain longer.

Many people who, although they had not been presented, were nonetheless known to the king and queen, and to whom Their Majesties were very gracious, remained until dinner was over. The Gentlemen of the King's Household usually did the same.

Then began a veritable race to pay court to the royal princes and princesses, who dined much later. Speed was of the essence. The first visit was to Monsieur,† later Louis XVIII, the next to the Comte d'Artois, then one to Madame Elisabeth, others to the king's aunts‡ and even one to the little Dauphin§ when in the charge of his tutor, the Duc d'Harcourt. Each visit lasted only three or four minutes for the princes' salons were so small that they had to dismiss the first comers to make room for the next.

For young ladies, the pleasantest of these visits was that paid to the Comte d'Artois. He, too, was young, with the charming

* A play on words. Literally, the stragglers. Used here because of the unusually long trains worn by these ladies. (Tr.)
† The Comte de Provence.
‡ Madame Marie-Adélaïde and Madame Marie-Louise-Thérèse-Victoire, daughters of Louis XV.
§ The first Dauphin, Louis-Joseph-Xavier-Françoise, 1781–1789.

good looks he never lost. Great efforts were made to please him, for to succeed ensured being noticed. He was on friendly terms with my aunt, whom he always greeted as 'Chère Princesse'.

By the time we returned to our own apartment, we were rather weary and as we had to be at the 'jeu' at seven o'clock in the evening, we stayed quietly in our rooms in order not to disarrange our hair, especially if it had been dressed by Léonard, the most famous of all the coiffeurs. People dined at three o'clock, the fashionable hour in those days. Afterwards, we talked until six o'clock and a few gentlemen of our close acquaintance would come to tell us the latest news, the gossip or intrigues they had heard during the morning. Then, once again arrayed in Court dress, we returned to the same salon of the Palace where we had waited during the morning. But this time, the gentlemen were there, too.

We had to arrive before the stroke of seven for the queen entered before the chiming of the clock. Near her door, she would find one of the two curés of Versailles who would hand her a bag. She would then go to everyone, men and women, taking up a collection with the words: 'For the poor, if you please'. Each lady had her écu* of six francs ready in her hand and the men had their louis.† The curé would follow the queen as she collected this small tax for her poor, a levy which often totalled as much as one hundred louis and never less than fifty.

I often heard some of the younger people, including the most spendthrift, complaining inordinately of this almsgiving being forced upon them. Yet they would not have thought twice of hazarding one hundred times as much in a game of chance, or of spending, in a morning, to no useful purpose, a far larger sum than that levied by the queen.

But it was fashionable to complain of everything. One was bored, weary of attendance at Court. The officers of the Garde du Corps, who were lodged in the château when on duty, bemoaned having to wear uniform all day. The Ladies of the Household in attendance could not bear to miss going two or three times to Paris for supper during the eight days of their attendance at Versailles. It was the height of style to complain of duties at Court, profiting from them nonetheless and sometimes, indeed often, abusing the privileges they carried. All the ties were being loosened and it was, alas, the upper classes who led the way. The bishops did not live in their dioceses and seized any pretext to come to Paris. Colonels, obliged to serve with their regiment for only four

* A silver coin. (Tr.)   † A gold coin. (Tr.)

months of the year, would not have dreamed of staying five minutes longer than the bare minimum. Unnoticed, the spirit of revolt was rampant in all classes of society.

The Minister of War, the Maréchal de Ségur, had been a guest at my wedding and gave my husband a month's leave. So, instead of leaving for Saint-Omer where his regiment was garrisoned, he remained with me at Montfermeil. It was there that my love of riding and driving gave him his first insight into my grandmother's character. Mme de Montfermeil, of whom I saw a great deal, suggested that I should ride with her. As she had a very quiet horse and as those of M. de La Tour du Pin* were very lively, she offered to put hers at my disposal. When I mentioned this to my grandmother, she was far from pleased but when she knew that my husband, anticipating my wish, had given me a charming riding dress and wanted me to accompany him on his rides, her displeasure turned into lively anger. My uncle no longer rode himself, but he, too, had instructed his groom to train a fine grey he had bought in England for my use. He made me a present of it, together with a pretty little carriage of a kind known today as a tilbury and I used to drive this equipage myself in the beautiful rides of the Forest of Bondy. My cousin, Mme Sheldon, was spending the summer with us and usually came with me.

During his month's leave at Montfermeil, M. de La Tour du Pin often took me hunting. All these youthful pastimes were utterly displeasing to my grandmother whose character grew daily more disagreeable. She did not yet feel sufficiently at ease with my husband to dare, in his presence, to attack those he loved. But whenever he left a room, she would launch into criticism of my aunt d'Hénin and her friends. She would talk of the inconvenience to the elderly of having young people living with them, of the difficulties it caused, and so on. She took a delight in making all kinds of hurtful, derogatory remarks. Noticing how frequently I reached our room with reddened eyes, M. de La Tour du Pin made me tell him the trouble. I used to refuse, as far as possible, to explain but he soon guessed the cause. He talked to his aunt and to many of my mother's contemporaries and soon learned of my grandmother's disgraceful conduct towards her daughter. He determined there and then that she would not behave in the same fashion to me and, seeing this determination, I lived in continual dread that his

* From this point, Mme de La Tour du Pin always refers to her husband by this title, and the translator has followed her practice. He was not created Marquis de La Tour du Pin until 1820. See Introduction, p 9. (Tr.)

vehemence would one day provoke him into rash outspokenness. However, he managed to restrain his feelings until he returned to his regiment at the end of June. I was very sad to see him go.

I remained at Montfermeil with my family, the butt of my grandmother's bad temper and in daily fear of scenes. Whenever my aunt wrote asking me to join her in Paris so that she could take me to Versailles or into society, I never knew how best to announce that I would be away for two or three days. I saw clearly that my grandmother's nature would make it impossible for us to live in my uncle's house. His very affection for me did him a dis-service. My grandmother also feared that my husband would gain too much influence over the archbishop, who had taken a great liking to him. From the time of my marriage, therefore, she determined to settle again at Hautefontaine with my uncle in order to remove him more surely from the danger of his own affections, which might draw him towards us.

Towards the middle of August, M. de La Tour du Pin came to spend another week at Montfermeil, the Maréchal de Ségur permitting it on condition that he did not show his face in Paris. Colonels who commanded garrisons in Flanders were at that time threatened with having to spend several months of the autumn and winter with their regiments. Owing to the troubles in Holland, it looked as if we might have to intervene. It would have been a very wise move but the king's indecision and the Government's weakness made it impossible to take a stand – one which, by giving the people of France something else to think about, might perhaps have diverted them from the ideas of revolution ripening in their minds.

❧❧❧❧❧❧❧❧❧❧❧ VII ❧❧❧❧❧❧❧❧❧❧❧

I am not writing history so I will not enter into the causes of the dissensions which split the United Provinces of the Netherlands into two parties: the supporters of the House of Orange-Nassau and the Patriots. The former wanted increased power for the Stadtholder, the senior official of the Republic. The Patriots wanted to restrict his power and keep it within the limits imposed by the families of de Witt and Barneveld.

The Stadtholder, William V, was a nonentity. But his wife – a niece of Frederick the Great and sister of his successor, Frederick-William II – was ambitious. She wanted crowns for her husband and herself. The aristocracy of the Guelder and the provinces of Over-Yssel and Utrecht watched with some unease the wealth of the merchants of Holland. The Princess of Orange fanned this discontent or, at least, kept it simmering. She was assured of the support of England and Prussia and had no fear of intervention by France, despite the very decided views of our ambassador, the Comte de Saint-Priest, who was continually asking his feeble Court to support the Patriot party since it stood for the preservation of the 'status quo'. At the urging of Prussia, which had assembled troops at Wesel, the Princess of Orange incited a rebellion in Amsterdam and the Hague: the Stadtholder was insulted by people posing as Patriots and his supporters exacted reprisals. The French Embassy was sacked and M. de Saint-Priest withdrew to the Austrian Netherlands. The Patriots of Amsterdam then took up arms. To give the Prussians an excuse for intervening, the Princess of Orange pretended a fear she was very far from feeling and openly left The Hague to retire into Prussian territory – to Wesel. The Patriots were maladroit enough to fall into the trap. The princess, pretending to be unaware that they had forward posts on the Utrecht road, took that route, in the hope of being stopped. This bold move succeeded beyond her hopes. She was captured and taken prisoner to Amsterdam. The Orangists straightway rushed to arms and called on the Prussians for help. The latter set out immediately and advanced as far as The Hague; their passage was marked by the firing and sacking of all property belonging to Patriots. In vain did M. de Saint-Priest send courier after courier to Versailles to urge his Government to send troops into Holland and not to abandon the party he supported; in vain did M. Esterhazy, appointed commander of the army corps which had been promised to the Patriots, go to Versailles to implore help from the queen. Nothing could overcome the indecision of the king and the weakness of his Government.

The affair dragged on. M. Esterhazy, whom the queen treated as a friend and called 'mon frère', continued to hope that she would eventually obtain the intervention of the French Government in favour of our allies and sent M. de La Tour du Pin to Antwerp to arrange with M. de Saint-Priest the action to be taken if the troops were allowed to advance.

But the ambassador knew his Government far too well to expect anything generous or decisive from it. We ignobly abandoned the Dutch Patriots to their unhappy fate and contented ourselves with recalling our legation, or rather, the ambassador, leaving a Chargé d'Affaires who was authorised to wear the orange cockade on the grounds that he would be assaulted if he or his household went into public without it.

Many Dutch Patriots took refuge in France, where they were not backward in spreading their very justifiable discontent. Their accusations were of the liveliest interest to all those who were already discontented with the Government and saw in the situation a possibility for reform. So it was that many good Frenchmen were carried away by the wish, very patriotic at the time, to see put into effect the changes which, to all thinking men of goodwill, seemed essential.

In 1787, my sister-in-law and very dear friend, Mme de Lameth, had to stay in Paris until October owing to the serious illness of her youngest son, who almost died. The colonels of M. Esterhazy's Division had been ordered to remain with their regiments and since M. de La Tour du Pin was in like case and could not return, my sister-in-law suggested that I should go with her when she left for the country on 1 October. Her brother would then be able to join us there, as his regiment was garrisoned at Saint-Omer, only a short ride from Hénéncourt.

I have such very happy memories of that journey. I had been so accustomed to the constraint which my grandmother's terrible character imposed on the entire household at Montfermeil that, to live with my husband and his amiable sister seemed to change my whole existence. They were both very witty and gay. We went to Lille to see my bother-in-law, the Marquis de Lameth, who was there with his *Régiment de la Couronne*. Never had I enjoyed myself so much.

We returned to Hénéncourt, and there found the good curé, an old man of ninety who lived in the château. He had celebrated his first Mass in the presence of Mme de Maintenon and remembered Saint-Cyr* in great detail. As a child, I had myself visited this admirable establishment with Mme Elisabeth,† who had had the kindness to take me walking or hunting with her when I was with my mother at Versailles.

When the colonels were allowed to return to Paris, my husband

* A boarding school founded by Mme de Maintenon for daughters of the nobility. Now a military academy. (Tr.)
† Sister of Louis XVI.

Marié-Antoinette. Painting by Drouais.

Louis XVI. Painting by Duplessis, at Versailles.

and I went back to Montfermeil. My sister-in-law was to remain in the country until the beginning of the winter. It was very fashionable then for colonels to travel in uniform redingotes, with two epaulettes, and for the ladies to wear very elegant riding dresses, the skirt slightly shorter than that normally used for riding. It was essential that this dress, including the hat, should come from London, as the vogue for English fashions was just then at the height of its extravagance. As a result, I looked quite English.

Shortly afterwards, I found I was pregnant and therefore could not go with my uncle and grandmother to Montpellier as we had planned. We had intended returning by way of Bordeaux and Le Bouilh in order to visit my father-in-law. Instead, it was arranged that while my family was away, I should stay with our aunt, Mme d'Hénin. As she took me out into society, this was both pleasanter and more convenient, for it was not customary in those days for a young lady to go alone into company during the first year of her marriage. Going out in the morning to visit young friends or to the shops, she had to take a maid in the carriage with her. There were even some of the older ladies who carried their strictness to the point of disapproving a young lady walking with her husband in the Champs Élysées or the Tuileries,* insisting they should be accompanied by a liveried footman. My husband found this convention intolerable and we never observed it.

Once settled in my aunt's house, where we were much happier and more at ease than in my grandmother's, we went nearly every day to the theatre. In those days, the plays finished early enough for people to go out to supper afterwards. My aunt and I had permission to sit in the queen's boxes, a favour accorded to only six or eight of the youngest ladies of her Household. The queen had boxes at the Opera, the Comédie Française and at the theatre known then as the Comédie Italienne,† where light operas were sung in French. All we had to to was to consult the *Journal de Paris* and choose our theatre. In each of them, the queen's box was a stage one, furnished like a very elegant salon, with a large, well-heated and well-lit ante-room. There was a fully-equipped dressing table with everything necessary for repairing one's coiffure, a writing table and so on. Stairs led to another ante-room where the servants waited. At the entrance was an usher in the king's livery. One was never kept waiting a single minute for one's carriage. It was customary

* The gardens of the royal palace of the Tuileries were open to the public (Tr.)
† Known today as the Opéra Comique.

to arrive at the Comédie Italienne in time for the first piece, always the best, and at the Opera in time for the ballet. I record these rather trifling details only to emphasise the contrast with my present situation when, at the age of seventy-one, I cannot even afford forty 'sols'* to hire a miserable sedan chair to take me to Mass on a wet Sunday.

Now that I am settled at my aunt's, this would seem to be the place to tell you about the people in her circle. It was the most elegant and highly-considered coterie in Paris and it received me into its midst during my very first winter in society. It consisted of four very distinguished women: Mme d'Hénin; the Princesse de Poix (née Beauvau); the Duchesse de Biron, who had recently lost her grandmother, the Maréchale de Luxembourg; the Princesse de Bouillon (née Princesse de Hesse-Rothenbourg). They had been linked since their youth in a friendship which was to them almost an article of faith, unfortunately perhaps the only one they had. They upheld one another, defended one another, adopted one another's ideas, friends, opinions and tastes. They protected any young woman connected with any one of them against all comers. By birth, they were all of importance and high rank and they were all what we then called 'philosophes',† or free-thinkers. Voltaire, Rousseau, d'Alembert, Condorcet, Suard and their like were not of this circle, but their principles and ideas were eagerly adopted by it and many gentlemen of these ladies' acquaintance did frequent this group of literary men which in those days was quite separate from the world of the Court.

It was M. Necker's ministry which was mainly responsible for the mingling of different classes which until then had kept themselves separate. When Mme Necker, that pedantic, pretentious Genevan, moved with her husband into the lodgings of the Contrôleur-Général,‡ she brought with her a double following: those who admired her wit and those who admired her cook. Her daughter, Mme de Staël, being married to an ambassador, moved in Court circles and she, in her turn, brought to M. Necker's house a number of people with intellectual leanings, including my aunt and her friends. The Maréchal de Beauvau, father of Mme de Poix,

---

* An old form of the word 'sou'.

† Literally, philosophers. A name given in France at this period to followers of the new intellectual movement led by Voltaire, Montesquieu, Diderot and Rousseau. Its principles were humanitarian, universal and not national, and it was critical of established religions. (Tr.)

‡ Comptroller-General of Finance. In effect, Prime Minister. (Tr.)

was a friend of M. Necker and his wife was one of the arbiters of Parisian society. It was essential, if you aspired to distinction, to have her approval and to be received by her. She gathered at her house and afforded a somewhat aloof patronage to a swarm of M. Turgot's old followers, known as the 'Economists'.*

But let us return to my aunt. At the time of my marriage, Mme d'Hénin was thirty-eight. At the age of fifteen, she had married the seventeen-year-old Prince d'Hénin, younger brother of the Prince de Chimay. They were much admired as the handsomest couple ever seen at Court. During the second year of her marriage, Mme d'Hénin caught smallpox and this illness, for which there was then no known treatment, left on her face weeping scars which were never cured.

When I first met her, she was still very beautiful, with lovely hair, delightful eyes, teeth like pearls, a magnificent figure and a most aristocractic bearing. Her marriage contract had stipulated separation of property and she lived with her mother, the Marquise de Monconseil, until the latter's death. Although M. d'Hénin had an apartment in Mme de Monconseil's house, and was not separated in law from his wife, he nonetheless lived with an actress of the Comédie Française, a Mlle Raucourt, who ruined him.

Unfortunately for morals, such a situation was only too frequent and the Court, by its very indifference, did nothing to discourage these situations. It was thought amusing and quite unimportant. The first time I went to Longchamp with my aunt, our carriage often overtook or was overtaken by the carriage of this actress, which resembled our own in every detail. Horses, trappings, liveries, all were so exactly similar that it was like looking at ourselves in a mirror. When society is so corrupt that corruption itself seems natural, and when no one is any longer shocked at anything, why should we wonder that the lower classes, faced with so bad an example, should have indulged in such excesses. Among the people there are no shades of feeling: as soon as they have reason to despise or hate something above them, they know no restraint and abandon themselves to their feelings.

The shamelessness with which the ladies of high society flaunted their love affairs was notorious. Liaisons were known almost as

* A group of eighteenth century writers concerned with economic problems, the first to make a study of this science. Anne-Robert-Jacques Turgot, Baron de l'Aulne (1727–1781) was one of the earliest economists. He was a great administrator and reformer and at one time Contrôleur-Général des Finances. (Tr.)

soon as they began and, if they lasted, acquired a measure of acceptance. In the circle of the 'princesses combinées', as they were known, there were, however, certain exceptions to these scandalous ways. Mme de Poix, deformed, lame, helpless for a large part of the year, had never been accused of any intrigue. When I met her, she still had a charming face, despite her forty years. She was the most amiable person in the world.

Mme de Lauzun, who later became the Duchesse de Biron, was an angel of sweetness and kindness. After the death of her grandmother, the Maréchale de Luxembourg,* who had owned the largest house in Paris and with whom she had lived, she bought a house in the Rue de Bourbon overlooking the river. She furnished it with a simple elegance as much in keeping with her great fortune as with the modesty of her nature. She lived there alone, for her husband followed the example of M. d'Hénin and lived with an actress of the Comédie Française. After the death of my mother, whose friendship and influence had kept him in good company, he had become caught up in the set which surrounded the Duc d'Orléans – Égalité – who corrupted everything that came near him.

The Duchesse de Lauzun had a library of rare works, including many of Rousseau's manuscripts. Among them was that of *La Nouvelle Heloïse,* written entirely in his own hand, as well as a quantity of letters and notes written by him to Mme de Luxembourg. I particularly remember the letter he wrote her explaining and justifying his quite incredible decision to send his children to a foundling home. In this letter, specious justification of his cruel decision was mingled with the most sympathetic, sensitive phrases of condolence on a misfortune which had just befallen Mme de Luxembourg: she had lost her dog! I believe that after Mme de Biron's sad death, all these precious manuscripts, as well as the rare editions in her collection were taken to the king's Library.

Mme la Princesse de Bouillon had been married very young to the last Duc de Bouillon, who was half-witted and legless. She lived with him in the Hotel de Bouillon on the Quai Malaquais. Naturally, he was never seen in public, remaining always in his apartments with his attendants But he was brought every day to dine with his wife and I have sometimes seen their two places laid opposite one another. Thank Heaven, I never had the mis-

* In her old age, the arbiter of society in Paris. Her grand-daughter married the young Duc de Lauzun, who became Duc de Biron on the death of his grandfather, the great Maréchal de Biron. They were both executed during the Revolution.

fortune to meet this deformed piece of humanity who had to be
carried in his servants' arms. In the summer he went to his home in
Navarre, that lovely place which has since belonged to the Empress
Josephine, but I believe that Mme de Bouillon went there rarely
or never at all.

She was a woman of prodigious wit and charm, to my mind the
most distinguished person I ever met. She had never, at any time,
been pretty. She was excessively thin, almost a skeleton, with a flat,
Germanic face, a turned-up nose, ugly teeth and yellow hair. Tall
and gangling, she would bury herself in the corner of a sofa, draw
her legs up under her, cross her long, thin arms under her mantle
and then, from that collection of fleshless bones, there would
sparkle forth such wit, originality and amusing conversation that
one was borne away on the wings of enchantment. She showed
me very great kindness and of this I was extremely proud. She was
forty and I was eighteen, but she allowed me to visit her as if I had
been her contemporary. My intense interest in her conversation
pleased her and she would say to my aunt: 'The young Gouvernet
came to be amused by me this morning.' I was well aware that, at a
quarter to two, one had to disappear in order to avoid meeting her
'cul de jatte'.* Such an encounter would have distressed her greatly,
for even after twenty years, she had not been able to accustom
herself to his condition.

Yet this ugly, brilliant princess had had at least one lover. She
even brought up a small girl who bore a striking resemblance both
to herself and to Prince Emmanuel de Salm-Salm. He was generally
accepted as her permanent lover, but at that time he was certainly
no more than a friend.

Until the time of my marriage, the Chevalier de Coigny,† a
brother of the Duc de Coigny and principal equerry to the king,
had been my aunt's accredited lover. Such, at least, was his reputation but even if it had once been the case, it was quite certain that
for a very long time only the reputation had persisted, for he had
formed another tie with Mme de Monsauge, widow of a 'fermier-
général'.‡ Later, he married her. I was much attached to this stout,
gay and amiable knight. He was fifty, so I talked to him as often
as I could and he told me hundreds of anecdotes which I still
remember. Since I was to live in the highest ranks of society and

* A person without legs or unable to use them. (Tr.)
† Marie-François-Henri de Franquetot, Marquis and later Duc de Coigny, a
peer and Marshal of France, 1737–1821.
‡ Someone who leased from the Crown the taxes collected in a given area. (Tr.)

at the Court, a knowledge of the past would be very useful to me.

I counted among my friends many people of the same age as the Chevalier de Coigny for they appreciated my evident pleasure in talking with them. My aunt's friends had decided that I ought to be *à la mode*. I, on the other hand, had decided not to listen to any unbecoming conversation from a young man, an easy decision since I was so deeply in love with my husband. There was no severity or prudishness in my attitude to young men, only that easy friendliness which is so disconcerting to the flirtatious. Archambault de Périgord used to say: 'Mme de Gouvernet is impossible; she treats all young men as if they were her brothers.'

Women did not dislike me. Since I envied no one, I drew attention to the good qualities of others, to their intelligence and their clothes. This exasperated my aunt who, despite her superior mind, had suffered many petty jealousies in her own youth and was now suffering them all over again on my behalf.

I also knew how important it was to make friends among the older women who, in those days, were all powerful. Before my grandmother withdrew from society, or rather, before society abandoned her, she had made many enemies and it was a handicap to me to have grown up in her charge. I had to win my way back into the favour of many who had loved my mother and who looked on my grandmother's charge of me as a misfortune, almost a fault. I had renewed my childhood friendship with the Rochechouart family. They moved in a quite different circle from that of my aunt, but she was not unwilling that I should also frequent theirs. I also saw many of my sister-in-law's friends, for although she frequented, as I did, the company surrounding my aunt, she also had certain friendships of her own.

One house where we all visited and where I was received with the most affectionate friendship was that of Mme de Montesson. She loved M. de La Tour du Pin like a son. He had gone to live with her after Mme de Monconseil's death and remained there until his marriage. She welcomed me with the greatest kindness and I became very friendly with her great-niece, Mme de Valence, daughter of Mme de Genlis.* She was three years older than me and considered the model of everything a young lady should be. Her first child had died and she was shortly expecting another.

Spiteful tongues suggested that Mme de Montesson, carried away by a strong attachment to M. de Valence, had persuaded him

* Tutor to the children of the Duc d'Orléans – Philippe Égalité. (Tr.)

to marry her niece in order to have an excuse for devoting herself entirely to him. I do not know what the truth was. She was old enough to have been his mother, but it cannot be denied that it was his influence which ruined her, for he advised her badly over the administration of the fine fortune left her by the Duc d'Orléans.*

It was well known that she had been the perfectly legitimate wife of the Duc d'Orléans. They were married by Loménie, Archbishop of Toulouse, in the church of Saint-Eustache in Paris, in the presence of the curé of the church. However, the king refused to recognise the marriage and Mme de Montesson no longer went to Court. The Duc d'Orléans left his apartments in the Palais Royal and went to live in the Rue de Provence, in a house communicating with one which Mme de Montesson had just bought in the Chaussée d'Antin. All the inside dividing walls were pulled down and the two gardens made into one. However, the Duc d'Orléans had his own entrance in the Rue de Provence, with a porter in his livery, and Mme de Montesson had hers, with a porter in grey livery. But they shared the courtyard.

When I entered society, Mme de Montesson had just put off her widow's mourning and emerged from retirement in the Convent of the Assumption. This retirement had been forced on her by the Court's refusal to allow her to wear mourning in public or to dress her servants in black. Invitations to her house were much sought after for she entertained the best company in Paris, also the most distinguished, from the very oldest ladies to the very youngest. She no longer gave fêtes or entertainments, as she had done while the Duc d'Orléans was alive, and this I much regretted. She adopted me immediately as if I had been a daughter, and thanks to her great knowledge of the world, her conversation and counsels were very useful to me. I could always ask her advice on any matter at all and could count on her support if ever I were attacked. Scarcely a day went by without my seeing Mme de Valence, and Mme de Montesson would often keep me to dinner if it was late. On other occasions, she would send a message asking me to return and dine with her, informally, in my morning dress.

Such was my introduction to society while staying with Mme d'Hénin. My family had prolonged their visit to Languedoc and when they returned, in about February 1788, I in my turn found myself in circumstances which prevented my leaving my aunt to rejoin them. As the result of a miscarriage, I was confined to my bed. It had been caused by an excess of blood, I believe, or perhaps it

* Louis-Philippe, Duc d'Orléans, 1725–1785. Father of Philippe Égalité.

was only the consequence of an imprudence at Versailles. One Sunday evening, hearing nine o'clock strike as I passed through the gallery and fearing the queen would already have entered, I started to run. But my paniers caught in a doorway and I was considerably shaken. At the time, I felt no ill effects and returned to Paris but two days later, I became ill. This accident caused me a two-fold grief: my own personal grief and the disappointment I knew it would cause my good father-in-law.

When my grandmother returned to Paris, she came to see me. Extreme weakness still forced me to remain in bed, but she pretended to think it was an excuse for not leaving my aunt's house. From our conversations, she soon learned of my success in society, of the warm welcome I had received from a large number of people whom she detested and of the attentions and kindnesses of my mother's friends. This roused in her a deadly spite and I think it must have been then that she resolved to seize upon the first pretext that offered to oblige us to leave my uncle's house. I did return, nevertheless, to the Hôtel Dillon. A charming suite of rooms had been arranged for me on the mansard floor, but unfortunately the only entrance was by way of a small, ugly, winding stair which passed close to my grandmother's dressing room.

I cannot remember the exact sequence of the events which led to the break with my relatives, but the principal reasons for this domestic catastrophe were my grandmother's unyielding hatred of M. de La Tour du Pin, her boundless jealousy of my uncle's liking for him and a fear that my uncle might be led into speaking to my husband of his affairs, thereby divulging her own and all the liabilities she had undertaken on his behalf. After many months of repeated clashes, incited by bad counsellors, my grandmother asked us to leave her house. Despite my tears and the pleading of my uncle, the archbishop, whose affection we had won but who was too frightened of my grandmother to oppose her, we had to leave the Hôtel Dillon and were never to return. It was about June, 1788.

My aunt most kindly took us into her house. But despite all the unhappiness which my grandmother's character had caused me, I felt a very deep grief at separating from my family. Society was divided in its sympathies. Some attributed to me wrongs of which I was innocent. Former friends of my mother defended me with warmth. The queen was one of them. Nor did M. de La Tour du Pin escape criticism. He was accused of violence, of hastiness and so on. In short, it was one of the most painful incidents of my life.

I knew then my first real grief and the memory of it still causes me a very lively regret. But I cannot reproach myself for any fault which might have caused it.

VIII

My aunt, Mme d'Hénin, lodged us in her house in the Rue de Verneuil, in a ground floor apartment looking out on to a small and exceedingly dismal garden. We did not want to be dependent on her and had a cook of our own to prepare meals for our servants and for ourselves when my aunt dined out or was in waiting at Court. My good Marguérite, who had never left me, withstood all my grandmother's offers, her advances, even her pleading, and remained with me. I had a great affection for this good woman and my trust in her was boundless.

We spent the summer of 1788 at Passy, in a house which Mme d'Hénin, Mme de Poix, Mme de Bouillon and Mme de Biron rented together. My aunt and I lived there all the time; the others came to stay in turn. I was again expecting a baby and took the greatest care to avoid another mischance. But for the first three months of my pregnancy, I continued to attend the Court at Versailles; it was not customary to do so beyond that period.

The queen was kind enough to excuse me from accompanying her to Mass, fearing I might walk too fast and slip on the parquet. I used to remain in her room while she was in chapel and so came to know in detail the routine of the waiting women. It consisted in making the bed, removing every trace of the queen's toilet and dusting the tables and other pieces of furniture. To anyone used to the ways of today, it would seem very odd that their first action was to open the great double curtains which surrounded the bed. The next was to remove the bed linen and pillows, tossing them into immense baskets lined with green taffetas. Four footmen in livery then came to turn the mattresses, which were too heavy for women to lift. The footmen then withdrew and four women came to put on white sheets and arrange the covers. The whole task took five minutes so that, although Mass, including the walk to and from chapel, did not last more than twenty-five to thirty minutes, I was there alone for a fairly long time, sitting in an armchair near the window. When there were large numbers of people present, the queen, who was always thoughtful, would tell me as she passed, to go and sit in the card-room so that I would not have to stand too long and grow tired.

These precautions prevented me from attending the reception given for the ambassadors of Tippoo-Sahib, which was a very splendid affair. They had come to ask the support of France against the English, but we gave them only words, as we had done to the Dutch. These three Indians stayed several months in Paris at the king's expense, taken everywhere in a carriage and six. I often saw them at the Opera and in other public places. They were all of that fine, light Hindu colouring, with white beards to their waists and very richly dressed. At the Opera, a fine stage box was reserved for them. Seated in large armchairs, they often propped their yellow babouche-shod feet on the padded edge of the box, to the delight of the public who, let it be said, had no fault to find with this custom.

M. de La Tour du Pin had just been appointed colonel of the Régiment de Royal-Vaisseaux. Discipline in this Regiment was very slack, not among the soldiers and non-commissioned officers, where it was excellent, but among the officers, who had been spoiled by their former colonel, M. d'Ossun, husband of the queen's Mistress of the Robes. My husband was very strict in matters of discipline and when he took command of the Regiment, he found that, despite having twenty-two Knights of Malta in their ranks, these gentlemen were not carrying out their duties. Noticing that the Regiment's daily drill was taken by the non-commissioned officers and the lieutenant-colonel, M. de Kergaradec, M. de La Tour du Pin announced that as he himself would attend the drill every day at sunrise, he expected all officers to be present. This roused a storm of fury.

There was to be a camp that year at Saint-Omer, under the command of the Prince de Condé. The Régiment de Royal-Vaisseaux had been chosen to demonstrate certain new tactical groupings which had just been issued. The officers were annoyed rather than flattered at being chosen for this distinction for it meant an end to the lazy, negligent ways into which they had been allowed to fall. They felt no shame at combining together to resist all their commanding officer's reproofs. Punishments, arrests, imprisonments – nothing would induce them to carry out their duties. The officers even passed a resolution not to see their colonel, except on official occasions, when it could not be avoided. All his invitations to dinner were refused. It was almost open revolt and lasted right through the summer. Then the camp was set up and the Regiment reported there for duty. The first manoeuvre at which it was to demonstrate the new methods was a failure. M. de La Tour du Pin was furious. He told the Prince de Condé of the bad spirit in the Regiment, or rather, among its officers and the prince said that if they had not improved by the next manoeuvres, he would have them all put under arrest for the entire duration of the camp. Command of the companies would be given to the non-commissioned officers. This threat was effective. When the camp broke up, the inspector, the Duc de Guines, also made it known that there would be no awards to officers of the Royal-Vaisseaux, neither Crosses of Saint-Louis nor the customary six months' leave. The colonel would spend the whole winter in garrison. At that, these fine gentlemen submitted, made their apologies to M. de La Tour du Pin and conducted themselves properly. Unfortunately, they had set a bad example which, a year later, was only too readily followed.

While all this was going on at Saint-Omer, I was leading a pleasant existence at Passy with my aunt and one or two of her friends. I went often to Paris and also spent some time at Berny with Mme de Montesson, who continued to show me great kindness. At Berny, I often met the aged Prince Henry of Prussia, brother of Frederick the Great. He was a man of considerable military and literary ability, a great admirer of all the *philosophes* whom his brother had made so welcome at his Court, Voltaire in particular. He had a more thorough knowledge of our literature than any Frenchman. He knew all our plays by heart and would recite whole speeches in an incredibly bad German accent and with a foreign intonation so ridiculous that we found it very difficult not to laugh.

As I am not writing a history of the Revolution, I will not speak of all the conversations, discussions, or even arguments to which differing opinions gave rise in society. At eighteen, I found them all very tedious and sought distraction by going as often as possible to a charming house to which I was drawn by childhood friendships. This was the Hôtel de Rochechouart, one of those patriarchal houses whose like will not be seen again, in which several generations mingled without any sense of strain, without tedium and without making exacting demands on one another.

Mme de Courteille, a very rich widow, had married her only daughter to the Comte de Rochechouart. She lived with her daughter, her son-in-law and their two daughters in a fine and very large house they had built in the Rue de Grenelle. Mme de

Rochechouart had been my mother's closest friend and I had spent my childhood with her two daughters. It was the younger, Rosalie, who was my closest friend. She had been married at the age of twelve years and one day to the Comte de Chinon, the fifteen-year-old grandson of the Maréchal de Richelieu. She was still a little girl, charming but thin and very delicate. He was an unamiable, pedantic boy whom we all disliked at our children's balls. The marriage took place before my mother's death and I had attended it. The wedding dinner was held at the Hôtel de Richelieu and all generations were represented, from that of the Maréchal, whose first marriage had taken place during the reign of Louis XIV, to that of the bride's friends, little girls of my own age. Immediately after this dinner, the bridegroom left with his tutor to travel throughout Europe. It was early in 1782 when he set out and he did not return to France until the winter of 1788 or 1789. He had become a tall, handsome, young man of fine character.

There were rejoicings in the Hôtel de Rochechouart on his return, but his poor wife was far from sharing the general joy. At fourteen, she had become completely hunchbacked and feared her husband would find this deformity repulsive. She had no illusions that her musical talent, her lovely voice, her wide knowledge, her adorable nature and lofty mind would make her husband, almost unknown to her, forget such an infirmity. She realised that her pleasant face, her intelligent expression, her beautiful hair and her pearly teeth would not make up for her misshapen body.

Misfortune was heaped on misfortune, for the poor young man found on his return that his two sisters, born of his father's second marriage, were as misshapen as his wife.* This trio of hunchbacks gave him a horror of France. At the first sign of the approaching Revolution, he emigrated and went to Russia where he served as a volunteer in the armies of the Empress Catherine II, covering himself with glory in the Russian war against the Turks. He was with the army which captured Ismail and fought with the greatest distinction. After the deaths of his grandfather and his father, he was appointed First Gentleman of the Bedchamber. He returned to France during the Consulate, but later went back to Russia, not returning for good until the Restoration. He spent many of the intervening years as Governor of Odessa.†

* Later, as Mme de Montcalm and Mme de Jumilhac, they became two of the most witty, informed women of their generation. (Tr.)
† He was virtually the founder of Odessa as a major trading centre with southern Europe. The prosperity of its hinterland and the port were both due to him. In

My baby was born in December 1788, but with such difficulty that I nearly died. After twenty-four hours of terrible pain, I brought into the world a child who was still born, strangled during its birth. I was not immediately aware of this for I was unconscious and, two hours later, suffering the agony of puerperal fever.

Towards the end of the winter I began to pick up the threads of my social life and went once again to sing at the Hôtel de Rochechouart. The musical gatherings there were very distinguished. They were held once a week, but if a piece called for several players or singers, there were rehearsals as well. Mme Mongéroux, a famous pianist of the day, played the piano; an Italian singer from the Opera took the tenor parts; Mandini, another Italian, sang the bass; Mme de Richelieu was the prima donna; I sang the contralto; M. de Duras was the baritone and the choruses were sung by other talented amateurs. Viotti accompanied us on the violin. We executed the most difficult finales in this way. Everyone took the greatest pains and Viotti was extremely demanding. Another critic at our rehearsals was M. de Rochechouart himself, a born musician, who let no fault pass unremarked.

When dinner time came, we would often be in the middle of a finale. As soon as we heard the bell, we took up our hats and then Mme de Rochechouart would come in saying there was enough for us all. And so we would stay and continue the rehearsal after dinner. It was no longer a morning's music, but a day's music.

On the evening of the final performance, there would always be an audience of about fifty people of all generations. Mme de Courteille would be in her sitting-room playing trictrac with her old friends, but from time to time she would come to the music room to watch what was known as 'la belle jeunesse'.

Nowadays, I live in retirement and cannot judge today's society. But from what I hear, I doubt if there exists anywhere the ease, harmony, good manners and absence of all pretension which was to be found then in the great houses of Paris. Usually, three generations lived together in the same house, but they did not irk one another or clash in any way. It seems that these gatherings of all the generations are now things of the past and, as M. de Talleyrand remarked with regret, old ladies no longer go into society.

It must have been in about the spring of this year that the Duke of Dorset was succeeded as English Ambassador by Lord Gower

1814, Louis XVIII summoned him back to France to form a government and he returned with many misgivings for he had been twenty-five years away from France. (Tr.)

and his charming wife, Lady Sutherland. Before the duke left Paris, he gave a grand ball. At supper, we sat at small tables in a gallery whose walls were entirely decorated with foliage. At the bottom of the invitation cards was the blunt instruction: 'Ladies will wear white'. This kind of command annoyed me and, in protest, I wore a charming dress in blue crêpe, with flowers of the same colour. My gloves were trimmed with blue ribbons, my fan was of a similar shade and there were blue feathers in my hair, which was dressed by Léonard. This small revolt had a certain success and people quoted endlessly: 'Blue bird, blue skies'. Even the Duke of Dorset was amused at the jest and observed that the Irish had always been an unruly race.

Amid all these pleasures, we were drawing nearer to the month of May 1789, laughing and dancing our way towards the precipice. Thinking people were content to talk of abolishing all the abuses. France, they said, was about to be reborn. The word 'revolution' was never uttered. Had anyone dared to use it, he would have been thought mad. In the upper classes, this illusion of security misled the wise who wanted only to see an end to abuses and the waste of public money. That is why so many upright and honourable people, including the king himself, could enjoy the illusion that they were about to enter a Golden Age.

Now that a long life has enabled me to see the course events have taken, I am amazed at the utter blindness of the unfortunate king and his ministers. It is certain that the Duc d'Orléans began his sinister preparations long before the meeting of the States-General. But the proclamation he sent to all the bailiwicks where he owned property, appeared on the surface to be a most patriotic document professing the loftiest intentions. It was carried by a number of people of the highest birth who represented him in the local assemblies of nobles. These representations were candidates for nomination as deputies to the States-General. M. de La Tour du Pin went to Nemours with the Vicomte de Noailles, brother of the Prince de Poix; but M. de Noailles won more votes than my husband, who also failed to get himself elected at Grenoble, where he went to represent his father. His father was elected in Saintonge.

I remember that some presentiment made me very glad that M. de La Tour du Pin was not elected to that Assembly which was to prove so disastrous to us. But the immediate cause of my gladness lay in the fact that I was released from the long, tedious hours of never-ending political conversations to which I had had to listen every day. People who frequented my aunt's company and my aunt herself were never at a loss for ideas for reforming abuses and establishing a fairer distribution of taxes. People were particularly insistent on the need to base the new French Constitution on that of England, which very few people knew anything about. M. de Lally* himself, despite his claim to know it thoroughly, was ignorant of its details. Yet he was consulted as an authority. He spoke so well that he charmed the ladies, who listened to him with delight. He had completely turned my aunt's head and she had no doubt at all that he would be a great success in the States-General. He had just been elected a deputy to the Assembly of Nobles in Paris and nominated by them as one of its two secretaries.

In the early spring of 1789, after the terrible winter which had caused so much suffering amongst the poor, the Duc d'Orléans – Égalité – was very popular in Paris. The previous year he had sold many paintings from the fine collection in the palace and it was generally believed that the eight millions raised by the sale had been devoted to relieving the sufferings of the people during the hard winter which had just ended. In contrast, whether rightly or wrongly, there was no mention of any charitable gifts from the royal princes or from the king and queen. That unfortunate princess had fallen entirely under the influence of the Polignac family. She no longer went to the theatre in Paris. The people never saw her or her children. Nor did the king ever show himself. Hidden away at Versailles, or hunting in the nearby forests, he suspected nothing, foresaw nothing and believed nothing he was told.

The queen hated the Duc d'Orléans, who had spoken ill of her. He had wanted his son, the Duc de Chartres, to marry Madame Royale.† The Comte d'Artois also wanted the hand of this princess for his son, the Duc d'Angoulême, and this was the marriage favoured by the queen. The Duc d'Orléans took this preference as a mortal affront. His visits to Versailles were rare and I do not remember ever having met him in the queen's apartments at the hour when all the princes came, that is to say, just before Mass. Since he was never in his apartments at Versailles, I had not been officially presented to

---

* Trophime-Gérard, Marquis de Lally-Tollendal, illegitimate son of Thomas-Arthur, Comte de Lally, Baron de Tollendal, Governor-General of French possessions in India, who was executed in Pondicherry in 1766 for failing to hold the territory in his charge. The Lally family was of Irish origin, closely connected by marriage with the Dillons.
† Marie-Thérèse, only daughter of Louis XVI and Marie-Antoinette. She was imprisoned with her family and was the only survivor. She was eventually freed, joined Louis XVIII in exile, married the Duc d'Angoulême and returned to France at the Restoration, 1778–1851. (Tr.)

him and whenever he met me at the house of Mme de Montesson, he always jokingly asked Mme d'Hénin my name. I nonetheless attended the suppers at the Palais-Royal, which were very brilliant that winter.

I attended that given to christen the fine silver service which the Duc d'Orléans had ordered from Arthur, the great silversmith of the day. I remember that it seemed to me too light and too English in shape, but that was the fashion. Everything had to be copied from our neighbours, from the Constitution to horses and carriages. Some young men, like Charles de Noailles, went so far as to affect an English accent and studied all the awkwardnesses of manner, the style of walking, in fact, all the outward signs of an Englishman, so that they could copy them. They envied me that people in public places would often exclaim at sight of me: 'There goes an English-woman!' To them, it was a compliment.

⚜⚜⚜⚜⚜⚜⚜⚜⚜⚜⚜⚜⚜ IX ⚜⚜⚜⚜⚜⚜⚜⚜⚜⚜⚜⚜⚜

Early in 1789, I happened to make a strange acquaintance: Mme de Genlis, tutor* to the young Princes of Orléans† and their thirteen-year-old sister, Mademoiselle.‡ She lived with Mademoiselle at the Convent of Belle-Chasse, in a very small pavilion built especially for her. Also living in the pavilion were Pamela, later Lady Edward FitzGerald, of whom I will tell you more, and Henriette de Sercey, both of whom were educated with the princess. Mme de Genlis was also responsible for the princes' education, but they did not sleep at the pavilion. They came very early each morning and stayed until after supper, when they returned with their assistant-tutor to the Palais-Royal. As I had often met them and was a close friend of

* The Duc d'Orléans (Égalité) insisted on Mme de Genlis being called a 'tutor' – implicitly, it emphasised his children's royalty. It was customary for royal princes to have a 'gouverneur' (tutor) to arrange their education. When the Duc d'Orleans asked the king's permission to use the term, Louis XVI shrugged his shoulders and replied, as he walked away: 'Tutor or Governess, you are entitled to call her as you please. In any case, the Comte d'Artois has children.'
† The Duc de Chartres (1773–1850), later King Louis-Philippe of the French; the Duc de Montpensier (1775–1807) and the Comte de Beaujolais (1779–1808).
‡ Louise-Eugénie-Adélaïde d'Orléans, whose influence over her eldest brother was considerable, even in matters of government, after he became king. (Tr.)

Mme de Genlis' daughter, Mme de Valence, Mme de Montesson used to invite me to her house when the young princes were there. Mme de Genlis took a great liking to me and wanted me to come to the small evening dances which were given once a week that winter. They always ended before eleven o'clock and were not followed by a supper.

The Duc de Chartres was beginning to go out into society, that is to say, he was sometimes present at the Palais-Royal suppers. He had entered the army and been admitted to the Order of the Holy Ghost. He was heavily-built, very ungraceful and awkward, with pale, heavy cheeks, a secretive expression, a solemn, shy boy. He was considered cultivated, even learned, but in those frivolous, care-free days, it was very easy to appear more learned than was the case. But it would be unjust to claim that the system of education adopted by Mme de Genlis, strange though it may have seemed then, in a world so full of affectations and absurdities, did not, in fact, have advantages, particularly when compared with the education given by the Duc de Sérent to the two children of the Comte d'Artois. They were never seen and knew as little of France as if they had been heirs to the throne of China. The Princes of the House of Orléans, on the other hand, devoted their walks and their leisure to everything that was instructive. They knew something of the different trades, of machines, libraries, restaurants, public monuments and the arts. They learned from their pleasures. They became known to the people and in the case of the only one of the princes to survive,* events have shown this to have been an advantage. In the days of which I am speaking, the two younger princes were still children. I was often present at their supper on the evenings when there was dancing. The other guests had supper at home or with friends, for there was never any question of eating at Belle-Chasse or of drinking anything there except water. The princes' supper was extremely frugal, perhaps exaggeratedly so. Mme de Genlis did not have supper with them and Henriette de Sercey and Pamela found great satisfaction in making their soup go further by adding a large glass of water and then breaking pieces of bread into it.

Since I have mentioned Pamela, I will tell you something of her origin. Mme de Genlis let it be known that she had adopted the child in England, but everyone was perfectly certain that she was her own daughter by the Duc d'Orléans. I have, however, reason to believe that Mme de Genlis was telling the truth. My aunt, Lady Jerningham, whose husband had large estates in Shropshire, was

* The eldest, who eventually became King Louis-Philippe. (Tr.)

closely acquainted with a cleryman in that county who was in touch with Mme de Genlis. One day he received a letter from her saying that 'for reasons of particularly great importance' she wished to undertake the education of a little girl of five or six. She went on to describe the child in great detail. A large sum was to be paid to the child's parents on condition that they kept the whole affair absolutely secret. They were not even to know the name of the person to whom the child's education was entrusted, only that the education would be greatly superior to her station and that she was destined to very great fortune.

The clergyman found a child exactly answering to the description given by Mme de Genlis and sent her to the place in London that had been arranged. Lady Jerningham was certain that this child was Pamela. Nothing could have been more charming than the girl's appearance at fifteen, when I first met her. Her face was quite flawless, her every movement graceful, her smile angelic and her teeth pearly white. When she was eighteen, that is to say, in 1792, Lord Edward FitzGerald, fifth son of the Duke of Leinster, fell madly in love with her, married her and took her to Ireland, where he was the leader of the rebel United Irishmen. When her husband died,* she returned to the Continent and settled at Hamburg, where she married the American consul, Mr Pitcairn. Her schoolroom companion, Henriette de Sercey, a niece of Mme de Genlis, was generously built, not without wit and had the merit of not being at all jealous of Pamela. I do not think she liked her and she pitied her for the fuss which Madame de Genlis made of her.

The really strange part of the story of this establishment is that Mme de Genlis did, in fact, have a daughter by Philippe Égalité. But she hated her from the moment she was born and when her legitimate daughter married M. de Valence, she gave her this illegitimate child, Hermine, who was then eight or ten years old and generally thought to be a foundling, saying that in educating her, Mme de Valence would be serving an apprenticeship for the education she would later have to give her own children. Hermine, a very sensible, very taciturn girl, married a stockbroker named Collard and one of her many daughters was the mother of the notorious Mme Lafarge.†

* Having arranged French assistance for an Irish rising, he returned to Ireland in 1798 to organise the rebellion. In evading arrest, he was wounded and died on 4 June 1798. (Tr.)
† Born in 1816 and married against her will, this grand-daughter of Mme de Genlis and King Louis-Philippe was eventually accused of murdering her

Never had people sought more after pleasure than during the Spring of 1789, before the meeting of the States-General.* For the poor, the winter had been very hard, but there was no concern for the misery of the people. There were races at Vincennes, where the horses of the Duc d'Orléans ran against those of the Comte d'Artois. It was after the last of these races, as we were driving home along the Rue Saint-Antoine with Mme de Valence, that we found ourselves in the midst of the first riot, the one which destroyed good Réveillon's wallpaper factory. It was not until long afterwards that I realised the true significance of that mob, which was a hired one.

M. de Valence was at the time First Equerry to the Duc d'Orléans and as we passed through the crowd of four or five hundred people which filled the street, the sight of the Orléans livery roused their enthusiasm. For a few minutes they held up the carriage shouting 'Long Live our Father! Long Live King d'Orléans!' At the time, I paid little attention to these cries, but a few months later, when I had certain knowledge of the activities of the scheming Duc d'Orléans, they returned to my mind. The popular movement which ruined Réveillon had been organised, I have not the slightest doubt, in order to get rid of him. He was a good man, employing three to four hundred workers, and he enjoyed an excellent reputation in the Faubourg Saint-Antoine. I do not know what became of him after that dreadful evening when his printing blocks, his machines and his warehouses were burned and destroyed.

As soon as the elections were over, everyone prepared to move to Versailles. All the members of the States-General sought lodgings in the town, those who were attached to the Court transferred their families and households to the apartments reserved for them in the château. At that time, my aunt had an apartment there and I lodged with her. It was on an upper floor, above the Galérie des Princes.† The room I occupied opened on to the roofs but my aunt's room overlooked the terrace and had a very fine view. It was only on Saturday nights that we slept there. As Governor of Versailles, M. de Poix had a charming small house with a pretty garden at the

* The oldest and most important of the nation's assemblies. It consisted of representatives of the three estates of the realm and each order had a collective vote. It could be summoned only by the king and represented his real power against factional interests. (Tr.)

† In the wing overlooking the south garden and the terrace of the Orangery, between the terrace and the Rue de la Sur-Intendance.

husband. After twelve years' hard labour, she was pardoned but died a year later, in 1853. (Tr.)

Ménagérie* and this he lent to my aunt who established herself there with all her servants, her cook, her horses, my own saddle-horses and my English groom. It was a very pleasant house. All one's acquaintance was at Versailles and we waited, amid much gaiety and without the least anxiety – visible anxiety, at any rate – the opening of that assembly which was to give birth to a new France. Looking back at our blindness, I can understand it in young people like myself, but find it inexplicable in men of the world, in ministers and, above all, in the king.

I have forgotten why I did not accompany the queen and all her Household to the procession which took place after Mass on the Feast of Pentecost. I went to watch it cross the Place d'Armes, as it always did, on its way from one parish of Versailles to the other.† We were with Mme de Poix in one of the windows of the Grande Écurie. The queen looked sad and cross. Was it, perhaps, some presentiment of what lay ahead?

M. de la Tour du Pin was so vexed at not being elected to the States-General that he even refused to attend the opening session. It was a magnificent spectacle but has been described so often in memoirs of the period that I shall not do so. The king wore the robes of the Order of the Holy Ghost, as did all the princes, with the difference that the king's were more richly embroidered and very closely sewn with diamonds. In appearance, this good prince lacked dignity, he stood badly and walked with a waddle; his movements were abrupt and without grace; he was very short-sighted and since it was not customary to wear spectacles, he used to screw up his face. His speech was very short and delivered in firm tones. The queen's great dignity was much commented on, but it was plain from the almost convulsive way she used her fan that she was very agitated. She often looked towards that part of the Chamber where the Third Estate was seated and seemed to be searching for a face in the ranks of men among whom she already had so many enemies.

A few minutes before the king entered, there was an incident which I saw with my own eyes. It was seen by everyone there but I cannot recall seeing it mentioned in any account of that historic session. Everyone knows that the Marquis de Mirabeau, whose dreadful reputation had prevented his election to the Assembly of Notables for Provence, was afterwards elected by the Third Estate. He entered the Chamber alone and took his place towards the middle

* A house standing alone in the Great Park, at the end of one arm of the canal, facing the Trianon.
† Saint Louis in the Rue Satory and Notre Dame in the Rue de la Paroisse.

of the rows of backless benches which stretched one behind the other. There arose a very low, but widespread murmur – a '*sussurro*' – and the deputies already seated in front of him moved one bench forward, those behind him moved farther back and those beside him increased their distance. He found himself isolated, surrounded by a very noticeable space. Smiling contemptuously, he sat down. This situation lasted several minutes and then, as the crush of members increased, those who had moved away were forced nearer and the empty space was gradually filled. The queen had probably been told there would be such an incident, one which was perhaps to influence her fate more than she suspected at the time, and this is the probable explanation of her curious glances towards the benches of the Third Estate.

The speech of M. Necker, the Minister of Finance, seemed to me unbearably dull. It lasted more than two hours and, to my nineteen-year-old ears, seemed never-ending. The ladies were seated on fairly wide benches which rose in tiers and they had nothing to lean against except the knees of the person above and behind them. The first row was naturally reserved for the ladies of the Court who were not in attendance and this obliged them to maintain an impeccable posture throughout the entire proceedings, which was exceedingly tiring. I think I have never felt so weary as during that speech, though M. Necker's supporters praised it to the skies.

On 1 June, my husband, like the other colonels, joined his Regiment. He was garrisoned at Valenciennes and was therefore not with the troops assembled at the gates of Paris under the command of the Maréchal de Broglie, those troops which, as a result of that fatal hesitancy whenever a firm decision was essential, were not used when the crucial moment came. The queen knew only how to show displeasure, not how to act. She merely retreated. It must also be admitted that encroachments on the royal authority were so novel that neither the king nor the queen realised there was real danger. It did not occur to them that there was anything worse to fear from the people than some small revolt like that against the shortage of food – the 'flour war', as it was called – at the beginning of their reign.

It was soon apparent that the Constituent Assembly would go further than had at first been expected but it was still thought it would be easy to check the spirit of change which was penetrating everywhere. When the king went to the Assembly on 23 June, he had no doubt, poor prince, but that his presence would discredit the innovators. If anyone had told him that his army was being corrupted, that the entire Régiment des Gardes Françaises had been won over, that foodstuffs were being purposely held up to create hunger in Paris and drive the people to revolt, he would have been dismissed as mad. Ah, it is very easy now, fifty years later, having seen all the consequences of this weakness at Court, to say what should have been done! But at the time, when no one even knew what a revolution was, it was less easy to decide on a course of action. Someone who, in June 1789, congratulated himself on his good, patriotic ideas might, three months later, regard those same ideas with horror.

There was no great change in the web of Court ceremonial. There were arguments in the salons, people were beginning to exchange sharp remarks, nothing more. The first event to strike me as serious was the departure of M. Necker from the Government. It was the extraordinary manner of his leaving rather than the likely consequences which struck me. I had called at the Contrôle-Général the day before that on which my aunt and I were to leave on a visit to the Maréchal de Beauvau at Le Val. His daughter, Mme de Poix, was there with an extremely select company, all of them *philosophes*. I was only nineteen and did not find such company very amusing. Mme la Maréchale de Beauvau was earnest, pedantic and unbending. She terrified me. One had to conform to her standards in absolutely everything, from dress to conversation. Charles de Noailles, the son of Mme de Poix, and his cousin, Amédée de Duras, both a year older than me, were there and we would all three have liked to escape into the garden to enjoy our own light-hearted company. But the timetable and arrangements, the strictness of the proprieties, did not permit such departures from the rule. However, in the evening, we made music, accompanied by Mme de Poix who was an excellent musician. Mme la Maréchale amused herself by watching a tableau made by me and a small negress, Ourika. I took her on my knee and she put her arms around my neck and leaned her little face, black as ebony, on my fair cheek. Madame de Beauvau never wearied of this tableau, which I found most tiresome because I have always disliked contrived effects.

While we were at lunch in a summer-house in the garden, a footman arrived in a state of great anxiety to ask the Maréchal if he knew where M. Necker was. He said that on the previous evening, after returning from the Council, the minister and Mme Necker had gone out in the carriage, saying they were going to supper at Le Val. They had not been seen since and no one knew where to find them. The news was becoming known and crowds were collecting outside the windows of the Contrôle-Général in Versailles. A mounted groom had been sent to all the places where it was thought M. and Mme

Necker might have gone but they were nowhere to be found. This disappearance was extremely disquieting and my aunt wanted to return to Versailles – or rather, to the Ménagerie, where we were staying. When we reached home, the mystery was explained. M. Necker's horses had been sent back to Versailles after taking their owners to Le Bourget. There, the Neckers had taken a postchaise to return to Switzerland by way of the Low Countries. M. Necker's purpose in leaving his Ministry in this way was to avoid the demonstrations of popularity which his departure was certain to arouse. I have since heard this manoeuvre attributed to excessive pride. Personally, I think M. Necker was acting in good faith and realising, as he already did, that the country was racing towards catastrophe, he did not want to excite the people who were already beginning to make themselves feared.

Mme de Montesson was in Paris, preparing to leave for Berny where she was to spend the summer. Loving the social whirl as she did, she would doubtless have preferred to establish herself for that season in Versailles, which was then the centre both of social life and of business affairs. Everyone who could, tried to live as near to it as possible. But her relations with the Court made this impossible. On the other hand, it was no longer possible to remain in Paris where attempts were being made to stir up anxiety about food, one of the means used by the revolutionaries to rouse the people. As Berny was not far from Versailles, which could be reached in two hours by the road to Sceaux, Mme de Montesson decided to stay there with Mme de Valence and made me promise to spend a month or six weeks with her there.

On 13 July, therefore, I sent off my saddle horses in the charge of my English groom, who spoke very little French, telling him to go by way of Paris to get certain things he needed. I tell you this little detail to show that we had not the slightest inkling of what was to happen in Paris the next day. All we had heard was that there had been a few isolated disturbances at the doors of certain bakers accused by the people of adulterating the flour. The Court put its entire trust in the small army gathered on the Grenelle plain and the Champs de Mars and despite the daily desertions from this force, no one was worried.

When you think that I myself was so placed as to hear about all that went on, that M. de Lally, an influential member of the Assembly, was living with my aunt and me in the small house at the Ménagérie, that I went every day to Versailles for supper with Mme de Poix whose husband was the Captain of the Guard and a member of the Assembly and saw the king every evening at his 'coucher' or at Orders, what I am about to tell you is amazing.

So secure did we feel in our safety that at midday, and even later, on 14 July, neither my aunt nor I had any idea that there had been the slightest disturbance in Paris. I set out in my carriage, with a maid and a manservant on the box, to drive to Berny by the main Sceaux road, which runs through the Forest of Verrières. It is true that this road, the one from Versailles to Choisy-le-Roi, does not pass through a single village and is very lonely. I remember still that I had dined early at Versailles in order to reach Berny in time to be settled into my apartment before supper which, in the country, was at nine o'clock. That fact alone makes our unawareness even more extra-ordinary. When we entered the outer courtyard at Berny, I was surprised to see no sign of activity, to find the stables deserted and the doors shut. The courtyard of the château was equally deserted. Hearing a carriage, the concierge, who knew me well, came out on to the steps, looking very worried and frightened, exclaiming: 'It is terrible Madame! Madame is not here. No one has left Paris. They have fired the cannon of the Bastille. There has been a massacre and it is impossible to leave the city. The gates are barricaded and manned by the Gardes Françaises who have risen with the people.' You can imagine my astonishment – it was even greater than my anxiety. But, although only nineteen, I was not in the least dis-concerted by this unexpected news. I ordered the carriage to return by the way it had come and take me to the staging post at Berny. I knew the owner was a good man, very devoted to Mme de Montesson and her friends. I told him that I was most anxious to return immediately to Versailles. He confirmed the concierge's story, which had been entirely supposition since no one had been able to leave Paris. But the city banners were flying from the barricades and, inside, could be seen the sentinels shouting 'Long Live the Nation' and wearing tri-coloured cockades in their hats.

My livery coachman said that nothing would persuade him to return to Versailles, so I had four post horses harnessed up and, with two postilions recommended by the postmaster as resolute lads, set out for Versailles at full gallop. I arrived there at about 11 o'clock. My aunt had had a migraine and was in bed. She had not been to see Mme de Poix. M. de Lally had not yet returned. She knew nothing. As for me, I admit that the fate of my English groom and my three horses was my over-riding anxiety. I had a terrible fear they might have been offered in holocaust to the nation.

Next morning, we were early at the château. My aunt went to

get news and I called on my father-in-law for the same purpose: From him I learned what had happened: the capture of the Bastille,* the revolt of the Régiment des Gardes Françaises, the deaths of M. de Launay, M. de Flesselles and many other less well known people, the badly-timed and pointless charge on the Place Louis XV† by a squadron of the *Royal Allemand* commanded by the Prince de Lambesc. The following day, a deputation from the people forced M. de La Fayette to put himself at the head of the newly-formed Garde Nationale. A few days later came the news that M. Foulon and M. Bertier had also been murdered. The Régiment des Gardes expelled all officers who refused to recognise the new organisation. The non-commissioned officers took their place and this act of insubordination, imitated throughout the French Army, did at least have one advantage for Paris: it ensured the existence, at the very outset of the rebellion, of an organised body to prevent the rabble from the excesses they would otherwise have committed.

The small army of the Plain of Grenelle was disbanded. The regiments, their ranks thinned by desertion, were sent to garrisons in the provinces where they spread that same fatal spirit of insubordination that they had learned in Paris and which it was afterwards to prove impossible to eradicate.

Seven or eight days after 14 July, M. de La Tour du Pin arrived secretly at Versailles from his garrison, unable any longer to endure the anxiety he felt for both his father and myself. At Valenciennes, where his Regiment was confined, fresh rumours were arriving all the time, as false and contradictory as could be. This minor breach of orders was condoned and, at his father's request, my husband was granted leave. My father-in-law realised that he would probably soon be offered a high office. He was too modest to desire such a responsibility and very glad to have his son at hand. My husband did not want his father to accept the post of Minister for War which was offered him and, after the king's visit to Paris at the demand of the commune and the return of M. Necker, who was recalled in the hope that he would be able to restore calm, was anxious to leave Versailles in order to avoid influencing his father's decision.

I had been ordered to take the waters at Forges, in Normandy. It was thought they would strengthen me, for my illness after the birth

* This ancient fortress and prison, though no longer of any military significance, represented, in the eyes of the people, the old royal despotism. Its capture represented the power of the people over the king and marked the real beginning of the Revolution. (Tr.)
† Today, the Place de la Concorde. (Tr.)

of our last child had so weakened my kidneys that it was even feared I might not be able to have any more children, a possibility which reduced me to despair. We went, therefore, to Forges and the month we spent there is one of the periods of my life that I most enjoy recalling. We sent our saddle-horses ahead and went every day for long rides in the beautiful woods and pretty countryside surrounding this small town. We had taken a wide choice of books with us and my husband, an indefatigable reader, would read to me while I worked, for I already had that keen pleasure in handiwork which remains with me still, even at the advanced age at which I am trying to write these memoirs.

On 28 July, there occurred one of the most extraordinary phenomena of the Revolution, one which has never yet been properly explained. It is, in fact, incomprehensible unless one accepts the existence of some gigantic network stretching to every corner of France, permitting one single action to communicate revolt, agitation and terror to every commune in the kingdom simultaneously. This is what happened at Forges that day – I saw it with my own eyes – and the same thing was happening everywhere else.

Our apartment was a modest one on the first floor, low and overlooking a small square on the high road to Neufchatel and Dieppe. It was morning and seven o'clock was striking. I was dressed, ready to go riding and was waiting for my husband who had gone alone to the spring that day. For some reason which I have forgotten, I had not wanted to go with him. I was standing at the window watching the road by which he would return when, along it but from the opposite direction, I heard a mass of people rushing into the square beneath my window – our house stood on a corner – all of them showing every sign of desperate fear. Women were weeping and wailing, men were raging, swearing, threatening, others raised their hands to Heaven crying 'We are lost!' In their midst, haranguing them, was a man on horseback. He wore a disreputable green coat, which looked torn, and was hatless. His dapple-grey was covered in lather, its cruppers cut and flecked with blood. He stopped under my window and began a sort of harangue in the style of quacks in public places, saying: 'They* will be here in three hours; they are pillaging everything at Gaillefontaine;† they are setting fire to the barns . . .' and

---

* The Austrians. Since Austria governed the Low Countries on the northern border of France and controlled the principalities to the east, it would not be difficult to rouse fears of invasion and one of the deepest fears of the French people was that Marie-Antoinette would summon her brother's troops to her aid. (Tr.)
† A small town two leagues from Forges.

so on. After a few sentences in this vein, he clapped spurs to his horse and galloped off towards Neufchatel.

Since I am not by nature fearful, I went downstairs, mounted my horse and rode at a walking pace along the street which was filling with people who thought their last day had come. I talked to them and tried to convince them that there was not one word of truth in what they had been told, that it was impossible for the Austrians, with whom we were not at war, to have arrived, as the impostor had been saying, in the heart of Normandy without anyone having heard that they were on the march. When I reached the door of the church, I found the curé arriving to sound the tocsin. At that moment, M. de La Tour du Pin rode up, fetched from the fountain by my groom. They found me still mounted and holding on to the curé by the collar of his cassock, trying to explain to him what folly it would be to alarm his flock by sounding the tocsin, instead of joining his efforts to mine to prove to them that their fears were groundless.

My husband then took charge and told the crowd that there was no vestige of truth in what they had been told. To reassure them, he said we would go over to Gaillefontaine and bring back news. Meantime, they were not to sound the alarm but return to their homes. We set off at a canter, followed by my groom who, since 14 July when he had happened to be in Paris, was convinced that all Frenchmen were mad.

After about an hour, we reached the country town where we had been told we would find the Austrians. As we rode down a sunken path leading to the main square, a man armed with a rusty pistol stopped us with the challenge: 'Who goes there?' Then, advancing on us, he asked if the Austrians were not at Forges. When we replied that they were not, he took us to the square and shouted to all the people gathered there: 'It isn't true! It isn't true!' At that moment, a large man, rather prosperous-looking, came up to me and cried: 'Eh, citizens, 'tis the queen!' From all sides came the shout that I should be taken to the Commune* and, although not at all frightened by my own predicament, I was greatly frightened by the danger to a crowd of women and children who were thrusting themselves in front of my horse, a very excitable animal. Luckily, a locksmith's apprentice who had come out of his shop to look at me, began to laugh heartily, saying that the queen was at least twice as old as that young lady and twice as large, that he had seen her only two months earlier and that I was not she. This assurance gained me my liberty

* A territorial area administered by a mayor and municipal council. By extension, the municipal council itself. (Tr.)

and we left immediately to return to Forges, where the rumour was already rife that we had been captured by the enemy. We found the men armed with anything they had been able to lay hands on and the Garde Nationale standing by. And that was the sole purpose of the scare: to ensure that, throughout France, on the same day and almost at the same hour, the entire population should resort to arms.

✿✿✿✿✿✿✿✿✿✿✿✿ X ✿✿✿✿✿✿✿✿✿✿✿✿

A few days after these events, my husband learned that his father had been appointed Minister for War. We left immediately for Versailles. It was the beginning of my public life. My father-in-law gave my husband and me a fine apartment on the first floor of the Ministry for War,* put his household in my charge and entrusted the honours of his house to my sister-in-law and me. My sister-in-law also had lodgings in the Ministry, but had to leave us two months later. At Montpellier and in Paris, I had been so accustomed to big dinners that my new position did not worry me in the slightest. In any case, I took great care to concern myself only with doing the honours of the house. Every week there were two dinners for twenty-four people to which all the members of the Constituent Assembly were invited in turn. Their wives were never asked. Mme de Lameth and I used to sit opposite one another and seat next to us the four most important guests, taking care to choose them from among all the parties. So long as we were at Versailles, the men always wore formal dress at these dinners and I remember M. de Robespierre in an apple-green coat, with his thick white hair wonderfully dressed. Mirabeau alone never called on us and was never invited. I often went out to supper, either to my colleagues or to people staying in Versailles for the session of the National Assembly, as it was called.

On 14 July itself,† the Comte d'Artois left France to visit his father-in-law‡ in Turin, taking his children with him. He was accompanied by many members of his Household, including M. d'Hénin, the captain of his Guard. Fearing that popular agitation might endanger the safety of the Polignac family, the queen made them,

* In the south wing of the Cour des Ministres at Versailles.
† The Comte d'Artois actually left Paris on the night of 16/17 July 1789.
‡ Victor-Amédée III, King of Sardinia.

too, promise to leave France. Mme de Polignac resigned her appointment as governess to the Children of France and took with her her daughter, the Duchesse de Gramont.

France is a country much given to fashions and just then emigration was becoming the vogue. People started raising money on their estates so that they would have ample funds to take with them and very large numbers of them who were in debt saw in this fashion a means of escape from their creditors. The very young looked on it either as a heaven-sent excuse to travel, or a pretext for setting off to join their friends and companions. No one yet realised the consequences of the decision.

Yet the happenings of the night of 4 August when, on the motion of the Vicomte de Noailles, feudal rights were abolished, should have convinced even the most incredulous that the National Assembly was unlikely to stop at this first measure of dispossession. This decree ruined my father-in-law and our family fortunes never recovered from the effect of that night's session. It was a veritable orgy of iniquities. The value of the property at La Roche-Chalais lay entirely in feudal dues, income from invested money and leases or from the mills. There was also a toll river-crossing. The total income from all these sources was 30,000 francs a year and the only charge on that sum was the salary of the agent who, on an appointed day, received payments in grain or the money equivalent of the grain at the current market price. This type of property, where there were, in effect, two proprietors to each piece of land, was very common in south-western France. The decree did not at first order complete seizure of the land, it merely fixed a rate at which it could be redeemed. But before the day fixed for this payment came round, it had been decided that no payments would be accepted. And so everything was lost.

We also lost the toll crossing at Cubzac, on the Dordogne, which was worth 12,000 francs, and the income from Le Bouilh, Ambleville, Tesson and Cénévrières, a fine property in the Quercy which my father-in-law was forced to sell the following year. And that was how we were ruined by the stroke of a pen. Since then, we have been forced to contrive a living, sometimes by the sale of some of the few possessions remaining to us, sometimes by taking salaried posts – though the salaries rarely covered the expense the posts involved. And so it is that, inch by inch, over a long period of years, we have gradually slid to the bottom of an abyss from which we shall not emerge in our generation.

I was far from thinking, then, that my grandmother, who had

removed six months earlier to Hautefontaine with my uncle, was also to deprive me of her fortune on which I had every reason to count. I could not foresee that my uncle, who had not been appointed to the States-General, whose income the Decree had reduced by only five or six thousand francs and who therefore still enjoyed a yearly revenue of 420,000 francs from Church appointments, whose quiet life at Hautefontaine could not have cost him even a quarter of that amount, would leave behind him when he emigrated the following year, debts amounting to 1,800,000 francs in which my grandmother's fortune would be heavily pledged.

We did not immediately feel the full extent of our ruin. As a minister, my father-in-law received a salary of 300,000 francs, in addition to his pay as Lieutenant-General and Commander of a Province. But he had, in fact, to maintain considerable state and as well as the two weekly dinners for twenty-four people, there were also every week the two lavish and elegant supper parties to which I invited twenty-five to thirty ladies of all ages. Only my sister-in-law and I were able to enjoy these supper parties as my father-in-law, who rose very early in the morning, usually retired to bed at the end of the council meetings. This, however, did not prevent his colleagues and their wives from calling on us.

Mme Necker, the wife of the Contrôleur-Général, lived in more or less the same style as we did. But as she seldom went out, she gave daily suppers for deputies, men of learning and her daughter's admirers. In this salon, her daughter reigned over a group of intellectuals. She was then at the full height of her youthful enthusiasms, interested alike in politics, science, learning, intrigue and love. Mme de Staël lived with her parents at the Contrôle-Général in Versailles and went to Court only on Tuesdays, the day ambassadors were received. She was at that time more than friendly with Alexandre de Lameth, who was still a friend of my husband, a friendship which dated from their childhood and caused me some anxiety. I had a very poor opinion of this young man's morals and was particularly anxious lest he should obtain any political influence. My sister-in-law shared my opinion and when, a few months later, my husband openly dissociated himself from him and his brother, Charles, we were delighted.

I have never pretended to be a woman of intellect, I have only tried to use wisely the common sense which Providence gave me. I knew Mme de Staël intimately, though not to the point of exchanging confidences with her. But she had sufficient trust in my husband to confide everything to him and he told me about her life in great detail. I profited from this to remain on terms of easy acquaintance with her, but not of friendship. We sometimes had conversations which are amusing to recall. Mme de Staël could not understand why I was not enthusiastic about my looks, my colouring, my figure and when I admitted that I did not attach more importance to these personal attributes than they warranted, for they would disappear with age, she exclaimed naïvely that if she had had them, she would have wanted to rouse the world. Her greatest pleasure, a very odd one, was to imagine a set of circumstances which, at the time, still seemed imaginary, and then ask me: 'Would you do this, or that?' And since my answers always showed that I was happy and ready to put into practice the ideals of devotion, self-sacrifice, abnegation and courage which her lively imagination had conjured up, she declared that I thought like a romantic. What she found less easy to understand was that one should be ready to make every possible sacrifice for one's husband, and she could only understand it in the following terms: 'It seems to me that you love him as a lover.'

That woman was an odd mixture and I have often tried to understand the mingling of virtue and vice in her. Vice is too harsh a word. Her great qualities were merely tarnished by the passions to which she abandoned herself the more easily since it was always a pleasant surprise to her that a man should seek from her those pleasures from which her unfortunate looks seemed to have debarred her for ever. Indeed, I have every reason to believe that she surrendered without the slightest struggle to any man who showed himself more aware of the beauty of her embrace than the charms of her mind. Yet you would be wrong to conclude that I considered her shameless, for she did insist on a certain delicacy of feeling and has shown herself capable of passions that were very deep and devoted while they lasted. It was in such a manner that she loved M. de Narbonne, who deserted her, so far as I remember, in a most shameful manner.

Groups of Gardes Nationales were organising themselves throughout the kingdom on the model of the Garde Nationale of Paris commanded by M. de La Fayette. The king himself gave instructions that a similar Garde be formed at Versailles from among the messengers and employees of the ministries, partly because he hoped that such a step would improve the spirit of the corps and partly in the hope that a Garde which included so many people dependent on the Court for their livelihood would be less likely to forsake it. But the commanding officer was badly chosen: he was the Comte d'Estaing, who had acquired a reputation he was far from deserving. I knew from my father how to regard his appointment. M. Dillon had served under him at the beginning of the war in America and had the most positive proof that M. d'Estaing lacked not only skill, but even courage. Yet, when he returned to France, favours were heaped upon him while my father, to whom he owed his first victory, since it was Dillon's Regiment which captured Grenada, had only the frustration and disappointment of seeing others promoted over him. It was at the queen's request that M. d'Estaing was appointed Commander-in-Chief of the Garde Nationale at Versailles. But my father-in-law, in an attempt to retain some measure of control over the force, appointed his son as second-in-command. This meant, in fact, that he became the effective commander for M. d'Estaing's arrogance and disdain gave him the greatest distaste for dealing with such a middle-class force and he avoided doing so on every possible occasion. He therefore took no part in organising the Garde or in the appointment of its officers. Berthier, who has since become the Prince de Wagram and a very distinguished staff officer, was made Chief of Staff. He was a good man with a talent for organisation, but his weakness of character left him a prey to intriguers. He recommended as officers certain merchants of Versailles who already belonged to the revolutionary party and who were eventually to sow discord in the force.

Even before the end of August, it had been discovered that there existed schemes to create a shortage of food and many of the plotters were surprised and arrested. Two of them were brought to trial, admitted their guilt and were condemned to be hanged. On the day of their execution, a crowd gathered in the square. The mounted police, not numerous enough to keep order and prevent the crowd from freeing the condemned men, thought it best to take the two men back to prison and the execution was put off until the following day. The mob pulled down the gallows and pillaged the bakeries, accusing the bakers of denouncing those who had tried to subvert them. But the law had to be upheld. On the day of the execution, M. d'Estaing being unwilling to come to Versailles, it was M. de La Tour du Pin who assembled the Garde Nationale and ordered it to ensure, by force of arms, the execution of the condemned men. There were strong protests, but his unshakeable firmness had its effect. He told the Garde that he himself would lead them and that any who refused to march would immediately be struck from the roll. After that, they no longer dared resist. Seeing that the commander of the Garde was not a man to be alarmed by threats, the people no longer opposed the execution. The men were hanged and the Garde Nationale was left with the feeling that it had emerged from a campaign covered in glory. M. de

The opening of the States-General, 5 May 1789.

The Regimental Banquet, held in the Opera House at Versailles, 1789.

La Tour du Pin had never before had anything to do with carrying out the death penalty and returned home greatly distressed.

On the feast of St Louis, it was customary for the magistrates and municipal authorities of the City of Paris to wait on the king and offer him their good wishes. This year, the Garde Nationale wanted to share this privilege and the commanding general, M. de La Fayette, brought his entire staff to Versailles at the same time as M. Bailly, the Mayor of Paris and all the municipal authorities. The fishwives came too, as was their custom, to bring the king a bouquet. The queen received them all in state in the green salon next to her bedroom. The usual procedure for such audiences was followed. The queen was not in Court dress but sparkled with many diamonds and other precious stones. She sat in a large chair with a back, her feet on a small stool. To right and left of her, a few duchesses in Court dress were seated on their stools and behind her stood the entire Household, both Ladies and Gentlemen.

I had managed to be near enough to the front to be able to see and hear. The usher announced: 'The City of Paris!' The queen waited for the mayor to go down on one knee, as he had done in previous years, but M. Bailly made only a very deep bow as he entered. The queen replied with an inclination of the head which was not sufficiently amiable. M. Bailly then made a little speech, very well composed, in which he spoke of devotion, attachment and also a little of the fears of the people at the daily threat of a food shortage.

Next came M. de La Fayette, who presented his staff officers of the Garde Nationale. The queen's colour rose and I could see that she was under the stress of strong emotion. She stammered a few words in a trembling voice and nodded her head in dismissal.

They all left, feeling – as I heard later – very annoyed with her, for that unfortunate princess was incapable of judging the importance of an occasion. She allowed her feelings to be seen without reflecting on the possible consequences. These officers of the Garde Nationale, who could have been won by a gracious word, went off instead in a very bad humour and spread their discontent throughout Paris, increasing the ill-will which was being stirred up there against the queen, mainly at the instigation of the Duc d'Orléans.

The fishwives were also badly received and resolved to take their revenge.

The Garde Nationale at Versailles, as elsewhere, wanted its own standards and it was decided to have them solemnly blessed at Nôtre Dâme de Versailles. A group of senior officers, headed by M. d'Estaing, came to ask me to take the collection at this ceremony.

It had been arranged that I would agree to do so. But my gravity was sorely tried when, in the middle of my polite words of acceptance, I saw behind M. d'Estaing a servant from the château, armed to the teeth. He was Simon and had charge of my aunt's apartment, often preparing our supper. These incongruities were still new, and to the young, merely amusing. If I had been told that Berthier, the modest chief of staff, whose father was in charge of the offices of the Ministry for War, would one day be sovereign prince of Neuchatel and marry a German princess, I would have laughed at such a fairy tale. But we have since seen many others far stranger.

I went, therefore, to this very brilliant and solemn ceremony which was attended by representatives of all the military corps in Versailles. During the very long High Mass, I had plenty of time to meditate on the course of events. Scarcely fourteen months before, on the Feast of Pentecost, I had taken the collection in the Chapel of Versailles at a Chapter of the Order of the Holy Ghost presided over by the king and attended by all the princes of the blood, many of whom had by now left France.

A very handsome young man whom I did not know came to give me his hand, obviously much embarrassed at his rôle. Perhaps he, too, like Simon, was some servant from the château or a shopkeeper from Versailles. I did not ask his name. The collection was good and the curé and his poor were very pleased with it, which was all I sought to know. My aristocratic notions were somewhat confused by having to play this kind of rôle. But my father-in-law wished it so and so did the king, which was sufficient to make me accept with good grace. I had put on a pretty toilette which brought me many compliments and afterwards we had to entertain to dinner the staff officers of the Versailles Garde. Perhaps it was presentiment which made me dislike them.

The summer wore on. I was again pregnant and it seemed likely there would be a happy outcome. My health was good and as my father-in-law had twelve carriage horses which he never used, my sister-in-law and I used them to go driving in the beautiful forests around Versailles.

Every day there was news of small riots in Paris caused by the increasingly difficult food situation, for which no one could produce a convincing explanation. The Court, stricken sublimely blind, could not see disaster approaching. The Garde Nationale of Paris was behaving quite well. It had a nucleus of soldiers – no officers – from the former Régiment des Gardes Françaises and they had, as it were, inoculated the citizens who joined its ranks with certain military traditions. The sergeants and corporals of the Gardes Françaises had been appointed to officers' duties and it was they who trained the new Garde. It was at full strength from the outset. M. de La Fayette paraded about on his white horse and, in his foolishness, had not the slightest suspicion that the Duc d'Orléans was dreaming of a throne and plotting to seize it. It is absurdly unjust to believe that M. de La Fayette was the instigator of the events of 5 and 6 October 1789. He thought himself supreme in Paris but his reign ended on the day the king and the Assembly returned to the city. Then, he was given a responsibility he did not want. He was overwhelmed by the revolutionaries and carried along by them despite himself. I will tell you later what I remember of those days, when the weakness of the king was at the root of all the trouble.

The Régiment de Flandre-Infantérie, whose colonel, the Marquis de Lusignan, was a deputy, had been summoned to Versailles. After the presentation of the standards, the Gardes du Corps expressed a wish to give a regimental dinner for the officers of the Régiment de Flandre and the Garde Nationale of Versailles and asked to borrow for the occasion the great theatre of the château, which lies at the end of the Chapel gallery. This magnificent hall could be transformed into a ballroom by laying a floor which raised the pit to the level of the boxes. There was a splendid, heavily-gilded screen which fitted in front of the stage, continuing the design of the other walls. They were given permission to set up their table. The dinner began quite late and the theatre was brilliantly lit, as would, in any case, have been necessary, for there were no windows.

Towards the end of dinner, my sister-in-law and I went to watch the spectacle, which was magnificent. Healths were being drunk and my husband, who had come to meet us and take us to one of the stage boxes, had time to whisper that people were getting very heated and that some rash things had been said.

Suddenly, it was announced that the king and queen were to appear at the banquet: an imprudent step which made a bad impression. The sovereigns did indeed appear in the centre box, accompanied by the young Dauphin, who was nearly five years old.* Enthusiastic cries of 'Vive le Roi!' could be heard. I myself heard no others, despite declarations that such there were. A Swiss officer approached the box and asked the queen's permission to take the Dauphin round the banqueting room. She consented and the small boy was not in the least afraid. The officer put him on the table and he

* The second Dauphin, Louis-Charles, born in 1785. His elder brother had died earlier in 1789.

walked boldly round it, smiling, quite undismayed by the shouting all about him. The queen was less happy and when he was taken back to her, embraced him tenderly. We left after the king and queen had gone. Since everyone was leaving, my husband, worried for me in such a crush, came to join us. During the evening, we heard that certain ladies in the Chapel gallery, including the Duchesse de Maillé, had distributed white ribbons from their hats to some of the officers. It was a most foolish thing to do, for the next day the dis-affected papers, of which there were already a number, did not omit a description of the 'orgy' at Versailles which ended, they said, with a distribution of white cockades to all the guests. I have since seen this absurd story printed in serious history books yet, in reality, this thoughtless prank consisted of one bunch of ribbons which Mme de Maillé, a heedless chit of nineteen, had taken from her hat.

On 4 October, many of the Paris bakeries had no bread and a great outcry arose. One unfortunate baker was hanged on the spot, despite the efforts of M. de La Fayette and the Garde Nationale. But at Versailles there was no alarm. It was thought that this riot would resemble the earlier ones when the Garde Nationale, on which the Court thought it could rely, had been sufficient to control the people. Many messages sent to the king and the President of the Chamber had been so reassuring that, on 5 October, at ten o'clock in the morning, the king went hunting in the Forest of Verrières and, after lunch, I myself went to visit Mme de Valence who had come to Versailles for the birth of her child. We went driving in Madame Elisabeth's garden at the end of the main avenue and as we were leaving the carriage to cross the side avenue, we saw a man ride past at full gallop. It was the Duc de Maillé, who shouted to us: 'Paris is marching here with guns.' Greatly alarmed, we returned at once to Versailles, where the alarm had already been given.

My husband had gone to the Assembly unaware of what was on foot. We all knew there was a great deal of unrest in Paris, but no one had been able to get any precise details, for the people had rushed to the barricades, shut the gates and refused to allow anyone to leave the city. M. de La Tour du Pin was walking along the corridors in search of someone to whom he wished to speak, when he passed behind a big man, whom he did not at first recognise, and heard him say to the Comte de La Marck: 'Paris is marching here with twelve guns.' The big man was Mirabeau, at that time a close associate of the Duc d'Orléans. My husband hurried to his father who was already in conference with other ministers. Their first step was to send messengers in every direction the hunt might have taken to warn the king to return. A number of people who had come to Versailles about their own affairs, offered their services as aides-de-camp. My father-in-law accepted their offer. My husband busied himself assembling his Garde Nationale, in which he felt little confidence. The Régiment de Flandre was ordered to stand to and occupy the Place d'Armes. The Garde du Corps saddled their horses. Couriers were sent to summon the Swiss Guards from Courbevoie. People were sent every other minute to the highway to gather news of what was happening. It was learned that a huge mob was marching on Versailles, women far outnumbering men, that behind this advance guard was the Garde Nationale of Paris, armed with cannons and followed by a large, unorganised rabble marching without any attempt at order. It was too late to try to close the bridge at Sèvres. The local Garde Nationale had already surrendered it to the women and was fraternising with the Garde from Paris. My father-in-law wanted the Régiment de Flandre and some workmen sent to close the Paris road but the National Assembly had declared itself in session, the king was not there and no one had the authority to initiate a hostile act.

My father-in-law and M. de Saint-Priest were desperate, the former saying: 'We are going to allow ourselves to be taken here, perhaps massacred, without doing anything in our own defence.' Meantime, the recall to arms was being sounded for the Garde Nationale. It assembled on the Place d'Armes and put itself in battle order, facing outwards from the entrance gate to the Cour Royale. The Régiment de Flandre stationed itself between the Grande Écurie on its left and the gate on its right. The positions inside the Cour Royale and in the Chapel arch were held by the Swiss Guard, a strong detachment being always stationed in Versailles. All the gates were closed. All the entrances to the château were barricaded and doors that had not turned on their hinges since the days of Louis XIV were shut.

At last, towards three o'clock, the king and his suite returned at full gallop up the Grande Avénue. This ill-starred prince, instead of stopping for a moment to say something heartening to the fine Régiment de Flandre, which was shouting *Vive le Roi!* passed them without a word. He went straight to his apartment, shut himself in and did not reappear. The Garde Nationale of Versailles, which was on active duty for the first time, began to grumble and say that it would not fire on the people of Paris. There were no cannons at Versailles.

The advance guard of three or four hundred women began to

arrive and spread along the avenue. Many of them entered the
Assembly, saying they had come for bread and to take the deputies to
Paris. Many of them, drunk and very weary, took possession of the
rostrums and a number of the benches inside the Chamber. Night fell
and some pistol shots could be heard. They came from the ranks
of the Garde Nationale and were aimed at my husband, their commanding officer. He had ordered them to remain in position and they
were refusing to obey. One shot hit M. de Savonnières and broke
his arm at the elbow. I refused to leave the window and watched
it all. My husband escaped by a miracle, and seeing that his troops
were deserting him, took up a position before the Garde du Corps,
where it stood in battle order near the Petite Écurie. But they were
so few in number – only de Gramont's company – that it was decided
in council that any attempt at defence was impossible. My husband
had reported the disaffection of the Garde Nationale and it was
agreed that, since it would inevitably fraternise with the Garde
Nationale of Paris as soon as the latter appeared on the scene, it
would be best to make no attempt to re-assemble it.

At this point, my father-in-law and M. de Saint-Priest proposed
that the king and his family should withdraw to Rambouillet and
there wait to see what conditions the Paris rebels and the National
Assembly would put before him. At first, the king agreed to this suggestion. At about eight or nine o'clock, the company of the Garde du
Corps was therefore summoned to the Cour Royale, entering through
the gate from the Rue de l'Orangerie. The Garde marched along the
terrace,* crossed the small park† and reached the Saint-Cyr road by
way of the Ménagerie. There remained at Versailles only enough
men of this troop to assure a continuous guard in the apartment of
the king and that of the queen. The Swiss Guard‡ and the Cent
Suisses§ stayed at their posts.

At this juncture, two or three hundred women who had been
wandering from gate to gate for about an hour discovered a small
door that opened on to a secret stair leading to the Cour Royale, just
under that part of the building where we were. This entrance was
probably revealed by someone who knew about these stairs. The
women rushed through in a body and, surprising the Swiss Guards on
duty at the top, spread into the courtyard and entered the apartments

* The terrace of the Orangerie, under the windows of the queen's apartments.
† The gardens to the west of the château.
‡ A corps of Swiss soldiers who served in foreign armies, particularly the French
Army. (Tr.)
§ A corps of Swiss infantry attached to the king's personal guard.

of the four ministers lodged in that part of the building. So many came into our apartment that the entrance, the ante-rooms and the staircase were packed. My husband returned at that moment to bring my sister and me the latest news. Worried at finding us so surrounded, he decided to take us to the château itself. My sister-in-law had taken the precaution of sending her children to a friend of ours, a deputy who had lodgings in the town. Led by M. de La Tour du Pin, we went up to the gallery* where a number of people who lived in the château, mortally anxious at the turn events were taking, had come to the royal apartments in order to be as close as possible to the source of news.

While all this was going on, the king, still hesitating over the best course of action, decided not to go to Rambouillet. He consulted everyone. The queen, just as undecided as he, could not bring herself to undertake a flight by night. My father-in-law besought the king on his knees to place his person and his family in a place of safety, telling him that the ministers would remain to deal with the rebels and the Assembly. But this good prince, repeating over and over again: 'I do not want to compromise anyone', lost precious time. At one moment, it was thought he would give way and orders were given to bring round the carriages which had been standing ready for two hours in the Grande Écurie. It is doubtless very difficult to believe that it did not occur to a single equerry in the king's entourage that the people of Versailles might oppose the royal family's departure. Yet this was just what happened. As soon as the mob of citizens from Paris and Versailles gathered on the Place d'Armes saw the courtyard gates of the Grande Écurie opening, there was a terrified, angry shout of 'The king is leaving'. They fell immediately upon the carriages, cut the traces and led the horses away. Word had to be sent to the château that departure was impossible. My father-in-law and M. de Saint-Priest then offered our own carriages which were standing ready outside the gate of the Orangerie, but the king and queen would not accept this suggestion. Discouraged, alarmed and fearful of the direst misfortunes, everyone remained there in silence, waiting.

Silently, people walked up and down that gallery which had seen all the splendours of the monarchy since the days of Louis XIV. The queen remained in her room with Madame Elisabeth and Madame. The card-room, which was almost in darkness, was filled with women who spoke in whispers, some sitting on the tabourets, others on the tables. I myself was so agitated that I could not remain still a

* The Great Gallery of the château. (Tr.)

minute. I went constantly to the 'Oeuil de Boeuf'* where it was possible to see the comings and goings of visitors to the king's apartments, hoping to meet my husband or my father-in-law there and to learn the latest news from them. The waiting seemed unbearable.

It was midnight when my husband, who had been in the courtyard for a long time, came at last to tell us that M. de La Fayette had arrived at the gate of the Cour Royale with the Garde Nationale of Paris, and was asking to speak to the king. My husband reported that that part of the Garde composed of former members of the Régiment de la Garde was showing great impatience and the slightest delay might cause difficulties, if not danger.

The king then commanded that M. de La Fayette be admitted. M. de La Tour du Pin hurried to the gate and M. de La Fayette, so tired that, when he dismounted, he could hardly stand, took no more than seven or eight officers of his staff and went up to see the king. He was much agitated and told the king: 'Sire, I thought it better to come here and die at the feet of Your Majesty than to die uselessly on the Place de Grève.' Those were his exact words. The king then asked him what they wanted and M. de La Fayette told him: 'The people are asking for bread and the Garde wants to resume its former duties at Your Majesty's side'. To which the king replied: 'Well, let it do so.'

This conversation was repeated to me immediately it had taken place. My husband went down again with M. de La Fayette and the Garde Nationale of Paris, almost entirely composed of former Gardes Françaises, resumed their former duties there and then. Some immediately replaced the Swiss Guards on sentry duty at each outer gate and the remainder, numbering several hundreds, formed a main guard and bivouacked, as was customary, on the Place d'Armes in a long building composed of several great rooms built in the shape of tents and painted to resemble them.

While all this was going on, the people of Paris began to wander away from the château towards the town and the wineshops. A multitude of people, dropping with weariness and soaked to the skin, found shelter in the stables and coach-houses. The women who had invaded the ministries ate everything that could be found for them, and then went to sleep on the floor in the kitchens. Many of them

* The long inner room behind the Great Gallery, lit only by a round window above a door leading directly to the king's bedroom; it was there that the courtiers waited for the king, discussing intrigues and the latest news. The name of this room, literally 'The Ox Eye' after the shape of the window, thus became synonymous with gossip and intrigue in high places. (Tr.)

The women of Les Halles set out for Versailles, 5 October 1789.

The return from Versailles, 5 October 1789.

wept, saying they had been forced to march and did not know why they were there. It seemed that their leaders had taken refuge in the Chamber of the National Assembly, where they spent the entire night among the Deputies who were taking it in turn to keep the session open.

I think that M. de La Fayette, after posting his sentries of the Garde Nationale, went briefly to the Assembly and then to the apartment of Mme de Poix in the château. She was lodged near the Chapel. My husband, who had accompanied him down, left him outside the courtyard. As for M. d'Estaing, he had not made a single appearance the whole evening. He remained in the king's study, paying no more heed to the Garde Nationale of Versailles than if he had no connection with them. M. de La Tour du Pin had gathered the few officers of his staff whom he knew to be reliable, including Major Berthier. But at that late hour, most of them had gone home or to stay with friends.

The king, being assured that the most complete calm reigned at Versailles, as indeed it did, dismissed all those still in attendance in the Oeuil de Boeuf or in his study. The footman came to the gallery to tell those ladies who were still there that the queen had retired. The doors were closed, the candles put out and my husband accompanied us back to my aunt's apartment. He did not wish us to return to the ministry on account of the women sleeping in the ante-rooms, who were a most revolting sight.

As soon as he had seen us safely to this apartment, he went down again to his father and begged him to go to bed, saying that he himself would keep watch all night. He went home to put a riding coat over his uniform – for the night was cold and damp – and then, taking a round hat, went down to the courtyard and began a tour of the various posts, the courtyards, passages and garden to make sure all was quiet. He heard no sound at all, either near the château or in the nearby streets. The various sentry posts were being diligently relieved and the Garde, reinstalled in the big tent on the Place d'Armes, had put its cannons in battery formation before the entrance and was carrying out its duties with the same precision as before 14 July.

Such is the real story of what happened at Versailles on 5 October. M. de La Fayette's error, if error it were, lay not in the much-criticised hour of sleep which he snatched, fully dressed, on a sofa in the salon of Mme de Poix, but in his total unawareness of the Duc d'Orléans' plot. The conspirators travelled to Versailles at the same time as M. de La Fayette, but unknown to him. The traitor duke took his seat in the Assembly a number of times during the day of 5 October and, in the evening, left for Paris – or at least, appeared to do so. But as you will see later, I discovered beyond any possibility of doubt, that he was at Versailles at the time of the attempt to assassinate the queen.

After making his night inspection without hearing anything to rouse the least fear of disorder, M. de La Tour du Pin returned to the Ministry of War. But instead of going to his study, or to his room, which opened, as did my own, on to the rue du Grand Commun, he stayed in the dining-room by the open window, for fear of falling asleep. It might be as well to explain here that the entrance to the Cour des Princes was, in those days, through an iron gate and that a soldier of the Garde du Corps stood sentry beside it because it was at this point that the king's personal guard took over, principally the Garde du Corps and the Cent Suisses. Inside this small courtyard was a passage communicating with the Cour Royale. It enabled the sentries at the post in the Cour Royale near the Chapel arch at the corner of the Cour de Marbre, to relieve one another without having to pass out through the middle gate of the Cour Royale and return by that of the Cour des Princes. You will see later how necessary a knowledge of this passage was to the assassins.

Dawn was just breaking. It was after six o'clock and the deepest silence still reigned over the courtyard. As he leaned against the window, M. de La Tour du Pin thought he heard the sound of many feet, as if a large number of people were climbing the slope from the Rue de la Sur-Intendance* to the Cour des Ministres. To his amazement, he saw a ragged crowd, armed with axes and sabres, entering through a locked gate, the key of which could only have been got through treachery. At the same moment, my husband heard a pistol shot. In the time it took him to rush down the stairs and have the doors of the ministry opened, the assassins had killed M. de Vallori,† the guard on duty at the gateway to the Cour des Princes. They had crossed the passage I have just mentioned and were advancing on the main body of the Garde in the Cour Royale. Part of the mob, fewer than two hundred, rushed up the marble staircase and the remainder threw themselves upon the sentry on duty.‡ His comrades had shut themselves into the guardroom, leaving him outside, quite defenceless. The assassins did not attempt to force the guardroom door, yet ten or twelve of the Garde du Corps were inside. They could have

---

* Mme de La Tour du Pin mistakenly called it the Rue de l'Orangerie.
† In most contemporary papers, he is called M. de Varicourt.
‡ His name was Deshuttes.

attacked the mob with firearms or sabres in an attempt to defend their companion, but they did nothing and so the unfortunate man, after firing his musket and killing the nearest of his assailants, was torn to pieces by the rest. This cowardly deed completed, the invaders hurried to rejoin the remainder of the mob which had just managed to force its way into the guardroom of the Swiss Guards at the head of the marble stairs. These giants have been much blamed for not defending this stair with their long halberds, but it is probable that, in accordance with custom, only one of their number was on duty at the stair for everyone had been certain that nothing would happen and that the strong iron railings and gates, all securely closed, would withstand attack long enough to permit the defenders to take up their positions.

One proof that no unusual precautions had been taken was the fact that the murderers, once at the head of the stairs and guided, without a doubt, by someone who knew the way, turned into the queen's guardroom and came suddenly upon the only Garde on duty there. He rushed to the door of the bedroom, which was locked on the inside, and knocking again and again with the butt of his musket, shouted 'Madame, you must flee, they have come to kill you'. Then, resolved to sell his life dearly, he set his back to the door, fired first his musket and then defended himself with his sabre. But he was soon cut down by those wretches who, fortunately, had no firearms. He fell against the door and as his body prevented the murderers from forcing it open, they bundled him into a window recess. This saved his life. He lay there unconscious until after the king had left for Paris and then his friends came to collect him. This brave man – Sainte-Marie* by name – was still alive at the Restoration.

While all this was going on, my sister-in-law and I were asleep in a room in the apartment of my aunt, Mme d'Hénin. I was exceedingly tired and my sister-in-law had difficulty in waking me to tell me that she thought she could hear a noise outside. She asked me to go and listen at the window which looked out over the leads, for the noise seemed to be coming from that direction. I shook myself, for I had been very fast asleep, and then climbed on to the window and leaned out over the leads. But they jutted out so far that I could not see the street.† I could distinctly hear a number of voices shouting: 'Kill them! Kill them! Kill the Garde du Corps!' I was terrified. Neither my sister-in-law nor I had undressed, so we rushed into my aunt's room, which overlooked the park, and from which she could hear nothing. Her fear was as great as ours. We immediately sent for

* M. de Miomandre de Sainte-Marie.   † The Rue de La Sur-Intendance.

her servants, but before they had been roused, my good, devoted Marguérite came in, pale as death. She collapsed on the first chair within reach, crying: 'Oh, Heaven, we shall all be murdered.' This was not exactly reassuring. The poor woman was so out of breath that she could scarcely speak. However, after a minute or two, she told us that she had left my room in the ministry in order to find me and ask if I would need her. On her way down the outside stair, she had come upon a large mass of people, the dregs of the town, one of them a man with a long beard, a well known model* at the Academy, in the act of beheading the body of a Garde du Corps who had just been killed.† As she passed the gate into the Rue de L'Orangerie, she had seen a gentleman arrive, his boots splashed with mud and a riding whip still in his hand. It was none other than the Duc d'Orléans, whom she knew very well by sight. She told us also that, at sight of him, the wretches had cried joyfully: 'Long Live our King d'Orléans!', he meantime signing to them with his hand to be quiet. My good Marguérite added that, realising her white apron and spotless gown might make her conspicuous among such a bedraggled mob, she had fled, stepping across the body of a Garde‡ who had fallen across the gate to the Cour des Princes.

Hardly had she finished this exciting tale when my husband arrived. He told us that when he had seen the assassins enter the Cour Royale, he had immediately rushed to the main Garde on the Place d'Armes to have the call to arms sounded. We also learned from him that the queen had managed to escape to the king's apartment by the little passage under the Oeuil de Boeuf which linked her bedchamber with the king's. He persuaded us to leave my aunt's apartment, which he thought too close to those of the king and queen, and advised us to join Mme de Simiane at a house near the Orangerie belonging to one of her former waiting women. The Abbé de Damas came to escort us. I left in a state of despair and great anxiety at all the dangers threatening my husband. He had to order me to go to this woman's house, but promised to keep me informed of everything that happened to him.

At the end of two hours, which to me seemed centuries, my husband sent his servant, as he had promised, to tell me that the king and queen were being taken to Paris, that the ministers and members of the Administration and the National Assembly were leaving Versailles and that he himself had been ordered to remain there to

* Nicolas Jourdan, an artists' model, who became known later as 'coupe-tête' (the beheader).
† i.e., Deshuttes.   ‡ M. de Vallori, or de Varicourt.

prevent looting in the château after the king had left. He said that he had been given for the purpose a battalion of the Swiss Guard, the Garde Nationale of Versailles – whose commanding officer, M. d'Estaing, had resigned – and a battalion of the Garde Nationale from Paris. He strictly forbade me to leave my refuge for the time being. I remained there alone for several hours, as my aunt had gone to join Mme de Poix, who was also leaving for Paris, and my sister-in-law had left me to fetch her children and re-join her husband. He had just arrived from Hénéncourt and wanted her to leave straight away for the country. I do not think I have ever in my life – certainly never until then – passed such cruel hours as during that morning. The cries of people being murdered, which had awakened me, still rang in my ears. The slightest noise made me tremble. My imagination conjured up all the dangers which my husband might be running. Even my good Marguérite was not there to give me courage. She had gone back to the ministry to help my servants pack our belongings, which were to be sent off to Paris in my father-in-law's waggons.

I had no news of Mme de Valence, except that on the previous evening she had felt the first labour pains. But she was unlikely to be in any danger as she lived in the Orléans coach houses and that livery was a protection in itself. But what fears might she not have had to endure at such a moment! My presentiments were justified. A member of the Garde du Corps was killed under her very window, a low mezzanine one. She was so frightened that the labour pains stopped completely and it was as if they had never begun. She left for Paris by way of Marly and her daughter, Rosamonde,* was not born until three days later.

Towards three o'clock, Mme d'Hénin came back for me and told me that the sad procession had left for Paris, the heads of the murdered guards being carried by their murderers on pikes immediately in front of the king's carriage. The Garde Nationale of Paris, which surrounded the carriage, had discarded their own hats and crossbelts in favour of those of the Garde du Corps and the Swiss Guard, and they tramped along with the women and the people. This horrible masquerade made its way slowly to the Tuileries, followed by a stream of carriages of all kinds conveying the National Assembly.

Meanwhile, Louis XVI, as he climbed into his carriage, had said to M. de La Tour du Pin: 'You are in complete charge here. Try to save my poor Versailles for me.' This was a command my husband was firmly determined to obey. He made his arrangements with the officer commanding the battalion of the Garde Nationale of Paris that

* Later Mme Gérard, wife of Maréchal Gérard. (Tr.)

had been left with him, a very determined man who showed the utmost good will – none other than Santerre!*

Accompanied by my aunt, I left my shelter and went back to the ministry. A terrible solitude already weighed heavily over Versailles. The only sound to be heard in the château was the fastening of doors and shutters which had not been closed since the time of Louis XIV. My husband made his preparations for the defence of the château, certain that as soon as night fell, the strange, sinister figures to be seen wandering about the streets and inside the still open courtyards would band together to pillage it. Fearful for me in the rioting he expected, he obliged me to leave with my aunt.

We did not want to go to Paris in case the gates should be closed and I should be separated from my husband and unable to rejoin him. I would have liked to stay at Versailles. Near my husband, I was not afraid of anything that might befall. But he feared the dangerous consequences to my health of any further terrors like those we had just experienced. He said that my presence would paralyse the effort which it was his duty to make to justify the king's trust in him. In the end, he persuaded me to go to Saint-Germain and await developments in the château there, in the apartment of M. de Lally.

We made the journey in a miserable little conveyance, my aunt and I, accompanied by a maid whose home was in Saint-Germain. My father-in-law's horses and carriages had gone to Paris, and in Versailles it would have been impossible to find any means of transport, no matter how large the fee one offered. The journey lasted three long hours. The bumpy paving of the road and the hundred and eighty steps I had to climb to reach the apartment – where the old concierge was amazed to see me – completely exhausted me. I became very ill and before the night was over, all the symptoms of a miscarriage threatened. Drastic cupping prevented this misfortune, but left me so weak that it took me several months to recover.

* Antoine-Joseph Santerre (1752–1809), owner of an ale-house in the Faubourg Saint-Antoine and known for his kindness and generosity. As an officer in the Parisian Garde Nationale, he did all in his power to restrain the violence of the mob. At the moment of Louis XVI's execution, he ordered a roll of drums to ensure silence, but this was misconstrued as an attempt to drown the king's voice and his name became anathema to royalists. (Tr.)

A fortnight later, I left for Paris and stayed with my aunt in the Rue de Verneuil until the Hôtel de Choiseul, which had been taken over by the Ministry of War, should be ready for occupation. My father-in-law was lodging temporarily in a house near the Louvre and I went there every day to dine with him and receive for him in the salon. But although suffering scarcely at all, I had remained so frighteningly pale that people who did not know me were shocked at my appearance. I had quite lost my appetite and my husband and father-in-law were distressed that nothing could be found to tempt me to eat. But my pregnancy continued in spite of everything, though so unnoticeably that there was much discussion as to whether it really existed.

After the revolution of 6 October, my aunt had persuaded M. de Lally, whom she dominated completely, to desert the National Assembly. She also forced him to leave France with M. Mounier. They both retired to Switzerland, a great mistake. It was deserting one's post in the face of the enemy and although their two voices in the Assembly would probably not have prevented any of the events which followed, they must have reproached one another bitterly for having acted in a manner which could be interpreted as arising from fear. However that may be, my aunt followed M. de Lally to Switzerland.

At the beginning of the winter, we moved into the Hôtel de Choiseul, a fine house where I had a charming apartment quite separate from my father-in-law's but communicating with it by a door opening into one of his salons. There was a pretty, separate stair which led only to my apartment. It was just like having a charming house of our own and our windows opened on to gardens. As my father-in-law entrusted many important matters to my husband, he was kept very busy and I seldom saw him except at luncheon, which we ate alone, and at dinner.

In Paris, my father-in-law no longer gave big dinner parties but every day we were twelve to fifteen at table, the guests being deputies, foreigners or persons of note. We dined at four o'clock. An hour later, and after talking in the salon to those who still followed the Versailles custom of coming for coffee, my father-in-law would go off to his study. I would then return to my own apartment or go visiting.

When the queen returned to Paris, she gave up her boxes at the theatres, an expression of resentment which, though very natural, was most unfortunate for it made the people of Paris more hostile than ever towards her. This unfortunate princess was either without tact or unwilling to use it. She would openly show temper to those whose presence displeased her, yielding to impulse without any thought of the consequences and, by so doing, greatly harmed the king's cause. She was blessed with great courage but little intelligence, absolutely no tact and, worst of all, a mistrust – always misplaced – of those most willing to serve her. She refused to recognise that the terrible danger which had threatened her on the night of 6 October was the result of an unspeakable plot by the Duc d'Orléans. Instead, she vented her resentment on the people of Paris as a whole and avoided appearing in public.

I greatly missed being able to use the queen's boxes at the theatre and, fearing the crowd, did not go to any plays during the winter of 1789–1790. I often arranged small supper parties of eight or ten people in my apartment. My father-in-law never joined us on these occasions as he went early to bed and rose correspondingly early in the morning.

It was during the first months of 1790 that the demagogues set out to corrupt the army. Every day some piece of disturbing news reached us: one regiment had seized its funds; another had refused to change garrison; in one place, the officers had emigrated; in another, a town sent a representative to the Assembly to ask for the transfer of the regiment stationed there because the officers were aristocrats and did not fraternise with the citizens. My poor father-in-law was worked to death trying to deal with all these bad reports. Many officers absented themselves without leave in order to leave the country, and their lack of discipline, exploited to the full by the non-commissioned officers, encouraged revolt.

On 19 May, I gave birth to a healthy son who was to be my joy for twenty-five years.* His godparents were my father-in-law and Mme d'Hénin, who had come from Switzerland to be with me when he was born. We called the baby Humbert-Frédéric. Priests were still free to exercise their office without taking the oath,† and my son was baptised in the parish of Saint-Eustache. I was not allowed to feed him myself as I had hoped, for my health had been over-taxed in the early weeks of my pregnancy and I was still very weak. A good

* He was tragically killed in a duel. (Tr.)
† Of obedience 'to the King, the Law and the Nation'. It was promulgated in 1790. (Tr.)

foster-mother took charge of him and although only skin and bone when he was born, he soon became quite plump.

In Paris, the Court followed the same routine as at Versailles, except that after the publication of the Decree which required priests to take the oath, we no longer went to Mass. The dinner ceremonial was unchanged. When I had recovered from my son's birth, I waited on the queen in full Court dress. She welcomed me most amiably. Mme d'Hénin had resigned when she went to Switzerland and there was some question of my taking her place. The queen, however, was unwilling. There was already talk of appointing my husband to be minister in Holland and since I would naturally accompany him, the queen did not think it worth while for me to begin my service. 'And also', she added, 'who knows if I might not expose her to further dangers like those of 5 October?'

I have forgotten the origin of the idea that all the military organisations in the country should 'fraternise', as it was then called, by sending the senior members of every rank to Paris for 14 July, anniversary of the capture of the Bastille. The Gardes Nationales, organised throughout the kingdom during the previous year, also sent deputations of their highest-ranking officers and their oldest guardsmen.

Preparations began at the end of June. The Champ de Mars, in front of the École Militaire,* was in those days a very smooth green used by the students from the School for their exercises and by the Régiment des Gardes Françaises for their manoeuvres. There was, in those days, no garrison either in Paris or its neighbourhood. The only troops in the city were the Gardes Françaises, who numbered, I believe, two thousand at the most. They provided a detachment for Versailles which was relieved every week. The regiment of the Swiss Guards, which was never seen in Paris, was stationed at Courbevoie. The Gardes du Corps consisted of four companies and only one was on duty at Versailles. The remainder were garrisoned in the neighbouring towns of Chartres, Beauvais and Saint-Germain. No other regiment ever appeared at Versailles or in Paris. No other uniforms were seen than those of the recruiting sergeants from various regiments. These sergeants were usually based either under the Pont-Neuf or on the Quai de la Ferraille, watching their chance to enlist some discontented young workman or ne'er-do-well, whom they proceeded to remove from the city.

My father-in-law gave my husband the task of checking all the deputations, seeing to their accommodation, their food and even their

* Founded in 1752 as a military academy.

entertainment, for all the theatres had been ordered to reserve free seats for the veteran soldiers and boxes for the officers. Many were lodged in the Invalides* and the École Militaire. The people of Paris set to with enthusiasm on the work which had to be done on the Champ de Mars. In a fortnight, everything was ready. The great semi-circle or amphitheatre of earth which you see there today was raised by two hundred thousand people of every age and station, both men and women. Such an extraordinary spectacle will never be seen again. The first step was to mark out the semi-circle and then raise its level by four feet, using the earth from the centre of the arena. But that proved insufficient, so more was brought from the Plain of Grenelle and from the area between the École Militaire and the Invalides, where the slightly raised ground was levelled. Thousands of barrows were pushed by people of every quality. There were still many monasteries in Paris where the monks continued to wear their habits and you would see Capuchin monks and friars pulling beside the ladies of the town, both harnessed to small tip carts known as 'camions'. Next to them would be laundresses and Knights of St Louis and in that great gathering of all the people there was not the slightest disorder or the smallest dispute. Everyone was moved by one and the same impulse: fellowship. Everyone who owned a carriage horse sent it for a few hours every day to pull earth. There was not a single shop boy in Paris who was not busy on the Champ de Mars. All other work was suspended, all the workshops were empty. People toiled until midnight and at daybreak were back again. Many of the workers camped in the tree-lined walks on either side of the Champ de Mars. The great reinforced ditches girdling it were filled with small travelling taverns, tables laden with coarse food and barrels of wine. At last, on the evening of 13 July, I went with my sister-in-law, who had just returned to Paris, to stay in a small apartment in the École Militaire overlooking the Champ de Mars, so that we would be on the spot the following morning. My father-in-law had had an excellent meal and other food sent over, with all that was necessary to provide a generous luncheon for the military who might come to see us during the ceremony. This precaution was the more appreciated because it had been forgotten at the Tuileries to bring any food for the king's children and as the misleading spectacle, intended to unite for ever the king and his people, went on long after the royal children's usual dinner hour, Monsieur le Dauphin was very glad to be able to share our luncheon.

* Founded in 1670 by Louis XIV to house officers and soldiers wounded in his wars. (Tr.)

The poor little prince was wearing the uniform of the Garde Nationale. As he passed a group of officers of the Garde gathered at the foot of the stairs to receive the king, the queen said graciously to them, as she showed them her son: 'He does not have the cap yet.' 'No Madame', replied one of the officers, 'but he has many at his service.' It is true that this first Garde Nationale included all the more balanced elements of the population of Paris. It was regarded as a means of raising a barrier against the spirit of revolution. All the shop-keepers, the great merchants, bankers, proprietors and members of the upper classes who had not yet left France were enrolled in it. In society, every man under fifty had joined and duties were scrupu-lously carried out. M. de La Fayette himself, who has been so greatly criticised, was not yet dreaming of a republic for France, whatever ideas he had brought back from America concerning that particular form of government. He was as fervent as any of us in his desire for the establishment of a wise freedom and the removal of abuses. I am certain that neither then nor ever did he have the slightest inclination or desire to overthrow the monarchy. The queen's unbounded hatred of him, which she showed whenever she dared, did, however, embitter him as much as his gentle, almost foolish good nature allowed. But he was not weak and his conduct during the Empire amply proved it. He resisted all Napoleon's approaches, bribes and cajolery. The Restoration has been unjust towards him. Mme la Dauphine* inherited the queen's hatred of him. She listened to all the absurd tales told about him, from that of his having fallen asleep on 6 October 1789 to that which reproached him for having acted as the king's gaoler after the royal family's flight to Varennes. But let us return to the Federation† of 1790.

An altar had been set up on the Champ de Mars and Mass was celebrated there by that least estimable of all French priests, the Abbé de Périgord who, when M. de Marboeuf was raised to the See of Lyon, had been appointed Bishop of Autun.‡ Later, he was to become the Prince de Talleyrand. Although he had been the Representative of the Clergy, which assured him of a bishopric after five years in office, the king was so displeased – and rightly so – with his un-priestly behaviour that he had refused to grant him a See. This refusal had about it a firmness which was far from usual in the king,

* Marie-Thérèse-Charlotte, Duchesse d'Angoulême, daughter of Louis XVI and Marie-Antoinette. Her husband became Dauphin when his father, the Comte d'Artois, succeeded to the throne as Charles X.
† The name given to the celebrations on the Champ de Mars on 14 July. (Tr.)
‡ In 1789. (Tr.)

but his decision was stiffened on this occasion by his conscience in matters of religion. However, when the abbé's father, the Comte de Talleyrand, was dying, he asked it as a last favour and the king, who had until then withstood his petitions, could do so no longer and nominated the Abbé de Perigord Bishop of Autun.

It was he who celebrated Mass at that Federation of 1790. His brother, Archambauld, served the Mass for him and although he strenuously denied this when he joined the princes at Coblentz, I saw him with my own eyes at the steps of the altar, wearing an embroidered coat and a sword.

There is nothing in the world exactly comparable with this assembly which might give you some idea of what it was like: the troops drawn up in good order in the middle of the arena; the multitude of different uniforms mingling with that of the Garde Nationale, which was dazzlingly new; a closely-packed crowd standing on the embankment which girdled the arena, the thousands of umbrellas of every conceivable hue which opened suddenly when there was a fairly heavy shower of rain. It was a most amazing spectacle and I enjoyed it all from my place at a window of the École Militaire.

In front of the middle balcony, a very handsome, ornate stand had been erected. It jutted out almost to the entrance of the amphitheatre and brought the Royal Family close to both the altar and the spectators. The members of that unfortunate family who were present included the king, the queen, their two children, Mme Elisabeth, Monsieur and Madame.* It was only two months since my confinement and I was still very weak, so I did not go down to the stand. The queen, however, had to pass close to me and, being long accustomed to her various expressions, I could see that she was making a tremendous effort to hide ill-humour. But she was not succeeding sufficiently well for her own good or the king's.

Towards the end of July 1790, I was fairly well recovered from my son's birth. My aunt wanted to return to Lausanne and my husband, knowing how much I wished to visit Switzerland, let me go with her for six weeks. Mme de Valence, whose conduct was still exemplary, was at Sécheron, near Geneva, with Mme de Montesson, who was spending the summer there. It had been agreed that she would take a small house separate from her aunt's and that I should spend some time with her there. I left my son with his good foster-mother and Marguérite at the Ministry of War.

My aunt took with her a young cousin who had just left her convent, Pauline de Pully. We had armed ourselves with every

* The Comte and Comtesse de Provence.

possible kind of passport, both for the civil authorities and the Gardes Nationales, as well as for the various other military authorities. But a careless remark of my aunt's nearly cost us very dear. The relay stage at Dôle was outside the town, on the Besançon road. We therefore crossed the town by a rather deserted road and, except for a few shouted insults from passers-by, such as 'There go some more on the way out, those dogs of aristocrats', we managed to leave without incident. We had already met similar behaviour in other places and had become used to it.

When we reached the staging post, my aunt asked the postmaster if we were on the right road for Geneva. He told her that if she wanted the Geneva road, the Route des Rousses, she would have to go back through the town. Vainly did I point out to her that our passports stated that we had to leave France by Pontarlier. She said it didn't matter and when our horses were put to, gave instructions to re-trace our steps and return through the town to pick up the Route des Rousses. Her excuse was that she had told M. de Lally to meet her in Geneva and that she would find M. Mounier there, too.

So back we went into the town. But what we had not realised was that our road would oblige us to cross the crowded market in the main square. We were forced to a walking pace by the press of baskets and people and were at first greeted with insults. Then, as we advanced, the storm increased and a voice suddenly shouted: 'It's the queen!' We were stopped, the horses were unharnessed and the courier dragged from his horse to shouts of '*À la lanterne!*' The door was opened and we were told to get out, which we did, but with many misgivings. I said I was the daughter of the Minister for War and demanded to be taken before the local commander or that he should be fetched. My aunt said she had a letter from M. de La Fayette for M. de Malet, the commander of the Garde Nationale. 'There's his house,' shouted someone, and indeed we could see two sentries at a door over which floated a large tricolour flag. It was only a few steps away so I dragged my aunt and Pauline with me and we went into the house. The mass of people did not dare to follow, out of respect for the commander, who was a popular man. I must add, however, that he did not exactly rush to our defence. We went into a dining-room where a very well-laden table was set for seven or eight people and showed every sign of having been abandoned in a hurry. Two or three over-turned chairs showed the haste in which the guests had left and a table napkin on the floor near a door showed the direction they had taken. My aunt refused to go any further, but said loudly, towards the door in question, that she had a letter from M. de La Fayette which she wished to deliver to M. de Malet. No reply. Not a sound. After a quarter of an hour, my aunt rang a bell she had noticed, in the hope that someone would appear. To leave again was out of the question, for we could see that our carriage in the square outside was still surrounded by the mob, although we could not see what they were doing. Pauline and I had not had any lunch. Seeing that my aunt had seated herself resignedly, saying 'We'll just have to wait', we sat down too, close to the table and began to eat the abandoned dinner. An excellent stew, some meat pâté and choice fruits soon satisfied our young appetites and we laughed heartily at our adventure and the cowardice of the chief of the national militia.

After waiting three hours and having seen from the window that our carriages had been taken away, we at last heard steps in the room above us, though no one had ever answered the bell which we had rung so often. Soon a solemn-faced man came in, a solid middle-class citizen, accompanied by two or three other men of respectable age. He asked my aunt her name and then, indicating me, said: 'And this is your daughter?' She told them that I was the daughter-in-law of the Minister for War, that I knew there was a cavalry regiment in garrison at Dôle and wished to speak to its commander, who would doubtless be able to persuade the President of the Commune – for such was the title of the official nowadays known as the mayor – to set us at liberty. At this point, the man to whom she was speaking announced that he was himself the President of the Commune. He added that the people were very excited, that my aunt's name sounded false, that many thought she was the queen and a hundred other stupidities of the kind. My aunt, realising that they wanted to hold us prisoner, suggested verification should be obtained by sending one of her servants to Paris, and asked that we should meantime be permitted to move to an inn. One member of the Commune suggested taking us to his house. It would be safer than the inn, where we might have to put up with further insults. We agreed to this and he offered me his arm – for the possibility that the officers might decide to intervene on my behalf had made a considerable impression on him and may perhaps even have frightened him a little.

Our host took us to his house and lodged us in rooms that were very simple but very comfortable. My maid and the three men-servants joined us there. While we were writing to Paris to describe what had happened, my aunt to M. de La Fayette and I to my husband, and just as our cook, who was a fast horseman, was preparing to leave, the Commune assembled to make out a passport for our messenger which would serve also as a safe-conduct. At the same time they drew up a declaration praising the 'high civic spirit of the people of Dôle who had been unwilling to allow past their boundaries persons who were suspected of being other than they claimed. A man who had been to Paris had declared that the eldest of the three was the queen, that the youngest might well be Madame Royale and the tall one Madame Elisabeth.' This fine story was believed throughout the town.

Our host made us promise not to try to go out. We were, in fact, forbidden to do so and resigned ourselves to remaining in our cheerless ground-floor lodging, which opened on to a minute garden where the light of day scarcely penetrated, even at noon.

The next morning, two members of the Commune came to question us. They asked hundreds of questions, looked at our papers, our escritoires, our wallets. They asked me to give them an account of everything I had in the postchaise, wanted to know why I had so many new shoes if I was to spend only six weeks in Switzerland, as I had stated, and a hundred similar absurdities. And then, suddenly, it occurred to me to tell them that the officers from the town who had been sent to Paris for the Federation would probably have returned to their regiment. It was likely they had dined with my father-in-law and would recognise me. This was acclaimed as a brilliant idea and they set out in search of them.

And so, towards the end of our first day's imprisonment, the officers of the Royal-Étranger arrived and offered me their services and their protection. The youngest were quite ready to draw their sabres in defence of a woman of twenty who was the daughter of their minister. The older ones wanted to take me to the garrison quarters. They said there was a very fine apartment there where we would be very comfortable while we waited for our messenger to return. I begged them to hide their anger, assuring them that my father-in-law would be furious with me if I allowed them to do anything on my behalf which might endanger the public peace. But I could not stop them coming in succession to visit me throughout the day, to such an extent that by the end of the fourth day even the members of the municipality realised they had been foolish to arrest us and gave us permission to leave. It took a few hours to re-load our carriages and, as we wanted to reach Nyon by night, we decided not to set out until the following morning at five o'clock. The carriages were not brought to the house where we had been detained but waited for us outside the town and I hoped that we would be able to leave on foot, unrecognised, at that early hour. But as I was putting on my hat, I heard the sound of sabres on the tiles in the hall. All the officers were there and, whether we liked it or not, we had to accept their escort to our carriages.

Our vindication arrived that very evening. The President of the National Assembly had written to the President of the Commune by the courier we had sent, reprimanding him in strong terms for arresting us. M. de La Fayette sent a message to the commander of the National Guard who had so prudently remained invisible. My father-in-law recommended our safety to the lieutenant-colonel commanding in the area and we congratulated ourselves on having managed, by such prompt flight, to escape all the very tedious honours that would have been showered upon us to make amends for our unjustifiable detention.

We arrived at Nyon at midnight, passing the frontier without any difficulty. My aunt did not find M. de Lally there. He was at Sécheron, where it was agreed we would go the following morning. I woke at dawn in my eagerness to see that beautiful lake* of which I had read so many descriptions. I ran to the window and cannot find words to describe the wonder and emotion I felt on opening the shutters and seeing that lovely stretch of water shining in the rising sun.

The following day we arrived at Sécheron, where we found M. de Lally and M. Mounier. There were also letters from my husband who, I thought, sounded anxious about the revolt of numerous garrisons in Lorraine, and particularly in Nancy. But that did not worry me then. M. Mounier persuaded my aunt to make an expedition to Chamonix, so we left the following day and were away nearly a week.

On our return, I found a letter from my husband sent on from Lausanne where he thought I was staying. He told me he was leaving for Nancy carrying orders from the king to M. de Bouillé† to group some of the French and Swiss regiments and then march on Nancy where the Régiment du Roi-Infanterie and the Régiment de Châteauvieux-Suisse had barricaded themselves in, having first seized their funds and arrested M. de Malseigne, the commandant of the town. A cavalry regiment belonging to the garrison, the Régiment Mestre, had gone over to the rebels and it had been decided that the strongest measures must be taken against them to set an example. I was extremely worried at this news and asked to go to Lausanne,

* The Lake of Geneva. Nyon is on the outskirts of Geneva. (Tr.)
† Commander-in-Chief of the army in that area.

The General Federation of 14 July 1790, held in the Champ de Mars.

The Arrest of Louis XVI at Varennes, 22 June 1791.

where my letters were being sent. My aunt, equally worried, readily agreed and we left with livery horses, for there were then no posting stages between Geneva and Lausanne.

Stopping to rest the horses at Rolle, we learned at the inn that M. Plantamour of Geneva was there on his way to Nancy. My aunt asked to have a private word with him. A few minutes later, she returned to the room where I had waited with Pauline, looking very troubled, which increased my anxiety. She told me there had been fighting in Nancy, but that details were not yet known, that M. Plantamour was going there to deliver a sum of money equal to that which the Régiment de Châteauvieux had stolen from its regimental funds, a sum which the aged general whose name the regiment bore, wished to replace from his personal fortune. But she was most careful not to tell me of the rumour that the son of the Minister of War had been killed before Nancy. It seemed to her most unlikely. She thought that if such a misfortune had happened, a courier would have been sent to tell me. However, she was extremely anxious and we left for Lausanne. She told me later that never in her life had she suffered so intensely as during that journey.

When we arrived, M. de Lally – who had gone on ahead – gave me a number of letters written by my husband after his return to Paris. He told me all that had passed at Nancy. The facts belong to history, but I will tell you those which concern M. de La Tour du Pin. He had left Paris with an order from the king to act with the utmost severity towards the mutinous garrison in Nancy if, after being summoned more than once to submit, it persisted in its revolt. M. le Marquis de Bouillé, who had acquired a great reputation as a soldier during the war in America, was commander-in-chief in Lorraine and Alsace. He was instructed to assemble those infantry and cavalry regiments on which he could depend and move towards Nancy. M. de La Tour du Pin, whom he sent into the town to parley, went to the house of the local commander, M. de Malseigne, whom the mutineers were holding prisoner, along with other officers who had remained faithful to their duties. When my husband had exhausted every means of conciliation, he left Nancy to inform the general of the obstinate resistance of the three regiments. They did not dare to prevent his departure, either because his presence as a prisoner would have been an embarrassment, or because, being prudent, they hoped to persuade him to intervene on their behalf should they lose their struggle and be forced to submit. M. de La Tour du Pin rejoined M. de Bouillé at Toul and preparations were made to march on Nancy. The imprisonment of M. de Malseigne was causing great anxiety.

But he managed to have his horse saddled without his gaolers becoming aware of it and presented himself so coolly at the gate that the sentinel mistook him for someone setting out on a peaceful ride and let him pass. Once outside, he took a short cut he knew and reached the highway from Nancy to Lunéville, where his former regiment of cuirassiers was stationed. Nancy was five post leagues distant from Lunéville. M. de Malseigne covered the first three leagues at a canter, but realising he was being followed, set spurs to his horse. As he approached Lunéville, he began to fear he might be stopped on the bridge. But, at that moment, he saw the cuirassiers on the manoeuvre field across the river beside which he was galloping, so he forced his horse into the water and swam across. His pursuers did not dare to follow and returned, looking rather foolish, to Nancy.

M. de Bouillé, relieved of the fear that he might be endangering the life of M. de Malseigne, marched next day on Nancy. A Swiss regiment, that of Salis-Samade, was in the van. As it drew near the entrance to the city, a single arch with a gate, the leading troop saw a company of the Régiment du Roi guarding a cannon set in the middle of the gateway. Before it stood a young officer shouting to his men not to fire and making signs that he wished to speak. M. de La Tour du Pin rode forward, but as he did so, the rebel soldiers fired and the gunners lit the fuse of their cannon, which was loaded with grapeshot. This shot hit the Swiss regiment broadside and killed many, especially of the officers who were nearly all in the van. M. de La Tour du Pin's horse was killed and he had a terrible fall. Until his servant, who was there as a volunteer, managed to reach him in the field where his horse had carried him before collapsing, it was thought he was dead. Meantime, the remainder of the column was forcing the gate and entering the city. Young M. Désilles, the officer who had tried to stop the rebels from firing, was riddled with the shot fired by his own men. He fell, wounded in seventeen places, but lived for another six weeks, dying eventually from the effects of only one wound from which it had been impossible to extract the lead.

After making its submission, the Régiment de Châteauvieux asked permission to hold its own trials and pass its own sentences, a privilege accorded to Swiss regiments. The day after the affair, officers from three of these corps formed themselves into a council of war, held an open-air session and condemned twenty-seven of the ringleaders to death. They were executed on the spot. The two French regiments were disbanded and their troops dispersed among other units. Some of the French mutineers were shot and an even larger number were sent to penal servitude, but none of these measures curbed the spirit of revolt. The army was lost to the throne on the day that its officers, instead of facing the storm, decided to emigrate, imagining they could abandon their standards without incurring dishonour. The non-commissioned officers were there, ready to take their place and it was they who formed the kernel of the army which conquered Europe.

As soon as the Nancy garrison had laid down its arms, my husband returned to Paris with the news. My father took him, travel-stained as he was, directly to the king and this time, the rule prohibiting the wearing of uniform at Court was laid aside.

While all this was going on, I was in Lausanne, where I spent a very gay fortnight. Many English people were staying there and they gave dances. I met a very famous man, Mr Gibbon, whose appearance was so grotesque that it was difficult not to laugh. There were many émigrés, too. I did not enjoy their company, for they were much given to exaggeration and as soon as Mme de Montesson arrived at Paquis, near Geneva, I went to join her. Mme de Valence and I shared a small house.

The inn at Sécheron was then greatly in fashion. Many émigrés I knew had come to stay there for the summer. A number of the young people who had gone with the Comte d'Artois to Turin had already tired somewhat of Piedmont and they, too, came to Switzerland. Archambauld de Périgord was among them. He had emigrated straight from the foot of the altar after the Federation. They all brought the airs and insolence of Paris society into the midst of Swiss customs, which were then even simpler than they are today. They mocked at everything and were everlastingly amazed that there should exist in the world anything besides themselves and their ways. They referred to the people of the country, who were offering them a safe and honourable asylum, as 'those people', they were convinced that the Swiss were only too pleased to have them in their midst and pitied those who did not rush to imitate them. I hope that I, personally, was not so ridiculous, but cannot be certain that I did not sometimes fall into the same errors. They were, after all, the manners of all the people I knew and among whom I had always lived.

Fortunately, I remained only three or four weeks in Geneva or, more exactly, at Paquis. My husband then came to fetch me and took me back to Paris. As he was in a hurry and wanted to return by way of Alsace in order to see M. de Bouillé, we left Geneva very early in the morning so as to have a few hours of daylight in which to visit Berne, Soleure and Bâle.

M. de Bouillé came to meet us between Huningue and Neuf-Brisach, and I waited patiently in the carriage while my husband talked with him as they walked up and down in the road. After spending a morning in Strasbourg, we stopped for the night at Saverne and from there went on to Nancy. As we crossed that town in the moonlight, we passed the lodging of the unfortunate M. Désilles, who was dying. A sentinel had been placed at the door to prevent people stopping to talk under his window. He died a few days later.

We travelled from Nancy to Paris without any further stops and there I found again my dear child, in excellent health and much improved in looks. He had an excellent foster-mother and my good Marguérite watched over her and the baby with incomparable, unfailing care.

✤✤✤✤✤✤✤✤✤✤ XII ✤✤✤✤✤✤✤✤✤✤

At the Ministry of War, I resumed my usual Paris life. Nearly every morning, I went riding with my cousin, Dominic Sheldon. I went often to the theatre with young Mme de Noailles whose mother, Mme de Laborde,* did not go into society. In any case, the pride of the families of Poix, Mouchy and de Noailles would never have been satisfied with such a chaperon. The fortune of Mlle de Laborde had been most welcome, her family less so. Her father-in-law, the Prince de Poix, was very fond of me and delighted that I should accompany his daughter-in-law, whose sixteen years deferred with a certain respect to my twenty. The Princesse de Poix also showed me much friendship and kindness and was delighted for her son's wife to go with me into society. I have never suffered from that smallness of mind which makes some women jealous of the success of other young women and I rejoiced sincerely in the success of Mme de Noailles. To me, Nathalie was like a younger sister and we often wore matching dresses and had our hair dressed in a similar style.

I cannot remember now why I never went to Méréville, M. de Laborde's magnificent house in Beauce, but I often went with Mme de Poix to supper at the Hôtel de Laborde in the Rue d'Artois.

* Wife of the Marquis de Laborde, a very wealthy banker, who helped finance the Seven Years' War. He was guillotined in 1794. (Tr.)

One could be sure of hearing very good music there, played by some of the finest musicians in Paris. As for my friends at the Hôtel Rochechouart, it was always quite late in the season before they returned to Paris from their lovely château de Courteilles.

My father-in-law's distaste for his ministry increased daily. Nearly all the regiments in the army were in a state of revolt. Most of the officers, instead of opposing the efforts of the revolutionaries with a steady firmness, sent in their resignations and left France. To emigrate became a point of honour. Those who remained with their regiments or in their province, received letters from the émigré officers reproaching them for cowardice and lack of loyalty to the royal family. Elderly gentlemen who had retired to their manors received through the post small parcels containing a white feather or an insulting caricature. It was an attempt to convince them that it had become their duty to abandon their sovereign. They were promised the intervention of innumerable foreign armies. The king, as weak as he was good, scrupled to stem this torrent and so, day by day, he was able to note the departure of yet another supporter, sometimes even some member of his Household.

My father-in-law, powerless before the intrigues of the Assembly and not finding in the king the firmness he had a right to expect, decided to resign his office.* It was suggested to my husband that he should take his father's place. He had just finished working out a plan for the reorganisation of the entire army and the king himself thought the originator of the plan quite capable of putting it into effect. But my husband refused, fearing that if he took his father's place, it might be wrongly interpreted. It was then, during the last days of December 1790, that he was appointed Minister Plenipotentiary in Holland, but it was agreed that he would not take up his new duties until the king had accepted the Constitution.† The National Assembly was expected to complete it before the end of the winter.

When we left the Ministry of War, we went to live in Mme d'Hénin's house in the Rue de Varenne. She had had all her furniture sent over there from the Rue de Verneuil, which she had given up. The house was most convenient. We moved in with my sister-in-law, Mme de Lameth, her two children and my father-in-law. My husband kept the saddle horses and another for his cabriolet. My father-in-law gave up his carriage and kept only two carriage horses for my

* He did so on 15 November 1790.
† The National Assembly started work on a new Constitution for France in July 1789 and completed its task in September 1791.

sister-in-law and me. My sister-in-law de Lameth hardly ever went out in the evening. But she went every morning to the meetings of the Assemblée which was housed in the riding-school at the Tuileries. I went sometimes to the sessions which interested me, but not regularly as my sister-in-law did. My mornings were more usefully employed. I had masters for drawing, singing and Italian and, if there was time, I also rode from three o'clock until nightfall. When my cousin Sheldon could accompany me, I went to the Bois de Boulogne, but usually I went, by way of the Plain of Grenelle, to the Bois de Meudon, and on those days rode a very lively thoroughbred whose step and manner I enjoyed tremendously. But in the Bois de Boulogne he was a great trial to me for he could never bear another horse in front of him and when that happened, always tried to seize the bit.

Towards the Spring of 1791, I was returning home one day from a long, solitary ride with only my English groom for company. It was about half-past four. On reaching the Rue de Varenne, I found the road barred by a picket of the Garde Nationale. In vain did I explain that I lived in the street and ask why it was barred, a measure likely to deprive me of my dinner. I was merely told there had been a little trouble at the Hôtel de Castries and that no one was allowed to pass. I tried to pass by the Rue de Grenelle, hoping that the picket there, which I had seen from the distance, might be less intransigent. It was not. The guards at the Rue Saint-Dominique were no better. Eventually, at the Rue de l'Université, I found the way clear and managed to make my way up the Rue de Bourgogne, telling a sentinel at the corner of the Rue de Varenne that I was coming from the house of M. de La Fayette.

When I reached the Hôtel de Castries, I learned that a riot had been organised by Charles and Alexandre de Lameth and directed by their secretary, a good-for-nothing Italian called Cavalcanti, as a consequence of the duel fought that very morning between M. de Castries, a Deputy of the Right, and Charles de Lameth. The latter had been slightly wounded in the arm. The two Lameth brothers, in an attempt to show that they were the idols of the people, had organised this popular manifestation at a cost of some thousand francs and a few barrels of Brie wine. The rioters reached the apartment of the Duc de Castries, who was living alone in the house. Fortunately, he was not at home. All the furniture in the apartment was thrown out of the windows, mirrors were shattered, windows lifted off their hinges and thrown into the courtyard. In fact, only the walls remained.

This disaster could have been avoided if it had not been for the laziness of M. de La Fayette, for I would not like to think that his inaction arose from any other motive. An Englishman of my acquaintance, Captain (later Admiral) Hardy, met the Lameth faction in the Rue de Sèvres. Out of curiosity, he asked the reason of the expedition and then thought it best to run to M. de La Fayette's house in the Place du Palais Bourbon where the headquarters of the Garde Nationale had been established. He arrived 'au grand galop' and rushed up to see the generalissimo, only to be terribly taken aback by the calm with which he took the news of the danger threatening the Duc de Castries' house. He took so long to give orders for the suppression of the riot that the Garde Nationale did not arrive until it was all over, and the posting of sentries at all the doors when the enemy had already left was greeted with nothing but scorn. From her window, my sister-in-law had seen Cavalcanti urging the people on and, from what she saw, was firmly convinced that her brothers-in-law were the instigators of the disorder. Like us, she no longer had anything to do with them and we did not even greet one another when we met.

In the spring of 1791, my husband began preparing to leave for Holland. We packed our belongings and the cases were sent by sea to Rotterdam. We sold our saddle horses and I set out with my son and his wet-nurse for Hénéncourt, where my sister-in-law was already staying. M. de La Tour du Pin joined us there for a while and then returned to Paris to complete his arrangements. However, M. de Montmorin told him the king did not wish him to leave until the day after the constitution, so soon to be presented, had received the royal assent. M. de La Tour du Pin therefore remained in Paris. I joined him there for a few days to see the unseemly splendour of Voltaire's funeral procession on its way to his last resting-place in the Panthéon.

I was living quietly at Hénéncourt with my sister-in-law when, one morning at about nine o'clock, my blackamoor, Zamore, came to my room in a state of great agitation. He told me that two strangers had just passed the gate and had said that on the evening of the previous day the king, his two children, the queen and Mme Elisabeth had left Paris and that no one knew where they had gone. This news worried me greatly and I wanted to speak to the men. I ran to the courtyard gate, but they had already disappeared and no one knew what had become of them. I have always been convinced that they hid in the village, for it was set in the midst of one of the great Picardy plains and they certainly could not have left unseen. They must have remained hidden until evening.

My anxiety was considerable. I was afraid my husband might be involved and decided to send Zamore to Paris to get reliable news of what had really happened. He left an hour later, but before his return, I had received by post a letter from M. de La Tour du Pin confirming what we had been told. My brother-in-law came back from Amiens, where he had been, and we spent two days in a state of indescribable anxiety. We had no news of the outcome of this attempt and the days seemed like centuries. My brother-in-law would not allow us to go to Amiens for fear that the gates might be shut and make it impossible for us to return to the country. We hoped the king had crossed the frontier but did not dare to imagine the consequences that might provoke in Paris. My anxiety for my husband was at its height, though I did not dare join him as he had forbidden it, when, on the evening of the third day, a man coming from Amiens told us of the king's arrest and his return to Paris as a prisoner. An hour later, Zamore arrived with a long, despondent letter from my husband.

I will not describe here the details of that unfortunate flight, so clumsily organised. Memoirs of the day have described it in all its aspects. But what I did learn from Charles de Damas was that, at the moment of the arrest, he had asked the Queen to let him take the Dauphin up on his horse, that he could in this way have saved him, but that the queen would not consent. Unhappy Princess, mistrustful of even the most faithful among her servants!

Before the king left Paris, it had been suggested to him that it might be better to take two trustworthy young men used to riding post, rather than the two soldiers of the Garde du Corps who did, in the event, accompany him and who had never ridden anything but troop horses. The king refused. The entire flight, organised by M. de Fersen, who was a fool, was a succession of blunders and imprudences.

Monsieur* and Madame travelled by another route, guided by M. d'Avaray. Louis XVIII has published an account of it in all its burlesque detail.†

It was only after two months of imprisonment that the King decided to accept the Constitution‡ presented to him. My husband

* The king's second brother, the Comte de Provence and his wife. He later became Louis XVIII.
† *Relation d'un Voyage à Bruxelles et à Coblentz, 1791* and *Mémoires sur l'Emigration 1791–1800.*
‡ The king accepted it on 13 September 1791 and signed it the following day at a session of the National Assembly.

had drawn up a long memorandum advising him not to accept it. This note was all in my husband's own hand, but unsigned. M. de La Tour du Pin gave it to the king himself. After 10 August, it was found in the famous iron cupboard and the king had written at the top 'Handed to me by M. de G. to persuade me to refuse the Constitution'. Friends spread the tale that the initials were those of M. de Gouvion, killed in the first engagement of the war, and I believe it was under his name that the memorandum appeared when it was published with the other documents from that iron cupboard.

After the acceptance of the constitution during the second Assembly, known as the Legislative Assembly,* there was a few months' lull. I am convinced that if war had not been declared† and if the émigrés had returned, as the king seemed to wish, the excesses of the Revolution would have been over. But the king and queen believed in the good faith of the European powers. There was mutual misunderstanding but France lived on and won glory in the defence of her territory. As Napoleon said to Siéyès‡: 'If I had been in La Fayette's place, the king would still be on his throne and', he added, tapping Siéyès on the shoulder, 'you, Abbé, would be only too glad to say Mass for me.'

We left for The Hague at the beginning of October 1791. My sister-in-law came with us, accompanied by her two sons and their tutor. Her health was very poor and the consumption from which she was to die the following year already very advanced. As she loved fashionable company, she found the idea of spending the winter alone at Hénéncourt quite unbearable.

Since 1787, when the French Embassy had been virtually driven out of Holland and the Comte de Saint-Priest had withdrawn to Antwerp, France had been represented at The Hague by a Chargé d'Affaires, M. Caillard. He was an experienced diplomat, and very useful to my husband who had never before concerned himself with diplomacy, except through the reading of history, which was his favourite study. But in character, M. Caillard and M. de La Tour du Pin were poles apart. M. Caillard was prudent to the point of timidity and had kept his post only by sending despatches exaggerating the difficulties. He had managed in this way to convince M. d'Osmond

* The first session was held on 1 October 1791.
† By France on Austria, in April 1792. (Tr.)
‡ A member of the Third Estate in the States-General of 1789, an authority on constitutional forms. Later, a member of the Directorate and an ally of Napoleon in his coup d'état of 1799. (Tr.)

who, thanks to his standing with the king's aunts, had for the previous two years been minister in Holland, that any French envoy who appeared at The Hague would do so at the peril of his life. Since the day when the Stadtholder's Party, with the help of English gold and Prussian soldiery, had defeated the Patriot's Party, both conquerors and conquered had worn a piece of orange ribbon either in their buttonhole or their hat. Women attached a small piece to the end of their belt or to their fichu, and servants wore it as a cockade. Only the Spanish Minister, acting on instructions from his Court, refused to wear this favour – or, to be more correct, this badge of servitude. My husband had told the Minister he would follow the example of the House of Bourbon. In any case, ever since some decree abolishing liveries in France, ministers to foreign countries had had permission to use the king's livery and we had adopted it for our household. It was quite out of the question for the royal livery of the Bourbons to be cluttered with the insignia of a private person, for such, after all, was the Stadtholder's true standing.* He was no more than the senior military officer of the Republic, though certainly of excellent family and married to a Royal Highness. It may even have been lingering resentment which prevented the Court of Spain from wearing the insignia of the House of Orange. However that may be, the Spanish Legation was the only one not to do so. When M. de Montmorin, our excellent but weak Minister of Foreign Affairs, was consulted, he told my husband: 'Oh well, try it, but at your own risk!'

We arrived at The Hague at nine o'clock in the evening and, after supper, my husband went with M. Caillard to call on the Spanish Minister. He told him he would follow his example in not wearing the orange ribbon and that his household would certainly not wear it. The household, he added, would not even wear the French cockade, for its resemblance to the colours of the Dutch Patriots' Party might irritate the people of The Hague, who were all supporters of the House of Orange. This decision pleased the Spanish Minister, the strong-minded Comte de Llano.

The following morning, my son was taken for a walk by his nurse. At the courtyard gate stood a group of people watching to see if she would wear the orange ribbon. When they saw that she did not, they began shouting insults in Dutch which she, knowing not a word of the language, did not understand. But she was frightened and came

* The Stadtholder was William V, Prince of Orange. The Principality itself, in southern France, had been ceded to France by the Treaty of Utrecht in 1713. Only the title survived. In 1805, William VI of Orange, brother of William V became the first King of the Netherlands.

straight back. When the carriages arrived to take M. de La Tour du
Pin to call on the Grand Pensionary, a small crowd of some fifty
people soon collected but mainly to admire the fine, elegant clothes
of our blackamoor, Zamore. Until then, M. Caillard had worn the
Orange colours. That day, he was half-dead with fright and accused
my husband of imprudence, which greatly amused M. de La Tour
du Pin. The credentials were presented to the Grand Pensionary
who, according to the constitution of the country, was the first
minister of the States. He then carried them to the States-General to
have them registered by the Recorder.

When we arrived at The Hague, the Stadtholder was in Berlin
where he had just married his eldest son to the young Princess of
Prussia. They all returned to The Hague a few weeks later and then
there began a series of fêtes, balls, suppers and amusements of every
kind, which suited my twenty-one years to perfection. I had brought
many elegant toilettes with me from France and soon became very
much the fashion. People sought to copy me in everything. I danced
very well and was a great success at balls. My enjoyment was child-
like, no thought of the morrow ever troubled my head. I was the
acknowledged leader at all society gatherings. The Princess of
Orange herself did not disdain to dress like me and have her hair
dressed by my manservant. In short, I was dazzled by my success,
little realising how short a time it would endure.

When Dumouriez was appointed Minister of Foreign Affairs in
March 1792, his first thought was to avenge some personal grudge he
bore my father-in-law for something the latter had done during his
Ministry. He dismissed my husband on the false ground that he had
not put sufficient firmness into a demand for reparations for an alleged
insult to the French flag.

We hurriedly rented a small, unfurnished and very pretty house for
ourselves, my sister-in-law and her children. My sister-in-law did not
want to return to France and preferred to remain with me at The
Hague. That very day, all the furniture we wanted to keep was
transferred to this house. The remainder of the furnishings, including
the wines, services of porcelain, horses and carriages, remained at
the Hôtel de France to be sold after the arrival of the new Minister,
should he not wish to buy them from us. As my husband did not have
a Secretary of Legation, M. Caillard having been recently transferred
to St Petersburg as Chargé d'Affaires, he entrusted the archives to
his private secretary, none other than M. Combes, my old tutor, who
looked after our interests better than we could have done ourselves.

M. de La Tour du Pin then went to England to visit his father, who had just arrived there, intending to persuade him to join us at The Hague. From England, he travelled to Paris and from there sent me, by every courier, letters which became more and more alarming.

M. de Maulde, who had been appointed Minister at The Hague, arrived on about 10 August and was very badly received. His calls were not returned, except by the English Ambassador whose country was not yet at war with France. He did not want any of our things and sent his secretary to tell me that he refused to allow them to be auctioned in the salons on the ground floor of the Hôtel de France, although he himself was occupying only a mezzanine floor and had with him only one servant. This secretary, though certainly very common, bore a name which did not yet arouse in me the horror it was later to inspire: he was the brother of Fouquier-Tinville.*

The weather being very fine, I obtained permission to hold the sale of our possessions on the small Voorhout, a charming promenade right in front of the Embassy. It was an occasion. All our friends came. Even the least important pieces fetched the wildest prices, not the tiniest piece remained unsold and I collected a sum certainly more than double the original cost of the goods. These funds were put into the keeping of a reputable Dutch banker who looked after them and later sent them to me in America.

My aunt, Mme d'Hénin, had emigrated to England and often urged me to join her there. But my sister-in-law's health was worsening so visibly that I was unwilling to leave her. My father-in-law, too, was thinking of joining us in Holland. My husband spent a few days in The Hague between 10 August and the September massacres of 1792 and then his father summoned him to London.

As I was in a position to know a great many details of the plight of the wretched émigrés in Belgium after the Battle of Jémappes,† I will tell you about it here. The Prince de Starhemberg, Austrian minister at The Hague, was a close friend of mine. He was young, only twenty-eight, and so irresponsible that he gave more thought to his dress and his horses than to the affairs of his Legation. Nearly every day, a messenger arrived from Brussels bringing him despatches from Prince de Metternich – father of that Prince de Metternich who today 'reigns' over Austria – who was accredited to the Archduchess Marie-Christine, Governor of the Netherlands. M. de Starhemberg

* This brother, Antoine Quentin Fouquier-Tinville (1746–1795) became Public Prosecutor of the Revolutionary Tribunal in 1793. Notorious for his pitiless zeal in accusing his victims, who included the queen and even his own cousin, Camille Desmoulins, he was, in his turn, accused and guillotined in 1795.
† In this battle of 1792, the French defeated the Austrians, who fled from Brussels.

sent these despatches on to England by way of Hellevoetsluis. This young diplomat unsuspectingly confided to me everything he learned. His wife, formerly a Mlle d'Aremberg, took me to the Court of the Princess of Orange whenever there was a Drawing-Room and the diplomatic corps were as friendly and courteous to me as if I were still a member. As I had kept a large wardrobe, I could go everywhere without incurring much expense. I had kept with me only my good Marguérite, who looked after my son, and my faithful Zamore, who dressed my hair as best he could, for it was difficult to do it oneself. As for my poor sister-in-law, she went early to bed and after dinner went directly to her rooms with her children and their tutor.

One day, then, there was a Drawing-Room and the Starhembergs were to fetch me. I was in my room, dressed and ready, when Prince de Starhemberg arrived, quite distraught, saying: 'All is lost. The French have defeated us completely. They now occupy Brussels.' He told me the news as we entered his carriage and advised me to reveal nothing of this at Court, where no one as yet knew anything of these grave events. But when the Princess of Orange came in and walked towards me, I realised she knew. Resting her fan on my hand, she asked me what news I brought and our eyes, as they met, were full of meaning. She already foresaw the fate awaiting her.

The flight of the émigrés, more than a thousand of whom had taken refuge in Brussels, was the saddest, most lamentable thing imaginable. Secure in the declarations of the ministers of the archduchess, who had promised to give them warning of any French approach, they lived there without the slightest misgiving. With that heedlessness and lack of foresight which so often brought disaster upon them, they thought themselves perfectly safe in Brussels, despite the Prussian retreat in Champagne. M. de Vauban, from whom I have these details, was returning home across the Place Royale at about midnight when he thought he heard the sound of the hooves of many horses in the courtyard of the Palace, which stood then where the Museum stands today. He waited, hidden in a recess, and after a moment, saw all the carriages of the Court setting out, waggons and drays piled high with luggage, all heading in silence towards the Namur Gate. Convinced that the archduchess was leaving Brussels secretly, he rushed to warn the nearest Frenchmen. Those who had been that very evening at Court, refused to believe in such a breach of faith, but it took only a few minutes to convince them of the truth. It is difficult to convey an idea of the tumult and panic which then overtook all those wretched people in their haste to get away. The whole night was spent packing the few belongings they had with them and, at daybreak, every available boat, carriage and waggon was hired at an extortionate price to carry them to Liège or Maestricht. The wisest, and those most plentifully provided with funds, decided to cross to England. I had numerous acquaintances among those who fled. Many of them still persisted in the attitude formerly fashionable in Paris and Versailles and presented a sorry spectacle of the most shocking heartlessness towards their companions in misfortune. I hastened to offer my services to the most heavily stricken, but paid very little attention to the richer people, not concealing from them that those who had the means to help themselves and thought not at all of others need not count on my assistance.

During the last days of November 1792, the Convention passed a decree against émigrés, ordering them to return within a given period, a very short one, under pain of confiscation of their property. My good father-in-law was in England and thinking of rejoining us at The Hague. When he heard of this decree he wrote to us that not for any personal consideration would he act against the interests of his children and that he was returning to Paris. In this most fatherly of letters, were expressions of sadness so profound that if it had been possible even then, after the massacres of September, to conceive the excesses to which the Revolution was to lead, it might have been thought inspired by presentiment.

I do not know why I have not yet mentioned the flight of M. de La Fayette, M. Alexandre de Lameth and M. de La Tour Maubourg.* All three secretly left the army division commanded by M. de La Fayette, intending, with a confidence so inconceivably foolish that it is inexplicable, to cross the frontier into foreign territory. When they reached the Austrian outposts, they were at once arrested. The authorities wanted to hold them hostage for the safety of the king and his family, imprisoned in the Temple since 10 August. M. Alexandre de Lameth was allowed to write to his sister-in-law, who was with me at The Hague, to ask her to send money. M. de La Fayette, in his turn, wrote to Mr Short, the American Minister at The Hague. I saw Mr Short the very same day and suggested he should use the good offices of a man whom I knew to be both able and discreet. This man was Dulong, and he had for many years been

---

* In 1791, the Marquis de La Fayette tried to persuade the Court to fight to regain its authority. In 1792, he came to Paris to protest at the treatment of the king and the suspension of his power. Finding his efforts fruitless, he and his companions crossed into the Austrian Netherlands but were imprisoned as hostages for the safety of the king and queen. (Tr.)

employed by the French Legation, to which he was still attached. He was very devoted to me and from him I was able to learn all the news sent to the new French Minister, almost to the contents of the despatches. M. de La Fayette was held in Liège and Dulong undertook to organise his escape. The essentials were speed, secrecy and money. Dulong thought that at least 20,000 francs would be needed. Mr Short refused to provide this sum. My own interest in M. de La Fayette was limited, but I knew him to be a friend of Mme d'Hénin and was most indignant at Mr Short's refusal to intervene on behalf of a man who was a friend of Washington. Mr Short was himself a very rich man and could have found this sum from his own money. He turned down all the plans suggested and was afterwards strongly reprimanded by his own Government. M. de La Fayette and his two companions were transferred to the prisons of Olmutz, where they remained until the Treaty of Campo-Formio.*

After the Terror, Mme de La Fayette went to Vienna with her two daughters and persuaded the Emperor of Austria to allow her to be imprisoned with her husband at Olmutz, sharing all the rigours of his confinement. It was something of a miracle that she herself had escaped death, for so many of her family perished under the guillotine. In her self-imposed captivity, she showed a resignation and courage which drew their strength from religion alone, for her husband had never treated her with anything but the most cruel indifference and she could certainly not have forgotten the numerous infidelities to which she had had to accustom herself.

My father, who was in command of the army division at the Famars camp, between Quesnoy and Charleroi,† did not follow M. de La Fayette's example. When he learned of all that had happened in Paris during August 1792: the attack on the Tuileries and the overthrow of the monarchy, he addressed an Order of the Day to his troops in which he renewed his own oath of loyalty to the king and recommended them to do likewise. The result of this gallant declaration was his removal from command on 23 August 1792 and an order to return to Paris. In vain did I beg him not to go and my fears were only too well-founded.‡

As I owned a house in Paris and certain State or City of Paris bonds, my husband feared I might be included in the list of émigrés which had just been published. He sent a very trustworthy servant to The Hague to fetch me back to Paris, charging him to tell me that,

---

* The Treaty of Peace between France and Austria signed in 1797. (Tr.)
† The camp was, in fact, between Quesnoy and Valenciennes.
‡ He was guillotined on 13 April 1794.

at the Belgian frontier, a few leagues from Antwerp, I should find
one of my father's former aides-de-camp who had become aide-de-
camp to Dumouriez. He would carry orders to ensure that I was
treated with respect and even given an escort if necessary. I bade
farewell to my poor sister-in-law, who died two months later, and set
out with my son, aged two and a half, my faithful Marguérite, a
manservant and Zamore. The winter was becoming very severe and
this made the journey most difficult. In those days, I was no cam-
paigner but as delicate, as fine a lady and as spoiled as it was possible
to be. Flattered and fêted during my stay in The Hague, I still
thought I had accepted the greatest sacrifice anyone could require
of me when I agreed to do without the services of my elegant maid
and my footman-hairdresser. I realised, it is true, that I might not be
able to have a carriage in Paris, that I might no longer go to balls,
that it might even be necessary to spend the winter in the country.
I had resolved to bear all these reverses with courage and determination, unlike the émigrés from Paris with whom I had just spent two
months and who, after spending, as they admitted, a most amusing
time in Brussels, counted on enjoying the same in London, their final
destination. I record these weaknesses and illusions so that my son*
may judge, now that he knows my beginnings, how far I have risen
above them.

I left The Hague on 1 December 1792, buried in the depths of an
excellent berline, well wrapped in pelisses and bearskin rugs, with
my small Humbert bundled up like a little eskimo and my good
Marguérite. So far as I can remember, we spent the first night at
Gorkum. Throughout the day we could hear the sound of gunfire.
My footman said it must be the French laying siege to the citadel of
Antwerp, but that it would take them a long time to capture it for the
garrison was very strong and the city well-provisioned. The next
day, at Breda, a town still in Dutch territory, there was the same
sound of cannon. Since there was nothing alarming in the news that
had been published, I set out without any fear and on the frontier of
the Austrian Netherlands, found M. Schnetz, a brave soldier and a
friend of my father's. I was very glad to see him.

On arriving there the previous day, he had been astonished at the
absence of news from Antwerp. He said laughingly that perhaps the
town had been captured, not for one moment thinking that might
really be the case. But when, towards midday, the gunfire ceased, he

* Frédéric-Claude-Aymar, Comte de La Tour du Pin de Gouvernet, later
Marquis de La Tour du Pin and Marquis de Gouvernet, the only child to survive
his parents.

said in rather military language that that outpost of the Austrian power had ... capitulated. It had. A French sentry posted at the outer gate of the city confirmed that we were masters of the great fortress and when we stopped at the 'Bon Laboureur' inn* on the vast Place de Meir, we had the greatest difficulty in obtaining a room. It was thanks to the intervention of a general whose name I have forgotten that an officer gave up to me the room in which he was already installed and from which he rather unwillingly had his baggage removed. As I went up the stairs, I met a crowd of officers both young and old, who made the most improper suggestions concerning the general's reasons for intervening.

My good Marguérite and I, once in our room and with the door safely locked, tried to get little Humbert to sleep. He was very frightened by the noise he could hear in the inn. M. Schnetz came to suggest that I should go down to supper and declared that I had nothing to fear as the general, a friend of my father's, had put a guard in the corridor. That he should think this precaution necessary frightened me still more. M. Schnetz, seeing that I was not tempted by the proposal of supper, went off. Marguérite got Humbert to sleep and I barricaded the door with the bed and everything else I could find in the room.

Just then my attention was drawn to the window, which opened on to the Place, for there was a great glow which I thought must come from some illuminations. I shall never forget the sight which met my eyes. In the midst of that vast Place had been lit a fire whose flames were leaping as high as the roof tops. Numbers of soldiers, drunk, reeling, unsteady, swayed around it, flinging in any furnishings they could find: bedsteads, chests of drawers, sideboards, screens, clothes, baskets full of papers and then a mass of chairs, tables and armchairs with gilded wooden frames The fire blazed higher by the minute. Dreadful looking women, their hair loose and their dress in disorder, mingled with this gang of madmen, giving them wine, perhaps vintage wine from the cellars of the rich citizens of Antwerp. Wild laughter, foul oaths and obscene songs added to the general horror of this diabolic fling. For me, it was the embodiment of all that I had ever read about the capture of a town by assault, of the pillaging and terrible disorders which followed. I stood at the window throughout the night, fascinated and terrified, unable to tear myself away, despite my horror.

Towards morning, M. Schnetz told me we would have to set out for Mons where the general had decided we were to sleep. As we left

* Known today as the 'Grand Laboureur'.

Antwerp, I was struck by the rare spectacle spread before us. Between the forward line of the fortifications and the first sentry post, that of Contich, we drove through the entire French army which was encamped there. These victorious soldiers, who were already making the fine armies of Austria and Prussia quake in their shoes, looked like a horde of bandits. Few had a uniform. After requisitioning everything in all the cloth shops in Paris and other big cities, the Convention had hurriedly had cloaks made from materials of every imaginable hue. This medley, a vast human rainbow, stood out curiously clear against the snow-covered ground. The camp looked like some gigantic, vivid flower-bed. It would have been a sight to enjoy had it not been for the red bonnets worn by most of the soldiers, which reminded us of all that we had to fear from them. Only the officers were in uniform, but with none of the brilliant embroideries which Napoleon has since scattered so liberally.

Forced to travel nearly all the time at a walking pace, the way seemed long. The roads, cut up by the artillery, were cluttered with waggons, ammunition carts and guns. Slowly, we advanced, to the accompaniment of the shouts and oaths of the drivers and the coarse pleasantries of the soldiers. Schnetz was clearly worried and regretted not having brought an escort. Eventually, at nightfall, we reached Malines where we spent a calmer night than at Antwerp, though there were still many troops about.

The following morning, we set out for Brussels, where we had not intended to stop, but M. de Moreton de Chabrillan, the local commander, decided otherwise. The horses had just been put to and M. Schnetz had had my passport franked, when there arrived an order from the general that I was not to be allowed to pass. The horses were unharnessed and when I tried to leave the carriage to seek shelter in the postmaster's house, the guards refused to let me pass. M. Schnetz went immediately to Headquarters for an explanation. After a while, my son and his nurse were permitted to go into the postmaster's house, and I waited alone.

Eventually, three hours later, without any explanation of his odd display of officious authority, M. de Chabrillan authorised my departure. He was of good family and I had met him hundreds of times, though I had never spoken to him. He was very short-sighted and strongly revolutionary in his sympathies.

That was not the last of my alarms. It was late when we reached Mons and we had the greatest difficulty in finding a lodging. All the inns were full. In the end, one of them offered us two small rooms for my maid and me, on a very low first floor, overlooking the street.

They told me the officers who had been occupying these rooms had just left. M. Schnetz and my two menservants would have to sleep on the far side of a very large courtyard, an arrangement which meant that my maid and I would be quite separated from them. It was far from satisfactory but there was no alternative. My son was tired. I put him into my bed and did not undress. I was, nonetheless, growing sleepy when the noise in the street, near my windows, awakened me. There was a loud knocking on the door of the house and terrible swearing. I soon heard the innkeeper shouting that a general's wife was sleeping in the room and that an aide-de-camp who was accompanying her was also in the inn. A drunken voice replied that he was coming to see if it was true. He had with him a number of other men in the same state and as I threw myself under the bed, I saw two hands grasp the balcony as someone tried to haul himself up. I was frozen with terror, but did not lose my head. Calling loudly for my maid, I prepared to throw at the intruder a great log that was burning in the hearth. At that moment, I heard him fall back into the street and he was either hurt in the fall or his comrades feared the consequences, for they carried him off and my fears subsided.

The next day, as we left, we met a squadron composed entirely of negroes, all very well mounted and perfectly equipped. The Duc d'Orléans' fine negro, Edward, was in command. As he was a great friend of Zamore, the latter asked my permission to spend the day with his fellow negroes. I feared they would enlist him and that I wouldn't see him again, but I was wrong. That good boy was given a wonderful time by his comrades but in the evening he was back with me, telling me in his simple way all that had been done to persuade him to stay. His loyalty to me had won the day and I was most grateful to him.

The rest of my journey passed without any incident worthy of note. M. Schnetz left me, I think, at Péronne and I took the road to Hénéncourt where I found my brother-in-law, the Marquis de Lameth.

In Holland, I had been spoiled, admired and flattered. Returning to
France, I had scarcely crossed the border when the Revolution was
all about me, dark and menacing, heavy with danger. I returned, it is
true, to the very same room from which I had set out so light-
heartedly only fifteen months before, but the light-heartedness had
gone. My heart was filled with a bitter sadness as I realised the
frivolity of the life I had led until then. Yet I felt I possessed qualities
which fitted me for more useful things and so was not discouraged
but felt rather that in such disastrous times ı should refresh and
strengthen the springs of my being.

I found pleasure in inventing all the situations in which I might be
called on to show very great courage. In my mind, I conjured up
every conceivable loyalty, every kind of hazardous undertaking.
I dismissed none of the possibilities, feeling that if they came to pass,
they could but better my life by permitting me to devote it to the
carrying out of my duty, however painful or dangerous that might
be. I felt that by this means I was finding my way back to the path
Providence had ordained for me. In those troubled times, and without my being aware of it, God had enlightened me. But later, when
He gave me the grace to draw closer to Him and to know Him,
I remembered the change wrought in me by those hours of serious
thought. From that day forward, my life was different, my moral
outlook transformed.

It was very late when I reached Hénéncourt. My brother-in-law
was there, feeling very gloomy about his own chances and very
thankful that his wife and children were out of France. It had been
arranged that I would stay twenty-four hours at Hénéncourt in
order to get the necessary papers to take me safely to Paris. These
included a certificate stating that I had been living at Hénéncourt
since the recall of M. de La Tour du Pin. My hope that he would be
there to meet me was disappointed, for travel within France had
already become as difficult as it was dangerous. A traveller not only
needed a passport, but in order to obtain it had to be accompanied by
two guarantors who, on their personal responsibility, undertook that
he would not travel in any direction other than that indicated.
Furthermore, no one could enter the outer suburbs of Paris without
a special pass and every post of the Garde Nationale had the right to

demand a sight of it. In short, to the really important difficulties had been added a thousand petty vexations and life in France had become intolerable.

I had to set out from Hénéncourt alone and arrived the following day in Passy, though not without some difficulty. At the Saint-Denis stage, the post-master at first flatly refused to take me to Passy,* on the pretext that my passport was for Paris and he was bound to take me there by the shortest route. After an hour of argument and explanation throughout which, being little accustomed to such situations, I was terrified in case I compromised myself, my servant had the idea of showing his own pass for Passy and then, on payment of two or three supplementary stages, we were allowed to leave.

At Passy, I was at last reunited with my husband, who was living in a house belonging to Mme de Poix. As it was too big for our household, we were able to leave all the windows on the street front shut and thus give the impression that the house was unoccupied. We used the concierge's small entrance. There were two or three other entrances as well, which made it a good hiding-place. Another advantage was that, being the last house on the Auteuil side of the village, we were easily able to keep in touch with my father-in-law who, since his return from England, had been living in Auteuil in a house belonging to a relative, the Marquis de Gouvernet.† The latter's house, 'La Tuilerie', stood in an isolated position between Auteuil and Passy. Fortunately, we could reach it by paths on which there was no danger of meeting anyone. An old cabriolet with a rather broken-down horse, whose real owner I never discovered, used to take us to Paris and we were therefore able to avoid sharing the secret of our hiding-place with all the cab-drivers in the city.

After luncheon, my husband and I went every day to 'La Tuilerie' for my husband had to look after his father's affairs and his own. We usually dined in Paris, either with my father or with Mme de Montesson, whose house was always open to us.

My father was living in a furnished house in the Chaussée d'Antin, doing all he could to help the king, calling on his judges, inviting them to meet in his own house and trying to organise the party which was later to be known as that of the Girondins, explaining to them that it was to their interest to safeguard the life of the king, to get him away from Paris and hold him as a hostage in some stronghold in the interior of the country where he could communicate neither with

* Now a fashionable residential quarter of Paris itself but then a village outside the capital. (Tr.)
† Philippe-Antoine-Gabriel-Victor-Charles de La Tour du Pin la Charce.

foreign powers nor with the royalists who were just beginning to organise themselves in La Vendée. But the Terrorist party, whom my father had no hope of convincing, and above all, the Commune of Paris which was entirely Orleanist, were too powerful for any human effort to turn them from their terrible purpose.

My poor father tried an urgent appeal to Dumouriez who came to Paris in the middle of January and was deceived by his false promises. Dumouriez had been completely won over by Egalité and his son, proudly claiming to be the latter's mentor in all things military. His journey to Paris had had no other purpose than to serve them.

I shall not describe all our terrible anxieties and disappointments during January 1793. My only wish here is to vindicate my father's honour and refute the hateful aspersions which people do not hesitate to cast upon it. His interviews with the judges of Louis XVI had but one purpose: to save, if not the freedom, at least the life of the king. On the very morning sentence was pronounced, my father remained convinced that the vote would be for imprisonment until the restoration of peace. Indeed, that is the resolution that would have been passed had it not been for cowardly changes of mind when the moment of voting arrived. We were at my father's house throughout that unforgettable session, suffering a degree of anxiety it is impossible to convey. When we left, we knew the king had been condemned but still hoped for the revolt my father so confidently expected. Everyone in Paris who felt as we did had planned, independently, to mingle with the Garde Nationale in order to draw it into action helpful to the unfortunate king. But this action, if it was taken, certainly failed.

On the morning of 21 January, the gates of Paris were closed and orders given that no reply was to be made to those outside who asked the reason why. We guessed the reason only too well, my husband and I, and leaning from a window of our house overlooking Paris, listened for the rattle of musketry which would give us some hope that so great a crime would not be committed unchallenged. We waited in a shocked silence, hardly daring to say a word to one another. We could not believe that such a price would be exacted and my husband was greatly distressed at having left Paris, refusing to believe such a tragedy possible. Alas! The deepest silence lay like a pall over the regicide city. At half-past ten, the gates were opened and the life of the city resumed its course, unchanged. A great nation had that day soiled its history with a crime of which future centuries would hold it guilty, yet not the smallest detail of the daily round had changed.

We walked towards Paris, trying to keep our faces calm and our thoughts unspoken. Avoiding the Place Louis XV,* we went first to see my father, then to Mme de Montesson and to Mme de Poix. People scarcely spoke, so terrified were they. It was as if each carried the burden of his share in the crime which had just been committed.

Returning early to Passy, we found Mathieu de Montmorency and the Abbé de Damas waiting at our house. Both had been at the place of execution with their battalion of the Garde Nationale. They had made certain comments which would now endanger their safety and had therefore left Paris to avoid arrest. They had come to ask us to hide them until they could either leave or return to their homes. They feared a house search, that first infliction which usually preceded by several months a person's actual arrest. During such searches, all papers of every kind were seized and carried off to the offices of the 'section'† where even the most private correspondence served to while away the time for the young Gardes Nationales on duty.

Towards the middle of March, my father-in-law was arrested at 'La Tuilerie' and brought, with the Maréchal de Mouchy and the Marquis de Gouvernet, before the Commune of Paris. It seems that the similarity of name had caused the marquis to be mistaken for my husband. They did indeed question him about the affair at Nancy, blaming him for the death of good patriots. After much questioning, they were all released but my father-in-law, more anxious for the safety of his son than for his own, decided that we ought to go to Le Bouilh from where my husband could make his way to La Vendée or leave with us for Spain. The second alternative seemed the wiser, as our good friend, M. de Brouquens, had been living in Bordeaux for a year. He had been allowed to continue as Director of Food Supplies to the army fighting in Spain.

We decided to go. It grieved me profoundly to leave my father, though I was still very far indeed from imagining that I was embracing him for the last time. The difference in our ages was so slight, barely nineteen years, that I looked on him more as a brother than a father. He had an aquiline nose, a very small mouth, large black eyes and light chestnut hair. Madame de Boufflers declared that he resembled a parrot eating a cherry. Owing to his height, his handsome face and fine bearing, he had remained very youthful in appearance. No one

* Today, the Place de la Concorde. (Tr.)
† Local popular assemblies whose resolutions could be sent as high as the National Assembly itself. (Tr.)

was ever nobler in manner or more aristocratic in bearing. His originality of mind and evenness of temper made him a most agreeable companion. He was my best friend and, to my husband, a comrade whom he could never remember to address otherwise than with the familiar 'thou'. Of my father's aristocratic appearance, M. de La Tour du Pin used to say laughingly that Edward Dillon's* nickname, 'Beau Dillon', was a double usurpation: of name and of personal good looks.

My father-in-law was impatient to see us well away from Paris and made us promise to leave as soon as possible. We set out on 1 April 1793. Not one of the petty vexations of the day was spared us, though we had passports covered in visas, renewed at almost every stage. But we travelled post and that superior manner of travel did us great disservice among all good patriots. It had been decided that we would travel by short stages for I was two months' pregnant and, having been ill the previous year at The Hague from a miscarriage, was afraid of injuring myself again.

We eventually arrived at Le Bouilh towards the middle of April and it was a great joy to me to be in a place so beloved of my poor father-in-law. His attachment to it had even made inroads into his fortune for he had made many improvements and added a number of buildings. At the time, his fortune was such as to permit embellishments to the place where he intended to spend in tranquillity the last days of his good and honourable life. But on the very day he was appointed minister, he had given instructions so final that we found the masons' scaffoldings and the diggers' wheelbarrows just where they had been left when the order arrived.

The house did not please me the less for that. The four months we spent there have remained in my memory, and particularly in my affection, as the most precious of my life. There was a fine library to occupy our evenings and my husband, who read for hours at a time without wearying, devoted them to giving me a course in history and literature which was as pleasant as it was instructive. I also made clothes for my baby and realised then the value of having learned in my youth all the feminine accomplishments. There was no flaw in our domestic happiness, it was more complete than it had ever been. My husband's perfect good humour, his adorable nature, his pleasant wit, combined with the mutual trust which bound us and our complete devotion to one another, ensured our happiness despite the dangers which surrounded us. None of the disasters which threatened had power to alarm us so long as we could bear them together.

* The second son of the Bordeaux Dillons – see p. 37.

Thanks to the Girondins, who had not voted for the death of the king, the town of Bordeaux was in a state of partial revolt against the Convention. Many royalists had joined the revolt in the hope that it would persuade the Departments of the south, particularly that of the Gironde, to join the movement recently organised in the Departments of the west. But Bordeaux was very far from having the energetic courage of the Vendée.* However, an armed troop of eight hundred to a thousand young men from the town's leading families had been formed. They drilled on the slopes of the Château-Trompette and made a great deal of noise at the theatre in the evenings. But not one of them shouted 'Long Live the King!' The organisers of this party had only one aim: to become independent of Paris and the Convention, to establish for the south of France a federal government similar to that of the United States. M. de La Tour du Pin went to Bordeaux. He saw the leaders of the proposed federation but was so disgusted by his talks with them that he refused to join a movement which was to include even such regicides as Fonfrède and Ducos.

At the end of the summer, while we waited for the birth of my baby, we began to feel anxious about the municipality of Saint-André-en-Cubzac. A rascally lawyer named Surget, who had been called in before the Revolution to put my father-in-law's papers in order when the old château was being pulled down and everything transferred to the new one, spread the tale that the barony of Cubzagues had been subject to a lien since the time of Edward III and that the instrument was among our papers. The story was correct, but it was not a royal domain. Surget wrote a memorandum on the subject and we had reason to believe he sent it to Paris for, two months later, when the Representatives of the People arrived in Bordeaux, they immediately ordered the sequestration of Le Bouilh.

My husband was worried at the possibility of a house search or the stationing of a garrison in the château at the time of my baby's birth. He was also anxious for me to have the care of a good accoucheur and nurse from Bordeaux. My father-in-law had just been arrested. Seals had been put on the Château of Tesson, near Saintes, and the Department of Charente-Inferieure had taken possession of the fine

---

* An area south of the River Loire where most nobles lived on their land and the peasantry were devoted to the Church and not inimical to the nobles. There was little resistance to the Revolution until priests were required to swear allegiance to the State and the men of the region were required to join the Army. Rebellion broke out in February 1793, by October it had become serious. Despite brutal repression, the war did not end until February 1795. (Tr.)

house we owned in Saintes itself and intended using it for its offices.

In the circumstances, we thought it prudent to accept the suggestion of our excellent friend, M. de Brouquens, that we should stay in a small house he owned about a quarter of a league from Bordeaux. This house, named Canoles, offered every advantage from the point of view of safety. It was isolated, in the middle of a vineyard, surrounded on three sides by small local roads leading in different directions and on the fourth by a fair stretch of sandy heath. There was no village in the neighbourhood and all the country thereabouts, known as Haut-Brion, consisted of a number of fairly large estates, planted with vines and nearly all adjoining.

We moved to Canoles on, I think, 1 September 1793 and M. de Brouquens, who was himself obliged to remain in Bordeaux to superintend the administration of his food supplies, came to dine with us daily. One day, he arranged a meeting at Canoles of all the officials of the municipality and the Department. They talked of nothing but the valiant deeds they were going to accomplish against the revolutionary army, whose advance was marked by a trail of severed heads. Lost in confused theories, these officials wanted to be neither royalist, like the people of La Vendée, nor revolutionary, like the Convention. Oblivious to what was happening on their very doorstep, these unfortunates thought that Tallien and Ysabeau would give them time to sort out their ideas. But Tallien and Ysabeau arrived only to sever their heads, and that but three days later.

This army of butchers, dragging a guillotine along with them, had already reached La Réole and claimed many victims there. I will tell you about one of them, so that you will have an idea of what it was like. The incident was so horrible that it ought to be recorded. M. de Lavessière was an inoffensive man who had retired to the country after the destruction of the *Parlement* of Bordeaux, of which he had been a member. His wife was the most beautiful woman in the city and they had two young sons. All four were arrested. The husband was condemned to death and, during his execution, his wife was put in a pillory, facing the guillotine, her two sons bound on either side of her. The executioner, more humane than the judges, stood so that she could not see the fall of the fatal knife. It was to such people as those judges that we were about to become subject.

If I had not been then in the ninth month of my pregnancy, we might perhaps have left for Spain, but even if such a journey had been possible, it would still have been necessary to make our way through the entire French army. Besides, who could have expected a city of eighty thousand people, its gates defended by a large battery and reinforced by an élite troop recruited from the leading families of the town, to submit without resistance to seven hundred criminals with only two guns between them?

Having taken refuge in Canoles, I awaited the baby's birth with some impatience, for my husband refused to leave me until it was over and the danger to him increased with every day that passed. The revolutionary army entered Bordeaux on the morning of 13 September. Less than an hour later, all the federalist leaders were arrested and imprisoned. The revolutionary tribunal was set up immediately and remained in session for six months. Not a day passed without the execution of some innocent person.

The guillotine was set up permanently in the Place Dauphine. The small group of frenzied agitators who escorted it had met with no opposition when they brought it into Bordeaux, though a few cannon shots fired into their close ranks as they passed along the Rue de Faubourg-Saint-Julien would certainly have put them to flight. But the people of Bordeaux who, only the previous day, had been declaring with true Gascon flourish their intention to resist, did not even show themselves in the deserted streets. The boldest shut their shops, the young men hid or fled and, by evening, terror reigned in the city. So great was this terror that when an order was published directing every holder of arms, under pain of death, to take them before midday the next day to the lawns of Chateau-Trompette, barrows could be seen passing along the streets and people stealthily throwing into them every weapon they possessed. It was noticed that some of these had probably not been used for at least two generations. All these arms were piled up at the place indicated. It does not seem to have occurred to anyone that it would have been far braver to use them in self-defence.

While all this was going on, I gave birth during the night to a daughter whom I named Séraphine, after her father who stayed just long enough to give her his blessing. At the very moment of her birth, we learned of the arrest of many people in neighbouring country houses. My doctor's maidservant had come out from the town to tell him they were looking for him to order to arrest him and that seals had been put on his house. That night, we posted a trustworthy woman on the road leading to Canoles, telling her to give us warning of any sound of people approaching so that, if danger threatened, my husband and the doctor would be able to escape through the vineyards. I suffered more from fear than from the actual pain of my daughter's birth. An hour later, her father left us, neither of us knowing what fate held in store or when we would see one another again.

It was a terrible moment and in the state in which I was, should have proved fatal to me. However, my health fortunately did not suffer at all. I had only one wish: to get well again as quickly as possible in order to be ready to deal with whatever might arise. The poor surgeon, not daring to return to his own house, hid in the newborn baby's room. A small bed was put there for him, in the depths of a kind of alcove, unused and hidden by the maid's bed and Humbert's cradle.

Three days later, our friend and host, M. de Brouquens, greatly distressed by the death of M. Saige, Mayor of Bordeaux, who had been guillotined the previous day, the first victim in the massacre of the municipal authorities, returned to Bordeaux where he usually lived. Scarcely had he entered his house than they came to arrest him and take him to prison. He pointed out that since he was in sole charge of all food supplies to the army being sent to fight in Spain, his arrest would gravely hamper its administration and the Commander-in-Chief would therefore strongly disapprove of it. These good reasons, or rather, the fear that M. de Brouquens' colleagues in Paris might complain to the Convention, made the Representatives decide to put him under house arrest only. He could not go out but did retain his freedom inside the house, which was large and well provided with means of escape should the danger become too imminent. The twenty-five men of the Citizen Guard stationed at his door were nearly all of the district and beholden to him in one way or another. His kindness and willingness to be of assistance were, in fact, unbounded and the people of Bordeaux adored him. He had to feed these twenty-five men during the entire period of his arrest, which lasted most of the winter.

At about midnight on the night following his arrest, just as he was going to bed, an officer of the municipality, followed by the Chef de la Section and a number of Gardes, presented themselves at M. de Brouquens' house and ordered him to accompany them to Canoles, where they wanted to examine his papers. In vain did he point out that he spent only a few minutes there each morning in order to inspect his garden and see that his vineyard was being properly tended and that, therefore, he did not really live there. He had to go with them. His anxiety and concern were acute. He knew that my name, my rank in the world, the position of my father-in-law who had so recently been confronted with the queen during her trial, would inevitably mean imprisonment for me. He did not see how I could escape death and was desperate when he thought of my husband who had entrusted me to his care and whom he loved dearly, for he could think of no way to save me. However, there could be no question of avoiding the visit. Fortunately, one of his guards was particularly attached to him and, guessing his dilemma, took matters into his own hands and came to give the alarm.

I was sleeping peacefully, for at twenty-three one sleeps even at the steps of the scaffold. Suddenly I found myself being shaken by an old servant who had been left in charge, a trustworthy woman who, in tears and deathly pale, was crying: 'And now those cut-throats are coming to look through everything and put on the seals. We're all lost!' As she spoke, she slipped a fairly large packet under my pillow and disappeared by the way she had come. I felt the packet and realised it held a little bag containing five to six hundred louis. M. de Brouquens had told me of it and that he was saving it against some sudden need, either his own, or M. de La Tour du Pin's or mine. It was scarcely reassuring to find it there and when I took it from its hiding place, I had to take the greatest care to keep it hidden from the girl who looked after my child. I had never trusted her and, not long before, the doctor, M. Dupouy, had also discovered that she was there to spy on me. As the woman was under a great obligation to him personally, he also hoped she would not betray me.

My good Marguérite had tertian fever and was not sleeping in the children's room but in a quite different part of the house. I therefore had my small three-day-old daughter put into my bed. The maid pushed her own bed and Humbert's against the alcove where poor Dupouy was making himself as small as possible, feeling more dead than alive and convinced his last hour had come. Having made these preparations, I went back to bed for although it was only three days after my baby's birth, I had been up, and we all waited resolutely for the arrival of the enemy. M. de Brouquens declared afterwards that I had put all my faith in the effect of a certain rose-coloured batiste which I was wearing on my head. Despite this quip, I think I probably looked rather ill.

My room was on the ground floor and therefore an outpost. It opened into the drawing room, where my faithful Zamore was hurriedly setting out some pâté and, above all, wine and liqueurs to put our persecutors in a good humour. Half-an-hour later, though it seemed a century, they at last arrived. First, they examined the house from outside. Then they came into the salon. I heard the clatter of their sabots – to wear shoes or boots would have been proof of lack of patriotism – and then their terrible talk of what they were going to do. My blood froze in my veins. Every second I thought I heard a hand opening my door. I clasped my poor baby to me and my eyes were fixed in horror on that door which might suddenly open to admit those fierce men. Eventually, I clearly heard the question: 'What is there in that bedroom?' followed by M. de Brouquens' reply: 'Hush!' I could not hear the rest of what was said. M. de Brouquens told me later he had suddenly thought to tell them that the young daughter of some friends had been entrusted to him so that her baby could be born in secret in his isolated house. That the baby had been born only three days before and that the girl was very delicate and very ill.

How could such blood-thirsty hearts feel pity? But they did and the very men who, during the morning, had watched the severing of twenty innocent heads without a thought of mercy, took off their sabots so that they would not make a noise when they thought they were above my room during their search of the first floor. After two hours, which for me were hours of anguish, and having drunk and eaten everything in the house, they went away, taking their prisoner with them and sending the new mother their crude congratulations.

I stayed on at Canoles with my good doctor, who was beginning to feel slightly reassured, although the danger had not entirely passed – far from it. But I have always noticed that those who take fright easily are equally easily reassured. And so it was that, once the house search, with all its dangers, was over, he recovered his calm. He was a man of wit and a good and religious person. He was very skilled in his profession and following my rule of never ignoring an opportunity to learn, I profited from his presence to learn much about medicine and surgery. As we had no books on these subjects, he himself gave me a short viva voce course in midwifery and surgery. In return, I gave him lessons in dressmaking, embroidery and knitting. He was very deft and his progress in these accomplishments was rapid. We continued thus for more than six months, for he lay hidden with us all that time and has told me since that when he left Canoles shortly afterwards to live among the peasants of the Landes, where there were no books or other interests to occupy him, he would have died of boredom if, thanks to my teaching, he had not been able to occupy his days in making stockings and shirts for the family which sheltered him.

In the evenings, the good doctor read the gazettes to me. I had asked him to do so, though just then they made terrible reading. They became even more painful to me one day when we found an account of my revered father-in-law being confronted with the queen. The gazette described Fouquier-Tinville's anger when M. de La Tour du Pin continued to refer to her as 'The Queen' or 'Her Majesty' instead of 'The Woman Capet', as the Public Prosecutor wished. My fears reached their peak when I heard that my father-in-law, being asked the whereabouts of his son, had replied straightforwardly that he was on his estates near Bordeaux. The result of this only too frank reply was an order the very same day to Saint-André-en-Cubzac to arrest my husband and send him to Paris.

He was at Le Bouilh and had only an hour in which to make his escape. Fortunately, he had taken his precautions and, on the pretext of having to visit his farms, had kept a fairly good horse ready in the stables. Disguising himself as best he could, he left for his estate at Tesson, near Saintes, intending to hide in the château. True, it had been requisitioned but an excellent concierge and his wife were still there. He had plenty of funds with him: ten to twelve thousand francs in bills. He travelled all night. The weather was terrible, rain fell in sheets, the thunder was continuous and the lightning dazzled and frightened his excitable horse.

As he left Saint-Génis, a posting stage on the road from Blaye to Saintes, a man standing in front of a small house shouted to him 'Terrible weather, citizen! Would you like to stop here a while to let the worst of the storm pass?' M. de La Tour du Pin accepted his invitation, dismounted and tied his horse under a small shed placed, luckily for him, as you will shortly see, right beside the door.

'You yoke your oxen very early,' he remarked to the old peasant. 'Yes, I do,' replied his chance host. 'It isn't three o'clock, but I want to get there early in the morning.' 'Ah, you're going to the fair at Pons?' asked my husband with great presence of mind, 'So am I. I am going to buy grain for Bordeaux.' As he said this, they entered the house. An old man in the chimney corner seemed to be waiting for the peasant. A quarter of an hour passed in talk about the high cost of grain and cattle. Then the man near the fire left the house and when he returned some ten minutes later, he was wearing a sash. He was the mayor. 'Naturally you have a passport, citizen?' he asked my husband. 'Oh yes' was the bold answer, 'one doesn't travel nowadays without that.' So saying, he showed him a false passport in the name of de Gouvernet which he had been using all the summer during his journeys between Saint-André and Bordeaux. 'But', said the mayor, looking at it, 'your passport has no visa for the Charente-Inférieure. You must remain here until morning. I shall consult the Municipal Council.' And he returned to his place by the fire.

My husband felt he was lost unless he acted boldly. During this exchange, the master of the house, who seemed rather vexed by it all, had moved nearer to the open door and said aloud, as if talking to himself: 'Ah, the weather has completely cleared.' My husband rose very calmly. In those days, my dear son, your father was not as you remember him. He was thirty-four, very agile and at vaulting into the saddle could have competed with the best. Imperceptibly, talking all the time of the lull in the storm, he drew nearer to the open door, stretched a hand out into the darkness and unhooked his horse's bridle. With one leap he was in the saddle and, spurring hard, was already well away before the poor mayor had had time to rise from his seat near the hearth and reach the door. The passport, it is true, remained with him as evidence, but he never mentioned it, which was perhaps the wisest course at a time when every action roused suspicions.

M. de La Tour du Pin did not dare to ride through Pons where there was a fair during the day. He stopped in Mirambeau at the house of a former groom of his father's, a man whom he trusted completely and who belonged to the district. This man kept a small inn and drove a stage-waggon to Saintes once a week. His name was Tétard and he offered to hide my husband but he had young children and feared they might unwittingly betray him. He therefore suggested it would be safer to seek refuge with his brother-in-law, a good, well-to-do locksmith named Potier, who was married but childless. This man was quite willing to shelter my husband, though for a handsome consideration, and, the deal being concluded, he put him in a safe place in his house, in a small, window-less room leading off the bedroom, which was also the kitchen.

I have since visited this dreadful hole. Only a thin plank separated it from the shop where the boys worked and where the forge and bellows were installed. When the locksmith and his wife left their room, always taking the key with them, my husband had to lie quite still on his bed in order not to make the slightest sound. He was also strongly urged not to have any light, in case it was seen from the workshop below. But once the shop was shut, he would come out and have supper with the man and his wife. The groom often brought him news and sometimes gazettes or books he had fetched from Tesson.

That is how my poor husband passed the first three months of our separation. The postmaster at Saintes, on whose loyalty he could rely, advised him not to make his way into the Vendée for not only was it extremely difficult to pass through the lines of republican troops patrolling the countryside to the south, but royalist feelings had reached such a pitch of exaggerated fervour that it was no longer certain they would admit to their ranks someone like M. de La Tour du Pin who had remained in the service of the king after he had accepted the Constitution. Nor could my husband travel to the Vendée in his own name. To join the royalists openly would have been to sign death warrants for his father and for me.

XIV

As I said earlier, the house search at Canoles did not have any adverse effect on my recovery. On the contrary, it stiffened my resolve to regain my full strength as quickly as possible. After eight days, I was out walking in the garden with my Aesculapius. As we were passing a large heap of vine shoots piled against a boundary hedge between Canoles and the neighbouring property, we noticed that some of the branches closest to the ground had been cleared away and thrown against the hedge. In the hole thus formed, the earth was freshly trodden. There were also a few crusts of bread which led us to suppose that someone was hiding in the hole by day and probably in need of food. We decided to bring some and in the evening set out a well-filled plate, a loaf of bread and a bottle of wine. The following evening, M. Dupouy went back after dark and found the bottle empty and the food gone. For several days we carefully continued to do this, much intrigued. But a week later, when we went one evening as usual to collect the plate and bottle, we found the provisions untouched. We were very upset, knowing all that might have befallen our unknown boarder.

As I mentioned earlier, Surget, the lawyer, had presented a memorandum to the municipality of Saint-André-en-Cubzac claiming to prove that the Bouilh estate was a royal domain. To show its zeal, the municipality passed the information on to the Representatives of the People, who ordered its immediate seizure. They came to Le Bouilh without warning and affixed seals so generously that not a single door escaped. But the excellent woman I had left in the château had already hidden the most precious of the linen and portable objects and sent them to me in Bordeaux every week, a little at a time.

I was becoming anxious in case my prolonged stay in M. de Brouquens' house should attract too much attention. Above all, I feared that sooner or later my presence there would compromise him and I knew that he would never tell me if this should become the case. I discussed this difficulty on a number of occasions with a relative of M. de Brouquens, M. de Chambeau, who was himself under suspicion and obliged to remain in hiding. He had found a very well concealed refuge in the house of a man who kept a small, obscure apartment house in the Place Puy-Paulin. His name was Bonie. He was young and very active, his wife was dead, he had put his only child into the care of his mother-in-law and he lived quite alone in this house with one old servant. He looked after the affairs of M. de Sansac, an émigré who had been declared dead and whose estate had ostensibly been inherited by an unmarried sister. Bonie gave himself out to be a fervent demagogue and wore the rough frieze jacket known as the 'carmagnole',* sabots and a sabre. He frequented the local 'section' and the Jacobin Club and addressed everyone with the familiar 'thou'.

M. de Chambeau told Bonie of my difficulties: that I did not know where to go, that my husband was in hiding, my father and my father-in-law imprisoned, my house seized and my only friend, M. de Brouquens, under house arrest. At twenty-four years of age, with two young children, what was to become of me?

Bonie came to see me at Canoles. He was touched by my unhappy circumstances and suggested I should take refuge with him. His house was empty and M. de Brouquens advised me not to refuse the offer. So I accepted. Bonie gave me a very gloomy, dilapidated apartment overlooking a small garden and I moved in there with my two children, their nurse and my dear Marguérite, who was still suffering from a fever which nothing seemed to cure. My blackamoor, Zamore, passed for a liberated Negro waiting to join the army. My cook went to work for the People's Representatives but was able to lodge in Bonie's house and prepare dinner and supper for me. Two couriers who carried despatches to Bayonne and might prove very useful in case of need, also lived in the house. In short, the situation was, if not the best, certainly the least bad that could be hoped for.

The apartment was so situated that I could practise my music without any fear of being heard and since I was nearly always alone, this was a great comfort. My room was fairly large and reached through a kind of wood store where I had laid up large quantities of logs brought secretly from Le Bouilh, unknown to the official caretakers. They were stolen for me and brought by our own peasants. It was arranged through a woman from those parts, entirely devoted to our interests, who came to Bordeaux twice a

* Named after a song and dance of the Revolutionaries. (Tr.)

week to sell vegetables. She led a donkey with panier baskets, the bottom half filled with clothes and linen and the top with cabbages and potatoes. She very cleverly succeeded in making the men at the toll gate believe that these things had been stolen from the enemies of the people. Sometimes she would give them a few items and bring the rest to me.

My husband managed to send me a letter every week by a young boy who came to Bordeaux. These letters, which bore no address, were hidden in a loaf which the child brought to the Hôtel Puy-Paulin, ostensibly for the wet-nurse. As he always came on the same day of the week the cook used to go at high tide to meet him. This poor fifteen-year-old was quite unaware of the subterfuge. He had merely been told that there was a wet-nurse in the house who had been forbidden by the doctor to eat 'section' bread.

On the very day they arrived in town, the People's Representatives had published what they called a 'maximum' and had it posted up. It was an order imposing a small tax on all produce of whatever kind and the penalty for infringing this order was death. As a result, the supply of goods ceased immediately. Merchants with stocks of grain hid it rather than sell it at a lower price than they had paid for it and the famine which was the inevitable result of the breakdown in supplies was blamed on their lack of civic spirit. To meet the difficulty, each 'section' appointed one or more bakers to ensure the bread supply for their area and they were strictly instructed to distribute it only to those in possession of a card issued by the 'section'. Many bakers who refused were executed; others closed their shops. A similar system was instituted for the butchers. A tax was imposed on the quantity of meat to which people were entitled, regardless of its quality. Fishmongers and sellers of eggs, fruit and vegetables no longer went to market. Grocers hid their goods and it was only through influence that one could find a pound of coffee or sugar.

To avoid all fraud in the distribution of cards, an order was issued that a notice should be posted up at the entrance to every house giving the names of all the people living there. A copy had to be filed at the 'section'. The notices were on paper with a tricolour edging and at the top was written: 'Liberty, Equality, Fraternity or Death'. Everyone tried to fill in the required details as illegibly as possible. Ours was written in an excessively fine hand and posted up very high so that it was difficult to read. Many were written in an ink so pale that the first rain made them illegible. The bread cards were personal but one person was allowed to take to the shop the cards of an entire household. Men received a pound of bread, children under ten only half a pound. Wet-nurses were entitled to two pounds and I was able to take advantage of this privilege to increase my poor Zamore's ration. It will be difficult to believe that we reached such a degree of absurdity and cruelty, above all that a whole great city should have submitted docilely to such a régime.

The 'section' bread, made from all types of flour, was black and tacky and people today would hesitate to give it to their dogs. It was delivered straight from the oven and people stood in queues, as they were called, to buy it. It is a very odd fact that people found a kind of pleasure in those gatherings. The terror in which we lived prevented us from exchanging more than a word or two when we met in the street and the queue represented, as it were, a lawful assembly where the timid could talk to their neighbours or learn the latest news without exposing themselves to the imprudence of asking a question.

Another characteristic of the French is the ease with which they submit to authority. For example: two or three hundred persons, each waiting for his pound of meat, would be gathered before the butcher's shop. Then their ranks would open without a murmur or a single protest to make way for men who carried off fine pieces of appetising meat for the tables of the People's Representatives, this despite the fact that most of the waiting crowd would only be able to get scraps. My cook sometimes had to fetch the provisions for these monsters and he told me one evening that he could not understand why the people had not murdered him. The same thing happened at the baker's and if envious eyes dwelt for a moment on a basket of small white rolls intended for our masters, the complaints were not audible.

I cannot remember the political reasons behind the arrest of all the English and American merchants living in Bordeaux. They were sent to prison, as were all other nationals of those two countries – workmen, servants and others on whom the authorities managed to lay hands. This measure gave me good reason to fear being mistaken for an Englishwoman, as had so often happened in the past. Bonie became seriously alarmed. He advised me not to wear a hat when I went out in the daytime, but to dress like the women of Bordeaux. I rather liked the idea of disguising myself. I ordered waistcoats, which suited me admirably for I was then very slight, and which, with one red kerchief on my head and another knotted about my neck, changed me so completely that I sometimes met people I knew without being recognised. This gave me greater courage when I went out. M. de Brouquens, still confined to his house, was greatly amused at the bold comments of his twenty-five guards on the daily visits he received from *la belle grisette*.*

Despite all this, my situation in Bordeaux became daily more dangerous. Looking back, I cannot see how I escaped death. I was advised to try to have the sequestration on Le Bouilh removed, but it seemed to me that it would be fatal to draw any attention to my existence. I was in a state of most anxious uncertainty when Providence sent me a special protector.

Mme de Fontenay†, then known as Citizeness Thérèsia Cabarrus, arrived in Bordeaux. I had met her once in Paris, four years before. Mme Charles de Lameth, who had been at convent school with her, pointed her out to me one evening as we were leaving the theatre. She had seemed to me then about fourteen or fifteen and I remembered her as but a child. It was said that she had divorced her husband in order to preserve her fortune but it was more probably in order to be able to use – and abuse – her freedom. She had met Tallien at a spa in the Pyrenees and he had rendered her some service or other which she repaid with a boundless devotion she made no effort to conceal. She had come to Bordeaux to join him and was staying in the Hôtel d'Angleterre.

Two days after her arrival, I wrote her the following note: 'A woman who met Mme de Fontenay in Paris and knows that she is as good as she is beautiful, asks her to accord a moment's interview'. She replied by word of mouth that the lady might come whenever she wished. Half an hour later, I was at her door. When I entered, she came towards me, staring and crying: 'Heavens, Madame de Gouvernet!' Then, having embraced me effusively, she put herself at my service. It was her own expression. I told her my position. She thought it even more dangerous than I did myself and told me that I would have to flee and that she could see no other way of saving me. I replied that I could not leave without my husband and feared that if I abandoned my children's fortune, they would never see it again. She said to me: 'See Tallien, he will tell you what it would be best to do. You will be safe as soon as he knows that you are my first interest here.' I decided to ask him to remove the sequestration on Le Bouilh in the name of my children, and to give me permission to withdraw there with them. Then I left her, encouraged by the interest she had shown and wondering why she should have done so.

* 'The pretty jade'.
† Daughter of a Spanish banker.

Mme de Fontenay was not yet twenty. No more beautiful creature had ever come from the hands of the Creator and, in addition, she was highly accomplished. Every feature was perfect in its regularity. Her hair, which was ebony-black, was like the finest silk and nothing could dim the radiance of her wonderfully fair skin. An enchanting smile showed a glimpse of perfect teeth. Her height recalled that of Diana the Huntress. Her slightest movement had a matchless grace. As for her voice, its melody and very slightly foreign accent gave it a charm which is quite impossible to describe. It was painful to remember that all this youth, beauty, grace and wit were abandoned to a man who, every morning, signed the death warrants of so many innocent people.

The following morning I received this short message from her: 'This evening at ten o'clock.' I passed the day in a state of great agitation. Had I improved my position? was everything lost? Should I prepare for death? Should I flee immediately? All these questions thronged my mind and I was greatly troubled. And my poor children? What would become of them without me and without their father? Finally, God took pity on me. I summoned all my courage and when nine o'clock came, took the arm of M. de Chambeau, who was even more fearful than I, though he did not dare to let me see it. He accompanied me to Mme de Fontenay's door, promising to walk on the boulevard until I came out.

I went up. Tallien had not arrived. The waiting was anguishing. Mme de Fontenay could not talk to me. There were many people there whom I did not know. Eventually, the carriage was heard. It was impossible to mistake it, for in those days it was the only one abroad on the streets of that great city.

Mme de Fontenay went out and, returning after a moment, took my hand and said: 'He is waiting for you.' I felt as if she were announcing the executioner. She opened a door leading into a small passage at the end of which I could see a room with lights burning. It is no figure of speech to say that my feet were glued to the parquet. Involuntarily, I stopped. Mme de Fontenay gave me a push, saying: 'Go along, don't be so childish!' Then she turned back and shut the door of the room behind her. There was no alternative but to advance. I did not dare to raise my eyes. I walked, nevertheless, to the corner of the fireplace, on which two candles burned. Without the marble support, I would have fallen. Tallien was leaning against the opposite corner. He asked me quite gently what I wanted and I stammered my request to go to our house at Le Bouilh and my petition for the raising of the sequestration put in error on the property of my father-in-law, with whom I lived. He replied brusquely that that was no concern of his. Then, breaking off: 'But it is you, then, who are the daughter-in-law of the man who was confronted with the Woman Capet? And you have a father? . . . What is his name? . . . Ah, Dillon. The General? . . . All these enemies of the Republic will have to go,' he went on, at the same time making a beheading gesture with his hand. Indignation surged within me and, with it, my courage returned. I boldly raised my eyes to the monster. Until then, I had not looked at him. I saw before me a man of twenty-five or twenty-six with a rather pretty face which he tried to make severe. A mass of fair curls escaped on all sides from beneath a large military hat covered in shiny cloth and surmounted by a tricolour plume. He wore a long, tightly-fitting redingote of coarse blue cloth, over which were slung a cross belt and sabre from one shoulder and a long, silk tricolour scarf from the other.

'I have not come here, citizen', I told him, 'to hear the death warrant of my relatives and since you cannot grant my request, I will not importune you further.' So saying, I slightly inclined my head in farewell. He smiled as if to say 'You are very bold to speak to me thus.' I went out by the door through which he had entered and left without returning to the salon.

When I reached home, I thought my situation worsened rather than improved. If Tallien did not protect me, my death seemed inevitable. Mme de Fontenay realised, however, that I had made a good impression on him and was less easily discouraged. She accused him of not treating me kindly enough and told him I had decided not to return again to her house in case I should meet him there. He promised then that I would not be arrested, but at the same time told Mme de Fontenay that he knew that his colleague, Ysabeau, was denouncing him to the Committee of Public Safety in Paris for being too moderate and for protecting the aristocrats.

Towards midwinter, the locksmith who was hiding my husband arrived in Bordeaux to buy iron. He came to see me and I expressed my gratitude and trust in him. I showed him my children so that he would be able to tell their father that he had found them well. He was a good peasant from the Saintonge, very simple, very ignorant, understanding nothing of the state of the country, nor why, when he always got excellent white bread in Mirambeau, he had that morning seen people in Bordeaux buying bread so black that even his dog would have refused it. When he paid for the iron he had bought, he was amazed that people should want mere pieces of paper and not

the good golden louis he had in his strong-box. Nor could he understand why foodstuffs were taxed. While he waited for the tide in
order to return to Blaye, he walked about Bordeaux and unfortunately passed through the Place Dauphine where the executions
were taking place. A lady was climbing the fatal ladder. He asked
what she had done. 'She's an aristocrat,' he was told. This excellent
reason, though he did not understand it, seemed to satisfy him. But
then he saw a peasant like himself on the same ladder, about to meet
the same fate. Tremblingly, he asked again: 'And what about him,
what has he done?' It was explained that the man had given shelter
to a nobleman and was condemned for this to die along with him.

In that poor man's fate, he saw his own. He forgot what had
brought him to Bordeaux. He set out on foot and arrived home in the
middle of the night to tell my husband that he would not shelter him
an hour longer, that his own life and his wife's were at stake. He
hurried off to waken his brother-in-law, the groom, who was quite
unable to re-assure him. Seeing that he had completely lost his head
and, having also heard during the day that the guillotine was about
to make what was called a 'patriotic tour' and would pass through
Mirambeau within a few days, this groom decided to harness a horse
to a small cart. Into it, he heaped straw in which my husband concealed himself and set off by little-used roads for Tesson, which had
been put under seals but to which the concierge, Grégoire and his
wife, had a secret entrance. One of the windows of the lodge where
they lived opened on to the road. The groom knocked on the shutter.
It was still dark. My husband climbed in by the window and these
good people, who were most devoted to him, received him with joy.
They put him in a room next to their own, and as the two rooms
shared a chimney, my husband was able to have a fire all day without
attracting the attention of people outside. He was particularly glad
of this, for he suffered greatly from the cold.

There was a fine library at Tesson and neither it nor the furniture
had yet been inventoried. Only the outer doors had been sealed so it
was possible to walk about inside the house provided one did not
open the shutters. M. de La Tour du Pin therefore had as many
books as he wished. He also found means to remove certain papers
and old letters of his father's which might have caused problems if
they had become public. But he was not to be left undisturbed for
long in his enjoyment of this comparatively pleasant retreat. Seven or
eight days after his arrival, instructions arrived at the municipality of
Tesson for an inventory to be made of everything in the château,
which was large and well furnished. M. de La Tour du Pin's father

M. Tallien, leader of the Revolution in Bordeaux.

Honoré Gabriel Riquetti, Comte de Mirabeau.

Robespierre. Painting by Greuze.

had inherited it from his father-in-law, M. de Monconseil, who had lived there for forty years, bringing to it all the sumptuous elegance and noble magnificence which marked the reign of Louis XIV. This inventory would take two days to make and, given the attitude of the local people, it was certain that nothing would be spared and that no small corner would escape the search.

Grégoire did not hide his fears from the wretched fugitive. He told him he knew of nowhere to hide him or of anyone in the village or the neighbourhood who would take him in. They both agreed that Grégoire would go to Saintes, to Boucher, the postmaster, a former groom of M. de Monconseil's and much attached to my husband, to ask him either to house the fugitive himself or to help him get through to the provinces that had risen in revolt.

Despite his age – he was over seventy – Grégoire set off very early in the morning, on foot, in most terrible weather. He could not find Boucher, who was in charge of the convoys of carts needed by the army which was gathering to crush the Vendeans, and was always on the move. But his sister, equally devoted to our interests, agreed to take my husband and hide him in her brother's absence, though she made it clear that it would imperil their lives and fortunes. Grégoire returned immediately to Tesson without stopping to rest. At night, he left again with my husband for Saintes, a town where there is no outer wall and which could therefore be entered by paths known to Grégoire.

I have not told you yet that while my husband was still at Mirambeau, I had sent him a complete outfit of clothes such as were worn by better-class revolutionary peasants. When his slight figure was thoroughly muffled in them, he hardly recognised himself.

Mlle Boucher received him very well, but with such exaggerated precautions that he realised the shorter his stay there, the better she would be pleased. Grégoire went back to Tesson. He has often told me since that never in his life had he been more weary and that by the time he had completed his fourth trip, in the depth of winter, in terrible weather and along an almost impassable road, he had begun to fear he would die before reaching home.

The inventory at Tesson took three days to make and was as thorough as Grégoire had foreseen. But once it was completed, there was little likelihood of further disturbance. On the morning of the fourth day, Mlle Boucher came in great distress to the room where she had hidden my husband and told him that her brother was arriving that very evening with several generals and their staffs, that all the bedrooms in the house would be needed and that she could not keep him there any longer. She said she knew of no one in Saintes who would be willing to give him shelter and only an immediate departure could save him. M. de La Tour du Pin saw that the woman was petrified with fear and wanted, at any price, to rid herself of such an awkward guest. To accept his unhappy fate without a struggle was all that could be done. And so, at nightfall, he set out alone. He knew the road perfectly well, but when he arrived at Tesson, intending to take a path which led to the park and did not pass through the village, he mistook the road in the darkness. Soon the barking of dogs warned him that he was in the village square, in front of the Church. To reach the gates of the château, he had to find a plank thrown across a ditch at the entrance to the drive and the noise he made in feeling for it drew all the dogs of the village to his heels. He could hear shutters opening and voices calling the dogs or asking who was there. At last, he found the plank and hurried on as fast as he could. Silence returned. Grégoire was delighted to see him and gave him the same room as before. He lived there for two months, often receiving news of me from letters I wrote to Grégoire. It was a strange fact for such times, but I never heard of the privacy of the post being tampered with, or at least, of letters failing to reach their destination. In Bordeaux, I often received letters from Mme de Valence who was in prison in Paris, and in them she told me all the gossip of the place where she was confined.

Meantime, the terror in Bordeaux had reached its climax. Mme de Fontenay began to be anxious for her own safety and to fear that Ysabeau's denunciations would end in Tallien's recall. I shared her fears, for such a recall would have meant death for both of us. It was just after the horrible procession which marked the destruction, at one sweep, of all the precious objects belonging to the churches of the city. All the loose women of the town and the criminals had been assembled and decked out in the most beautiful of the ornaments to be found in the sacristies of the Cathedral, of St Seurin, St Michael, churches as old as the city itself and endowed since the days of Gallien with the rarest and most precious treasures. These villains paraded along the quays and main streets, everything that could not be worn on their persons being carried beside them in carts. In this manner, preceded by some horrible creature impersonating the Goddess of Reason, they reached the Place de la Comédie. There, on an enormous pyre, they burned all that magnificent treasure. And consider my terror that same evening when Mme de Fontenay said to me, as if it were a perfectly ordinary remark: 'Do you know what Tallien said this morning? That you would make a beautiful Goddess of Reason.' When I told her with horror that I would prefer to die, she was surprised and shrugged her shoulders.

Yet, she was a truly good woman. I had many proofs of it. One evening, I found her alone, in great trouble and anxiety. She was walking up and down her room and the least noise set her trembling. She explained that M. Martell, a dealer in Cognac, to whose wife and children she was most attached, was at that very moment before the tribunal and that although Tallien had promised her on his own head to save him, she feared Ysabeau, who wanted him executed. Eventually, after an hour of almost convulsive impatience, we heard someone running towards us. She became terribly pale. The door opened and a breathless man gasped 'He's acquitted.' It was Alexander, Tallien's secretary. Then, seizing my arm, she drew me headlong down the stairs, stopping for neither hat nor shawl. We rushed along the street, without her ever telling me where we were going in such breathless haste. We reached a house I did not know. She rushed in like a mad thing, crying: 'He's acquitted!' I followed her into a salon where a woman was lying prostrate on a sofa, surrounded by two or three young girls. Hearing the news, she revived and threw herself to the floor at Mme de Fontenay's knees, kissing her feet. The girls kissed her dress. I have never seen such a pathetic scene.

When I went in the evenings to call on Mme de Fontenay, I was always accompanied by my negro, for he had a police card and after a certain hour – seven o'clock, I think – every patrol had the right to ask to see it. I only went out after dark to avoid the danger which my English looks and appearance might provoke.

Fortunately, in the very inconspicuous house where I lodged, there was no common table at meal times, otherwise we might have been caught up in a 'sweep', a frequent operation in those days. It happened to M. de Chambeau when he was visiting a friend. He arrived at the house where his friend lived just as twenty-seven people were gathering at table. Among them was someone the police wanted to arrest. Since everyone denied all knowledge of this person, the police came in, closed all the doors, summoned several fiacres and made everyone climb in, six to a fiacre. They were all taken to the Fort du Hâ. M. de Chambeau was imprisoned there for twenty-eight days, in a state of unremitting anxiety. Two of his cell companions, people unknown to him, were taken off one morning for questioning and when they did not return, he concluded they had been sent to the guillotine. So he expected death daily. Fortunately, no one recognised him. After twenty-eight days, someone came to his room and told him he could go if he wished. Needless to say, he did!

Then there was Ferrari who, although he carried a paper accrediting him a secret agent of the Regent (later Louis XVIII) well hidden, sewn into the lining of his coat, was, being Italian, none the braver for that. He had been clever enough to scrape acquaintance even among the Representatives of the People. There, he often mentioned how necessary it was for him to return to Italy with his daughter. For, among all the ways we had considered of leaving France, was a plan that he and I should take a passport to Toulouse, with my husband as our servant. I was to pass as Ferrari's widowed daughter, taking her children back to Italy, to her husband's family. In the main cities along our route, such as Toulouse and Marseilles, we were to give concerts. Without boasting, I undeniably sang well enough to pass as a singer. Every day we practised different pieces for our repertory. One that I particularly remember was the duet of Paesiello: 'Nei giorni tuoi felici', which we were convinced would be a great success.

Our accompanist during these rehearsals was M. de Morin, a very talented young man. He had played a leading part in the Bordeaux Association of Young Men,* which had achieved so little but on whose account he was heavily compromised. He never slept two nights in the same place. He went out after dark, carefully avoiding patrols, for he had no identity card. I suspect, though I never asked him, that he sometimes slept in our house. When he had been hidden during the day in a house where there was little food, he would arrive to see me in the evening half-dead from hunger. I used to give him what remained of my dinner and my bread from Saintonge, often eggs as well, for I was kept plentifully supplied by the peasants at Le Bouilh. They were turned into excellent omelettes, with truffles which my cook had abstracted from the stores of the Representatives of the People. In our hiding-place, this was a source of much amusement and laughter.

One really had to be young and French to remain so gay when the blade of the guillotine was poised to strike. For we were all in danger from it and when we bade one another goodnight, did not dare to add an unqualified 'Until tomorrow'.

---

* A group of royalist opponents of the Revolution. During the terror in Bordeaux they were all executed without trial, having been proclaimed, as a body, outside the law. (Tr.)

But the situation was becoming hourly more alarming and not a day passed without executions. I lodged near enough to the Place Dauphine to hear the roll of drums which marked the fall of each head. I could count the victims before seeing their names in the evening papers.

The news I received from my husband described his position at Tesson as very precarious. Grégoire was continually being threatened with the occupation of the château by a body of troops, a military hospital or something of the kind, which would have forced my husband to move again. I did not know where else to put him with any measure of safety. To summon him back to join me in Bordeaux was out of the question because of the girl who looked after my child. From his hiding place, Dupouy had again had me warned to beware of her but I did not dare dismiss her in case worse should befall.

A recent incident had shown me that I was not so unknown in Bordeaux as I had hoped. My man of affairs had written from Paris that a law had just been passed establishing certificates of residence, signed by nine witnesses, renewable every three months under pain of confiscation of any property in communes where one was not living. As I had a house in Paris and certain state bonds, I had to get this certificate. Bonie undertook to find the nine witnesses, none of whom had seen me before, but who accepted his assurance concerning me. We went together one morning to the municipality and it was not without extreme distaste that I entered a room where there were about a dozen clerks, all wearing the red cap. I sat by the fire, while Bonie had the certificate made out and got the witnesses to sign it. He had asked that I should not be kept waiting as I was nursing my baby and this plea moved these cut-throats to compassion. One of them even rushed up to me and insisted on removing my sabots and warming them with hot cinders, a local courtesy among the people of Bordeaux. Then, going to a cupboard, he took out a nice little white loaf and made me a present of it, calling me *charmante nourrice* (charming wet-nurse). A look from Bonie warned me that I must not refuse it. But I took it with shame for I had seen a poor old lady on the other side of the fire, wrapped in a pale blue satin pelisse edged with swansdown, who had been waiting for perhaps two hours without any breakfast, doubtless cursing the young hussy with her gay madras kerchief knotted over one ear, her red waistcoat, her short skirt and her sabots. At last the moment came for me to sign and the municipal official, with a respect which startled me, gave me his chair so that I might sit down to write. Then, to my very great embarrassment, the certificate was read aloud from beginning to end. At the name of Dillon, one of these monsters interrupted: 'Ah, so the citizeness would seem to be a sister or niece of all the émigrés of that name who are on our list?' I was just about to deny it when the chief clerk broke in: 'You don't know what you're talking about. She isn't even a relation.' I looked at him in some surprise and he said to me in a low voice as he passed me his pen to sign: 'You're the niece of the Archbishop of Narbonne. I come from Sorèze.' I thanked him with a slight inclination of the head, but thought as I went away that if I was so well known in Bordeaux, I would have to move.

I was at my wits' end. I could see that Bonie was uneasy for me. Every day there were executions of people who had thought themselves safe. I could no longer sleep at night and every time I heard a sound, thought they had come to arrest me. I hardly dared to go out. My milk dried up and I was afraid of falling ill just at the very moment when I needed my health more than ever before so that I could be ready to act if it became necessary. Then, while paying a morning call on M. de Brouquens, who was still under house arrest, I happened to be standing by his table, deep in thought, when my eyes moved mechanically to that morning's paper, which lay open. There, in the trading news, I read that: 'The ship *Diana*, of Boston, 150 tons, will leave in eight days' time, in ballast, by permission of the Minister of Marine'. For over a year, eighty American ships had lain mouldering in the port unable to get permission to sail. Without a word, I rose immediately and was leaving when M. de Brouquens looked up from what he was writing and asked me where I was off to in such a hurry. 'I am going to America,' I told him.

I went straight to Mme de Fontenay. When I told her of my decision she was all the more approving as she had received bad news from Paris. Tallien had been denounced there by his colleague and was liable to be recalled from one minute to the next. She thought this recall would be the signal for even greater cruelty in Bordeaux and did not want to stay there if Tallien left. We had not a minute to lose if we wished to be saved.

I went home and called for Bonie, telling him that he must find me a man he trusted who would go and fetch my husband. He said without hesitation: 'The errand is dangerous. I know only one man to undertake it, and that is myself.' He assured me he would succeed and I put my trust in his zeal and intelligence. He was risking his life, for if they were discovered, his life as well as my husband's would be forfeit. However, if that happened, my own would be in similar case, so I did not scruple to accept his offer.

I lost not a minute. I went to find an old ship owner, a friend of my father, who was also a ship-broker. He was very devoted to me and undertook to reserve passages on the *Diana* for me, my husband and our two children. I should have liked to take my good Marguérite with me, but for six months she had been suffering from a double tertian fever and I feared that a sea journey in the bad season, for we were then in the last days of February, would be fatal to her. In any case, how would she manage in a country where she did not understand the language, for she was already advanced in years and even more accustomed than I to all the comforts of civilised living. I decided, therefore, to leave without her. When I returned to M. de Brouquens' house with everything already arranged, he was amazed. He told me then that an order had just arrived from Paris setting him free and that he himself intended leaving within a few days. He suggested that I should lunch the following day at Canoles, which he had not visited since the day of the search.

Returning home again, I confided my plans to my good Zamore, for the greatest problem was to find a way of packing our belongings without the maid being aware of it. She would certainly have denounced us immediately to the 'section'. She slept with my small daughter, then nearly six months old, in a long room lined with cupboards in which I had stored all that had been sent from Le Bouilh, as well as everything I had taken with me when I went to live at Canoles. On one side was a door leading into my room; on the other, a door into Marguérite's room from which a third door opened on to a small stair leading to the cellar. Bonie, always a man of foresight, had long ago arranged, without a word to me, that if they came to arrest me, I would go down to this cellar, full of old cases, and hide there for a few hours. Luckily, mistrusting the maid, I had always kept all the cupboards locked. I arranged with Zamore that I would take the maid and the children to Canoles with me the following morning and that during our absence he would empty all the cupboards, carry the contents down the small stair to the cellar and pack them in the cases there. I warned him not to drop even the smallest piece of thread for it might betray that the cupboards had been recently opened. He carried out the whole operation in his usual intelligent fashion.

The next day, therefore, I set out with M. de Chambeau to lunch with M. de Brouquens at Canoles. While we were all three at table, the garden gate opened and Mme de Fontenay appeared on Tallien's arm. I was greatly surprised, for she had not told me they were coming. Brouquens was dumbfounded, but quickly recovered. As for me, I was trying to master an emotion which had been much increased by the sight of a second man who had entered with Tallien, walking a little behind him. He had looked at me and put a finger to his mouth, so I immediately looked away. It was M. de Jumilhac, whom I had known very well and who was in hiding in Bordeaux, working under some other name. Tallien, after a courteous apology to de Brouquens for the liberty he had taken in crossing his garden on his way to visit the Swedish Consul, came up to me with all the grace of manner which had characterised the great gentlemen of the former Court and said in the kindest possible way: 'I understand, madame, that I can today make amends for the wrongs I have done you and I wish to do so.' At that, I allowed myself to unbend and putting aside the cold haughtiness I had at first assumed explained tolerably politely that I had certain financial interests in Martinique – it was almost true – and that, wishing to travel there to deal with them, I was asking him for a passport for myself, my husband and my children. He asked: 'But where, then, is your husband?' To which I replied laughingly: 'You must forgive me, Citizen Representative, if I do not tell you.' 'As you wish,' he said gaily. The monster was attempting to please. His beautiful mistress had threatened not to see him again if he did not save me and that had curbed his cruelty for a moment.

Two hours after my return to Bordeaux, Alexander, Tallien's secretary, brought me the order enjoining the municipality of Bordeaux to issue a passport to Citizen Latour, his wife and their two small children for the purpose of visiting Martinique on board the ship *Diana*. Once in possession of that precious document, it only remained for me to tell my husband to come to Bordeaux, for the American captain would not have agreed to take him on board if these papers had not been in order.

The journey from Tesson to Bordeaux was quite as difficult as it was dangerous. As I have said, Bonie did not hesitate for a moment. He left for Blaye as soon as the tide was on the ebb. He had previously obtained a valid passport for himself, for without one it was impossible to leave the Department or to enter that of the Charente-Inférieure where Tesson lay, only ten leagues from the borders of the Gironde. Once in the Gironde, a simple identity card, without any details, was sufficient for travel in any direction. Bonie, indeed, had his own identity card, but he also needed one for my husband. He therefore went to see one of his friends who was lying sick in bed and, on the pretext of having lost his own card, borrowed the friend's for a few days. The poor sick man, snug in his bed, had no idea of the danger he was running, for one thing was certain: if my husband had been caught with the card on him, its real owner would have gone with him to the guillotine. Bonie's passport stated that he was going to fetch grain. The Charente-Inférieure was overflowing with it, but in Bordeaux there was none at all and the bakers were putting all kinds of flour into their bread: oatmeal flour, bean flour, etc.

Bonie set out in the evening. If I had an enemy, I could not wish for him any worse punishment than to have to endure the mortal anxiety that I endured during the three days that followed. I had put the life of the man I loved most in all the world into the hands of another man whom I had known for barely six months. He played the part of a revolutionary so very well. Was it really a part? Might it not rather be his kindnesses which were the pretence? I tried to banish these terrible doubts but the more I reminded myself of the dangers Bonie was braving, the more difficult I found it to explain his devotion.

I had calculated every second of the time that dangerous journey would take. Anxiously I counted the minutes and on the third day, towards nine o'clock in the evening, I thought I might begin to hope that the ferry boat which came daily to Blaye on the tide would bring the passenger for whom I so anxiously waited. Burning with impatience, I could not remain indoors. As soon as it was dark, I went with M. de Chambeau to the Quai des Chartrons, to the place where I knew the boat from Blaye arrived. It was so dark that it was impossible to see even the water in the river. I did not dare to ask for news, as I knew that all the points on the river where passengers landed were thickly posted with police spies. Eventually, after a long wait, we heard half past nine striking and M. de Chambeau, who had no identity card, remarked that we had only half an hour left if we were to return home in safety. At that moment, two sailors passed me speaking together in English. I risked asking them, in their own tongue, the state of the tide. They told me without hesitation that it had been on the ebb for an hour. Hearing this, I lost all hope for that day and returned desolate to the house, where I spent the night imagining in anguish all the obstacles which might have delayed Bonie and his unfortunate companion. Seated on my bed, beside my two dear children, I listened for the slightest sound which might revive my hopes. Alas, never had the house been so still.

While I trembled thus with anxiety and impatience, haunted by terrible visions of my husband being recognised, arrested, taken before the tribunal and, from there, dragged to the scaffold, he was sleeping quietly on a comfortable bed which Bonie had prepared for him before he left in an unused room far from the other occupants of the house. In the morning, when the maid came to dress my small daughter, she said casually: 'By the way, Madame, M. Bonie is there and asks if you are up?' I made a prodigious effort not to cry out and you will understand that my toilette did not take me long. Bonie came in as soon as I was ready and told me that they had arrived at Blaye too late to take the usual boat, on which, in any case, my husband ran the risk of being recognised. Instead, he had hired a fishing boat and although the ebb still had three hours to run, the wind was favourable and very strong, so they had set sail and soon caught up and passed the regular boat. They had therefore already arrived when I was standing there on the bank, waiting so despairingly.

I was dying with impatience to go to the room which held the being I loved most in all the world. But Bonie advised me to dress as if I intended going out, so as to deceive the nurse, a very necessary precaution which was sheer torture to me. Finally, half an hour later, I went out on the pretext of doing some shopping and, having rejoined Bonie, went with him by a secret stair to my husband's room. And so, at last, we found one another again after six months of most painful separation.

In every lifetime there are a few luminous memories that shine like stars on a very dark night. The day of our reunion was one of them. We were not yet safe. Indeed, the danger which now threatened was closer and more real than any of the perils we had so far surmounted; yet we were happy, and death, which we felt so very close, no longer frightened us, for it was possible again to hope that if it struck, it would strike us down together.

Looking back, now, after many years, and recalling the depth of the mistrust, absurdity, unreasonableness and fear which held even intelligent minds in thrall during this period – so aptly known as the Terror – the whole situation seems inconceivable. The simplest of reasonings, even that of a ten-year-old child, should have been sufficient to banish this confusion and fear. No one asked, for example, how it was that people were dying of hunger in Bordeaux when, just across the river, the necessities of life abounded. No one could explain why, but the fact remains that no peasant from Blaye or Royan would have dared to bring two bags of flour to the great city.

He would immediately have been denounced for hoarding. These facts have not been explained in any memoirs of the period. I leave the task to historians and return to my own story.

❦❦❦❦❦❦❦❦❦❦ XVI ❦❦❦❦❦❦❦❦❦❦

I have already told you how, two months previously, I had obtained a certificate of residence in the name of Dillon Gouvernet,* attested by nine witnesses. Now it was necessary to go and ask for a passport in the name of Latour and to avoid that of Dillon which was too well known in Bordeaux. I decided to drop the Dillon and take the name of Lee, which my uncle, Lord Dillon,† had added to his own name.

There could be no turning back. The passport office shut at nine o'clock and at half past eight we went to the commune. It was quite dark. The date was 8 March 1794. My husband walked with Bonie and I followed at some distance with a friend of Bonie's, carrying my six months' old daughter and holding my three-year-old son by the hand. Because of the English or American name I intended to use, I had dressed as a lady, but very shabbily, and wore an old straw hat. In the Hôtel de Ville we went to a room crowded with people. There, one was given the card or permit which the passport office required before issuing a passport. I was terrified in case someone from Saint-André-en-Cubzac or Bordeaux should recognise us and, to reduce the danger, M. de La Tour du Pin and I were very careful to keep far apart and to avoid the lighted parts of the room.

Armed with the permit, we went up to the passport office and as we entered, heard the clerk saying: 'That's more than enough for today: the rest must wait until tomorrow.' Any delay would have cost us our lives. Bonie leapt over the counter saying: 'If you're tired, citizen, I'll do the writing for you.' The clerk agreed to this and Bonie drew up a collective passport for the Latour family. There were still many people in the office so that when the Town Clerk, in his red cap, said: 'Citizen Latour, take off your hat so that we can

---

* It is still customary in France for married women to retain their own family name, adding it to that of their husband.
† Charles, 12th Viscount Dillon, assumed the name Dillon-Lee in 1776 and conformed to the Established Church in order to comply with the terms of the will of his maternal great-uncle, Robert Lee, 4th and last Earl of Litchfield.

put down your description', my heart beat so violently that I almost fainted. Fortunately, I was sitting in a dark corner. At the same moment, my son looked up and threw himself upon me, burying his face in his little hands. Thinking it was only from fear of those men in red caps, I said nothing.

When the passport was signed, we carried it off with a feeling of deep relief, though indeed we were still very far from being safe. To avoid being in the same house and having to cross Bordeaux together the following morning in broad daylight, we had arranged that M. de La Tour du Pin should sleep at the house of M. Meyer, the Dutch Consul, who lived in the last house on the Quai des Chartrons. He was most devoted to us. As for me, after taking my children home, I went to see Mme de Fontenay, thinking I would meet Tallien at her house for he was to visa our passport. I found her in tears. Tallien had been recalled and had left two hours earlier. She herself was to leave the following day and did not hide from me her fear that Tallien's colleague, the fierce Ysabeau, would refuse us a visa. But Alexander, Tallien's secretary, swore by his own head that Ysabeau would do so. He said that since he always signed papers at ten o'clock, after the theatre, he was in a hurry to get his supper and did not look very closely at what was put before him. Providence in its goodness had ordained that Ysabeau should have asked Tallien to leave him his secretary who was not only very useful to him, but had also been sufficiently clever to make himself indispensable.

As I entered Mme de Fontenay's house, Alexander was on his way out with papers for signature. He took the passport and put it among many others. Ysabeau was that day very much preoccupied with the arrival of a new colleague, who was to reach Bordeaux the next day, and signed without paying any attention. As soon as Alexander was free to leave, he sped back to Mme de Fontenay's, where I was waiting for him, more dead than alive. I was not alone. A person of some distinction whom I did not know and who looked extremely worried, was also there. It was M. de Fontenay, who had ignored the most elementary notions of delicacy and come to ask his wife to save him.

Alexander arrived with the passport unfolded in his hand. He was so out of breath that he fell into an armchair, unable to say more than: 'Here it is.' Mme de Fontenay embraced him most warmly and so did I, for it was he who really saved us. I have never seen him since. He may have paid with his life for the services he rendered to so many people who have forgotten all about them.

I spent the last night packing some belongings which Zamore

took away very early the next morning. I had pretended to undress and was careful not to waken the maid. As soon as we were alone, my son, whose bed was beside mine, sat up and called me. I was terrified, fearing he might be ill, and went hurriedly over to him. Throwing his little arms about my neck and pressing his lips to my ear, he whispered: 'I saw Papa, you know, but I didn't say anything because of those wicked people!' The terror in the passport office had touched even a small child of less than four.

Our luggage had been aboard for three days and my spy was unaware that all the cupboards and drawers were empty. I bade a tender farewell to my good Marguérite, who thought only of me and was happy to see me escaping from the dangers which threatened. I left her under the protection of M. de Brouquens, who was well aware of my affection for her. At last, on 10 March, carrying my daughter, Séraphine, and holding Humbert by the hand, I told the nurse that I was taking them to the Allées de Tourny, which was still the usual place to take children walking, and that I would be back in an hour or two.

I set off, instead, in the direction of the slopes of the Château-Trompette where I joined M. de Chambeau whom I had arranged to meet there. He too, had obtained a passage in our boat. Not long before, he had heard that his father, a good Gascon country gentleman living on his estate near Auch, had been denounced by a servant who had been thirty years in his service and that he had been arrested and put into prison. From papers seized at the time of his arrest, they knew that his son was in hiding in Bordeaux so it was necessary for him to leave at once. But where could he go? During the morning of the day we were to fetch our passport, I happened to be at M. de Brouquens' house at the same time as M. de Chambeau. We talked of his predicament and I had said light-heartedly to him: 'If I were to give you a power of attorney to manage my house in Martinique, you could get a passport and leave on the *Diana*.' The idea had a greater success than I foresaw. M. de Brouquens went to his lawyer. The power of attorney was drawn up. I signed it with my true name and an hour later, M. de Chambeau was in possession of a valid passport, visaed probably – in fact, certainly – by Representative Ysabeau. It did not reach him until eleven o'clock in the morning. By midday, he was ready to leave, his only baggage being a dozen shirts and a purse with twenty-five louis given him by M. de Brouquens. He was delighted to be escaping and, being only twenty-five, was in the highest spirits, busily and effectively turning his hand to whatever needed doing. He was a charming and most pleasant companion in misfortune. His friendship for my husband grew into a devotion which never once wavered.

I found him, then, at the Château-Trompette, accompanied by a small boy carrying his portmanteau, which weighed very little. He took Humbert's hand and when we arrived at the end of the Quai des Chartrons and saw the dinghy from the *Diana*, we each of us experienced a depth of joy felt but seldom in any lifetime.

M. Meyer, at whose house my husband had spent the night, was waiting for us. We found, already at lunch, M. de Brouquens, Mme de Fontenay and three or four other people, including a councillor of the Parlement de Paris, whom Brouquens had hidden among the staff of his commissariat and whose real names I never knew. He was much teased because, charged with finding provisions for our journey, all he had been able to find in the space of three days was one lamb which he had brought bleating along. The famine was indeed so bad that we ourselves had been unable to obtain anything. A few jars of goose legs, a few sacks of potatoes or French beans, a small case of bottled jams and fifty bottles of Bordeaux wine composed our entire store. It is true that Captain Pease had some barrels of biscuits, but they were a year and a half old and had already made the journey from Baltimore. M. Meyer gave me a small bag of fresh biscuits, which I saved to make gruel for my small daughter. But what did it all matter in the face of what had been achieved: my husband's life was saved!

Mme de Fontenay rejoiced in the result of her work. Her lovely face was wet with tears of joy as we climbed into the dinghy. She has since told me that, thanks to our expressions of gratitude, that moment counted as one of her dearest memories.

When the captain seated himself at the tiller and shouted 'Off', an inexpressible happiness flowed through me. Seated opposite my husband, whose life I was saving, with my two children on my knee, nothing seemed impossible. Poverty, work, misery, nothing was difficult with him beside me. There is no doubt at all that the heave of the oar with which the sailor pushed us off from the shore marked the happiest moment in my life.

The *Diana* had gone down on the preceding tide to the Bec d'Ambez, where we were to join her. We were compelled by the authorities to stop alongside a warship stationed in the middle of the river, like a sentry, at the entrance to the port. The captain prepared his papers and our passports for inspection. It was a bad moment. We did not dare to speak in French or to look up towards the warship's deck. The captain went on board alone. He knew not a word of French, though his ship had been lying in embargo a whole year at Bordeaux. A voice shouted from the deck: 'Send the woman up as interpreter', and there followed some ribald enquiries as to whether she were young or old. I was filled with a deadly fear. Our captain leaned over the side and told me not to answer. I dared not even raise my eyes. At that moment, a French boat drew near, full of men in uniform, and in a great hurry. The captain took advantage of this to collect his papers, jumped into the dinghy and we made off as fast as possible.

At last we reached our small boat, the *Diana*, and settled ourselves on board as best we could. The next ebb tide took us down to Pauillac. There we had to endure yet another visit from two more guardships. My husband, already seasick, was in bed. The officers who came on board were very polite, but wanted to know a great deal. They took a fancy to my lamb which, unfortunately, was still alive. They coolly asked me to give it to them and promised to send a goat in exchange, which delighted me for my children's sake. But they took away the lamb and we never saw the goat, for shortly afterwards we weighed anchor to move in towards Pauillac, where the sea was less rough. My husband felt much better.

Our small ship was a vessel of only 150 tons. Its solitary mast was very tall, as in all American-built ships, and as there was no cargo except for our twenty-five cases, the rolling was horrible. My apprenticeship to the sea was grim indeed.

We had arranged that the captain should provide our food but he had found it as difficult as we did to get provisions and had been able to get only such victuals as his consignees had managed to obtain for him from the naval stores.

As we left Bordeaux, one of the four sailors had a terrible fall from the masthead to the hold. It naturally put him out of action and only three were left to man the ship. The entire crew consisted of these three sailors, a cabin boy who acted as steward, the captain, a young man of no great ability, his mate who came, like the captain, from Nantucket and an old sailor called Harper, well salted in experience who, though new to the ship, was consulted by the captain at every turn.

The captain's cabin, which he had to himself, was, as you may imagine, very small. He had given one cabin to my husband and me and another to M. de Chambeau. He himself slept in his own cabin on a sort of chest which served as a bench during the daytime. For thirty days, my husband did not leave his bed. He suffered terribly from seasickness and also from the bad food. The only nourishment he could take was tea made with water, and a few pieces of toasted biscuit soaked in sweet wine. As for me, when I look back across the years, I cannot conceive how I was able to withstand the weariness and hunger. I was nursing my baby at the time and, being only twenty-four, naturally had a most excellent appetite, but in this strange new life, I had not even time to eat.

Fortunately, the movement of the ship lulled my poor little daughter and she slept nearly all day. But for that very reason, she allowed me no peace when she felt me beside her at night and I could never sleep for more than half-an-hour at a time. I was so afraid of rolling over on her in my sleep and smothering her that I had a piece of cloth passed around the middle of my body and fastened to the wooden frame of the bed. My little daughter thus had all the room she needed. I could neither turn nor change my position but although it was torture at first, I soon grew used to it.

At that time, the Americans were at war with the Algerians who had already seized a number of their ships. Our captain's dread of these pirates was such that, when we were barely two leagues out from the Tour de Courdouan,* he headed due north, declaring that he would not feel safe until he had reached the waters north of Ireland. He had little faith in the French navy's powers of protection against these marauders and put all his trust in the English navy, thinking the Algerians would not dare risk provoking it.

In terrible equinoctial gales, we steered a course that kept us twenty leagues out from the coast of France, a course which, from our point of view, was not very reassuring. We had heard at Pauillac that a French frigate, the *Atalante*, I believe, had met an American boat carrying a number of French passengers at the entrance to the port of La Rochelle, seized it and taken the French passengers to Brest, where they were all guillotined.

This cheering story gave me something of a distaste for any course near the French coast. But however hard I pleaded with the captain to set a direct course for his own country, he could only repeat his fears of the Algerians and the danger of slavery. Since M. de La Tour du Pin felt as he did, he encouraged him to hold to his northerly route.

One day, when the seas were so high that we had had to fasten the scuttles and were confined to the living quarters with the lamps lit, even though it was midday, the hoarse voice of the sailor on watch was suddenly heard to shout the news we so dreaded: 'French man-o'-war ahead.' In one bound, the captain was on deck,

* A light-house on a rock at the entrance to the Gironde estuary.

ordering us to remain out of sight. We heard a cannon shot, the opening round in a parley which meant life or death for us. The frigate declared her French nationality, running up the flag. We hastily declared ours in the same manner and, after the customary questions, heard our captain's reply: 'No passengers, no cargo.' To this, the *Atalante* replied: 'Come aboard.' The captain said the seas were too high. It was indeed very rough and, being hove to, we were thrown around to such an extent that the only way to keep one's feet was to cling to some support. The imposing challenger ended the exchange with one word: 'Follow', and continued on her course. We unfurled our only sail and prepared to follow meekly in her wake.

The captain came down from the deck saying gaily: 'In an hour it will be dark and a fog is coming up.' Never was a fog welcomed more joyfully. We soon lost sight of the frigate in the darkness and as we had put on as little sail as possible, despite a cannon shot intended to hurry us up, she drew slowly ahead of us. She had signalled us that she was making for Brest and that we were to follow her there. As soon as it was dark, we set a directly opposite course and, the wind being favourable and very strong, we made off to the north-west with all canvas spread, caring not at all if it was in the direction of Boston, the port for which we were bound.

The incident threw us right off our course and as the thick fogs made it impossible to take a bearing for twelve or fifteen days, the colour of the water was the only indication that we had reached the vicinity of the Newfoundland bank. Strong westerly winds drove us back continually. Food was becoming short and water had to be rationed. We met an English boat coming from Ireland and the captain went on board. He returned with a sack of potatoes and two small jars of butter for me and my children. Having compared his position with that taken by the English captain, he found we were fifty leagues north of the Azores. In fact, for several days, feeling he was beyond the reach of the Algerians, he had been steering south-west by a good north-east wind.

Learning this, my husband besought him to land us in the Azores, for we could have found our way from there to England, but the captain refused. Providence had decided otherwise for us, and how very grateful I have since felt. But at the time, in our human blindness, we grumbled. If we had gone to England, we would have arrived just as the expedition was preparing to set out for Quiberon Bay. My husband would certainly have gone with it, along with his friends and he would, like them, have perished. But God did not want to take from me all the years of domestic happiness with which

I have since been blessed on this earth. If he has taken back to Himself the children I had then, and the later ones who made me such a happy, proud mother, I hope perhaps He will leave me, to close my eyes, the one I have loved most of all, the only son* remaining to me, and also my two grandchildren†, whom I truly adore. Of these, one grand-daughter has been entrusted to my care and I have had charge of her upbringing. I look on her as my own child and also as a very dear friend.

My life on board, hard though it was, had one advantage: all the small pleasures we do not value when we have always had them were perforce beyond my reach. Indeed, deprived of everything, without a moment of leisure, entirely occupied with caring for my children and my sick husband, not only had I not made what people call their 'toilette' since going on board, but I had not even had time to remove the Madras kerchief I wore on my head. Fashion still decreed excessive quantities of powder and pomade. One day, after the encounter with the *Atalante*, I decided to dress my hair while my daughter was asleep. It was very long hair and I found it so tangled that, despairing of ever being able to restore it to order, I took the scissors and cut it quite short, anticipating, as it happened, the 'Titus' fashion. My husband was very angry. I dropped the hair overboard and with it went all the frivolous ideas which my pretty fair curls had encouraged.

My recreation during the journey was the time I spent in the galley. In shape, it resembled a berline; there were no doors and it was secured to the mast. One sat in its depths and the pots boiled on a sort of furnace which had to be lit from outside. More than once, a wrong twist of the helm brought us a good wetting from some passing wave, but we were warm in there – or, to be more exact, our feet were warm. I say 'we' because I did not have this delightful kitchen to myself. A sailor known as the cook used to fetch me and install me there beside him to spend an hour or two cooking those haricot beans which had already crossed the ocean from Baltimore and which had spent at least a year in store at Bordeaux. The cook's name was Boyd. He was twenty-six and it was obvious that under his mask of grime and grease he was very good looking. He was the

* Frédéric-Claude-Aymar.
† The children of her daughter Alix, known as Charlotte, and Florent-Charles-Auguste, Comte de Liedekerke-Beaufort:
(a) Hadelin-Stanislas-Humbert, Comte de Liedekerke-Beaufort, 1816–1890. It was his son who first published the Journal.
(b) Cécile-Claire-Séraphine de Liedekerke-Beaufort, 1818–1893. Married in 1841 to Ferdinand-Joseph-Ghislain, Baron de Beeckman.

son of a farmer on the outskirts of Boston and much better educated
than would have been a Frenchman of similar station. He immediately realised that I was a lady and anxious to learn all I could about
rural life in his country. It was indeed thanks to him that I acquired a
knowledge of all the tasks that were to fall to me when I became a
farmer's wife. My husband used to say laughingly: 'The beans are
boiled to a mash because my wife forgot herself with Boyd!'

When water was rationed, he promised to see we did not go short.
This was particularly important for my husband, since tea was all he
could drink without causing a recurrence of seasickness. Personally,
I suffered greatly from the shortage of food. The biscuit had become
so hard that I could not eat it without making my gums bleed. When
I tried to soften it with liquid, the weevils came out and I found this
utterly disgusting. For my children, I crushed the biscuit into a kind
of gruel and in making such mixtures had already used up the two
small jars of butter given us by the English boat. The shortage of
food caused my milk to dry up and I could see my daughter shrink-
ing visibly. My son begged me, with tears, for one of our potatoes,
though he had eaten the last one several days before. Our plight was
terrible and I could not rid myself of the fear that I would see my
children die of hunger.

It was ten days since we had been able to take a bearing and the
fog was so thick that, even on our small ship, it was impossible to see
the bowsprit. The captain had no idea where he was. In vain did old
Harper declare that he felt land breezes: we thought he was only
trying to hearten us.

At last, on 12 May 1794, at daybreak, the weather being warm and
the sea calm, we went to sit on deck with our children to enjoy a
change of scene and the fresh air. The fog was as thick as ever and
the captain was certain that, whatever land we were approaching
was still at least some fifty to sixty leagues distant. I noticed, however, that the dog was very excited. It was a black terrier bitch of
which I was very fond and which had developed an affection for me,
to the very great disgust of its owner, the captain. The poor animal
kept rushing forward, barking loudly, and then returning to me,
licking my son's hands and face, and rushing off again. This odd
behaviour had been going on for at least an hour when a small
decked-in boat, a pilot boat, passed close to us and the man aboard
her shouted in English that if we didn't change our course, we would
founder on the point. We immediately threw him a rope and he
jumped aboard. It is quite impossible to describe our joy at seeing
this Boston pilot.

We were, all unaware, at the entrance to that magnificent road-stead which has no equal among even the most beautiful of the European lakes. Leaving a sea whose waves were breaking in fury against the rocks, we entered through a passage so narrow that two ships could not have passed abreast, into waters as quiet and smooth as a mirror. A slight land breeze sprang up to reveal, like the changing of scenery on a theatre stage, the friendly land waiting to welcome us.

My son's transports of joy defeat all description. For sixty days he had heard us talking of the dangers from which we had, thank God, escaped. With his four-year-old mind, he had grasped that, in order to avoid those men in red caps of whom he had been so frightened, and who had threatened to kill his father, he would have to live a life lacking in many of the good things to which he had been accustomed. He often remembered the fine, white bread and the good milk of earlier days, and found it very disagreeable to be without these things. Vague recollections such as these caused him to cry some-times without apparent reason. But when, from the narrow creek through which we were sailing, he saw the green fields, the flowering trees and all the beauty of a most luxuriant vegetation, his joy was beyond words.

Ours, though less exuberant, was quite as deep.

PART II

PART II

Lucca, the 7th of February 1843. It is probably very presumptuous to continue writing these memoirs when in ten days' time I shall enter on my seventy-fourth year. But today I finished copying out the part I had written on loose sheets of paper and I assure you, my dear son,* that you will have the remainder, God willing, either with or without crossings-out, so long as I retain a little strength, power of mind and the sight of my eyes to guide my pen.

But let us end these preliminaries and return to the entrance to the Boston Roads where I left your poor brother, Humbert, joyfully gazing once again on cows, fields, trees, flowers and all the other things his youthful imagination had almost forgotten. I admit with shame that the joy felt by the rest of us, the grown-ups, was entirely focussed on the enormous fish which the pilot had just caught and which, with a jar of milk, some fresh butter and white bread, was to provide what the captain called 'a welcome breakfast'. While we ate, satisfying our famished appetites, we were moving further into this magnificent bay, towed by our dinghy. The captain dropped anchor two cables' length from land and then left us, promising to return in the evening after finding lodgings for us.

We had not a single letter of introduction and waited patiently for his return. Meantime, supplies of fresh food were arriving from all sides. So also did a number of Frenchmen, very impatient for news and besieging us with questions to which we could give only the sketchiest of answers. One wanted to know what was happening in Lille, another in Grenoble, a third in Metz, and they were all amazed and, indeed, almost angry when we could only tell them about Paris or France in general. For the most part, they were very ordinary people: tradesmen who had been ruined, workmen seeking jobs. They all seemed to us more or less sympathetic towards the Revolution and they, in their turn, looked on us as aristocrats fortunate to have escaped the death which, according to them, we fully merited for our past tyranny. They left us angrily and we were rid of them for the remainder of our stay in Boston.

The rest of the day was spent in putting our belongings in order. In the evening, the captain returned. He had found us a small lodging on the Market Square and brought offers of help from the owner of

* Aymar.

the ship. My husband determined to call on him the following day when we landed. The captain told us he was a rich man and greatly esteemed, and that we were very fortunate to be under his protection.

As you will easily believe, I was awake before dawn the next day. I dressed my children and as soon as the dinghy was ready, said goodbye to all the crew, shaking hands warmly with each one, for these good men had been extremely kind and obliging. The cabin boy wept bitterly at parting from my son. Each had some personal regret to express and I myself was very sorry not to be able to take along with me 'Black', the dog, who had become so attached to me.

Only someone who has been exposed to the sufferings we had been enduring for two months, the restrictions I had had to bear before that, the anxiety for my husband's safety and also for my own, the anguish of mind caused by living for months in continual fear of imminent death, knowing that it would leave my two poor children entirely alone, without help or protection, will ever be able to appreciate fully the joy I felt when I set foot on that friendly shore. Our good captain was as happy about it as we were ourselves. He took us first to one of the best inns, where he had previously ordered an excellent lunch with everything we had lacked for so long. Although this gesture may seem trivial to people who have never lacked for anything, I would ask them to indulge me a moment while I confess that the sight of that plentiful table gave me a pleasure so vivid that it surpassed any pleasures I had known until then.

Afterwards, we set out for the small lodging chosen by our kind captain and my husband left me there while he went to call on Mr Geyer, the owner of the ship. He was one of the richest men in Boston. Although he had returned after the peace treaty to enjoy his fortune in the country of his birth, he had been among those who had supported England and had taken no part in the revolt against the mother-country. Like many other Boston merchants, he had taken his family to England. My husband was received by him with a warm friendliness which quite charmed him.

The house in which our captain had found us a lodging was the home of three generations of women: Mrs Pierce, her mother and her daughter. It stood on the Market Square, the busiest and liveliest part of the town. Our apartment consisted of, on one side, a small drawing-room with two windows looking out over the Square and, on the other side, beyond a very small staircase, a good bedroom intended for my husband, my children and me. This room looked out over an isolated shipyard where the builders were busy. Beyond, stretched the countryside. You will see later why I give you these details.

We boarded with these good ladies, who fed us very well in the English style. Sally, the young daughter, was passionately fond of children and she took my small daughter and insisted on looking after her. The grandmother took charge of Humbert, already very tall for his age and unusually intelligent. We could not have had a more fortunate start. By the evening of that first day, we felt as settled there as if no grief or anxiety had ever troubled our lives.

Towards the middle of the night, I was awakened by the barking of a dog and its whimpers as it scratched at the kitchen door, which opened on to the shipyard. The bark was familiar. I got up and opened the window. There, in the moonlight, I recognised Black. I went straight down to open the door for her and when I got her back to our room, saw that the poor creature was so soaked that she must have spent a very long time in the water. Next day, I learned that she had been kept tied up on board all day but that, at ten o'clock in the evening, the sailor had thought it safe to unfasten her. No sooner had he done so than she took a mighty leap over the side. Now, the *Diana* was anchored over a mile from the quay, so the good animal had probably swum all that distance and, having searched for us through that strange town, had eventually discovered the very door of the house closest to the room where we were sleeping. The captain was almost superstitious in his determination not to cross such well-proven attachment. Black never left us again and eventually returned with us to Europe.

The following morning, Mr Geyer came to call on me, bringing his wife and daughter. He himself spoke French fairly well but the ladies did not know a single word of the language. They were therefore delighted to find that their tongue was as familiar to me as to them. Their kindly hospitality did not need the formality of letters of introduction. The dangers through which we had passed in France evoked general sympathy and people marvelled at our story. They insisted on believing that my hair had been cut short at the back in preparation for execution. This intensified their interest in us and quite in vain did I explain that it had been cut for a very different reason.

Forty-five years ago, the town still had the appearance of an English colony yet it was there that the first uprising against the mother-country had taken place. We were shown with pride the column that had been erected on top of the hill where the people had gathered to pass the first resolutions against the unjust taxes with which England was crippling the colony; the place in the harbour where they had tipped two shiploads of tea into the sea rather than pay the exorbitant duty charged on it; the fine lawn where the first armed troops had gathered and the site of the first battle: Bunker's Hill. But the richest and most distinguished of the inhabitants, although they submitted to the new government, regretted, though they did not disapprove, the separation from the mother-country. They were still linked to England by ties of affection and family. They preserved the customs of that country quite unchanged and many of them who had taken refuge there, did not return until the peace had been signed. They were known as the Loyalists. Among them was Mr Jeffreys, brother of the famous editor of the *Edinburgh Review*, and a family named Russell who were at pains to make known their close connection with the Duke of Bedford. All these people welcomed us with the greatest kindness and took a lively interest in our welfare.

Mr Geyer suggested we should live on a farm of his about eighteen miles from Boston. Perhaps it would have been wise to accept, but my husband wanted to be nearer to Canada, where he hoped to settle eventually. He spoke English with difficulty, though he understood it perfectly, and the knowledge that French was spoken in Montreal, as it still is today, made him want to be close to that city.

Letters from England were waiting for us when we arrived, including one from our aunt, Mme d'Hénin. I forgot to tell you that, at Pauillac, we had anchored alongside a ship which, like ours, was waiting for a favourable wind and which was headed for England. I had therefore written a few hurried lines to Mme d'Hénin, who was living in London, asking her to write to us at Boston, in care of Mr Geyer, whose name the captain had given me. Our crossing took so long that there had been time for a reply to arrive from our aunt which settled for us the question of where we were to live in the United States. She wrote that she was sorry we had not joined her in England but sent letters of introduction from an American friend of hers, a Mrs Church, to her family in Albany. Mrs Church was a daughter of General Schuyler, who had so greatly distinguished himself during the War of Independence. Since the war, General Schuyler, who was of Dutch descent, had been living on his estates with all his family. His eldest daughter had married the head of the Renslaer family who lived in Albany and owned enormous wealth in the county.

And so, Mrs Church, seeing the deep and motherly interest taken in us by my aunt, who was a dear friend of hers, wrote to her parents and when we arrived in Boston, we found most pressing letters from General Schuyler telling us to come without delay to Albany, assuring us we would find it easy to settle there. He offered us his full support in the matter. This decided us and, having shipped our belongings by sea to New York and from there up the Hudson to Albany, we waited in Boston until we heard of their safe arrival and then set out to follow them by the land route. We preferred to travel this way as the five hundred mile journey would give us an opportunity to see the country without involving us in any extra expense.

Before despatching our belongings, we had had to empty all the cases and re-pack them. In his haste, Zamore had had to pile things in pell-mell and quite indiscriminately, so there were a multitude of things altogether useless to people who, like us, would be living very modestly in the country, in a manner similar to that of the peasants in Europe. There was nothing to indicate that the turmoil of the Revolution would allow us to return to Europe for many years to come and I admit that I was glad my husband had been so well received in the United States that he had lost all wish to return to England. I had a kind of presentiment that we might not be well received by my family.

In Boston, I sold everything we had that might fetch money. As the *Diana* had made the crossing in ballast, no charge had been made for our luggage and we had brought a considerable amount. We reduced it by more than half: clothing, materials, laces, a piano, music, porcelain, everything that would be superfluous in a small household was turned first into money and then into bills of exchange on reliable people in Albany.

We stayed a month in Boston, going nearly every day to visit the kindly people who showered us with attentions and kindnesses. I also received visits from many Creoles* from Martinique who had known my father. One of them, who had married in Boston, made us promise to spend a few days with him in the country and we did so with great pleasure. He lived in Wrentham, a village half way between Boston and Providence. It was a delightful spot, cool, unspoilt and fertile. There were lakes strewn with small wooded islands which looked like floating gardens; there were great trees, old as time itself, dipping their ancient trunks and their young shoots into water clear as crystal. It was a place of enchantment.

We all three† left Boston early in June, taking the children with us. A fortnight later, we arrived in Albany having travelled right

* French settlers in the West Indies.
† Mme de La Tour du Pin, her husband and M. de Chambeau.

across the State of Connecticut.* We greatly admired its fertility and
air of prosperity but some very sad news had made me so unhappy
that I could not enjoy any of it. Before leaving Boston, M. de La Tour
du Pin had learned of my father's death.† He did not tell me until we
had started out, hoping that the need to journey on and the changes of
scene would help to dull my grief. He decided to tell me at North-
ampton, the State capital, where we spent the night, fearing I might
see it in some gazette. Indeed, all the news from France was printed
in the American papers as soon as it arrived, no matter at which port
of the Union it was received.

My father's death distressed me very deeply, despite the fact that
I had been expecting it for a long time. For many years I had seen
him only very occasionally, but had nonetheless a most tender
affection for him. I wrote to my step-mother, who was living in
Martinique, and to my twelve-year-old step-sister, Fanny. Long
afterwards, I had a reply from Mme Dillon in which she told me
that she was leaving for England with Fanny and Mlle de la Touche,
her daughter by her first marriage. It was a very cold letter and
showed not the slightest concern for the conditions in which I was
living in America.

In spite of everything and as always happens when there are new
things to see, I did find distraction in the beauty of the forests we had
to cross on our way to Lebanon, our last stage, where we spent a
night before arriving in Albany. A fifty-mile stretch of unbroken
forest separated the State of Connecticut‡ from that of, I think, New
York, though it has doubtless disappeared by now. It offered a
spectacle I had never seen before: a forest in every stage of growth,
from the tree just emerging from the ground to the tree fallen back
to it through age. The road through these magnificent forests was
only wide enough for two carriages to pass. It was no more than a
cutting where the trees, felled at ground level, had been pushed to
right and left to clear a path. But, what jolting we had to endure
when those trunks had not been cut sufficiently level with the
ground! The remarkable fertility of this virgin land had encouraged
the growth of an enormous number of parasitic plants, wild vines
and lianas which wound from tree to tree. In the more open areas,
there were thickets of rhododendrons covered in blooms, some
purple, others pale lilac, and roses of every kind. The flowers made
a vivid splash of colour against the grassland, which was itself

* It was, in fact, the State of Massachusetts.
† Arthur Dillon was executed on 13 April 1794.
‡ Read Massachusetts.

studded with mosses and flowering plants, while in the low-lying parts, furrowed and watered by small streams – or creeks, as they are called – every kind of water plant was in full flower. This unspoiled nature so enchanted me that I spent the entire day in rapture.

Towards midday, we stopped for lunch at an inn set up not long before in the midst of this immense forest. In America, when a house is built in a forest and close to a road, even if only one traveller is likely to pass in the whole of the year, the owner's first purchase is a sign and his first task the raising of a pole on which to hang it. Then, under the sign, a letter box is nailed to the pole. The road may be barely visible, but thenceforward the place is marked on the map as a town.

The timber house at which we stopped had reached the second stage of civilisation for it was a frame house, that is to say, a house with glazed windows. But it is the incomparable beauty of the family who lived in it that particularly remains in my memory: first, the husband and wife, aged about forty to forty-five, both remarkable for their strength and beauty and gifted with that exquisite perfection of form found only in the paintings of the greatest masters; about them were grouped eight or ten children, boys and girls, and in them you could admire everything, from the young girl so like one of Raphael's beautiful virgins, to the smaller children with the faces of angels whom Rubens himself would not have disowned. Also in this house lived a grandfather, most venerable in appearance, his hair whitened by the years, but quite unhampered by infirmity. When we had finished lunch, which we all ate together, he stood up, took off his cap, and with great respect announced: 'Let us drink to the health of our beloved President.' In those days there was not a single cabin, no matter how deeply buried in the forests, where this expression of love for the great Washington was not observed after every meal. Sometimes the health of 'The Marquis' was added. M. de La Fayette had left a much-loved memory in the United States.

At Lebanon there was a sulphur bath establishment which was already quite well known. The inn was very good and, above all, impeccably clean. But the luxury of white sheets was still unknown in that part of the United States. To ask for sheets that had not been used by others would have been considered a quite unreasonable caprice and, when the bed was fairly wide, you would even be asked, as if it were the most normal thing in the world, to allow someone to share it with you. This happened to M. de Chambeau that very evening at Lebanon. In the middle of the night, we suddenly heard a stream of French oaths, which could come only from him. In the morning, he told us that at about midnight, he had been awakened by a gentleman who was sliding, without so much as a 'by your leave' into the empty half of the double bed in which he was sleeping. Furious at this invasion, he had promptly leapt out at the other side and spent the night in a chair listening to the snores of his companion, who had been in no way disturbed by M. de Chambeau's anger. This misadventure led to much teasing from everyone. When we arrived that evening at Albany, a small room was reserved for him alone and that consoled him.

The town of Albany, capital of the county, had been almost entirely burned down two years before, as the result of a negro plot. In the State of New York, slavery had not yet been abolished except for children born in 1794 and after, on attaining their twentieth year. This was a very wise measure as it obliged the owners of slaves to support them during childhood and compelled the slaves, for their part, to work sufficiently long for their master to repay the cost of their upbringing. One negro, a very bad lot, who had hoped that the Government's measure would give him unconditional liberty, resolved to avenge his disappointment. He collected a few other malcontents and they resolved to set fire to the city on a certain day. Most of the buildings were still of wood and this horrible plot succeeded beyond their wildest imaginings. The fire caught hold in twenty places at once and despite the efforts of the inhabitants, led by old General Schuyler and his entire family, houses, shops and merchandise were reduced to ashes. A small twelve-year-old negress was caught in the act of setting fire to her master's hay store. She revealed the names of the plotters and the following day the Court assembled in the smoking débris of the building where it always held its sessions and condemned the negro leader and six of his accomplices to be hanged. The sentence was carried out there and then.

The Renslaer and Schuyler families accomplished wonders of enlightened generosity and the energy with which they set about repairing the effects of the disaster set an example to everyone. Convoys arrived from New York laden with merchandise, bricks and furniture and a charming new town gradually rose on the ashes of the old. The new houses were of stone or brick, usually the latter, roofed with sheets of zinc and tin plate. By the time we arrived in Albany, no trace of the fire remained.

The houses of General Schuyler and his son-in-law, Mr Renslaer, were both surrounded by gardens and had not been touched by the fire. There, we found a welcome that was as flattering as it was kind. When General Schuyler saw me, he exclaimed: 'And now I shall have a sixth daughter.' He entered into all our plans, our wishes and our interests. He spoke French perfectly, as did all his family. This is the place to tell you something of his family, or rather, of that of his son-in-law. It was very powerful in the county of Albany which had been originally settled by the Dutch. Before William III usurped the throne of England,* in the days when he was still only Prince of Orange and Stadtholder of Holland, Dutch colonists had sailed up the North River, or Hudson, and settled on the flats at the confluence of the Hudson and the Mohawk, a fine plain stretching from Albany to Half Moon Point. One of William's young pages, a member of a noble Guelder family named Renslaer, had been able to win his master's goodwill and one day, as he served the Prince at table, told him of a dream he had had. It was that he had walked behind William, carrying the train of the royal mantle at his coronation as King of England. Hearing this, the Prince of Orange replied that if ever the dream came true, the page might ask any favour and be sure that it would be granted.

Time and events made Renslaer's dream a reality. He reminded William III of his promise, presented him with a map of the county of Orange in the United States and asked for a concession of land in the Mohawk country. Taking a pencil, the king traced a rectangle forty-two miles long and eighteen miles wide, with the North River running through the middle.

Renslaer crossed to America with his unchallengeably legal act of cession and settled in Albany, then a small settlement with few colonists. He attracted others by granting them land on perpetual lease in return for annual payments in grain or silver, usually such very small payments that their only value lay in establishing the rights of the overlord. He also sold lands and farms, thus considerably increasing his fortune. The Revolution enlarged it further still.

When we landed in America, the Renslaer family was divided into numerous branches, all of them wealthy. The eldest member of the family, its head, had married General Schuyler's eldest daughter. People called him 'The Patroon', a Dutch word meaning 'lord'. On the very day of our arrival in Albany we went walking in the evening down a long and lovely street at the end of which we discovered some enclosed grounds surrounded by a plain white fence. It was a

* The settlement referred to was founded in 1625. William III was born in 1650 and it was in 1688 that he was invited by the English Whigs to share the throne of England with his wife, Mary, daughter of James II. James abdicated in 1689 and was succeeded by his daughter and her husband, William of Orange. To Mme de La Tour du Pin it must indeed have been an usurpation. (Tr.)

well tended park, planted with beautiful trees and flowers and in it stood a pretty house, simple in style and with no outward pretentions to art or beauty. Behind it rose extensive outbuildings which gave the whole establishment the air and appearance of a splendid farm, wealthy and carefully tended.

Two days later, we were received in that same house with a kindness, an attentiveness and a friendliness which were never to change. Mrs Renslaer was a woman of thirty who spoke French well, for she had learned it when visiting the headquarters of the French and American armies with her father. She was blessed with a superior mind and a rare accuracy of judgement of both men and things. She had been unable to leave her house for many years and for months at a time would be confined to her armchair, for her health was poor and she suffered already from the illness which caused her death a few years later. From the newspapers she had learned the state of the parties in France, the blunders which had caused the Revolution, the vices of the upper classes and the follies of the middle classes. With extraordinary insight, she had grasped the causes and effects of the disorders in our country better than we had ourselves. She was very anxious to meet M. de Talleyrand, who had just arrived in Philadelphia, having been forced to leave England at eight days' notice. With his usual diabolical shrewdness, he realised that France had not yet completed all the phases of her revolution. He brought us important letters from Holland which Mme d'Hénin had entrusted to his care. She wrote, among other things, that M. de Talleyrand had come to the country of true liberty there to await the end of the period of cruel madness through which France was passing. M. de Talleyrand asked where he could find me on his return from a journey into the interior which he was planning to make with M. de Beaumetz, a friend of his, and an English millionaire from India.

❧❧❧❧❧❧❧❧❧❧ XVIII ❧❧❧❧❧❧❧❧❧❧

As we did not want to stay in Albany itself, General Schuyler undertook to find a nearby farm for us to buy. Meantime, he advised us to board for three months with a farmer of his acquaintance who had a farm not far from that on which his brother, Colonel Schuyler, lived

The *Diane*, 1794. The ship in which the family escaped to America.

Albany, from Van Renslaer's Island.

with his twelve children. We therefore spent only a few days in Albany and then went to stay with this Mr van Buren to learn American ways, for we had made it a condition that we should live with the family and that they should not change the smallest detail of their ordinary routine. It was also agreed that Mrs van Buren would let me help in the house as a daughter would have done. At the same time, M. de Chambeau apprenticed himself to a carpenter in the small new town of Troy, a quarter of a mile from the van Burens' farm. He used to leave on Monday mornings and return on Saturday evenings just to spend Sunday with us. The news of my father-in-law's tragic death* had just reached us and at the same time, M. de Chambeau learned of his own father's death. Being a very good dressmaker, I made my own mourning clothes and my good hostess, seeing my skill with the needle, found it very convenient to have an unpaid sewing woman at her disposal. To engage one from Albany would have cost her a piastre a day and food, including two lots of tea.

My husband went to look at a number of farms, but we waited for the arrival of our money from Holland before deciding which to buy. General Schuyler and Mr Renslaer advised M. de La Tour du Pin to divide these funds into three equal parts: one third for the purchase of the farm itself; another third for its furnishings – the provision of negroes, cows, agricultural implements and furniture; the remaining third to be added to what was left of the 12,000 francs we had brought with us from Bordeaux and set aside to meet any unexpected demands, such as the loss of negroes or cattle and to cover our living expenses during the first year. We adopted this guiding principle.

I resolved to equip myself to run my house as well as any good farmer's wife. I began by accustoming myself to never remaining in bed after sunrise. In summer, I was up and dressed by three o'clock in the morning. My room opened on to a small lawn stretching down to the river. When I say 'opened', I am not referring to a window, but to the door itself which was level with the lawn. From my bed I could, without moving, have watched the boats pass by.

The van Buren's farm, an old Dutch house, occupied a delightful position at the water's edge. It had no approach from landward, but was easily reached across the river. Opposite, on the road to Canada, stood a large inn where all the news, gazettes and sales notices were to be found. Two or three stage coaches stopped there every day. Van Buren owned two canoes and the river was always so calm that it could be crossed at any time. The property was unbroken by any

* He was executed on 28 April 1794.

road and its boundaries were marked a few hundred *toises** away by a hill covered with fine trees which also belonged to the van Burens. We used to say sometimes that this farm would suit us very well, but its price was more than we could afford. It was indeed only that which prevented us from buying it, for in the America of those days, and I think it may not have changed, no matter how attached a man might be to his house, his farm, his horse or his negro, if he were offered a price one-third higher than the real value, he could be relied upon to sell. It was a country where everything had a reckoned value.

A path led from the farm to the small new town of Troy. For a quarter of a mile, it passed between grasses which were cut each autumn to provide bedding for the cows. The speed at which plants grew in the soil near the stream was prodigious. Grasses which were only five or ten inches high when we arrived, had grown by the time we left in September, two months later, to a height of eight or ten feet. You could walk in their shade. Later on, I rode on horseback through fields of Indian corn which stood much taller than me mounted on my horse.

A few days after our arrival at the van Burens, I needed to go to Troy to buy various things. I was told to follow the path and to be careful not to leave it. I came in this way to the point where a creek, or stream, joined the Hudson River. It was filled with great logs floating on their way to a recently opened sawmill. They were bound together and could not separate. But not being, as yet, very seasoned, I hesitated to trust myself to this moving bridge, especially as the tide was high. I noticed that the path, which ended at the water's edge, began again on the opposite bank and that the logs bore traces of footsteps. Obviously, it was a crossing. Black was with me and went backwards and forwards over the logs several times. But Black was very light and I . . . ? However, I was ashamed to return to the house and admit that I had not dared to cross. Everyone would laugh at me. It was a bad moment. And then, realising that if there had been any danger, I would have been warned, I stepped on to the first log. It dipped a little, but I saw that was the worst it would do and that the danger was not, after all, very frightening. I was careful not to tell anyone of my fears and later on crossed there every day without hesitation.

In September, my husband opened negotiations with a farmer whose land lay two miles inland on the other side of the river, on the

* Literally, a fathom. An old French lineal measure equalling originally the distance between the extremities of both arms outstretched, i.e., 6 feet.

road from Troy to Schenectady. It lay on a hill overlooking a wide
stretch of country and we thought it a very pleasant situation. The
house was new and pretty, and in good condition. Only a part of the
land was in cultivation. There were 150 acres under crops, a similar
area of woodland and pasture, a small kitchen garden of a quarter of
an acre filled with vegetables, and a fine orchard sown with red
clover and planted with ten-year-old cider apple trees, all in fruit.
We were told that the price was twelve thousand francs, which
General Schuyler thought not excessive. The property was four
miles from Albany, on the route of the road it was planned to build
between Albany and Schenectady, a town which was then expand-
ing rapidly. In other words, it was 'in a thriving situation', an all-
important phrase over there.

The owner did not want to move until after the snow had settled.
Since our agreement with the van Burens had been for two months
only and since it was clear that they had had enough of us, this
meant we had to find other lodgings from 1 September to 1 November. At Troy, for a modest rent, we found a little wooden house
standing in a large yard enclosed by clapboard walls. We moved in
and, as it would eventually be necessary to buy certain furnishings
for the farm, decided to buy them now. These, added to what we had
brought from Europe, made it possible for us to move in without
delay. I had engaged a very reliable white girl. She was to be married
in two months' time and agreed to enter my service while waiting for
her future husband to finish building the log house where they were
to live after their marriage.

I must explain what is meant by a log house, though it is more
easily drawn than described. A site fourteen to fifteen feet square is
levelled off and, before any other work is begun, a brick chimney is
built. This is the most important part of the house. Next, the walls
are put up, built with large planks of wood still covered in bark and
cut to fit very closely together. On these, is set the roof, with a hole
for the chimney. A door is then cut into the south wall. You can see
many such buildings in Switzerland, in the pastures of the Upper
Alps, where they are used only for sheltering cattle and the herds-
men. In America, they represent the first step in settlement – and
often the last, for there are always the unlucky ones and, when a
town has prospered, these log houses become the refuge of the poor.

Betsey, then, was waiting until her future husband, an odd-job
man, had built a house for her to live in. He hired himself out by the
day, working sometimes in the small gardens of the townsfolk who
kept those shops where one found such an amazing assortment of

goods: nails and ribbons, muslin and salted pork, needles and ploughshares. The rest of the time, he took on a variety of jobs. He earned up to a dollar or piastre a day and is certainly by now a wealthy man and the owner of property.

One day, towards the end of September, I was   .t in the yard, chopper in hand, busy cutting the bone of a leg of mutton which I was about to roast on the spit for our dinner. As Betsey did not cook, I had been left in charge of everything concerned with food and, with the help of the *Cuisine Bourgeoise*, tried to acquit myself as well as possible. Suddenly, from behind me, a deep voice remarked in French: 'Never was a leg of mutton spitted with greater majesty.' Turning quickly round, I saw M. de Talleyrand and M. de Beaumetz. They had arrived in Albany the previous day and learned our where-abouts from General Schuyler. They had come, on his behalf, to invite us to dine and spend the next day with them at his house. These gentlemen were to stay only two days in Albany as the English friend travelling with them was extremely anxious to return to New York. However, as M. de Talleyrand was so amused at the sight of my leg of mutton, I insisted he should return the following day and share it with us. This he promised to do. Leaving the children in the care of M. de Chambeau and Betsey, we went off to Albany. And that is the whole story of my meeting with M. de Talleyrand, a meeting which Mme d'Abrantès and Mme de Genlis have invested with stupid and ridiculously romantic circumstances.

We had much to talk about on the road and passed from one subject to another as people do when they meet after a long interval. They had returned only the previous evening from their journey to Niagara and had therefore heard none of the latest news from Europe, which was worse than ever. Blood flowed everywhere in Paris. Mme Elisabeth* had perished. Each of us had relatives and friends among the victims of the Terror. Nor could we see where it would end.

When we reached the good general's house, he was on the steps making signs to us from afar and shouting: 'Come along, come along! There's fine news from France!' We hurried into the draw-ing-room and each seized a gazette. There were accounts of the revolt of 9 Thermidor, of the death of Robespierre† and his supporters, the end of the murders and the just execution of the members of the Revolutionary Tribunal. We all rejoiced together, but the deep

* Sister of Louis XVI, imprisoned with him and his family. Guillotined in May 1794.
† Robespierre: lawyer, ardent disciple of Rousseau and a Jacobin. In July 1793, he gained control of the all-powerful Committee of Public Safety and became

mourning worn by my husband and me bore sad witness to the fact that, for us, this divine justice had arrived too late. We, personally, had less cause for rejoicing than M. de Talleyrand and M. de Beaumetz.

The former rejoiced especially that his sister-in-law, Mme Archambauld de Périgord, had escaped death, but much later in the evening, taking up a gazette he thought he had already read, he found the terrible list of victims executed on the morning of 9 Thermidor itself, during the actual session at which Robespierre was denounced, and in that list he found her name. He was grievously stricken at the news. His brother, who had never troubled about his wife, had left France as early as 1790 and as their fortune belonged to her, he had found it more fitting and, above all, more convenient, that it should be she who remained behind in France to ensure that the property was not confiscated. This virtuous woman had obeyed his wishes and when, after she had been condemned, it was suggested to her that she should declare herself pregnant, which would have ensured her safety within a few hours, she had refused to do so. She left three children: Mme Juste de Noailles, now the Duchesse de Poix, and two sons: Louis, who died with the Army under Napoleon, and Edmond, who married the youngest daughter of the Duchesse de Courlande. If it had not been for this very sad piece of news, our evening with General Schuyler would have been extremely pleasant.

Mr Law, who was travelling with M. de Talleyrand and M. de Beaumetz, might well be considered the most eccentric of Englishmen, though they are all eccentric in a greater or lesser degree. He was a tall, fair man, between forty and forty-five, with a handsome, melancholy face. When preoccupied with some idea, the entire house might fall about his ears without making him look up. In the evening, on their way back to the inn, he suddenly said to M. de Talleyrand:

'Mon cher, we won't leave tomorrow.'

'Why not? You have booked your passage on the sloop sailing down to New York.'

the most powerful man in France. He did not start the Terror but used it to further his ideal: a France based on his interpretation of Rousseau's theories of Virtue, Peace and Religion. Christianity was banned. On 7 May 1793, he had secured from the National Convention a decree recognising Rousseau's 'Supreme Being', and on 25 July made a long speech in the Convention for the establishment of a more concentrated form of Government, perhaps even Rousseau's dictatorship. But the Convention mustered courage to protest and when he tried again the following day, 9 Thermidor, he was refused a hearing, arrested and executed. With his death, the Terror came to an end.

'Oh, that doesn't matter. I don't want to go. These people from Troy whom you went to fetch . . . .'

'Well, what about them?'

'I wish to see them again, often. Will you be going to see them tomorrow?'

'Yes.'

'Then I will come to fetch you there in the evening. I want to see that woman in her own home.'

And he fell silent again. Nothing would persuade him to say more.

Next morning, M. de Talleyrand and my husband lunched with our fatherly general before returning to Troy. I had left earlier in the morning since I had to prepare dinner for our guest. A little negro boy driving a carriole, a carriage rather like the horse-drawn chairs – the 'baroccini' – which cover Tuscan roads at such a pace, and easily hired in Albany for a dollar, had carried me back to my duties as cook and steward.

M. de Talleyrand was amiable, as he unvaryingly was to me, and his conversation had a peerless grace and ease. He had known me since my childhood and so talked to me in a fatherly, kindly manner which had great charm. One might, in one's innermost mind, regret having so many reasons for not holding him in respect but memories of his failings were always dispelled by an hour of his conversation. Worthless himself, he had, oddly enough, a horror of faults in others. Listening to him without knowing him, one might have believed him a virtuous man. Only his exquisite sense of propriety prevented him from saying things to me which would have displeased me and if, as sometimes happened, they did escape him, he would recollect himself immediately, and say: 'Ah yes, you do not approve of that.'

In the evening, Mr Law came with M. de Beaumetz to take tea with us. I already had a cow, and was able to give them excellent cream. We went walking. Mr Law offered me his arm and we talked for a long time together. He was a brother of Lord Llandaff and when still very young had gone to India where for fourteen years he was Governor of Patna, or something of the kind. There, he married a very rich Brahmin widow, by whom he had two sons, who were still children. His wife had died, leaving him a considerable fortune. He returned to England, but grew bored and decided to come to America and use part of the money he had brought from India to buy land. His intention was to discover if this new nation merited the esteem he was ready to give it. I doubted if it did and said so, but he did not agree with me. He had created for himself an imaginary America and clung to his own idea. He was an idealist, but witty and cultivated, both a poet and an historian. He had written a number of interesting pieces in English concerning the history of the Mogol* and had translated a Hindu poem written by the last ruler,† whose eyes had been put out and who had been in prison for I do not know how many years.

After promising to send me this translation the next day, he fell into a deep reverie and did not speak again till the end of our walk. Then, as he re-entered the house, he sighed deeply, saying to himself: 'Poor Mogol.'

Two days later, we went to spend the day at Mrs Renslaer's house with all the Schuylers. M. de Talleyrand had been extremely impressed by Mrs Renslaer's outstanding qualities of mind and found it difficult to believe, from her manner of judging men and events, that she had not spent many years in Europe. It was also very interesting to hear her talk of America and the revolution there, for she had a wide and very profound knowledge of it, thanks to her brother-in-law, Colonel Hamilton, Washington's friend and closest confidant.

Colonel Hamilton was expected in Albany, where he intended to spend some time with his father-in-law, General Schuyler. He had just left the Ministry of Finance of which he had had charge ever since the peace, and it was thanks to him that such excellent order had been established in that branch of the United States' Government. M. de Talleyrand knew him and had the highest regard for him. But he found it very strange that a man of his quality, blessed with such oustanding gifts, should resign a ministry in order to return to the practice of law, giving as his reason that in ministerial office he did not earn enough to bring up his eight children. Such an excuse seemed more than a little odd to M. de Talleyrand and even rather silly.

After dinner, Mr Law took M. de Talleyrand by the arm and led him into the garden where they remained quite a long time. The departure of these gentlemen had been arranged for the following day and they had decided they would come to Troy during the morning to say goodbye to us. After talking with M. de Talleyrand, Mr Law said he had letters to write and returned to his inn. M. de Talleyrand, taking my husband and me into a corner of the drawing-room, told us that Mr Law had said to him, using these very words: 'My dear friend, I like those people – meaning us – very much and it

* The Grand Mogol, ruler of the former empire of the Mogols, or Mongols, in Hindustan, from the sixteenth to nineteenth centuries.
† Chah-Alem II, 1759–1806.

is my intention to lend them a thousand louis. They have just bought a farm. They need cattle, horses, negroes and so on. So long as they live in this country, they will not repay my loan . . . in any case, I would not allow them to do so . . . I feel that to be useful to them will procure my own happiness and if they refuse . . . my nerves are very bad . . . I shall fall ill. Truly, they will render me a service in accepting my offer.' Then he added: 'That woman, so well bred! Who does her own cooking . . . who milks the cow . . . who does her own washing. I find it intolerable . . . the thought of it kills me . . . for two nights now, I have not been able to sleep because of it.'

M. de Talleyrand was too well bred to ridicule such a state of mind. He asked us very seriously what answer he was to give. To tell the truth, we felt very deeply touched by this proposal, despite the odd manner in which it was made. We asked him to express to his friend our sincere gratitude and to assure him that for the moment we were able to meet all the needs of our establishment, but that if, later on, for some unexpected reason, we should find ourselves in difficulty, we promised to have recourse to him. This promise, of which he was informed that same evening, calmed Mr Law a little. The following morning, he came to say goodbye. The poor man was as embarrassed as if he had done something wrong. I shook his hand warmly and most sincerely, but made no mention of what had passed. He had brought me his translation of the Mogol's poem into English verse. To my great surprise, I recognised it to be the story of Joseph and his love for the wife of Potiphar, word for word as it is told in the Bible.

We waited impatiently for the first snow to fall and for the moment when the river would freeze over for three or four months. The freeze-up happens suddenly and, if the ice is to be solid, it has to harden within twenty-four hours to a depth of two or three feet. This was a local peculiarity, due solely to the enormous stretches of forest which covered that huge continent to the west and north of the settlements in the United States, and quite unconnected with the latitude of the region. Since the lakes are today – that is to say, in 1843 – almost entirely surrounded by cultivated land, it is very probable that the climate of the region where we lived has greatly changed. However that may be, at the time of which I am writing, things were as I shall describe them.

Between 25 October and 1 November, the sky would become covered by a mass of cloud so thick that the daylight grew dark. These clouds were driven very violently before a horribly cold north-west wind and everyone began preparing to put under cover

everything that could not be left out and buried under the snow.
Boats, canoes and ferries were hauled out of the water and those
which were not decked in were turned keel upward. It was a time of
intense activity for everyone. Then the snow would begin to fall, so
thickly that it was impossible to see a man at ten paces. Usually, the
river would have frozen hard two or three days earlier. The first
precaution was to mark with pine branches a wide path along one of
the river banks. Places where the bank was not steep and where it
was safe to walk on the ice were similarly marked. It would have
been dangerous to walk anywhere except between these markers for
in many places the ice at the edge was not very solid. Every year
there were accidents through lack of care. Indeed, since the tidal
rise and fall at Albany, and as far up as the junction of the Mohawk,
was some seven or eight feet, the ice was often unsupported by
water. It therefore sometimes happened that careless people drove
their sledges down the bank at a trot or a gallop and, instead of
gliding over the ice, were engulfed beneath it and perished, for there
was no means of rescuing them.

We had bought moccasins, which resemble slippers, of buffalo-
hide, made and sold by the savages. Sometimes, as for instance,
when they are embroidered with dyed bark or porcupine quills, they
are quite costly. It was when buying these shoes that I saw the
savages for the first time, the last survivors of the Mohawk people
whose territory had been bought or seized by the Americans after
the war. At about the same time, the Onondagas, who lived near
Lake Champlain, had also sold their forests and dispersed. Occasionally some of them would be seen in the neighbourhood. I was
rather startled, it must be admitted, the first time I met a man and a
woman, both stark naked, walking calmly along the road. But no one
seemed to find it strange and I soon grew used to it. When I was
living at the farm, I saw these people nearly every day during the
summer time.

We took advantage of the days immediately following the marking out of the road and the treading of the snow to begin our removal.
The funds we had been waiting for from Holland had arrived and my
grandmother, Lady Dillon, who was still alive, sent me – although
she had never seen me – three hundred louis* which we used to buy
farm implements. We already owned four good horses and two work
sledges. A third was kept for our personal use and was known as the

* In fact, Lady Dillon, who had died on 19 June 1794, had left Mme de La Tour
du Pin a legacy of three hundred guineas for the purpose, as her will states, of
'wearing mourning for her'.

'pleasure sledge'. It held six people and was rather like a very shallow box. At the back was the main bench, a little wider than the remainder of the sledge, mounted above a cupboard which served to hold small packages, and with a back-piece higher than head level to shelter us from the wind. The other benches, two in number, were just simple planks. Buffalo skins protected our feet. The sledge was drawn by two horses and travelled very fast.

When this equipage was complete, we moved into the farm, although the people from whom we were buying it had not yet moved out. They showed little regard for our wishes or convenience and, as they were in no hurry to leave, we found ourselves obliged literally to force them out.

During this time, we bought a negro and this purchase, which seemed so very normal, gave me such a strange sensation that I shall always remember the smallest circumstance connected with it. As I said earlier, the Government had decreed that negroes born in 1794 would be set free on reaching the age of twenty. But some had already been freed, either by their masters as a reward, or for some other reason. A custom had also been established which no owner would have dared to disregard for fear of incurring public disapproval: when a negro was dissatisfied with his situation he could go to a Justice of the Peace and send his master an official request to be sold. By common usage, the owner was then compelled to allow him to seek another master willing to pay a certain sum for him. The owner could enforce a delay of three months or six, but rarely did so, not usually wishing to keep a worker or servant known to be anxious to leave him. The negro, for his part, would look for someone willing to buy him. Usually, he would find a new master before telling the one he wished to leave. That is what happened in our case. Betsey, who was very well thought of, had sung our praises and was very sad at leaving us. A few pieces of ribbon and some old gowns that I had given her had secured me, at very little expense, a surprising reputation for generosity, a reputation which had reached even the farmers in the old Dutch colony. A young negro there, named Minck, wished to leave the master on whose property he had been born, in order to escape from the severity of his father, a negro like himself, and of his mother. He brought us written permission to find another situation and when we made enquiries, we learned that he was indeed treated with extreme harshness and, as the boy's father himself asked us to buy his son, we agreed to do so.

We climbed into our red and yellow sledge, drawn by our two excellent black horses and drove about four miles to a part of the country – a tract of land, as they call it – where there were eight or ten neighbouring farms, all owned by people named Lansing. This arose from the fact that the first man to settle there would have bought the land when it was covered with forest and cost only four or five sous an acre. He would have begun the work of clearing the ground and his children would have continued it. Each son would then build on the land he had cleared a house exactly like the original from which they came. For this reason, it is not uncommon to spend an entire day going from farm to farm, finding them all occupied by owners of the same name, yet none of them the person one is seeking.

However, since we knew the baptismal name of our negro – always supposing that he had been baptised – we reached the pretty house of Mr Henry Lansing. It was in brick, which indicated a standing to which we ourselves did not aspire. There, we asked Mrs Lansing for Minck. True to the Dutch tradition still strong in her, she was anxious to discover, in her rather halting English, if we had brought the money. My husband counted out on the table the thousand francs I had been holding under my cloak and, at that moment, Mr Lansing came in. He was a tall man, dressed in a good coat of home-spun grey cloth. He called Minck in and, taking his hand, put it into my husband's saying: 'This is your master.' When that had been done, we told Minck that we were leaving. But Mrs Lansing had set out Madeira wine and cake for us and we had to accept them under pain of being thought unneighbourly. In the course of conversation, Mr Lansing learned that my husband had represented the King of France in Holland, his mother country, as he called it. His opinion of us rose prodigiously. We took our leave and found Minck already installed in the sledge. He had gone up to his room and put on his best clothes. These belonged to him, for he took nothing that had been bought with his master's money, not even his moccasins. All his other personal belongings, few enough to have been carried in the crown of a hat, he put into the sledge locker and then, turning to us and touching his hat in a manner that would have done honour to a well-trained English coachman, pointed to the horses and asked me: 'Are they *my* horses?' Told that they were, he took up the reins and set off at a gallop for his new home, much more carefree than I, for it was the first time I had ever bought a man and I still felt quite overcome by the way in which it had been done.

A few days later, the people from whom we had bought the farm moved out, leaving the house dirty and in poor condition, which considerably lowered their reputation. They were English colonists, that is to say, from the coast. They had lived several years on the farm and were leaving because it had become too small for them. They intended clearing fresh land on the far side of the river. These people had not been able to raise sufficient money to permit the different generations of the family to separate and form their own establishments. To continue living together was a sign of poverty, bad management or lack of intelligence. The Americans are like bees: swarms must leave the hive from time to time, never to return.

As soon as we had the house to ourselves, we devoted a little of our money to setting it in order. It consisted of only a ground floor, raised five feet above the earth. The builders had first sunk a wall six feet into the ground, leaving only two feet above ground level. This formed the cellar and the dairy. Above it, the remainder of the house was of wood, of a type still frequently seen in the Emmenthal region of Switzerland. The gaps in the wooden frame were filled with sun-dried bricks which made the wall compact and very warm. We had the inside walls covered with a layer of plaster into which some colour had been mixed and the general effect was very pretty.

M. de Chambeau had put his four months' apprenticeship to the master carpenter to excellent use and had become a very skilled workman. It would, in any case, have been impossible for him to dream of growing careless, for my own activity allowed no excuse. My husband and M. de Chambeau might well have said of me as M. de Talleyrand said of Napoleon: 'Anyone who could teach a little idleness to that man would benefit the universe.'

By taking a new situation, Minck had sought to escape not only from his master's severity but also from his father's. He was therefore cruelly disappointed a few days later when he saw his father arrive at our farm to arrange with us the price for his purchase. He was a negro of between forty-five and forty-eight years of age, with a considerable reputation for intelligence, industry and knowledge in agricultural matters. He had cleverly and rightly calculated that, with masters of good social standing but without experience, it would be easy for him to assume control of the house and make himself indispensable. His really superior mind had often thought of improvements but old Lansing had never been willing to listen. He longed to be with new people who would not be ruled entirely by prejudice, unlike his Dutch master who would not allow the slightest change in practices that dated back a hundred years.

We went to consult General Schuyler and Mr Renslaer, both of whom knew this negro by reputation. They congratulated us on his wish to belong to us and made us promise to take him, even advising us to consult him on all the details of farm methods. We bought him very cheaply because of his age, for it was no longer permitted to sell a negro aged more than fifty. Mr Lansing even used this as a reason for not selling him to us but the negro, producing his certificate of baptism, proved he was only forty-eight. We were glad to have him on the farm. The only person who did not share our satisfaction was his son. The father's name was Prime, a nickname given him because of his general superiority.

To conclude this tale of our settling-in and of our negroes, I will tell you that we bought two more and made them very happy. One was a woman. She had been married for fifteen years and had lost all hope of being reunited to the husband she adored because her master, a brutal and wicked man, always refused to sell her. Prime persuaded us to buy the husband, an excellent man and a good worker, and I thought it would be a good idea to buy the woman as well. I needed a negress for I had too much to do and a daily woman would have cost me too much.

I therefore went by sledge one morning, with a bag of money, to fetch this negress, whose name was Judith, from her master's house. His name was Wilbeck and he was a brother of Mr Renslaer's agent. I told him that I had learned from the Patroon of his intention to sell Judith. He refused, saying she was very useful to him. I replied that he must know it was impossible to refuse to sell a negro who wished to be sold. I added that this woman had told him such was her wish and that, thereupon, he had beaten her almost to death and that she was still ill as a result of it. Brutally, he replied that she could find another master when she was cured. 'Send for her,' I told him, 'she has found one.' She came. Learning that I had bought her husband and wished to buy her also so that they might be reunited, the poor woman sank fainting on to a chair. Then Wilbeck, who knew of our friendship with Mr Renslaer, dropped his opposition. I counted out the money before him and told Judith that her husband would come the following day to fetch her and her small daughter. This three-year-old child had, by law, to go with her mother. And that is how we collected our negro staff. We were indeed exceedingly fortunate. The woman, like her husband, was excellent, both of them being active, hard-working and intelligent. They became passionately devoted to us, for negroes, when they are good, are exceedingly good. Their devotion could be counted on to death itself. Judith was thirty-four and very ugly, but that did not prevent her husband being madly attached to her. M. de Chambeau arranged that they should have a room in the granary entirely to themselves, a comfort they had not dared to hope for in even their wildest dreams.

I remember these good people with pleasure. After serving me well, they gave me, as you will see later, what I have rightly called the finest day in my life.

❦❦❦❦❦❦❦❦❦❦❦ XIX ❦❦❦❦❦❦❦❦❦❦❦❦

Two French families with whom we had become acquainted lived in Albany. They were quite different from one another. The first was the family of a small shopkeeper named Genetz, a very common man who had arrived in the district with a certain amount of money and a great variety of drapery goods. He was outwardly amiable but at heart a thorough blackguard and a secret supporter of the Revolution. However, as he rented his small lodging from a French Creole who was a friend of ours, we were careful to treat him as a compatriot.

This Creole was from San Domingo and had known my father well. I had myself met him at my father's house in Paris. His name was Bonamy and he had been completely ruined by the fire which destroyed the Cape.* All that remained to him was a small sum of money invested in France, where his wife, who came from Nantes, had taken refuge with her two daughters. She had since died and the daughters, still children, had gone to live with uncles who were bringing them up. M. Bonamy had been declared an émigré and could return neither to San Domingo nor to France. He was therefore looking for some way of earning his living when the ten or twelve thousand francs he had saved from the Cape should be exhausted. He was a very well-bred man, knowledgeable, even learned, witty, charming and adaptable. He often came to our house, usually arriving on Saturday and staying until Monday. Prime used to fetch him in the sledge on his way back from market, where he went nearly every day to sell a load of wood, as well as butter and cream for breakfast.

My butter was much in demand. Using a mould with our monogram, I used to cut it into neat pats and arrange them in a very clean basket on a fine cloth. We sold it to whoever was willing to buy. We

* The town of Cap-Français, burned down in 1793. It was the capital of the French colony of San Domingo. It is today in the republic of Haïti and known as Cap-Haïtien.

had eight well-fed cows and our butter did not taste of winter feed. My cream was always fresh. Every day, the butter and cream earned me a fair sum and the sledge-load of wood brought in at least two piastres.

Prime could neither read nor write but he kept his accounts so accurately that there was never the smallest mistake. He often brought fresh meat back from Albany and, when he returned, my husband would set down the receipts and expenditures according to what Prime told him.

The second of the two French families I mentioned was staying in Albany until they could settle in Blackriver, near Lake Erie. The head of the family, M. Desjardin, was agent for a company owning immense tracts of land and it was his job to re-sell parcels of it to poor Irish, Scottish or even French colonists sent to him by agents in New York.

Let us follow one such group of colonists, people whom I knew, so that you can see how this system worked. The household consisted of the husband, wife, a son of about fifteen, or seventeen, and two daughters. I saw them set off on foot, across the snow, the first three carrying shoulder packs. The husband led a poor horse harnessed to a small sledge on which he had packed two casks, one containing flour and the other salted pork, several axes, gardening and other tools, some bundles and the two small girls.

On reaching Kentucky, a State which flourishes today but where there were then very few settlers, they would have sought out the representative of the person who had sold or rented them the land on which they were to settle. Their first task would have been to cut down trees for the log house, and they would have lodged with neighbours until it was ready. Then they would burn off the brushwood to clear the ground, inevitably scorching the lower branches of the trees in the process. When the snows melted, they would rake the charred pieces with a harrow and sow the corn. Nothing more was needed to ensure a good crop. Little by little, they would use the big trees for building fences to divide the property into sections and the best watered of these would be turned into a meadow or pasture. And there you had a family on the road to prosperity. Any passing traveller would see seven or eight children of all ages about the house, all fresh-looking and healthy, fed on maize flour, milk and butter and busy, from the age of four, at some useful task.

Usually, a small rent would be levied on the property, either in wheat or in money. Our farm paid Patroon Renslaer a rent of fifteen bushels of corn, or an equivalent in money, and a similar rent was payable on all the other farms on his immense property which was eighteen miles wide and forty-two miles long.

M. Desjardin had brought a household of furniture from Europe, including a good library of between 1,000 and 1,500 books. He used to lend them to us and my husband or M. de Chambeau would read to me in the evening while I worked.

We breakfasted at eight o'clock and dined at one. In the evening, we had tea at nine o'clock, with slices of bread spread with our own excellent butter and the good Stilton cheese M. de Talleyrand sent us. With this gift, he had sent another which gave me the greatest pleasure: it was a fine and good lady's saddle, complete with bridle, saddle-cloth and other accessories. Never had a gift been more timely for, when we bought the farm, we had also bought two pretty mares with similar markings and of the same height, though vastly different in temperament. One was lamb-like and although she had never before had a bit in her mouth, I was able to ride her the very first day she was saddled. Within a few days, I was able to teach her manners quite as good as those of a manège-trained horse. She had a very easy movement and followed me around like a dog whenever she could. The other mare was a demon and not all the skill of M. de Chambeau, who had once been a cavalry officer, could tame her. We did not master her until the spring and then it was by making her work between two powerful horses, all three fastened by the nostrils to a wooden bar. The first few times, she was so furious at this treatment that she was in a lather in less than ten minutes. But gradually we succeeded in quietening her. She was a fine mare, worth at least twenty-five to thirty louis.

Speaking of the spring, it is interesting to note the suddenness of its arrival in those regions. It is then that the latitude – 43° – comes into its own and takes charge of the climate. During the first days of March, the north-westerly wind which had been blowing throughout the winter, suddenly dropped. The winds veered to the south. The snow melted so quickly that for two days the roads were raging torrents. As our house was on a hillside, our white blanket disappeared in a very short time. The winter snow had been three or four feet deep, protecting the grass and plants from the ice and so, within a week, the meadows were green and carpeted with flowers and the woods were filled with countless varieties of plants unknown in Europe.

The savages, whom we had not seen during the winter, began to call again at the farms. At the beginning of the cold weather, one of them had asked me if he might cut branches from a kind of willow which has shoots five to six feet long and as thick as a finger, promising to weave baskets for me during the winter. I had put no trust in this promise, being very doubtful if savages were accustomed to keeping their word to such an extent, although I had been assured that they did. I was wrong to doubt, for scarcely a week after the snow had disappeared, my Indian reappeared with a load of baskets. He gave me six, all fitting into one another. The first, round and very large, was so closely woven that it held water as well as any earthenware bowl. I wanted to pay for them, but he firmly refused and would only accept a jar of buttermilk, which the Indians like very much indeed. I had been warned never to give them rum, for which they have an immoderate passion. I was therefore careful not to do so, but in an old box I had some remains of artificial flowers, feathers, ends of ribbon of all colours, balls of blown glass which once upon a time had been very fashionable and these I distributed among the women, who were delighted with them. One of these Indian women, who was very old and very repulsive looking, was called the 'Old Squaw' and, whenever she appeared, my negress was terribly worried for she had the reputation of being a witch and casting spells. If she appeared when chickens were about to hatch, cows to calve, sows to produce a litter, or when one was about to start some important household task, it was essential to ensure her goodwill by offering her something for her personal adornment.

An old woman is always very ugly, even in a civilised setting. Try to imagine this 'Old Squaw', a woman of seventy, with a black, leathery skin, who had spent her entire life with her body naked and exposed to all weathers, her head covered with grey hair that had never known a comb, whose only clothing was a sort of apron of coarse blue cloth and a small woollen shawl thrown over her shoulders and fastened at the two corners under her chin with a wooden brooch, a nail or an acacia thorn – garments which were never renewed until they had fallen away in shreds. Well, this woman, who spoke English quite well, had a mad passion for adornment. She would use anything for this purpose: the tip of an old pink feather, a knot of ribbon, an old flower, any such gift would please her. If, in addition, she were allowed to take a look at herself for a moment in the mirror, you could be certain that she would be favourable to your clutch of eggs and to your cows, that your cream would not turn and that your butter would be of the finest yellow.

But these savages, who knew only a word or two of English and spent all their time wandering from farm to farm, were as sensitive to good manners, to a friendly reception, as any Court gentleman. They soon realised that we did not belong to the same class as the other farmers living near us, and when they spoke of me, would say: 'Mrs Latour from the old country . . . great lady . . . very good to poor squaw.' This word 'squaw' means savage. It is used equally for every creature or object from countries where European civilisation has not yet penetrated. Thus, birds of passage would be called 'squaw pigeons', 'squaw turkeys' and objects brought in by the savages would be 'squaw baskets' and so on.

One day we received a visit from a Frenchman who had been an officer in my husband's regiment, M. de Novion. Having just arrived from Europe, he was delighted to learn that his former colonel had become a farmer. He had brought some funds with him and would have liked to use them to buy a small farm near us. But as he had no knowledge of agriculture, spoke not a single word of English and had neither wife nor children, he lacked all the essential qualifications for setting up a reasonable establishment of that kind. M. de La Tour du Pin explained this to him. But he still wanted to see something of the country, so we went riding together. After a few miles, I realised that I had forgotten my whip. As M. de Novion had no knife with which to cut me a stick, he could not help. The undergrowth in the wood was fairly thick and at that moment, seeing one of my Indian friends sitting behind a bush, I called to him: 'Squaw John.'

It is impossible to describe the surprise, almost horror, of M. de Novion at the apparition which emerged from the bush and came towards us with his hand held out to me: a very tall man wearing only a strip of blue cloth between his legs, fastened to a cord about his waist. His astonishment increased when he saw how well we knew one another and the calm way in which we engaged in a conversation of which he could not understand a single word. As we walked our horses on, and before I had had time to explain how I knew such an odd person in such extraordinary garments, Squaw John leaped lightly from the top of a hillock which dominated the road and politely offered me a stick which he had stripped of its bark with his tomahawk.

I am certain that, in that moment, M. de Novion resolved, deep in his heart, never to live in a country where one was exposed to such encounters. 'And if you had been alone, Madame?' he asked. 'I should have been just as little alarmed,' I told him, 'and, you know, if I had had to defend myself from you and had told him to throw his tomahawk at you, he would have done so without hesitation.' Such a manner of life did not seem to appeal to him. On our return, he told my husband that I had odd friends and that he, for his part, had decided to go and live in New York, where civilisation seemed slightly more advanced.

Our ride was rather long and tired me, which brought on a recurrence of the double tertian fever from which I had been suffering for two months. It had begun as the result of a severe fright about which I have forgotten to tell you.

One day that spring, I had had to go to Troy to fetch something I needed for my work. The negroes were working in the fields with my husband and M. de Chambeau was busy in his carpenter's shop, so I went to the stable, saddled my mare, as I often did, and set out at a canter. On the way back, I crossed in the ferry with the mare to call on a friend who lived in a mill about a mile from the town. She kept me to tea and as it was getting late, I rode back to the ferry at a good pace, which made me very hot. As we left the bank, four large oxen and their driver insisted on coming too, despite the protests of Mat the boatman, who had noticed that the oxen were making my mare nervous. My first impulse was to get out, but it was late and I was afraid my husband would be worried, so I stayed. In midstream, these four enormous beasts, naturally unyoked, all leaned over the same side of the ferry to drink. It heeled over and seemed about to capsize. Mat came to me and told me to let go of my horse and hold on to his belt. I had not, until then, realised the imminence of the danger, but Mat's words made the blood freeze in my veins. Fortunately, just at that critical moment, one of the passengers drew his knife and plunged it into the rump of one of the oxen. The pain made the animal jump overboard. The other three followed and the ferry returned to an even keel, though not before it had shipped so much water that we were standing in it up to our ankles.

Mat urged me to drink a small glass of rum but I refused, which was a big mistake. In a hurry, I mounted and rode back to the farm at a fast gallop. As soon as I arrived, my negress made me take a hot drink, but in spite of it, I had a fever the next day. It returned daily after that, always at the same hour and lasted for the same length of time. Nothing cured it, neither the excellent quinine which M. de Talleyrand sent me from Philadelphia, nor the medicaments of a French surgeon named Rousseau. He may have been no more a physician than I was myself but he was French and had rendered us several services, which was sufficient to give me confidence in him.

These attacks of fever, which lasted between five and six hours, hampered me greatly in my daily work. They weakened me, took away my appetite and, although I never remained in bed, set me shivering even when the temperature stood at 30°. In short, they rendered me quite incapable of work. When this happened, the daughter of some neighbours who lived in the woods not far from us used to come to my rescue. She was a good girl, a dressmaker by trade, and her work was perfect. She arrived at the farm in the morning and stayed all day, asking no wages, only her food.

My son, Humbert, was then five but so tall that he looked at least seven. He spoke English perfectly, much better even than French. A lady living in Albany, a friend of the Renslaers and of the Anglican minister's wife, had become very attached to him. He had spent many afternoons at her house and one day she suggested taking charge of him for the whole summer, promising to teach him to read and write. She pointed out that in the country I did not have sufficient time to devote to him, that he would catch my fever and gave a number of other reasons to persuade me to agree to her request.

This lady was a Mrs Ellison. She was forty years of age and had never had any children, which was an inconsolable grief to her. I ended by agreeing to let her have Humbert and he was very happy with her and very well cared for. This decision removed much of my anxiety. At the farm, I was always afraid of some accident befalling him among the horses, for he loved them dearly. It was almost impossible to prevent him from going out into the fields with the negroes and, above all, from mixing with the savages, with whom he always wanted to wander off. I had been told that the Indians did sometimes carry off children, so that when I saw them sitting for hours at a time motionless at my door, I used to imagine they were watching for an opportunity to steal my son.

A pretty cart laden with fine vegetables often passed through our yard. It belonged to the Quaker Shakers who had a settlement about six or seven miles from us. The driver always stopped at our house and I never missed an opportunity of talking to him about their way of life, their customs and their beliefs. He invited us to visit their settlement, and one day we decided to go.

They were a reformed branch of the original Quakers who had come to America with Penn. After the war of 1763, an Englishwoman proclaimed herself the apostle of reform. She made a number of converts in the States of Vermont and Massachusetts and many families pooled their belongings and bought land in the still un-inhabited parts of the country. However, as the clearances advanced and reached their settlement, they would sell it and retreat still further inland. But they moved only when the land immediately next to theirs had been acquired by someone not of their sect.

The Quakers of whom I am writing were at that time protected on all sides by several miles of thick forest and had therefore nothing as yet to fear from neighbours. Their settlement was bounded on one side by twenty thousand acres of forest belonging to the town of Albany and on the other by a river, the Mohawk. No doubt by now they have moved from the place where I knew them and withdrawn beyond the lakes. The settlement was an offshoot from their main settlement at Lebanon in the great forest we had crossed on our way from Boston to Albany.

Our negro, Prime, who knew every road in those parts, guided us to them. For the first three hours, we travelled through the forest, along a path which was nothing but a vague track. Then, after passing a barrier which marked the boundary of the Quakers' property, the path became clearer and even well kept. But we still had to cross a great stretch of forest interspersed here and there with meadows where cows and horses had been turned loose to graze. Finally, we came to a vast clearing surrounded on all sides by forest, with a fine stream running through it. In the middle of this clearing stood the settlement, consisting of a large number of fine wooden houses, a church, schools and the community house, which was built of brick.

The Quaker we knew gave us a kindly, though reserved welcome. Prime was directed to a stable where he could put up the horses, for there was no inn. We had been warned that no one would offer us anything and that only our guide would speak to us. He took us first to a magnificent kitchen garden, perfectly cultivated; everything in it was as flourishing as it could be, yet there was nothing attractive about it. Numbers of men and women were there, busy tilling and weeding, for the sale of the vegetables was the community's main source of income.

We visited the boys' school and the girls' school, the immense communal stables and the dairies where butter and cheese were made. Everywhere there was perfect order and total silence. All the children, both boys and girls, were dressed alike in clothes of the same shape and colour. The women, whatever their age, were also dressed exactly alike in grey woollen cloth, very neat and spotless. Through the windows could be seen the cloth looms, the lengths of newly-dyed cloth and the workrooms of the tailors and dressmakers. But not one word, not one song broke the silence.

Eventually, a bell rang. Our guide told us it was for prayers and asked if we would like to attend. We gladly agreed and he took us to the largest of the houses. Outwardly, it looked just like all the others. At the door, I was separated from my husband and M. de Chambeau and we were put at opposite ends of an immense room, separated by a chimney in which burned a magnificent fire. It was early spring and, in those great forests, still very cold. This room might have been 150 to 200 feet long and about 50 feet wide. It was entered through two doors, set into the side of the room. It was very light, bare of decoration, its smooth walls painted light blue. At each end was a small platform on which stood a wooden armchair.

I was given a seat in the chimney corner and my guide asked me to remain silent, a request which was easily obeyed since I was alone. While sitting absolutely still, I had time to admire the floor, which was of pine, free from knots, remarkably white and well made. On this beautiful floor, running in various directions, were lines of copper nails, shiningly clean, their heads level with the wood. I was trying to guess the purpose of these lines, for they seemed to have no connection with one another when, on the last peal of the bell, the two doors opened and through the one on my side came fifty to sixty young girls and women, led by another woman of considerable age, who seated herself in one of the armchairs. No children came with them.

The men entered in similar order through the door on the other side where M. de La Tour du Pin and M. de Chambeau were. I noticed then that the women stood on the lines of nails, careful not to allow even the tips of their toes to overlap them. They remained motionless until the woman seated in the armchair gave a sort of groan or shout which was neither speech nor chant. Then they all changed places, so I concluded that that rather stifled cry must have been some form of command. After several manoeuvres, they again stood still and the old woman muttered a fairly long passage in a language which was quite unintelligible to me, but in which I thought I caught a few English words. After this, they left in the same order in which they had entered. Having visited every corner of the settlement, we took leave of our kindly guide and climbed back into our waggon to return home, little impressed with Quaker hospitality.

Whenever the Quaker who took the community's vegetables and fruit to market passed our farm, I always bought something. He would never take money from my hand. If I said that some price was too high, he would say: 'Just as you please,' and I would put at the corner of the table the sum I thought reasonable. If the amount suited him, he took it, if not, he climbed back on to his waggon and went off without a word. He was a very respectable looking man, always impeccably dressed in a coat, waistcoat and trousers of grey homespun made at the settlement.

One action of mine had won me immediate popularity: on the day
I moved into the farm, without referring to the change, I adopted
the dress worn by the women on neighbouring farms – the blue and
black striped woollen skirt, the little bodice of dark calico and a
coloured handkerchief. I parted my hair in the style fashionable
today: swept up and held in place with a comb. In summer, I wore
cotton stockings and shoes. Only when I was going into town did
I wear a gown or stays. Among the things I had brought to America
were two or three riding habits. I used them to transform myself
into a lady of fashion when I was going to visit the Schuylers or the
Renslaers, for more often than not we dined and spent the remainder
of the evening with them, especially when there was a good moon
and, above all, snow. While the snow lasted, the road, once marked,
formed a track a foot or two deep and the horses never strayed from
it.

Many of our neighbours made a habit of passing through our yard
on the way to Albany. As we knew them all, we never objected.
Besides, in talking to them, I always learned some fresh piece of
news. As for them, they enjoyed talking of the 'old country'. They
also liked to admire our small improvements. It was an elegant small
pigsty of wood made by M. de Chambeau and my husband that
excited the greatest admiration. It was indeed a masterpiece of
carpentering, but the praise was so pompously worded that it always
amused us: 'Such a noble hog sty.'

Early in the summer of 1795, the Duc de Liancourt paid us a visit.
He makes a very kind reference to it in his book *Voyages en Amérique*.*
M. de Talleyrand had given him letters to the Schuylers and the
Renslaers and after he had spent a day with us, I suggested taking
him into Albany to introduce him to these two families. Had he
seriously thought I had only my woollen skirt and calico bodice?
I do not know, but the fact remains that it was only when he saw me
appear in a pretty gown and a very well made hat, though the
milliner had had no hand in it, and when my negro, Minck,
brought round the smart waggon drawn by two excellent horses in a
harness shining with polish, that he seemed to begin to realise we
had not yet been quite reduced to beggary. At that point, it was
I who had to say that nothing would persuade me to take him to call
on Mrs Renslaer and Mrs Schuyler unless he did something to
improve his appearance. His clothes were covered in mud and dust,
torn in a number of places and he looked like some shipwrecked

* *Voyages dans les Etats Unis d'Amérique fait de 1795–1798*, by the Duc de la
Rochefoucauld-Liancourt. Published in 8 vols in 1800.

sailor just escaped from pirates. No one would have guessed that such an odd collection of garments clothed a First Gentleman of the Bedchamber! We made a bargain: I agreed to take him to call on Mrs Renslaer and Mrs Schuyler and he agreed to open his trunk, which he had left at the inn at Albany, and dress more suitably. I went to pay a call in the town while he changed. The transformation was not to be so complete as M. de Liancourt had allowed me to hope. I reproached him bitterly, especially for the patch on the knee of a pair of nankeen breeches which must have come all the way from Europe, so worn were they from laundering.

When we had paid our calls, he promised to return to the farm the following day and I left him in Albany and took back with me his travelling companion, M. Dupetit-Thouars.

The latter remained a number of days with us while M. de Liancourt visited the country around the town. M. Dupetit-Thouars, a very amiable man, was on his way from Asilum, that French settlement in Carolina which had proved such a failure.* The settlers had disagreed among themselves and had not put their money to the best uses so that, by the end of a year, everything had had to be sold at a loss and they had all gone their separate ways. M. Dupetit-Thouars, who was witty and gay, gave us the most amusing descriptions of the breaking up of this settlement and the three or four days he spent at the farm left us with very pleasant and agreeable memories. He died gloriously some years later at Aboukir.†

As for M. de Liancourt, I never saw him again. The double tertian fever from which I suffered continuously, made it impossible for me to ride or go visiting. In any case, that philanthropic nobleman, always so ready to point out their shortcomings to the people of a country but never ready to learn from them, had displeased me greatly. The friends we visited together had liked him no better. Intelligent Mrs Renslaer had at first sight declared him to be a very mediocre man. I shall be thought ungrateful to speak so badly of him for, in his book, he has spoken of me most flatteringly, but I must admit, with shame, that the only part of the book I remember is the passage I inspired.

A few days after M. de Liancourt's visit, in June or thereabouts,

---

* Tradition has it that there were royalist plans to bring Queen Marie-Antoinette to this settlement. A house was prepared. After her execution, the plot centred around the Dauphin and one of the legends is that he did come, but was almost immediately kidnapped by revolutionary agents and never heard of again. (Tr.)
† M. Dupetit-Thouars, one of the leading settlers in Asilum, was by profession a naval officer. Nelson destroyed Napoleon's fleet in Aboukir Bay in 1802. (Tr.)

we received a letter from M. de Talleyrand telling us of something which might have had serious consequences for us, and of the very great service he had just rendered us in that connection. The balance of the funds we were to receive from Holland, some twenty to twenty-five thousand francs, had been consigned to the firm of Morris in Philadelphia. M. de Talleyrand had undertaken to withdraw this sum and was waiting for the necessary authorisation from my husband. By a truly providential piece of good fortune, he learned one evening, from an indiscreet conversation, that Mr Morris was to be declared bankrupt the following day. Losing not a minute, he hurried round to see the banker, forced an entrance when admittance was denied him, and reached his office. He told Mr Morris that he knew of his position and obliged him to hand over certain Dutch bills of exchange which he held only in trust. Mr Morris allowed himself to be persuaded, for he greatly feared the disgrace which would have fallen upon him if such a breach of trust had become known, a course M. de Talleyrand would not have hesitated to take. He made only one condition, that M. de La Tour du Pin should sign a statement that the funds had been paid. M. de Talleyrand undertook that my husband would go to Philadelphia to settle the matter. He also advised me to accompany him for, he said, having consulted a number of doctors on the persistent nature of my fever, they had all said that, in their opinion, only a change of air would rid me of it.

Mr Law had a charming house in New York and had several times suggested that we should visit him there. The harvest would not be ready for at least a month. M. de Chambeau knew every detail of the farm routine. There was nothing to prevent such a journey. Susy, the young neighbour whom I mentioned earlier, agreed to come and look after my small daughter. As for my son, Humbert, he was still with Mrs Ellison in Albany and would not even notice our absence.

⚜⚜⚜⚜⚜⚜⚜⚜ XX ⚜⚜⚜⚜⚜⚜⚜⚜

Steamships had not yet been invented, but steam was already being used to provide motive power in a number of factories. We ourselves even had a steam jack* which worked perfectly and which we used every week for our Sunday roast of beef or for those very large

* A contrivance for turning a spit.

brown and white turkeys which are so infinitely superior to the European varieties. But Fulton* had not yet applied his discovery to ships
and since the subject has arisen, I will tell you here what first gave
him the idea.

Between Long Island and New York is a channel about a mile or
so wide across which, when weather permitted, small boats plied
continually. There is no current, for it is not a river, and the only
movement is the rise and fall of the tide, which presents no difficulty
to navigation. There was a certain sailor who, poor man, had lost
both legs in battle. Being still young, he enjoyed excellent health and
had retained considerable strength in his arms. This man had the idea
of fixing across his bark canoe a round bar fitted at each end with
wings. These projected over the sides and could be controlled from
his seat in the stern. One day, he took Fulton across to Brooklyn on
Long Island and as Fulton watched him operate this ingenious
contrivance, he realised for the first time that it might be possible to
use steam power for ships.

The town of Albany did a considerable trade, the merchandise
being carried in large sloops or brigs. Nearly all these boats were
equipped to carry passengers and had good cabins and a pretty
saloon in the stern. The journey down to New York took about
twenty-six hours but a part of that time, the period of the rising tide,
was spent at anchor. Boats always tried to leave Albany at daybreak
so we spent the previous night on board and before sunrise were
already well on our way. The North River, or Hudson, is very
beautiful. Along the banks are a number of houses and pretty little
towns, and the river widens into a stretch of water several miles
broad before narrowing to enter the gorge through that chain of very
high, steeply rising mountains which run the whole length of the
continent of North America and are called by different names in different regions: the Black Mountains, the Appalachians, the Alle-
ghanies. The wide reach is very like that part of Lake Geneva known
as 'le fond du lac', but with this difference: the mountains rise only at
the very far end, and the point where the river flows between two
steep rocks into the gorge itself cannot be seen until one is upon it.
The water in this wonderful gorge is so deep that a large frigate
could tie up to the bank without any danger of running aground. We
sailed through these beautiful mountains during all the following
morning and, when the tide was against us, went ashore to visit West

* Robert Fulton, 1765–1815, an engineer from Pennsylvania. In Paris, in 1794,
he produced a submarine, the *Nautilus*. He produced by 1807 the first steam
vessel of note to ply between New York and Albany. (Tr.)

Point,* famous in history for the treason of General Arnold† and the execution of Major André.‡ The incident is well known, but I will tell you about it briefly.

There had never been any reason to doubt the loyalty of the American general, Arnold, to the cause of the independence of the United States and it was with every confidence that he was entrusted with the defence of the Hudson at the point where it traversed the mountains. The English general, Clinton, was cut off in New York, surrounded by the American army commanded by General Gates. The capture and occupation of West Point was essential to the English to enable them to re-establish communication with Canada. There was apparently reason to think that Arnold's greed would prove stronger than his patriotism. Negotiations with him had already been begun and were to be concluded by young André, a major in the English army, who had visited Arnold several times at West Point. When General Gates discovered the plot, he sent an armed boat to the place on the bank where André would re-embark. The crew of André's small boat warned him of the craft's presence and persuaded him – not foreseeing the sad consequences of their advice – to change into a sailor's clothing. Their small boat had gone less than a quarter of a mile when it was seized by the Americans and Major André was taken prisoner. Being in disguise, he was treated as a spy and, as such, condemned to be hanged.

General Gates offered to exchange him for the traitor, Arnold, who had escaped through the mountains. The English refused. Their need of Arnold's help was too great for them to hand him back. Instead, they sacrificed André, whose execution became the subject of many laments in prose and verse. This young man was only twenty, very distinguished in appearance and exceptionally well-bred. His death provided the motive – or pretext – for cruel reprisals by the English.

Although I have travelled in many lands and seen many of the grandeurs of nature, I have never seen anything to compare with that stretch of river at West Point. Today, it has probably lost much of its beauty, particularly if the fine trees which leaned their centuries-old

* West Point commands the Hudson valley route from New York to Canada. In the War of Independence, General Washington established a headquarters there. Today, it is the home of the U.S. Military Academy. (Tr.)

† Benedict Arnold, 1741–1801, a merchant from Connecticut. After his treachery, he was given a command in the English army. (Tr.)

‡ John André, 1751–80, son of a Genevan merchant. When Arnold offered to betray West Point, André was chosen to negotiate the surrender. There is a memorial to him in Westminster Abbey. (Tr.)

branches into the river, have been felled. However, the steep mountain sides are not suitable for cultivation, so my love of nature makes me hope that the soulless, frenzied clearing of land may have spared them.

We reached New York on the morning of the third day and found that M. de Talleyrand was staying with Mr Law. They gave us a most friendly welcome but were shocked by my thinness and changed appearance. I had intended to travel by the stage coach to Philadelphia with my husband, spending two nights on the way, but this they absolutely refused to allow. So my husband went alone and I was given into the care of Mrs Foster, Mr Law's housekeeper. This excellent lady tried every restorative in her medical repertory in an effort to help me. Four or five times a day she would arrive with a small cup of broth and, curtseying in the English fashion, say 'Pray, ma'am, you had better take this.' I submitted very willingly to her care, so weary was I of listening to M. de Talleyrand's lamentations about my wasting away.

The three weeks that we spent in New York are among my happiest memories. My husband was away only four days, but was able to admire the fine city of Philadelphia and, what I envied still more, to see my hero, the great Washington. Even today, I still regret not having looked on the face of that great man about whom I heard so much from his friend, Mr Hamilton.

In New York, I met all the Hamilton family again. I had been in Albany when they arrived there in a waggon driven by Mr Hamilton himself. He had just retired from the Ministry of Finance to resume his legal practice, a profession more likely to enable him to leave some kind of fortune to his children. Mr Hamilton was then between thirty-six and forty years of age. Although he had never been in Europe, he spoke our language like a Frenchman and his distinguished mind and the clarity of his thought mingled very agreeably with the originality of M. de Talleyrand and the vivacity of M. de La Tour du Pin. Every evening, these three distinguished men, together with M. Emmery,* a member of the Constituent Assembly, Mr Law and two or three other persons of note would forgather after tea and sit on the verandah conversing together until midnight, or even later, under the beautiful starry sky of the 40th latitude. Whether it was Mr Hamilton describing the beginnings of the War of Independence, Mr Law talking of his years in India, of the administration of Patna where he had been Governor, of his elephants and his palanquins, or

* Emmery, Comte de Grozyeulx, President of the Constituent Assembly of 4 January 1790.

my husband raising some argument over the absurd theories of the Constituent Assembly which M. de Talleyrand abandoned so readily, the conversation never dried up.

We also made the acquaintance of a very interesting French merchant family, M. and Mme Olive, who had eight charming children, all under ten. I often went to see them in the country, where they had bought a pretty house in which to spend their summers.

Three weeks passed and then the rumour spread one evening that yellow fever had broken out in a street very close to Broadway where we were staying. That very night, either because we had the first symptoms of the illness or because we had eaten too many bananas, pineapples and other fruit brought from the Caribbean in the same ship that had brought the fever, my husband and I were terribly ill. Fearing to be kept in New York by quarantine measures, I decided to leave immediately. We packed our trunk and went at daybreak to reserve places on a sloop which was ready to sail. We then returned to the house to say goodbye to Mr Law. He decided to leave too, on the pretext of visiting certain properties he had bought in the new town of Washington, where building had just begun. He had invested the greater part of his fortune in these purchases. Our departure was so hurried that I did not even see M. de Talleyrand. By the time he had begun to think of rising, we were already far from New York.

We saw again the fine scenery near West Point, this time from the opposite direction, but with quite as much appreciation. On this occasion, we went for a long walk ashore during the six hours the boat lay at anchor. We climbed the hill on which stood the inn where Arnold had had his last meeting with André. I had seen old General Gates in New York. He had known all the French officers and liked to talk of them. But I had been strongly warned not to mention the Major André incident as the subject was very painful to him. Not because he reproached himself for condemning him to death, a sentence which was in accordance with military law, but because it reminded him of the terrible reprisals taken by the English, who had executed several American prisoners.

We had crossed the wide part of the river beyond the mountains when our progress was suddenly halted by one of those accidents which are fairly frequent in summer when the water is low. The sloop went aground on a sandbank and although it suffered no damage, the accident happened when the tide was at its highest point and the boat lay there, in midstream, unable to move. The captain feared the next tide might not be high enough to refloat it and that it would probably be necessary to wait for another boat travelling downstream to tow us off, re-float us, and set us back into the channel from which a false turn of the wheel had diverted us.

The prospect of lying for several days in the middle of that great river did not appeal to us. I remembered that some Creoles from San Domingo, friends of M. Bonamy, were living on the banks of a small river nearby, not far from a town we had just passed. The captain told us we were exactly opposite the point where this stream joined the main river and offered us his boat to take us to these French people, whom we already knew as they had visited us. We accepted his offer and were soon in the boat, with the one trunk which constituted all our luggage. We entered the smaller river and travelled for three or four miles between steep, rocky banks, so close that parasitic plants and wild vines at the top of the banks grew across the water in garlands. It was delightful. Our journey ended at a small farm where we were given a cart to take us to our destination. Our two compatriots, still fairly young men, were as delighted as they were surprised by our unexpected arrival. They understood nothing at all about the life they had adopted. They knew very little English and, being unable to use any of the agricultural methods they had employed in San Domingo, had almost died of cold and boredom during the winter. From the fire at the Cape they had saved a number of very fine trifles whose luxury contrasted strangely with the poverty and disorder of their establishment, in which the only woman was an old negress. We slept at their house, but before going to bed talked for a long time with them about their farm and household arrangements. The following day, we were given our breakfast in wonderful, but unmatching porcelain cups, so chipped that I would have preferred an honest set of matching earthenware crockery like our own. Afterwards, we rode in their waggon to the highway and, from there, regained our house. At our invitation, these two friends accompanied us to Albany and from there to the farm, where they were very astonished to find us able to sell them several bags of oats and a dozen bushels of potatoes.

I found my house in perfect order, although M. de Chambeau was not expecting us. My poor little daughter was in excellent health. We had been away a month and it had seemed long to me, despite the amiability of the people among whom we had spent it. Yellow fever caused terrible ravages in New York that year so I was very glad I had decided to leave in such a hurry.

I returned to my country tasks with fresh ardour, for the change of air had cured my fever and I had recovered my strength. I resumed my dairy work and the pretty patterns stamped on my butter told my customers I was back. Our orchard promised a magnificent crop of apples and our loft held enough grain for the entire year. Our negroes, spurred on by our example, worked with a will. They were better clothed and better fed than any of those belonging to our neighbours.

I was very happy in this life when, suddenly, God dealt me the most unexpected and what seemed to me then the most cruel blow that any mortal could endure. Alas, I have since suffered others far more severe. My small Séraphine was taken from us by a sudden illness very common in that part of the continent: a sudden paralysis of the stomach and intestines without any accompanying fever or convulsions. She died within a few hours and was conscious until the end. The Albany doctor whom M. de Chambeau had ridden to fetch as soon as the illness began, told us immediately he saw her that there was no hope. He said that the illness was very widespread in the country just then and that there was no known remedy for it. The Schuyler's small son, who had played with my daughter all the afternoon of the previous day, also died a few hours later from the same illness and joined Séraphine in heaven. His mother adored him and called him my dear child's little husband. This cruel loss threw us all into the deepest sadness and despondency. We brought Humbert home to live with us and I tried to find distraction from my grief in teaching him myself. He was then five and a half years old. His intelligence was very well developed and he spoke English perfectly and read it fluently.

There was no Catholic priest in Albany or anywhere else in the neighbourhood and, as my husband did not want a Protestant minister summoned, he himself performed the last rites for our child and buried her in a small enclosure intended as a cemetery for the people of the farm. It was in the middle of our wood. Nearly every day I went to prostrate myself on that earth which was the last home of a child I had so dearly cherished and it was there, my beloved son,* that God was waiting for me, to work a change of heart in me.

Until then, although far from irreligious, I had not been much concerned with religion. During my childhood, no one had ever talked to me about it. During my early youth, I had been constantly surrounded by the worst possible examples. In the highest circles of Paris society I had seen the same scandalous behaviour repeated so often that it had become familiar and no longer distressed me. It was as if all concern with morality had been stifled in my heart. But the hour had come when I was to be forced to recognise the hand that

* Aymar, her only surviving child.

had stricken me. I could not describe exactly the change which took place in me. It was as if a voice cried out to me to change my whole nature. Kneeling on my child's grave, I implored her to obtain forgiveness for me from God, who had taken her back to be with Him, and to give me a little comfort in my distress. My prayer was heard. God granted me then the grace of knowing Him and serving Him. He gave me the courage to bow very humbly beneath the blow I had received and to prepare myself to endure without complaint those future griefs which, in his justice, he was to send to try me. Since that day, the divine will has found me submissive and resigned.

Although all the joy had gone from our home, we still had to go about our daily tasks and we encouraged one another, my husband and I, to seek distraction in the necessity in which we found ourselves of finding employment for every single minute. It was almost apple-picking time. The orchard looked most promising and it was likely that the crop would be very plentiful. There were almost as many apples as leaves. The previous autumn we had followed an old Bordeaux custom and, with a spade, had turned the earth in a patch four or five feet square around each tree. It was the first time this had been done to them. Indeed, Americans were ignorant of the benefit which this practice has on growth and when we told them that we had owned vines where this operation was repeated three times a year, they thought we were exaggerating. But when spring came and they saw our trees covered in blossom, they decided we must have some special power.

Another idea also brought us considerable respect. Instead of buying new barrels of very porous wood for our cider, we hunted in Albany for a number of Bordeaux casks and for some marked 'Cognac', of a type well known to us. Then we arranged our cellar with as much care as if it had been going to house the wines of Médoc.

We were lent a mill for pressing the apples and to it we harnessed an ancient, twenty-three-year-old horse which General Schuyler had given me. The mill was exceedingly primitive: there were two interlocking, grooved pieces of wood, like ratchets, and these were turned by the horse, which was harnessed to a wooden bar. The apples fell from a hopper into the interlocking pieces of wood and when there was enough juice to fill a large basket, it was taken to the cellar and poured into the casks.

The whole operation was exceedingly simple and as the weather was very fine, this harvesting became a delightful recreation for us. My son, who spent the whole of every day astride the horse, was convinced that his presence was vital to the task!

Mme de La Tour du Pin on her farm, near Albany.

West Point, New York. Engraving by James D. Smillie.

When the work was finished, we found that, after putting aside enough for our own use, we had eight or ten casks to sell. Our reputation for honest dealing was a guarantee that not a drop of water had been added to the cider so that it fetched more than twice the customary price. It was all sold immediately. As for that which we kept for ourselves, we treated it just as we would have done our white wine at Le Bouilh.

The apple-picking was followed by the harvesting of the maize. We had an abundance of it, for it is indigenous to the United States and grows there better than any other plant. As the corn must not be left in the husk for more than two days, the neighbours collect to help and they work without stopping until it is all done. This is called a 'frolic'. First, the floor of the barn is swept with as much care as for a ball. Then, when darkness falls, candles are lit and the people gather, about thirty in number, both black and white, and they set to work. All night long someone sings or tells stories and in the middle of the night everyone is given a bowl of boiling milk, previously turned with cider, to which have been added cloves, cinnamon, nutmeg and other spices, and about five or six pounds of brown sugar if one is being very grand, or a similar quantity of molasses if one is not. Our good workers paid us the compliment of drinking a great kitchen boiler full of this mixture with their toast and they left us at five o'clock in the morning, going out into the sharp cold, saying: 'Famous good people, those from the old country!' Our negroes were often asked to similar frolics, but my negress never went.

When all our crops had been gathered in and stored, we began the ploughing and all the other tasks which had to be finished before winter. The wood we intended to sell was stacked under a shelter. The sledges were repaired and repainted. I bought a length of coarse blue and white checked flannel to make two shirts each for my negroes. A journeyman tailor installed himself at the farm to make them good waistcoats and well-lined cloaks. Being white, this man took his meals with us. He would certainly have refused, had we suggested it, to eat with the 'slaves', though they were incomparably better dressed and far better mannered than he. But I was very careful to avoid even the slightest reference to this custom. My neighbours acted thus and I followed their example, never making in any of our dealings the slightest allusion to my former station. I was the owner of a 250-acre farm and I lived as did all owners of such farms, neither better nor worse. This simplicity and renunciation of the past earned me far more respect and consideration than I would have had if I had tried to play the lady.

The work which tired me most was the laundering. Judith and I did it all between us. Every fortnight, Judith washed the negroes' clothes, her own and the kitchen linen. I washed my own clothes, my husband's and those of M. de Chambeau and I did all the ironing. This latter task I greatly enjoyed: I excelled at it and could compete with the best. In my early girlhood, before my marriage, I often went to the linen-room at Montfermeil and there, as if by presentiment, had learned to iron. Being naturally dexterous, I was soon as skilful as the girls who taught me.

I never wasted a minute. Every day, winter and summer, I was up at dawn and my toilet took very little time. Before the negroes went to their work, they helped the negress to milk the cows, of which we had at one time as many as eight. While they were doing that, I busied myself in the dairy, skimming the milk. On the days butter was made, which was twice a week, Minck stayed behind to turn the handle of the churn, a task too heavy for a woman. The remainder of the butter-making, much of it still quite tiring, fell to me. I had a remarkable collection of bowls, ladles and wooden spatulae, all made by my good friends the savages. My dairy was reputed the cleanest and even the most elegant in the neighbourhood.

Winter came early that year. In the first days of November, the black clouds which heralded the snow began to gather in the west. Everything happened in the proper order: eight days of extreme cold, the river frozen within twenty-four hours to a depth of three feet, and then the first falls of snow. We passed the winter in the same way as the previous one, dining frequently with the Schuylers and Renslaers, whose friendship was undiminished. M. de Talleyrand, who was again living in Philadelphia, had managed under strange circumstances, to retrieve certain objects belonging to me: a cameo of the queen, the casket you* still have and a watch which had belonged to my mother. He knew from me that my banker in The Hague had told me that he had entrusted these objects to a young American diplomat – luckily for him, I have forgotten his name – asking him to deliver them to me. Despite numerous enquiries, M. de Talleyrand had never managed to discover this man. Eventually, one evening in Philadelphia, when visiting a lady of his acquaintance, he was told by her of a portrait of the queen which Mr X had obtained in Paris and had lent to her to show some of her friends. She asked M. de Talleyrand if it was a good likeness. As soon as he saw it, he recognised it as mine and

* Aymar.

took possession of it, telling the lady it did not belong to the young diplomat. Then, going straight to call on him, he demanded without preamble the casket and the watch which the banker at The Hague had given him at the same time as the portrait. The young man was frightened and ended by returning everything. M. de Talleyrand sent these things on to us at the farm.

✤✤✤✤✤✤✤✤✤✤✤✤ XXI ✤✤✤✤✤✤✤✤✤✤✤✤

At Pisa, the 14*th of May* 1843. Towards the end of the winter of 1795–96, I caught measles. It was a fairly severe attack, aggravated by the fact that I was in the first months of a pregnancy. We were afraid Humbert would also catch it, but he did not, despite the fact that he slept in my room. I recovered quickly and was no sooner better than we received letters from Bonie in France telling us that he and M. de Brouquens had, by their combined efforts, succeeded in having the sequestration removed from Le Bouilh.

The property of those condemned to death had been restored. My mother-in-law, with the assistance of her daughter's husband, the Marquis de Lameth, had acted on behalf of her children and re-taken possession of the properties of Tesson and Ambleville, as well as the house at Saintes. But when they asked for the removal of the seals on Le Bouilh, they were told this could not be done in the owner's absence. They replied that he had settled in America with a valid passport and that neither M. de La Tour du Pin nor I, who owned a house in Paris, had been included on the list of émigrés. After much discussion the authorities agreed to allow us one year's grace in which to present ourselves. If we did not do so Le Bouilh would be offered for sale as national property unless M. de Lameth could claim his own children's rights as the grandchildren of the previous owner. We were urged therefore, to return as soon as possible. However, the stability of the French government of the day inspired little confidence, so we were advised to take passage to a Spanish port instead of a French one, for the Republic had just signed a treaty of peace with Spain which seemed likely to last for a while.

These letters erupted into our peaceful lives rather like fire-brands, setting aflame in the hearts of all about me thoughts of the possibility of returning to our own country, anticipation of a better life, hopes of achieving our ambition for the future—in short, all those sentiments which animate the life of man. My own feelings were quite different. Of France, I had only memories of horror. It was there that I had lost my youth, crushed out of being by numberless, unforgettable terrors. Only two sentiments had remained alive in me and, to this day, they are my only guide: love of my husband and love of my children. Religion, henceforth to be the only motive power of all my actions, bade me raise no obstacle, however slight, to a departure which terrified me and filled me with dismay. I had a presentiment that I was embarking on a fresh series of troubles and anxieties. M. de La Tour du Pin never realised the intensity of my regret when I learned that the day on which we were to leave the farm had been fixed. I set only one condition to this departure: that our negroes should be given their freedom. My husband agreed and reserved the joy of telling them to me alone.

When these poor people saw the letters arriving from Europe, they feared there would be changes in our way of life. They were anxious, frightened, and it was tremblingly that they came, all four of them, to the drawing-room in answer to my summons. Judith was carrying her small daughter, three-years-old Maria and was soon to give birth to her second child. They found me alone and I said to them with deep emotion: 'My friends, we are returning to Europe. What are we to do with you?' The poor things were stricken. Judith sank on to a chair, sobbing, and the three men hid their faces in their hands. All four remained motionless. I went on: 'We have been so pleased with you that it is right you should be rewarded. My husband has charged me to tell you that he gives you your freedom.' Hearing this, our good servants were so amazed that for a few seconds they could not speak. Then, falling on their knees at my feet, they cried: 'Is it possible? Do you mean that we are free?' I replied: 'Yes, upon my honour. From this moment you are as free as I am myself.'

The poignancy of such a scene cannot be described. Never have I known a happier moment. These people whom I had just freed, surrounded me, weeping. They kissed my hands, my feet, my gown; and then, suddenly, their joy vanished and they said: 'We would prefer to remain slaves all our lives and for you to stay here.'

The following day, my husband took them before the Justice in Albany for the ceremony of manumission, which had to take place in public. All the negroes of the town were there. The Justice of the Peace, who was also the manager of Mr Renslaer's properties, was in a very bad humour. He tried to object that Prime, being fifty years old, could not, under the law, be given his freedom unless he had an assured pension of one hundred dollars. But Prime had foreseen this difficulty and produced his certificate of baptism which showed that he was only forty-nine. They were told to kneel in front of my husband who laid his hand on the head of each in turn in token of liberation, exactly as used to be done in ancient Rome.

We leased our house with its land to the very man from whom we had had it and sold most of the furnishings. The horses fetched quite good prices. I distributed as keepsakes many small pieces of porcelain that I had brought from Europe. To my poor Judith, I gave some of my old silk gowns, which will doubtless have been handed down to her descendants.

About the middle of April, we embarked at Albany for New York, having taken affectionate and grateful farewell of all those who, for two years, had showered on us care, friendship and attentions of every kind. Two years later, when we were forced once more into exile, I was often to regret my farm and those good neighbours.

In New York we stayed with M. and Mme Olive at their pretty little country house. There we also found M. de Talleyrand who, like us, had decided to go back to Europe. Mme de Staël, who was back in Paris with Benjamin Constant, had urged him to return and serve the Directory* which was anxious to make use of his ability. At one time we thought we would be able to sail in the same ship with him but when he learned of our intention to land at a Spanish port and travel from there to Bordeaux, he changed his plans. He had no wish to put himself, even for such a short time, in the power of his Most Catholic Majesty who might, and not without reason, consider him a somewhat unedifying bishop. He decided, therefore, to take a ship sailing for Hamburg. We ourselves had hoped to find one leaving for Corunna or Bilbao, but there was only one, a superb English vessel of four hundred tons, sailing for Cadiz and due to raise anchor at any moment. For lack of an alternative we decided to book our passages in her, despite the long journey it would mean through Spain. She was sailing under the Spanish flag, though she belonged, as did her cargo, to an Englishman. I believe the cargo was corn. The owner, a Mr Ensdel, was on board travelling as a passenger. He had formerly owned whaling vessels. He knew not one word of French but the captain, who came from

* A government of five directors who governed France from 1795–1799 with the help of two Chambers: the Council of the Elders (*Conseil des Anciens*) and the Council of the Five Hundred (*Conseil des Cinq-Cents*). (Tr.)

Jamaica, spoke English. In any case, he immediately found a very intelligent interpreter in my son who, although only six, was of great service to him. We spent a further three weeks with Mme Olive, as did M. de Talleyrand, while we completed our arrangements and settled ourselves on board.

Anchored in the roadstead was a French sloop of war commanded by a Captain Barre. My husband had known his father in the household of the old Duc d'Orléans.* Captain Barre was a very pleasant man, though a true sea dog, and he came every day in his barge to take us out to different parts of the roadstead. He was very careful, however, to avoid Sandy Hook where Captain Cochrane, later Admiral Cochrane, had been lying in wait for two months to seize him should he try to leave. We visited his sloop, which was armed with fifteen guns. It was gem of order, cleanliness and care. How I should have liked to return to Europe in that lovely ship.

But the *Maria-Josepha* was waiting for us. We all four† went on board on 6 May 1796 and set sail the same day. There were a number of other passengers, including a French merchant, a M. Tisserandot, whose wife, like me, was expecting a baby.

I did not suffer from seasickness and, as the weather was splendid, was busy all day long. This meant that I had soon exhausted the work I had brought with me for my husband and myself, so I set up as wardrobe-mistress to all on board and sent out an appeal for work. Everyone brought me something. There were shirts to be made, cravats to be hemmed, linen to be marked. The crossing lasted forty days because the captain, refusing to accept Mr Ensdel's advice, had sailed southwards with the currents. It gave me enough time to put the crew's entire wardrobe in order.

Eventually, towards 10 June, we saw Cape St Vincent and the next day we entered the Cadiz roads. We dropped anchor alongside a French three-decker, the *Jupiter*, one of a French fleet prevented from sailing by an even larger force of English warships which patrolled daily almost within sight of the port.

A quarantine boat visited us and told us we would have to spend eight days on board in quarantine. We preferred this to going to the quarantine station where we would have been devoured by the many varieties of insect life with which Spain abounds. If there had been a boat sailing even to Bilbao or Barcelona, we would have taken passage in it for the journey would have been much shorter, as well as less tiring and less expensive than by road.

* Louis-Philippe, Duc d'Orléans (1725–1785), father of Philippe Égalité.
† M. and Mme de La Tour du Pin, Humbert and M. de Chambeau.

M. de Chambeau had not been crossed off the list of émigrés and so could not return to France. He wanted to go to Madrid, where he knew several people, but would nonetheless have been only too willing to accompany us to Barcelona, for it would have been so much closer to the town of Auch near which he owned several properties.

The uncertainty of our plans was the topic of all our conversations during the quarantine period, which lasted ten days. It might have been much longer, for one of our sailors deserted and we could not be allowed to leave until he had been found. This man, who was French, had been captured after a fight on a war sloop. He had recognised a sailor on board the *Jupiter* which was lying very close to us and had spoken to him through the hailer. That same night he swam over to the *Jupiter* and when the health officials called the roll the following morning, all that was left of him was his shirt and trousers. He was eventually discovered in the French ship.

This quarantine nearly proved fatal to me. Fruit sellers came alongside all day long and Mme Tisserandot and I spent our time lowering a basket on a string to be filled with figs, oranges and strawberries. This surfeit of fruit gave me violent dysentery and I was very ill.

At last we were declared out of quarantine. The captain set us ashore and never in my life have I been so embarrassed as then. On landing, Mme Tisserandot and I were taken to a small room opening on to the street while our luggage was examined with quite excessive thoroughness. Our coloured gowns and straw hats soon drew a huge crowd of people of all ages and kinds: sailors and monks, dockers and gentlemen, all curious to see what they doubtless regarded as two strange animals. As for our husbands, they had to stay in the room where our luggage was being examined. Mme Tisserandot and I were therefore alone, with only my son for company. He was not at all frightened, but asked me a thousand questions, especially about the monks, the first he had ever seen. At one point, when a young, beardless monk was passing, he cried: 'Oh, I see now. That one is a woman!'

The indiscreet curiosity quickly determined my companion and me to dress like the Spanish women. And so, even before going to the inn, we bought a black shirt each and a mantilla so that we would be able to go out without shocking the inhabitants. We lodged at an hotel said to be the best in Cadiz, but I had become so accustomed to the exquisite cleanliness of America that it seemed to me disgustingly dirty and I would willingly have returned on board.

I remembered that one of the sisters of poor Theobald Dillon, who had been massacred in Lille in 1792, had married an English merchant living in Cadiz, a Mr Langton. I wrote him a civil note and he came at once, all courteous solicitude. Mrs Langton was in Madrid, staying with her daughter, the Baronne d'Andilla, and had taken their youngest daughter, Miss Carmen Langton, with her. Mr Langton invited us nonetheless to dine with him and even wanted to take us to stay with him, but it was impossible to accept as I was too unwell to face the strain of visiting. It was agreed that the dinner would be postponed until the first day I felt better.

The day after our arrival, my husband took our passport to be visaed by the French Consul-General, a certain M. de Roquesante, a *ci-devant* comte or marquis turned ardent republican, perhaps even terrorist. He asked my husband innumerable questions and noted down all his answers. It was remarkably like an interrogation. Then, doubtless to see what effect it would have, he said to my husband: 'Today we have received excellent news from France, Citizen,' – such being still the form of address – 'that wretched Charette* has at last been captured and shot.' 'That is a pity,' replied M. de La Tour du Pin, 'it means one brave man the less.' The consul said no more, signed the passport and reminded us that it would have to be presented again at the French Embassy in Madrid. Later, we were to hear what he reported to Bayonne about us.

At that time, after concluding a peace treaty with the French Republic, Spain had disbanded the greater part of her army, probably without pay. The roads were therefore infested with brigands, especially in the mountains of the Sierra Morena which we had to cross, and people would only travel in convoys of several carriages at a time. They did not hire a military escort for fear it might be in league with the brigands, all of whom were ex-soldiers, but any mounted travellers who accompanied the convoys took the precaution of arming themselves to the teeth. A convoy usually consisted of fifteen to eighteen covered waggons drawn by mules.

It was in one such convoy that we left Cadiz. My husband, my son and I occupied one of the waggons, lying at full length on the mattress we had used on board ship. Beneath it, on the floor of the waggon, was our luggage. It was covered with a layer of straw, and straw had also been stuffed into the spaces between the trunks.

* François-Athanase Charette (1763–1796), a royalist leader in the Vendean war. He was defeated in 1796 at Prélinière by Hoche, captured and executed.

A wicker hood artistically fashioned and covered with tarred cloth sheltered us from the sun during the daytime and from the damp at night, for we often preferred sleeping in the waggon to staying at the inn.

But I anticipate. We stayed a week in Cadiz, walking every evening along the fine Boulevard de l'Alameda which overlooks the sea and where people go to enjoy the cooler air after enduring a daytime temperature of 35°. My small Humbert came with me and one day we met a young gentleman of seven summers wearing a silk dress coat, richly embroidered, a sword at his side, his hair powdered white and his hat under his arm. My son looked at him in astonishment and then, thinking it might be one of the performing monkeys I had taken him to see in New York, asked: 'But, is it a real boy or is it a monkey?'

A spectacle he never forgot and one which I, too, remember still was the magnificent bull fight on the Feast of St John. This national feast has been so often described that I will not try to do so here. The amphitheatre was enormous and there were at least five thousand people on the steps, sheltered from the sun by a cloth stretched above them, like the awnings in a Roman amphitheatre. With the help of pumps, a fine spray kept this cloth damp on the underside and even when the fight began after midday Mass and did not end until sunset, I do not remember ever suffering a moment's discomfort from the heat. Ten bulls were killed, of such magnificent strain that any one of them would have made the fortune of any American farmer. The matador was the leading one of the day, a fine young man of twenty-five. Despite the terrible dangers he courted, he was so agile that one felt not the slightest anxiety for him. But it cannot be denied that, at the moment when the two adversaries faced one another alone, in the second before the bull hurled himself at the matador, the spectators were held in the grip of a most exquisite emotion. No sound broke the stillness. But it must be realised that it is not the matador who delivers the sword thrust. He only directs the weapon so that the bull impales itself upon it. This spectacle was epoch-making in my life: none other has left such a deep impression.

On the day fixed for our departure, we let the convoy start out without us, my husband, my son and I remaining behind to dine with Mr Langton. He had arranged for a boat to take us to the other side of the bay to rejoin the convoy at Port-Sainte-Marie, where it was to spend the night, for it was never to travel at more than a walking pace during the whole of that long journey.

I was so ill from the terrible attack of dysentery, complicated by fever, that my husband hesitated to let me set out. But it was impossible to delay. Our luggage was loaded. We had paid half the cost of the journey as far as Madrid. Our passport had been visaed and M. de Roquesante would have taken umbrage at any postponement. He would have thought it some pretext, though I cannot imagine for what, and as I have always believed that it is possible to overcome any handicap, no matter what it may be – except a broken leg – it did not even enter my head to remain in Cadiz. We dined, therefore, with Mr Langton, after assisting at the departure of our travelling companions for Port-Sainte-Marie.

Nothing could have been more delightful than Mr Langton's house. It was English in style, impeccably clean and well cared for. The only Spanish customs that Mr Langton had adopted were those which eased the difficulties of living in a torrid climate. The house was built around a square courtyard filled with flowers. On the ground floor was a cloister-like loggia and on the first floor, an open gallery. Stretched at roof level over the whole courtyard was a sheltering cloth sprayed by a fountain. This gave a delicious coolness to the whole house. I admit it was very distressing to think that, despite a pregnancy already six months advanced, I had to set out on a long journey in a temperature of 35° instead of remaining in such an agreeable place. But the die was cast: departure was unavoidable. After this farewell dinner we went on board the boat towards evening and, an hour and a half later, the wind being favourable, we reached Port-Sainte-Marie. There we found our convoy, consisting of fourteen coaches and six or seven gentlemen armed from head to toe.

The second day's stage was to Xérès, only five leagues further on. As I needed to rest, we decided once again to let the caravan leave without us and to rejoin it at Xérès in the evening. We therefore dined early in the pretty town of Port-Sainte-Marie and then the three of us climbed into a 'calesa' or cabriolet drawn by a huge mule. It had no bridle, which seemed very odd to me, but on its head waved a tall plume hung with small bells. A young boy armed with a whip leapt lightly on to the shaft, uttered a few cabalistic sounds and the mule set off at a trot as rapid as a good hunting gallop. The road was superb, we went like the wind and the mule, docile to the voice of its small driver, avoided all the obstacles and wound through village streets with a wisdom that savoured of the miraculous. At first I was frightened. Then, thinking it must be the local custom to travel like that, I resigned myself. On arriving at

Xérès, I was curious to know what such a mule might be worth. I was told sixty to seventy louis, which seemed to me expensive.

The next day, the real journey began. I was still ill, but lying at full length on a good mattress, and the road being excellent, I suffered no more than if I had remained quietly in one place. We always stopped two hours for dinner at appalling inns and on several occasions preferred to spend the night in our waggon rather than to sleep in revoltingly dirty beds.

We were approaching Cordova when poor Mme Tisserandot was seized with the pains of labour. We were still four leagues from the town, in a great plain where there was no sign of a house. She gave birth safely to a small daughter, whom the muleteer washed in wine from his flask. We had no coverings for her as the mother happened to be lying on the trunks containing the baby linen. We could not delay longer for the remainder of the convoy had continued on its way and was already far enough ahead to make it dangerous. The Cordovan plain had a very bad reputation. The muleteer handed me the poor baby, quite naked, and I wrapped it as well as I could in the cravats of our travelling companions. Then we continued on our way at a trot, trying to catch up with the caravan. Poor Mme Tisserandot suffered terribly from the speed, but it had to be endured.

It was night by the time we reached Cordova. As we were a long way behind the others, they were already settled by the time the inn servants reached our carriage. Seeing someone sick lying there, they thought she had been the victim of an attack. Now, it is a well known fact that, whenever there has been a crime and circumstances are likely to require local people to give witness in a court of law, they inevitably disappear so that they can say, with truth, that they have seen nothing. These inn servants, true to tradition, set their lamps on the ground and disappeared. The muleteer guessed why they had gone but although he called them back, they did not come. I spent part of the night unpacking the sick woman's cases to find the things she needed for herself and for the baby. But first we had to eat, and in that inn there was only sleeping accommodation so we were forced to go and look for a tavern. With enormous difficulty, because of the lateness of the hour, we did eventually manage to get some bread and a few slices of fried bacon.

Next morning, the departure of the convoy was delayed an hour so that I could have the poor baby baptised. She was healthy despite her adventures. It was thanks to this ceremony that I saw

the magnificent cathedral of Cordova. As you will readily understand, travelling in such discomfort, sick and six month's pregnant,
I felt little inclination in the heat which beats down on Andalusia
between noon and three o'clock – the time of our daily halt – to
visit historic buildings. But after the baptism, which was by immer-
sion, the baby's head being dipped into the water of the font, we
spent an hour wandering through the forest of pillars in that wonderful church. The muleteers came to urge us to hurry. They had with
them provisions for the two meals we would have to eat in the open
that day as there was no dwelling at all in the country we were to
cross.

For about an hour after leaving Cordova the road runs through
well-watered gardens of lemon trees and Moorish olive trees before
reaching the walls of the old city, parts of which can still be seen.
Like the boundaries of ancient Rome, they give some idea of the
immense area which this great Moorish city once covered.

We dined, as we had been told we would, near a well, in the
middle of a pasture full of grazing sheep. The plain stretched
farther than the eye could see, for it was several leagues long and
covered sometimes in fine grass and sometimes with dwarf myrtle.
Around the well stood a few pomegranate trees covered in blossom.
This halt had about it something very oriental, which appealed to
me in a strangely powerful way. I found it infinitely preferable to
those three-hour halts in horrible, dirty inns where the heat inside
was even worse than in the open.

The next day, and for several days afterwards, we crossed the
Sierra Morena. There, we saw the two pretty little towns of La
Carlota and La Carolina built for the German colonists invited to
Spain by M. de Florida Blanca,* the great minister of Charles III,
and we noticed that certain German characteristics still remained.
We met children with fair hair whose sun-tanned Spanish skins
contrasted with their blue eyes. These small towns are very picturesque, built as they are to a regular plan and in beautiful sur-
roundings. On all the slopes, the road is edged with a marble parapet
and is very lovely. At that time, it was the only road linking southern
Spain with Castille.

To my great regret, we did not pass through Toledo. We reached
Aranjuez in time for dinner on, I think, the fifteenth day of our

* The foreign agricultural colonies which gave rise to these two small towns were
actually founded in about 1768 by M. Olavides, a Spanish statesman and at that
time Administrator of Seville. The Comte de Florida Blanca did not become
Prime Minister to Charles III until 1777.

journey. We spent the remainder of the day there, admiring the cool shade, the beautiful weeping willows and the green fields which, to any traveller coming from Andalusia, exhausted, burned by the July sun, are like green oases in the midst of a desert. It is the Tagus, still a small stream wandering prettily through this charming valley, which keeps the place so deliciously cool. The Court was not at Aranjuez, but for some reason that I have now forgotten, we did not visit the castle.

The following day we arrived in Madrid, after a two-hour halt at the Puerta del Sol waiting for the luggage and the occupants of the fourteen waggons of our convoy to be examined, searched and inspected. Those who had already been cleared were not allowed to leave. Nothing is allowed to affect the deliberate manner of a Castilian. It would have been useless to show impatience: the customs officials would not even have recognised it for what it was. The signal to depart was eventually given and we were taken to the Hôtel Saint-Sebastian, a mediocre inn in a small street.

We took a fairly good room and my husband immediately sent off the letters and packages which Mr Langton had given us for his wife and two daughters. Then I made a more careful toilette than I had been accustomed to do in the waggon, intending to call on these ladies when we had dined. But they were before us. Within little more than half-an-hour, we saw two of the most beautiful women in the world arriving at our hotel: the Baronne d'Andilla and Mlle Carmen Langton. Their mother was indisposed and unable to go out, but a brother-in-law* accompanied them. He was the widower of a third Miss Langton who had been considered even more beautiful than her sisters. They proved to be of unequalled kindness and attentiveness, and their brother-in-law suggested we should take a small furnished lodging in that part of the city where these ladies were staying. He undertook to make all the necessary arrangements and put himself at our disposal for the whole of our stay in Madrid. We had to remain there a month or six weeks at least, as we had to wait for letters from Bordeaux in reply to those we had written from Cadiz.

But my pregnancy was advancing and I wanted to be at Le Bouilh before 10 November for the birth of my child. My husband went the next day to call on the Ambassador of the Government of the Directorate, to have his passport put in order. Remembering vividly the reception accorded him by Citizen, *ci-devant* Comte or Marquis, de Roquesante, he was most agreeably surprised at the

*Mr Broun.

ambassador's amiability. He was General Pérignon, later a Marshal. He had served under my father, who had greatly assisted him in his career. This he had not forgotten and he showed my husband every attention. His gratitude, however, did not stretch so far as calling on me. The former aristocracy had not yet attained the vogue it was to enjoy later.

We stayed six weeks in Madrid, surrounded by the care, attentions and kindnesses of the Langton and Andilla families. Mr Broun took us to visit all the most interesting parts of the city and every evening Mme d'Andilla took us to the Corso and afterwards to eat ices in a fashionable café at the bottom of the Rue d'Alcala.

✠✠✠✠✠✠✠✠✠✠ XXII ✠✠✠✠✠✠✠✠✠✠

At last a letter arrived from Bonie appointing a day when he would be at Bayonne to meet us. This time we engaged a returning 'collieras' to transport us and our baggage. M. de Chambeau was forced to remain in Madrid. The deep friendship he bore us, which had shown itself in so many different ways, made this separation very painful to him and to us. For nearly three years he had shared all our vicissitudes, our interests and our griefs. My husband loved him as a brother. During the long years of exile, we had shared our very thoughts. He had no money. No one had thought to send him any. Luckily, we were able to leave him fifty louis and, by very good fortune, he was able to go to stay in the house of the Comtesse de Galvez, where he remained until 1800.

We left Madrid at two o'clock in the afternoon in order to reach the Escurial by night. The 'collieras' was a berline, old but solid, drawn by seven mules and driven – or let us rather say, coaxed and exhorted – by a coachman who sat on the box and a postilion armed with a long whip who leaped from one mule to another in turn. They had no bridles and obeyed his voice. I think the mules next to the cross-beam must have had reins, but the other five certainly did not. One of them, the seventh, walked in front, alone. She was called the *generala*, and her job was to guide the others.

We spent nearly all the following day visiting the remarkable monastery of St Laurence of the Escurial, or the Escurial, as it is usually called. There have been many descriptions of it, but not one of all those I have read since our visit has seemed to me to give a true impression. None conveyed the melancholy, devout peace which fills the soul in this masterpiece of all the arts, set in the midst of a desert. It seems to have no other purpose than to make us aware of the futility and vanity of the works of man.

One of the priests showed us the crypt chapel where are buried all the Kings of Spain since Philip II. The tombs were all similar but one was still empty, the lid propped open. It was for the reigning King, Charles IV.

Every year since the discovery of America and the gold and silver mines of Peru, the Kings of Spain have presented a magnificent gift in these two precious metals to the Church of the Escurial. In consequence, its collection of treasure has become the richest in the whole of Europe. All these splendid gifts are arranged chronologically so that a sensitive eye can follow the steady decline in taste since the earliest of the gifts, which bear the signature of Benvenuto Cellini.

The reredos of the high altar was a bas-relief in silver representing the apotheosis of St Laurence, patron saint of the Escurial. In magnificence, it was unrivalled, but as a work of art it was unsatisfactory. I use the past tense for there is reason to believe that the misfortunes of Spain have resulted in the destruction of all these masterpieces. The various articles used in the ceremonies of the Church were arranged in glass-fronted cupboards made from the most beautiful of East Indian woods. I remember very clearly a ciborium in the form of a globe, surmounted by a cross with an enormous diamond mounted in the middle and a large pearl at the end of each of the four branches. There were monstrances glittering with precious stones. We were shown the Easter vestments of red velvet embroidered all over with millions of fine pearls graduated in size to form the design.

We climbed up to the rood loft where there was a wonderful collection of Church books. Their pages were of vellum and their margins ornamented with paintings by the pupils of Raphael, using their master's designs. These large folio volumes, silver-cornered and bound in soft brown leather, were kept in a kind of open cupboard, separated from one another by thin wooden partitions. It would normally have been difficult to take the books from their compartments on account of their great weight, but the problem had been solved by fitting the bottom of each compartment with small ivory rollers turning on iron rods. I have not seen this system in any other library.

Benvenuto Cellini's fine, life-sized Christ in silver is in the upper gallery of the Escurial. When we had explored and admired this magnificent Church, my husband and a companion left me there alone while they went off to visit the monastery and the library, which contained Raphael's fine painting known as 'The Pearl'.* They had not warned me in Madrid that a woman needed special permission to visit this library, which is inside the monastery itself. I greatly regretted not being able to see it.

I had to wait quite a long time for my travelling companions and had leisure to meditate on many things. I thought of the beauty of this building and then of the Battle of Saint-Quentin†, for the Escurial had been built‡ to commemorate that victory over the French. And so, when my husband returned and touched my shoulder saying: 'Let us go and see the Prince's House', I felt almost annoyed at having my thoughts interrupted. My son had been able to accompany his father to the library, and proudly told me of all he had seen.

We directed our steps towards this Prince's House, built by Charles IV when still Prince of the Asturias and used by him as a retreat when the Court was at the Escurial and he wanted to escape from the constraint of Spanish etiquette. It was like a very elegant villa and today would barely satisfy a modest stockbroker. Its elegant furniture, nondescript paintings, the doubtful taste of the ornaments and a quantity of exceedingly ugly hangings, all combined to make it resemble the lodging of some favourite. What a contrast with the fine Church we had just left.

We returned to the inn and soon set out for La Granja,§ where we were to spend the night. The Court was in residence and there we were to collect certain packets from the American Minister, Mr Rutledge, for his consul in Bayonne. He invited us to supper and next day we set out for Segovia, a very picturesque small town with a castle. All we saw of this castle was its courtyard, which was surrounded by arcades, in the Moorish style.

The rest of our journey was almost uneventful. We spent one day in Vittoria to rest *la generala*, without whom we would have been unable to proceed, and another in Burgos, where I visited the cathedral. Finally, we reached San Sebastian, where Bonie was waiting for us.

---

* Or 'The Virgin of the Pearl'.
† On 10 August 1557, the feast of St Laurence.
‡ By Philip II of Spain, 1527–1598.
§ A royal castle in the town of San Ildefonso.

I felt no pleasure in returning to France. In fact, the sufferings I had endured there during the six months before our departure had left me with feelings of horror and terror which I could not overcome. I could not forget that my husband had lost his fortune and was faced with the disagreeable task of tackling difficult problems of every kind, that we would be forced to live in a vast, empty château since everything in Le Bouilh had been pillaged and sold. My mother-in-law was still alive and had again taken possession of Tesson and Ambleville. She was not an intelligent woman and, being by nature very suspicious and exceedingly obstinate, trusted no one in business matters. How deeply I longed for my farm and the peace we had enjoyed there. It was with an aching heart that I crossed the bridge over the Bidassoa and realised I was back on the territory of the 'one and indivisible' Republic.

We reached Bayonne in the evening and had scarcely entered the inn when two Gardes Nationaux came to fetch M. de La Tour du Pin and take him to the local authority, represented at the time, so far as I recall, by the President of the Department. Such a beginning revived all my fears. My husband, accompanied by Bonie, was brought by the two Gardes before the assembled members of the tribunal who questioned him about his views, his plans, his actions, the causes and purposes of his recent absence, and of his return. He realised immediately that M. de Roquesante had denounced him and told the tribunal so, adding how favourably impressed he had been by the ambassador in Madrid. After at least two hours of parley – to me, waiting so anxiously at the inn, it seemed a century – my husband returned. He was authorised to continue his journey as far as Bordeaux, but was given a sort of official route map with every stage marked and this had to be countersigned at each halt. In fact, if I had felt tired or unwell, as might easily have happened for my pregnancy was far advanced, it would have been necessary to ask the local authority to provide an official declaration to that effect.

Bonie left us and returned to Bordeaux by mail coach. We ourselves engaged a bad coachman who took us by short stages. Our journey was marked by only one incident: at Mont de Marsan I sent for a hairdresser to dress my hair and to my amazement he offered me two hundred francs for it! Fair wigs were so much the fashion in Paris, he said, that we would certainly make a profit of at least one hundred francs if I would agree to sell it to him. I naturally refused, but from then on have held my hair in great respect. Modesty aside, it was very beautiful in those days.

At Bordeaux, we met the excellent Brouquens again. He had prospered during the war with Spain and had been re-engaged in the company which supplied food to the armies in Italy. He welcomed us with the affectionate friendliness that he has always unfailingly shown us but I was impatient to reach home and made all the necessary arrangements with my good Dr Dupouy, who was to look after me. Then, the matter of raising the sequestration being settled, we arrived at Le Bouilh to have the seals removed.

I must admit that the first moments strained my resolution to the uttermost. I had left this house well furnished, not perhaps in a particularly stylish or elegant manner, but with everything in it comfortable and plentiful, and I found it quite empty. Not a single chair was left to sit on, not a table nor a bed. I almost gave way to discouragement but to complain would not have helped. We set about opening the cases we had brought with us from the farm, for they had reached Bordeaux long before us, and the sight of the simple furniture in that vast house gave us much food for thought.

The next day, many of the inhabitants of Saint-André, ashamed at having attended the auction of our furniture, came to see us and suggested we should buy it back at the prices they had given for it. This enabled us to recover, for a reasonable sum, the articles we needed most and we were very careful to limit our dealings to those we thought had bought only from fear. As for the good republicans, they had no intention of showing such unpatriotic readiness to help. One of the most valuable possessions of the house had been a very fine collection of kitchen utensils. It had been removed to the district of Bourg, with the intention of sending it to the Mint. It was returned to us, however, as was the library, which had also been put into the official store. We spent many days in the agreeable task of putting the books back on the shelves and before Dr Dupouy arrived, had finished arranging the interior of the house, so that it looked as if we had been back for at least a year.

It was then that a very great happiness befell me: my dear Marguérite arrived. It was a deep pleasure to see that excellent woman again. A month after my departure for America, she had reached Paris, where a friend had taken her in. Some days later, she went out, dressed as always in the clothes normally worn by a maid in a good household, her apron white as snow. She had gone but a few steps along the street when a cook, her basket over her arm, pushed her into one of those dark passages known in Paris as alleys and said to her: 'Don't you know, you wretched woman, that you will be arrested and guillotined if you wear an apron like that?' My poor maid was astounded to find that she had risked death by observing a life-long habit. She thanked the woman for saving her, hid her anti-republican apron and hurried off to buy several lengths of coarse cloth to disguise herself, as she put it.

Shortly afterwards, passing through the Place Vendôme, she saw two children of six or seven playing in front of a carriage entrance and, finding them pretty, stopped and spoke to them. She learned that they were living with their grandfather, who was an invalid, that there were sentries in the house, that their father and mother were in prison, that all the servants had left and they were alone with their grandfather. Kind-hearted Marguérite did not hesitate. She asked the children to take her to their grandfather, who confirmed their story. She suggested she should remain in his service to look after him and the children. He was delighted and two hours later she had settled in. She lived there until the death of Robespierre, when Mme de Valence was released from prison and sent for her to come and look after her two daughters. But as soon as she heard of my return, nothing could dissuade her from rejoining me and she came to find me at Le Bouilh, in time to receive my dear daughter, Charlotte, who was born on 4 November 1796. I called her Charlotte because her godfather was M. de Chambeau. On the register of the Commune, however, she was named Alix, the only name, therefore, that she could use in legal documents.

In December, when I had recovered, my husband went to visit Tesson, Ambleville and La Roche Chalais where all that remained to us of the 30,000 franc income from the property was a few old, tumble-down towers. I remained alone in the great house at Le Bouilh with Marguérite, two maidservants and old Biquet, who got drunk every evening. The farm workers were some distance away. The unfinished part of the ground floor was secured only by a few dilapidated planks and it was the time when gangs of brigands known as *chauffeurs** were spreading terror throughout the south of France. Every day fresh horrors were told of them. Only two leagues away from Le Bouilh they had burned the feet of a certain M. Chicous, a Bordeaux shop-keeper, to force him to tell them where he kept his money. Many years later, I saw this unfortunate man, still on crutches. I am ashamed to admit it, but these gangs filled me with a paralysing terror. I often spent half the night sitting on my bed, listening to the barking watch-dogs, thinking that at any moment the brigands would break through the flimsy planks covering the ground floor windows. How I longed for

* Robbers who tortured their victims with fire.

my farm, my good negroes and the peace of those months. My days were no happier than my nights. It was midwinter, and all my thoughts were with my husband, travelling about the countryside on a poor horse, over the terrible roads of the southern provinces, which in those days were especially bad.

Our financial position was another constant worry. My husband had been advised not to accept his father's estate without benefit of inventory,* and if only he had followed that advice. But the tragic manner of his father's death and the respect in which M. de La Tour du Pin held his memory made him unwilling to do so. I will not go into details of our ruin; in any case, I never knew them very exactly. I only know that when I married, my father-in-law was understood to have an income of eighty thousand francs. Since the Revolution, our losses have amounted to at least fifty-eight thousand francs a year.

We lived at Le Bouilh right through the winter and for a part of the Spring. Towards July 1797, my husband realised it would be necessary to go to Paris to see M. de Lameth and finish putting his affairs in order. As if driven by presentiment, I asked to go with him. Mme de Montesson, who had always shown me great kindness, suggested to me, through Mme de Valence, that I should stay in her house in Paris. She herself proposed to spend the summer in the country. The six weeks we intended to spend in Paris before returning to Le Bouilh for the gathering of the grapes and the vintage did not call for a great quantity of luggage, so we took with us only what was strictly necessary for ourselves and the children.

Many émigrés had come back under borrowed names. Mme d'Hénin had taken that of a milliner in Geneva, a Mlle Vauthier, and had gone to stay with Mme de Poix at Saint-Ouen. Mme de Staël, under the protection of Barras, one of the five Directors, and many others were in Paris. M. de Talleyrand wanted us to come, my husband in particular. There was beginning to be talk of a counter-revolution and everyone was in favour of it. There were many royalists in the Government itself. Barras was one of the most influential of the Directors and his salon, presided over by the Duchesse de Brancas, was always full of royalists. Although it seemed unlikely that the other four Directors would follow his example, there is no doubt that the Bourbon cause had never had such well-founded hopes of success as at that time.

* A legal device by which an heir secured himself against unlimited liability for his ancestor by providing an inventory of his actual heritage, to the extent of which alone he would then be liable. (Tr.)

We set out in a hired carriage, my husband, myself, my good Marguérite and our two children: Humbert, who was then seven and a half, and Charlotte who was eight months old and whom I was nursing.

We spent several days at Tesson. The house was in an appalling state. Not only had the furniture been carried off but the paper had been torn from the walls, the locks from many of the doors, the shutters from many of the windows, the iron pots and pans from the kitchen and the gratings from the ovens. The house had been devastated. Fortunately, Grégoire had piled as many mattresses as possible on his own bed and on those of his wife and daughter and it was on these that we slept during our stay.

It was with considerable emotion that I saw that good couple again for they had hidden my husband with so much care and devotion. On our way through Mirambeau, I had already seen the locksmith, Potier, and his wife, with whom M. de La Tour du Pin had taken refuge and lain hidden for three months in a space too dark even for reading. I thanked God again for having permitted him to escape from all the dangers of that dreadful Terror. The memory of it remained so deeply impressed on my mind that I still had frequent nightmares in which I thought they were searching for my husband, hunting him from room to room. Then I would suddenly wake up, covered in a cold sweat, my heart pounding painfully.

At last, we reached the end of our journey. Mme de Valence welcomed me with joy and Mme de Montesson, who had not yet left for the country, greeted me with the greatest kindness. My husband and I were at supper that very evening with Mme de Valence when M. de Talleyrand was announced. He was very pleased to see us and was soon asking: 'Well, Gouvernet, what are your plans?' Taken by surprise, my husband replied that he had come to settle some personal affairs. 'Ah,' said Talleyrand, 'I thought . . .' and changed the conversation to unimportant, trifling matters. A few minutes later, he began telling Mme de Valence, with that nonchalance which must be seen, for it cannot be described: 'By the way, you know the Government has been changed. New ministers have been appointed.' When she asked who they were, he hesitated a little, as if he had forgotten their names and was trying to recall them, then continued: 'Ah, yes. Let me see. So-and-so at the Admiralty and somebody else at the Treasury.' 'And who', I asked, 'is at the Foreign Office?' 'Ah, at the Foreign Office? Well, I expect I am!' And, taking up his hat, he left.

My husband and I looked at one another, but without surprise, for it was impossible to feel surprise at anything M. de Talleyrand did, unless, perhaps, it should be something lacking in taste. Although he served a government drawn from the dregs of the gutter, he himself remained a very great gentlemen. By the following day, he was already as much at home in the Foreign Office as if he had spent the last ten years there. The influence of Mme de Staël, all-powerful at that time through Benjamin Constant, had made him a Minister. He had arrived at her house one day and, flinging on the table his purse, which held only a few louis, had said: 'That is what remains of my fortune. I must have a ministry by tomorrow or I shall blow my brains out.' None of it was true, but it was dramatic and Mme de Staël loved drama. In any case, the appointment was not difficult to secure. The Directory, especially Barras, were only too honoured to have such a minister.

I will not re-tell the story of 18 Fructidor.* The royalists were full of hope, and intrigues and counter intrigues were legion. Many of the émigrés had returned, some under false names. They wore badges so that they would know one another and all these badges were well known to the police: the black velvet coat collars, some form of knot in a corner of the handkerchief and so on. It was by such absurdities that they thought they could save France. Mme de Montesson used to come back from the country to give dinners for deputies favourably disposed to the royalist cause. M. Brouquens, our very good friend, also gave such dinners and the talk was most incredibly unguarded.

Every day, my husband and I met people we had once known and for at least a month, the strangeness of the life I had led in America and my wish to return there made me quite the rage. We spent several days with Mme d'Hénin at Saint-Ouen, to the delight of Humbert who was very bored in Paris, where he could not go out.

I was struck by the extreme lack of prudence in the talk at table and before the servants. People loudly discussed the royalist plans and hopes, and talked by name of émigrés they had met during the morning who had returned with false papers. Nor were they any more careful in the presence of deputies on whom they thought

* The coup d'état of September 1797. The elections of the previous March had gone in favour of the moderates and anti-Jacobins. The three Jacobin Directors appealed to Napoleon for help and he sent troops, under the command of General Augereau. There was no military action but the extreme Jacobins were re-established and revolutionary rigours reimposed. A royalist coup was indeed preparing but the deputies concerned were arrested.

they could rely. I was thought ridiculous and pedantic when I said that M. de Talleyrand was aware of every single plot that was being discussed and was laughing at them. Yet I knew it was so.

I also saw Mme de Staël nearly every day. Despite her more than intimate friendship with Benjamin Constant, she was working for the royalists, or rather, for compromises. I dined with her one day when the guests included eight or ten of the most distinguished deputies: MM. Barbé-Marbois, Portalis, Villaret de Joyeuse, Dupont de Nemours and Tronson du Coudray, that champion of the queen. The latter said to Benjamin: 'You, who visit Barras every day, know well that the way lies clear for us.' To which Benjamin replied with a quotation from one of M. de Lally's poems: 'They shall not touch a hair of thy head.' 'I'm quite sure they won't,' flashed Tronson du Coudray, 'I wear a wig.' And that is how those unfortunate people joked and talked among themselves, unaware that a fortnight later they would all be on their way to Cayenne.

While all this was going on, a Turkish embassy arrived in Paris and M. de Talleyrand gave a magnificent luncheon in honour of the ambassador and his suite. Instead of having the luncheon at a table, a buffet was arranged along one side of a large salon. It rose in tiers half way up the windows and was laden with exquisite dishes of every kind and decorated with vases of the rarest flowers. Around the other three sides of the room were sofas for the guests and small tables, already laid, were carried in and set before them. M. de Talleyrand led the ambassador to a divan, seated himself in Eastern fashion and invited his guest, through an interpreter, to choose the lady whose company he would like at luncheon. The ambassador did not hesitate and indicated me. This was not unduly flattering for, of all the ladies present, none could stand the brilliant light of a mid-August noon, whereas my own complexion and fair hair had nothing to fear from it. I was, nonetheless, extremely embarrassed when M. de Talleyrand came to take me to this Moslem, who held out his hand most gracefully. He was a handsome man of between fifty and sixty, well dressed in the Turkish style of that day and wearing an enormous turban of white muslin. During the luncheon he was very attentive and I completed my conquest by refusing a glass of Malaga wine. Through his Greek interpreter, M. Angelo, who was well known in Parisian circles, he paid me a thousand amiable compliments. He asked me, among other things, if I liked perfume. As I replied that I liked what we in France called aromatic pastilles, he took my handkerchief, spread it on his knees and then, from an enormous pocket in his pelisse, filled both hands with small pastilles no larger than peas, of a kind which the Turks used to put in their pipes. Pouring these pastilles into my handkerchief, he gave them to me.

The following day, he sent me, by M. de Talleyrand, a great flask of attar of roses and a very fine piece of green and gold cloth woven in Turkey. And that was the extent of my triumph, which created a momentary stir. None of the ladies referred to as being of the Directory – the Duchesse de Brancas, Mme Tallien, Mme Bonaparte – had been invited to this luncheon.

As you will imagine, my son, my first care on arriving in Paris was to call on Mme Tallien,* to whom we owed our lives. I found her living in a small house called 'La Chaumière' at the end of the Cours la Reine. She received me most affectionately and wanted straight away to explain why she had found herself obliged to marry Tallien, by whom she had had a child. She was already finding life with this new husband unbearable. His readiness to take offence and his suspicious mind were, it seems, unequalled. She told me that once, when she returned home at one o'clock in the morning, he had been in such a fury of jealousy that he had been ready to kill her. Seeing him load a pistol, she had fled for shelter and protection to M. Martell, whose life she had saved at Bordeaux. But he had refused to let her into his house. She wept bitterly as she told me of this ingratitude. The expression of my own gratitude, into which I put all the warmth that I so sincerely felt, was very sweet to her. Tallien came into his wife's room for a moment. I thanked him fairly coolly and he told me I could always count on him. You will see later how he kept that promise.

XXIII

My husband was busy with his affairs and engaged in negotiations to buy back a part of the Hautefontaine property which had just been sold when, at daybreak on 18 Fructidor – 4 September 1797 – as I sat on the bed nursing my daughter, I heard what sounded like gun carriages on the boulevard. As my room opened on to the courtyard, I told Marguérite to go and see from the dining-room window what was happening. She returned to tell me that large

* Thérésia Cabarrus, formerly Mme de Fontenay.

numbers of generals, troops and guns were pouring into the boulevard. I rose hastily and sent to awaken my husband, who slept in
the room above mine. We both went to the window and were soon
joined by Mme de Valence. Augereau was there, giving orders.
Both the Rue des Capucines and the Rue Neuve-du-Luxembourg
had been closed. M. de La Tour du Pin then went off to M. Villaret
de Joyeuse who lived right at the beginning of the Rue Neuve-du-
Luxembourg and stayed with him until he was arrested.

By midday, as no one had brought us any news, Mme de Valence
and I had become so curious to discover what was going on that
we set out, modestly dressed in order not to attract attention, to
call on Mme de Staël. We had intended taking the Rue Neuve-du-
Luxembourg, but it was barred by a gun. So also was the Rue des
Capucines. The Rue de la Paix did not exist in those days, so we had
to go as far as the Rue de Richelieu to find a street still open. All
the shops were shut, the streets were full of people, silent people.
When we reached the archway passages, we found our way blocked
by a mass of men and women who were being refused access to the
Quai.* By pushing and threading our way between them, we finally
managed to reach the front of the crowd where a line of soldiers was
keeping a way clear for five or six very strongly escorted carriages
which were making their way at a foot pace towards the Pont
Royal. In one of them, the last, we recognised MM. Portalis and
Barbé-Marbois. They saw us and made friendly signs which seemed
to mean: 'We don't know what they're going to do with us.' Seeing
these gestures, a number of those horrible women who appear only
during revolutions or disorders, began insulting us, shouting:
'Down with the royalists.' I admit that I was terrified. Fortunately,
as we were standing immediately behind the soldiers, we were able
to slip between them and cross the road to reach Mme de Staël's
house.

She was with Benjamin Constant and very angry with him
because he maintained that by arresting the Deputies, the Directory
had made a coup d'état inevitable. When she expressed a fear that
the Deputies might be tried before a Government commission, he
did not deny the likelihood, saying with his usual hypocritical air:
'It would be unfortunate, but perhaps necessary!' Then he told us
that all émigrés who had returned would be ordered to leave France
again, under pain of trial by military tribunal. Dismayed at this
news, I hurried home to tell my husband. Alas, the Decree was
already being cried in the streets. When I reached home, I found

* The carriage road beside the Seine.

my husband wondering anxiously how he could warn his aunt at Saint-Ouen of what was happening. All the gates of Paris had been closed and no one could pass the barricades without special permission.

By an extraordinary piece of good fortune, I met Mme de Pontécoulant whom I knew through having met her often at the house of Mme de Valence. She was on her way to Saint-Denis, where she had a country house and had a pass from the Section for herself and her maid. I asked her to let me take the place of the maid and, with her usual kindness, she agreed. I was still nursing my small Charlotte and could not abandon her, so I asked Mme de Pontécoulant to take me not as a maid, but as a nursemaid. She liked the idea that at her age – she was between forty-five and fifty – the guards at the barricades should think her the mother of an eight-months-old baby, so we set out together. But the poor woman was quickly disillusioned. Indeed, when we reached the city gate, the toll collectors and soldiers, far from congratulating the mistress, directed all their flatteries at the nurse. Mme de Pontécoulant was very annoyed and instead of taking me to Saint-Ouen, a detour which would have added only ten minutes to her journey, she simply set me down in the road, at the end of a very long avenue. The weight of my plump small daughter made it seem even longer.

You will easily imagine the exclamations with which I was greeted by Mme de Poix and my aunt. The latter decided to return immediately to England. With these two ladies were a number of former émigrés who were in despair at being forced to leave France again. It put an abrupt and irrevocable end to all the negotiations which had been begun with those who had bought confiscated properties from the state and were at that time often willing to consider selling them back to their former owners. It can be truly said that the happenings of 18 Fructidor were as fatal to private fortunes as the revolution itself.

The Decree ordered all émigrés who had returned to French soil to leave Paris within twenty-four hours and France within a week. My own view was that we should set out immediately for Le Bouilh. Since we had left France with a valid passport and returned on the same document, duly visaed by the French and Spanish authorities, I thought the Decree might not apply to us. There had been nothing clandestine about our return. To obtain assurance on this point, my husband went to see M. de Talleyrand. He, however, was greatly preoccupied with his own future and had no time to spare for that of others. So he replied without hesitation that it was no concern of his and told us to submit the case to Sottin, Minister of Police. I went, then, to see Tallien, who welcomed me warmly. He drew up a statement of our circumstances, omitting our names: 'A private person, who left in 1794 with a passport . . .' and so on, setting out our circumstances as favourably as possible. He promised to go immediately to see Sottin to ask him to add his recommendation. Without it, it would be impossible to get a visa for the passport given us by the municipality of Saint-André-en-Cubzac for our journey to Paris, which had to be produced in order to pass the barricades when leaving the city.

I returned home in some anxiety and began to pack. A police order had just been posted up in Paris calling on all householders to report anyone living in their houses without the proper papers. We did not want to create difficulties for Mme de Montesson, who was lodging us. She was already sufficiently anxious on her own account, for she had been receiving the deported Deputies at her house for several months past, welcoming them with the greatest kindness, and feared that she might, as a result, be heavily compromised.

Eventually, after many hours of extremely anxious waiting, Tallien returned to me the request he had submitted to Sottin. The minister had added a signed note in his own hand: 'This person is within the law.' Tallien also sent a short letter, written in the third person, apologising very civilly for not having been able to obtain anything, but the end of the letter might have been construed to mean: 'I wish you a good journey'.

Two courses were open to us. We could ask for a passport to Spain and travel by way of Le Bouilh, where I would remain for a time while my husband went on to San Sebastian. It would have been the wiser course. The alternative was to go to England and from there, according to circumstances, return to America. My aunt, Mme d'Hénin, had considerable influence over my husband and she persuaded him to adopt the second course. We had very little money but, knowing that in London we would find my stepmother, Mme Dillon, and many other very close relatives who would doubtless be willing to help us, we decided to go to England.

As it had been our intention to spend only five or six weeks in Paris, we had brought very little with us. I had had a few gowns made for me there, but two very small trunks were all we needed for our meagre baggage, including that of my good Marguérite, who was fully determined, this time, to come with us. This departure was to have the most unfortunate consequences for us. We were in the midst of our negotiations with the buyers of Hautefontaine, intending merely to become the buyers of the estate in their stead, for my grandmother was still alive. However, it had been laid down in my marriage contract that I was her sole heir, so I thought it not unreasonable to consider that I could, with a clear conscience, acquire property that was hers. This new emigration ruined all these arrangements. Providence had decreed that my husband and I should end our lives in the most complete ruin. It also condemned us, unfortunately, to many other very cruel griefs. But I must not anticipate the sorrows that have befallen me. That tale will sadden the last pages of this account.

We spent the two or three days before our departure in a state of gloom and uncertainty. Perhaps we should have returned to Le Bouilh. There was a rumour that Barras, although giving way for the moment to the demands of his colleagues, would soon regain all his power and that, when that moment came, he would resume his favourable attitude towards the émigrés.

Everyone we met was distraught at this fresh emigration. We booked three places in a carriage which would take us to Calais in three days. Two other places were taken by a cousin. M. de Beauvau, and by young César Ducrest, a cousin of Mme de Valence. The French are by nature gay, so that although we were all desolate, ruined and furious, we nonetheless succeeded in preserving our good humour and laughter. We reported to each municipality along our route, including that of Calais, where we embarked on a packet at eleven o'clock in the evening.

I sat on a closed hatch on the deck, my daughter, Alix, in my arms. Marguérite put Humbert to bed. My husband felt sea sick the very moment he stepped on board, though there was little wind and the night was superb. Beside me was a gentleman who, seeing me burdened with a child, suggested in a very English voice that I should lean against him. I turned to thank him and, as I did so, the moonlight shone on my face and he exclaimed: 'Good God, is it possible?' It was young Jeffreys, son of the editor of the *Edinburgh Review*, whom I had met daily at his uncle's house in Boston during our visit to that hospitable city three years before. We spoke for a long time of America and my regret at having left it, a regret intensified by these new threats of emigration. I explained that, despite the presence of all my family in England, I was going there with but one idea and purpose: to return to my farm, if all hope of returning to France should fail or be postponed indefinitely.

As I talked to my companion, the night passed and the first

gleams of daylight revealed the white cliffs of Albion towards which we were being driven by a strong south-easterly wind. When we dropped anchor on British shores, the sad faces of the passengers could be seen emerging from the hatches, all in various stages of pallor and dishevelment. My poor maid, whose longest sea journey had been from Le Bouilh to Bordeaux, was enchanted to see dry land again. We disembarked and found ourselves at the mercy of the rough English excise men, who seemed to me far worse than their Spanish counterparts. When they saw my passport, which I presented at the office charged with examining them – the Aliens' Office – I was asked if I was a subject of the King of England. When I said that I was, I was told I would have to find someone of standing in England to vouch for me. When, without hesitation, I named my three uncles – Lord Dillon, Lord Kenmare and Sir William Jerningham – the tone and attitude of the officers changed at once. These formalities occupied the whole morning.

After an English luncheon, or more, exactly, dinner, we left Dover for London. We spent the night at Canterbury or Rochester, I can no longer recall which, and the following morning arrived in London at one of the inns in Piccadilly. From Dover, I had sent news of our arrival to my aunt, Lady Jerningham, and she had sent her dear, amiable Edward* to meet us and take us to her house in Bolton Row. She gave us a most motherly welcome, told us that she was leaving for the country, for Cossey, where she would be staying at least six months, and made us promise to come and spend them with her, saying this would give us plenty of time in which to settle our future plans. My good aunt was especially kind to my husband and since she dearly loved children, immediately conceived a great affection for Humbert. It is true to say that, at the age of seven and a half, he was a most extraordinarily intelligent child, speaking and writing fluently both English and French and already writing dictations in both languages.

We established ourselves, therefore, in Bolton Row as if we had been children of the house. There, I found my good old friend, the Chevalier Jerningham, brother of my aunt's husband. The faithful friendship shown me by the chevalier ever since my childhood was as heart-warming as it was useful during my stay in England.

I was preparing to call on my stepmother, Mme Dillon, who had been living in England for nearly two years, when she arrived at my aunt's house. She was very moved at seeing me again and hearing

* The third son of Sir William and Lady Jerningham.

from me about the last months of my poor father's life, for I had spent the winter of 1792–1793 with him.

My arrival in London was an event in the family. I saw again Betsy de La Touche, my stepmother's daughter, who had been entrusted to my care in 1789 and 1790 when she was in Paris at the Convent of the Assumption. I had gone often to visit her there and was the only person allowed to take her out occasionally. She had recently married Edward de Fitz-James and was expecting her first child. She was a gentle, sweet girl and deserved a better fate. She was deeply in love with her husband, who did not return her devotion and whose cruel and flagrant infidelities broke her heart.

Her brother, Alexandre de La Touche, was her junior by three years. He was a handsome young man, irresponsible and gay, of little intelligence and still less learning. He had all the faults of the young people forced into idleness by the emigration. He had no particular talent, loved horses, fashion and small intrigues but never opened a book. My stepmother who, to my knowledge, had never had a book on her table, was incapable of giving him a taste for them. She herself was not without a certain natural wit and was well bred and versed in the ways of society. But I often wondered why my father, gifted as he was with a superior mind and great learning, had married a woman older than himself. It is true that she was wealthy, but she could not have been considered an heiress. He longed above all for a son, and from his marriage with her had only three daughters. Two died in very early childhood and only the eldest, Fanny,* survived.

My uncle, the archbishop, and my grandmother were also living in London. I had not seen them since leaving their house in 1788, nine years before. My aunt, Lady Jerningham, thought I should show them some mark of respect and the good chevalier undertook to ask them if they would receive me. Seeing that the archbishop wished it, my grandmother did not dare to refuse, but she made it a condition that M. de La Tour du Pin should not accompany me. I could have used this as a pretext for not calling on them, but pretended not to know of it. In any case, my husband was delighted to be dispensed from the visit, for he already knew, he told me later, that my grandmother had spoken very maliciously of him since she had been in London. If I had known this at the time, I certainly would not have called on her.

* Frances, or Fanny, Dillon, who later married General Bertrand, Napoleon's devoted Grand Marshal, who accompanied him to St Helena and remained with him until his death. It was he who brought Napoleon's body back to France.

One morning, then, I set out for Thayer Street with my small Humbert. It was not without emotion and many conflicting feelings that I knocked on the door of the modest five-windowed house where my uncle and my grandmother were living. For me, there had been no intermediate stages between that house and the beautiful hôtel on the Faubourg-Saint-Germain where I had spent my childhood in luxury and splendour. The door was opened by an old servant who burst into tears when he saw me. He was from Hautefontaine and had been at my wedding. He preceded me and I heard him announce in a voice shaken by emotion: 'Mme de Gouvernet is here.' My grandmother rose and came to meet me. I kissed her hand. Her welcome was very cold and she addressed me as 'Madame'. At the same moment, the archbishop came in and, throwing his arms about me, kissed me tenderly. Then, seeing my son, he embraced him too, over and over again. He asked him a number of questions in both English and French and the child replied with a self-possession and shrewdness that charmed my uncle. When he asked me if Humbert might accompany him to a nearby house where he went every morning to have electric treatment for his deafness, I was a little afraid that Humbert would not wish to go. But I need not have worried: the child replied without hesitation that he would like very much to go 'with the old gentleman.'

I was extremely uneasy at being thus left to spend half-an-hour alone with my grandmother. I was afraid she would begin her long list of accusations and trembled also at the thought that she might turn the conversation to my poor father or my husband. She detested them both equally, and I never felt sufficiently mistress of myself to endure unmoved the attacks her inveterate hatred was capable of inspiring. Fortunately, she restrained herself until the archbishop returned, delighted with Humbert who had not been in the least frightened by the electrical apparatus and who had even received several shocks without flinching.

My uncle invited me to dine the following day with the six aged bishops of Languedoc whom he boarded at his table. They were all old acquaintances of mine. As for my husband, there was no question of his coming. I announced my plan to stay at Cossey with my aunt for the whole of her stay there. The archbishop was pleased to hear of this arrangement, but I could hear my grandmother muttering wordlessly to herself, a sign I remembered as heralding some disagreeable remark which she would not be able to keep back. So I rose to leave, kissed my grandmother's hand and was immediately embraced by the archbishop who complimented me on my looks.

Lady Jerningham had been very anxious about this visit and was pleased that it had passed off well. The following day I was taken to call on two other uncles.

One was Lord Dillon, my father's eldest brother. He received me courteously but coolly and clearly felt not the slightest interest in us. He offered us his box at the Opera for that very evening and we accepted. It was the only service he was ever to render me. He gave a pension of £1,000 a year to my eighty-four-year-old uncle, the archbishop, but so far as I myself was concerned, the fact that I was his brother's daughter availed me nothing and not once in the two and a half years I spent in England did he give me any help.

The second uncle I visited, this time with Lady Jerningham, was Lord Kenmare. He received me quite differently, although I was only his niece through his first wife, my father's sister. She had been dead for many years and he had re-married. By his first marriage, he had had a daughter, the Lady Charlotte Browne. Lord Kenmare, his daughter and all his family welcomed me with a kindness and a readiness to help that were unequalled. The friendship of Lady Charlotte, in particular, never failed me. She was then eighteen and much sought-after in marriage, as her dowry was a goodly £20,000.

I went to Richmond to see our aunt, Mme d'Hénin. She was very offended at our plan to stay at Cossey with Lady Jerningham. She was an exceedingly dominating woman, a veritable tyrant, and the slightest infringement of her authority or her influence roused her to unreasonable fury. Most of her tyranny was exercised on M. de Lally, but it must be admitted that her decisiveness and firmness were really of the greatest help to him. She would brook no rival and the fact that during the three or four months that Mme d'Hénin had been in France, M. de Lally had been so unwise as to stay at Cossey, as happy there as a schoolboy on holiday, had given my aunt the greatest dislike for Lady Jerningham. However, despite her choleric, authoritative nature, Mme d'Hénin did not lack a sense of justice. This forced her to admit that it was only natural for us, arriving in England without a penny, to be overjoyed at being adopted by a relative so close and so well esteemed in the world as my aunt Jerningham.

Mme d'Hénin and M. de Lally shared an establishment. Their ages should have guaranteed them from scandal, but they were

Mme d'Hénin, Mme de La Tour du Pin's aunt.

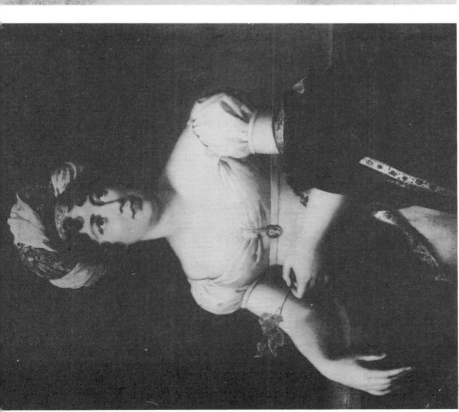

Mme de Staël, by Mlle E. de Godefroy at Versailles, from a painting by Gerard.

nonetheless the butt of considerable ridicule. Despite her real and great qualities, Mme d'Hénin was not generally liked. Some of her friends remained faithful, but her quick temper and dominating nature created enemies for her, almost without her being aware of it.

After three days in London, I realised it would give me no pleasure at all to stay there longer. Émigré society, with its gossip, petty intrigues and scandal-mongering had made the visit odious. I went one evening to visit Mme d'Hénnery, a friend and close relative of Mme d'Hénin, whose daughter, the young and pretentious Duchesse de Lévis, was one of the pale constellations about which fluttered all émigrés aspiring to fashion. There, I met Mme and Mlle de Kersaint and learned that that inveterate aristocrat, Amédée de Duras, so haughty and so intolerant, was by no means disdainful of Mlle de Kersaint's income of 25,000 francs. Mme de Kersaint had been able to save the fortune she had in Martinique. I was six years older than Mlle de Kersaint and she has told me since that she stood much in awe of me in those days.

To my great joy, the departure for Cossey was finally arranged. Lady Jerningham was to leave first and it was therefore decided that I would stay for a few days with my stepmother, Mme Dillon. There, I heard with pleasure that Edward de Fitz-James was taking some saddle horses and that, since I was known to be an excellent rider, he had included a lady's saddle for me. My stepmother gave me a charming habit and we looked forward to some good riding.

We resembled a convoy as we left London: in the first berline were my stepmother, myself, my daughter, my son, Marguérite and Flore, Mme Dillon's mulatto maid; in the second were Mme de Fitz-James, Alexandre de La Touche and my husband. Then there was Betsy's old governess and, last of all, M. de Fitz-James with his horses, grooms and so forth.

We spent the night at Newmarket where the famous races are held and which I was curious to see. We stayed there all the following day, the last of the racing season and therefore the day of the King's Cup race. We spent the whole day on the course and by a piece of good fortune very rare in England, the weather was heavenly. I still remember it as one of the most enjoyable and interesting days in my life. The next day we left for Cossey. It was, I think, the beginning of October 1797.

My aunt loved children and took charge of Humbert. She would take him to her room immediately after breakfast and keep him there the whole morning, giving him lessons and making him write and read in English and French. She even took charge of his wardrobe and I saw coats arriving and overcoats, linen and so on, a whole wardrobe for my children. She also showed me the very greatest kindness. She had noticed that I made my own dresses and, on the pretext of encouraging my cousin, Fanny Dillon,* who was also at Cossey, to do likewise, brought to my room and put at my disposal lengths of muslin and materials of every kind. I particularly appreciated this attention as I had arrived from France very lightly clad for the English climate.

Vaccine (against smallpox) had recently been discovered and when my aunt learned that my children had not been inoculated with it, she undertook to have it done and sent to Norwich for her own surgeon to perform the operation. In short, she surrounded us with attentions of every kind and the time I spent at Cossey was as agreeable as we could have wished.

We were a large party: nineteen, including the chaplain, and most of us very closely related. The French cook was excellent and the food plentiful and not too elaborate. Sir William had an income of about £18,000 sterling, which was not considered a great fortune in England, but which was sufficient to permit him to live liberally. The house was old but comfortable. The Chapel was up in the attics, as was customary in Catholic houses before the Emancipation.

The winter passed very pleasantly. Towards March, Mme Dillon, my sister Fanny and M. and Mme de Fitz-James returned to London for the birth of Mme de Fitz-James's baby, but we stayed on at Cossey until May. My aunt was to spend the summer in London, so Sir William suggested that while they were away, we should live in a pretty cottage he had had built in the park. As I was four months' pregnant and, in consequence, not very well, I preferred not to be so far away from everyone, fearing that something might go wrong and prevent my pregnancy reaching its full term. Mme d'Hénin, too, was breathing fire and brimstone at the idea that we might prolong our stay in the country and insisted that we should go to stay with her at Richmond where there would be room for us. We therefore accepted her invitation, though much against my inclination. However, my husband did not want to offend his aunt and there were also certain business matters to be attended to in London.

I am not re-reading the earlier parts of these memoirs, and so am not sure if I told you that when we reached Boston, I wrote to my

* Daughter of Lord Dillon.

good tutor, M. Combes, who was then with my stepmother in Martinique. My father had given him a good post as Registrar of the Island. He had previously held the same post in St Kitts and Tobago, and living, as he did, in my father's house, he had been able to lay aside all his earnings and had eventually accumulated 60,000 francs. Mme Dillon had borrowed this capital against payment of interest. When M. Combes heard that we intended buying a property near Boston, that excellent man, who loved me like a daughter, decided to add this sum, his entire savings, to the funds we already had, so that we could buy a larger property and then he would come to live with us.

He asked Mme Dillon for the capital he had loaned to her. She not only refused his request but would not even agree to repay it in instalments. Desperate at seeing his plans come to nothing, he begged and threatened. All in vain. Each boat from Martinique to the United States brought me a letter from him. He wrote that he did not dare to leave Mme Dillon, hoping by his presence to force her to repay at least something. At this point, Mme Dillon went to England. Before she left, poor M. Combes, who remained in Martinique, managed to extract from her a statement acknowledging her indebtedness for the 60,000 francs of capital and for the interest which by then amounted to nearly 10,000 francs.

While visiting Richmond, I received the sad news of my old friend's death. In his will, he left me this 70,000 francs which Mme Dillon owed him, together with the current interest, which amounted to 1,500 or 1,800 francs. From the day Mme Dillon heard of this bequest, her attitude towards us changed completely. She kept a good house in London and spent lavishly on dinners, evening parties and private theatricals. But whenever we stood in need of money, she sent us to a Creole émigré who looked after her affairs. To all our requests that she should come to some arrangement for paying the interest on our loan, she returned evasive answers. Sometimes the sugar crop was bad, sometimes funds had not arrived, in fact, each day there was a fresh excuse. I spoke to her personally about it and was very badly received. We spoke about it to her son, Alexandre de La Touche, and my husband spoke of it to her man of business, but all to no effect. In short, we were given as alms the revenue from what was really our own property. But we had to pay Mme d'Hénin our share of the household expenses and this was a fresh source of embarrassment. There was also the need to make a new layette for the baby, as all the baby clothes had been left behind in France. Oh, I very often regretted leaving Cossey.

I found sharing a house with Mme d'Hénin intolerable. She had given us such poor accommodation that we could not receive visitors – we had only two small bedrooms on the ground floor and it is not customary in England to receive visitors in the room where one sleeps. I shared one of these rooms with my daughter and M. de La Tour du Pin shared the other with our son. It was only in the evenings that we joined my aunt in a pretty salon on the first floor. It was certainly very uncomfortable, but if life had been pleasant, this would not have worried me. I was fully aware of the outstanding qualities of Mme d'Hénin and was never lacking in respect towards her, but I had to admit that our characters were not compatible. Perhaps it was my fault. Perhaps I should have remained impervious to the hail of pinpricks I received from her. M. de Lally, that most timorous of men, never dared risk the slightest jest which might have provided me with some amusement. I was still young and loved to laugh. At twenty-eight, it would surely have been unnatural for me to have acquired the serious mien proper to my aunt's fifty years? She was entirely wrapped up in politics and her sole interest was the future constitution of France. It bored me to death. And then, there were the writings of M. de Lally, which had to be read and re-read, word by word, sentence by sentence . . .!

In short, I longed for a house of my own, however small. But I could see no means of fulfilling this longing and had to resign myself.

✠✠✠✠✠✠✠✠✠ XXIV ✠✠✠✠✠✠✠✠✠

The Princesse de Bouillon, of whom I wrote in the first part of these memoirs, came to England early in the summer of 1798 with her son-in-law to settle certain matters connected with a legacy. Although she had always lived in France, she was by birth a German, a Princess of Hesse-Rothenbourg. There had been a long and faithful attachment between her and Prince Emmanuel de Salm by whom she had had a daughter, known as Thérésia. While an émigrée, Mme de Bouillon had married this daughter to M. deVitrolles.*

* At that time, M. de Vitrolles was a young councillor in the *Parlement* of Aix. Leaving his wife and three young children in Germany, he accompanied the Princesse de Bouillon to London, where he terrified her by declaring

My aunt had taken a small apartment for them not far from the house where we were living. Mme de Bouillon's visit to Richmond brought us a number of very enjoyable invitations. The Duchess of Devonshire gave a great luncheon party for the émigrés in her delicious country house at Chiswick. Her sister, Lady Bessborough, gave a fine dinner at Roehampton, where she was spending the summer in a lovely house. We were invited on both occasions and I went with the greatest pleasure, despite being more than seven months' pregnant.

People who had not seen Mme de Bouillon for some years hardly recognised her. She had never been pretty, or so I assume, but at the time of which I am writing, when she was fifty-four or fifty-five years old, she was a tall, stooping woman and looked literally dried up. Her dry, yellow skin clung to her bones and through her cheeks you could count her black and broken teeth. Her face was truly frightening and her health, which had been very bad for a number of years, showed no sign of improvement. But I must quickly add that her wit, grace and kindness had lost none of their charm. I frequently called on her in the mornings and she received me with the same kindness she had always shown.

One day, Mme d'Hénin came in and announced that she and Mme de Bouillon had arranged everything for me: 'M. de Vitrolles is leaving and Mme de Bouillon does not want to stay alone in her lodging. But the lease has still three months to run, so she will exchange apartments with you. You will be much more comfortable there for your lying-in.' My husband signed to me to accept this offer.

So I went to stay in Mme de Bouillon's lodgings and there gave birth to a son whom we called Edward, his godparents being Lady Jerningham and her son, Edward.

The good Chevalier Jerningham came to see me and from him I learned that Lady Jerningham considered that when I left my present lodging, it would be impossible for me, with three children, to return to the two small bedrooms of the modest apartment I had formerly occupied in Mme d'Hénin's house. Also, no matter how short of funds we might be, and, in fact, on that very account, she thought we would prefer to be on our own and independent. She had therefore charged him to find us a small house in Richmond and his search had been successful beyond anything we could have

a violent passion for her. His extraordinary conduct was said to have arisen from some temporary madness, real or feigned, and he was sent back to Germany.

wished. The house belonged to a former Drury Lane actress who had been very beautiful and much in fashion. She never lived there, but it was so clean and beautifully kept that she was not anxious to let it. However, the chevalier's eloquence and a gift of £45 from Lady Jerningham persuaded her to do so.

This little house was a real gem, with a frontage that could not have been more than fifteen feet in width. Downstairs was a corridor, a pretty drawing-room with two windows and, beyond it, a concealed staircase. On the first floor were two charming bed-rooms; above them, two servants' rooms. At the end of the corridor on the ground floor, a pleasant kitchen opened on to a minute garden with a path and two flower borders. There were carpets everywhere and good English oilcloth in the passages and on the stairs. Nowhere would you have found a daintier, cleaner or more elegantly furnished house, so small that it would have fitted into any room of medium size.

Yet, on the day we moved in, I was in a state of profound distress. On that very day, my poor baby son, a strong and beautiful child only three months old, died suddenly from a pleurisy for which I blame the carelessness of the English nurse who had the care of him. It was late autumn, which comes early in England. As I had been nursing the dear angel myself, my grief curdled my milk. I became very ill and was myself near to death when we arrived at the house with my two remaining children, Humbert, who was nine and a half and Charlotte who was just two. Having only these two children left to care for, we dismissed the English servant. While I had been in the United States, Marguérite had learned something of cookery and willingly turned her talents and, above all, her devotion, to feeding us

England, a country where there are immense fortunes and people who live in sumptuous elegance, is also the country where the poor can live most comfortably. For instance, there is no need to go to market. The butcher never fails to call regularly at the same hour every day, coming to the door and shouting 'Butcher' to announce his presence. You open and tell him what you want. A leg of lamb, perhaps? He will bring it to you all prepared and ready to be put on the spit. Cutlets? They are laid neatly on a little wooden tray, which he collects the following day. A small wooden skewer fastens a paper to the meat showing the weight and price. There are no useless pieces of what are known elsewhere as 'make-weights'. The same with all the other tradesmen. There are no arguments or problems to fear.

After a couple of days, my son, who spoke English like an Englishman, would call at the shops in the morning on his way to school, where he spent the entire day. On Saturdays, he would pay our accounts for the week. There were never any mistakes or muddles.

Humbert went to school every day after our lunch, stayed to dinner and returned home again at six o'clock. Then came the great pleasure of his day: a visit to a good French family, Monsieur and Madame de Thuisy, who lived quite near us at Richmond. They had four sons, whom M. de Thuisy was educating himself. Humbert went alone to their house every day after dinner and stayed from seven until nine o'clock. On the rare occasions when he returned after nine, the Chevalier de Thuisy would accompany him home. This excellent man, a Knight of Malta, was Providence itself to all the émigrés living in Richmond. Once a week, sometimes more often, he would go on foot to London and it is unbelievable how inconsiderate people were in the number of commissions with which they charged him.

I saw him every day. Once a week, I did our ironing. On those days, he would sit by the fire and hand me the irons, cleaning them first on brick and sandpaper, as has to be done when they are heated on coal. Sometimes when we met in the evening at the house of Mme d'Ennery, who always had a lot of company, or at that of Mrs Blount, an English lady, the chevalier would come up to me in his best company manner and ask quietly: 'Is it tomorrow that we iron?'

Many ladies among the émigrés of his acquaintance never went out into society. They had to earn a living. The chevalier knew of my skill with the needle and when they were particularly rushed, often brought me some of their work, especially linen for marking, because it was at that kind of work that I excelled.

After a while, we found ourselves very short of money because Mme Dillon was creating difficulties about payments. Our entire wealth consisted of five or six hundred francs and we said to one another that when that was spent, we would literally not know where to turn – not for shelter, since our little house cost us nothing, but for food. My friend, the Chevalier Jerningham, had told me that our uncle, Lord Dillon, had most hard-heartedly refused to help us. Nor could there be any help from France, for all communication had been cut.

It was just then that we received a despairing letter from M. de Chambeau, who was still living in Spain. He had had no news from France and no one had sent him a penny. His uncle, a former fermier général whose sole heir he was, had just died leaving a will in his favour, but the Government had confiscated the legacy as émigré property. On the day he wrote, he had but one louis left and could no longer count on the Spaniards of his acquaintance, for he had exhausted their charity. When M. de La Tour du Pin received this letter, he did not hesitate a moment to share with his friend the few francs left in the bottom of his purse. He hurried to a reliable banker and took out a bill of exchange for £10 sterling, payable on sight in Madrid. It was sent off that very same day. It represented nearly half our fortune, for we were left with only £12 in the exchequer and no means of meeting our needs when that was spent. Out of consideration for my family, particularly Lady Jerningham, we did not want to claim the help which the English Government offered to émigrés. So far as Lord Dillon was concerned, I felt under no obligation, but another consideration was respect for my father's memory which made me unwilling to let it be publicly known that his widow, my stepmother, who owned a house in London and gave dinners and evening parties with theatricals, refused to come to my assistance.

One last £5 note remained to us when my good and very kind cousin, Edward Jerningham, rode out one morning to see me. He was a charming young man and had just celebrated his twenty-first birthday. Everything about him justified his mother's adoring love. Witty, thoughtful and well read, he combined all the qualities of more mature years with the charm and gaiety of youth. The kindness of his nature equalled the loftiness of his sentiments and the distinction of his mind. He showed me great friendship and I, in return, loved him like a younger brother. He was about to leave for Cossey and told me that his father had just given him some sum or other from a legacy bequeathed to him in childhood. 'I wager that a good part of it will go to providing winter clothing for the good Fathers of Juilly,' I remarked. These were the Oratorians with whom he had spent many years of his childhood 'Not all,' he replied, blushed to the very roots of his hair and turned the conversation to other things.

As he rose to leave, I went to the door to see him mount. He remained behind a moment and I saw him slide something into my workbasket. I pretended not to notice, so great was his embarrassment. After he had gone, I found in the basket a sealed letter addressed to me. It contained the brief message: 'Given to my dear cousin by her friend, Ned' and a note for £100.

M. de La Tour du Pin returned a minute later and I told him it was a reward for what he had done for M. de Chambeau. As you may imagine, he went the very next morning to London to thank Edward, but found he had already left for Cossey.

A few days later, I too went to London with two English ladies of my acquaintance whom I saw often in Richmond. They were sisters, the elder, Miss Lydia White, being a well-known blue-stocking We made music together and they put their books at my disposal. When they decided to spend a week in London, they begged M. de La Tour du Pin to allow me to accompany them. We went to the Opera, where they were playing *Elfrida*. The singer was Mme Banti, whom I had already heard with Lady Bedingfield. I was also taken to a large gathering in the house of a lady whom I scarcely saw. People overflowed on to the stairs and no one even dreamed of trying to sit down. By chance, I was crowded into a corner of the salon where someone was playing the piano, though no one was paying the slightest attention to the music. The pianist was a man and I listened in some surprise, for I could not recall ever having heard anything so agreeable, in such excellent taste and expressing so much feeling and delicacy. After a quarter of an hour, the pianist realised no one was listening, so he got up and left. I asked his name . . . it was Cramer! There were so many guests that we had some difficulty in detaching ourselves from the throng, but the doorman's cry: 'Miss White's carriage stops the way' forced us to hasten. It is a summons that has to be obeyed under pain of losing one's turn in the line and being condemned to wait a further hour.

The week seemed long and tedious and by the end of it I was glad to return to Richmond.

During this time, Mme de Duras* had given birth to my dear Félicie, a friend who will perhaps read these memoirs when I am no longer here. I had come to know Claire quite well during a short visit she made to Richmond and although our characters were not particularly compatible, we grew to like one another very well. In those days, she was madly in love with her husband, whose in-fidelities, when she knew of them, roused her to storms of fury and despair scarcely calculated to bring him back to her. Shortly after Félicie's birth, they took a house at Teddington, a village two miles from Richmond. Amédée de Duras was the oldest of my friends. When we were very young, we had made music together. We resumed the habit at Teddington, where I often spent the day.

* Mlle Claire de Kersaint, who had married Amédée, Duc de Duras.

M. de Poix, who was living in Richmond, had a very good horse and a tilbury. I often walked over to Teddington and he would take me back to Richmond in his carriage. Thus did we pass the summer of 1798.

We made one excursion lasting a week of which I have the happiest memories. My children were in such safe hands with my good Marguérite that this short absence gave me no anxiety at all. M. de La Tour du Pin rode and I travelled with M. de Poix in his tilbury. After passing through Windsor, we spent the night at Maidenhead, where we stayed the following day, visiting Park Place and taking a boat on the river. From there, we went to Oxford, Blenheim, Stowe and other places, returning by way of Aylesbury and Uxbridge. I was charmed with the beautiful country houses we were fortunate enough to visit. Only in such settings do English gentlemen really become 'grands seigneurs'. We had very fine weather during the whole week we were away on this journey, the expenses of which we shared. I must say here that the English climate away from London is much maligned. I never found it any worse than that of Holland and it is incomparably better and less uncertain than that of Belgium. In my long life there have been a few, a very few, shining moments – rather like the paintings of Gherardo delle Notti* – and this short excursion is one of them.

When we returned to Richmond, I resumed my household occupations. The news from France seemed less black. My husband was even planning to send me over for a few days, armed with an English passport, which would not have been entirely false, as I would have signed it with my own name: Lucy Dillon. But just at that moment we heard that two émigrés who had returned with false papers, M. d'Oilliamson and M. d'Amnécourt, had been caught and shot. They had been given no form of trial. This tragic news reached us on the very day I intended leaving for France and caused us to renounce all thought of such a journey. Personally, I was delighted not to go, not because I feared the danger, but because I so greatly minded leaving my husband and children. I firmly resolved never again to try to return without them.

My life in Richmond was very monotonous. After some very forthright correspondence between M. de La Tour du Pin and Mme Dillon's man of business, we had finally managed to extract some money from Mme Dillon and, as a consequence, I no longer saw her. M. de Fitz-James and M. de La Touche no longer came

* Gerard Honthorst.

to Richmond to visit us and when I went to London, which was but once or twice, I saw only Lady Jerningham and Lord Kenmare who, for the past year, had been making me an allowance of six louis a month.

After the birth of her second daughter, Clara, Mme de Duras went with her husband to Hamburg. Louis XVIII was still in Mittau and officers of the Crown and members of the Household joined him there when their tours of duty came round. The First Gentlemen of the Bedchamber lived with the king during their year in waiting. M. de Duras' turn had come and he expressed a wish to take his wife with him. They, therefore, left their children in the care of Mme de Thuisy. But Mme de Duras' father, M. de Kersaint,* had been a member of the National Convention at the time of the king's trial and she feared this unfortunate circumstance might prevent her being received at Mittau. She thought it unlikely that her father's death would have effaced the blot and therefore gave as a reason for not continuing her journey the need to look after certain business matters for her mother, who was in Martinique to sell her house there. I have certainly had reason to believe that when M. de Duras did arrive in Hamburg, he found the Duc de Fleury waiting to tell him, on behalf of the king, that his wife would not be received. So Mme de Duras' journey ended there. I have forgotten if M. de Duras himself went on to Mittau but in any case, they returned to Teddington shortly afterwards.

Their marriage was unhappier than ever. M. de Duras' attitude towards his wife became increasingly difficult and she wept day and night, unfortunately putting on deplorable airs which bored her husband to death. With a wounding lack of dissimulation, for which I often reproached him, he let her see it. But he argued that love could not be commanded and said he hated scenes.

Having lectured the husband, I consoled the wife. I tried to instil a little independence into her, to convince her that jealousy and reproaches, by making their home unbearable, were alienating her husband. By day, it was not too difficult for there was a constant stream of visitors. But the evenings, when they were alone, were another matter. An old officer of the bodyguard, M. de La Sipière, almost invariably came to interrupt any tête-à-tête. Often Amédée de Duras took advantage of this to go off to London and then would follow endless tears and recriminations from his wife. Poor Claire wanted only romance and her husband was the least romantic

* The Comte de Kersaint was a member of the Convention for the Department of Seine et Oise.

of men. He would certainly have enjoyed his home if it had been made pleasanter for him. But under an outward show of passion, there were barely concealed in Mme de Duras an arrogance and a tyranny which have since become even more intense. Intelligent as she was, she brought great unhappiness on her family and on herself.

Towards the end of the winter, Miss White left Richmond. This was a grief to me, not because we had formed a lasting friendship, but because she had been so kind that I found it very pleasant to have her near. For some time, my health had not been as good as it should have been. I felt very listless but did not know exactly what was wrong. It was out of the question for me to have a carriage, yet our house was on the green on the outskirts of the town. I had therefore stopped going out after supper and spent my evenings reading the books which Miss White sent me in large numbers from her well-stocked library. Subscriptions were costly in England and I could not myself have afforded such a luxury. So you may imagine my joy when one day a box arrived addressed to me and I was handed the key by the messenger. On opening it, I found ten volumes from Hookham's Library in London – Hookham's Circulating Library. There was also a catalogue of the twenty thousand volumes of every kind, in English and French, which the library possessed. A receipt in my name for a year's subscription was attached to the parcel, together with the information that, if the box were fastened and put on the 7 a.m. stage coach, it would be returned by the evening stage with the new books that had been requested. No attention ever gave me greater pleasure. I decided it must have been arranged by Miss White. I wrote to thank her, but having no reply, concluded she did not wish it to be known.

❧❧❧❧❧❧❧❧❧❧❧ XXV ❧❧❧❧❧❧❧❧❧❧❧

The summer of 1799 was unremarkable. When it was over, Lady Jerningham went to Cossey and again invited me to join her for the six months she was to spend there. Since the rent of our house at Richmond was about to fall due, and since it was she who paid it, it would have been tactless in the extreme to ask her to renew it in order that we might avoid accepting her invitation. She was alone at Cossey except for her beloved Edward so that it would also have been most discourteous not to have gone. We were, therefore, preparing to join her when the news came of General Bonaparte's unexpected return from Egypt. He had landed at Fréjus.

We set out immediately for Cossey, hoping it might be possible to return before long to the Continent, perhaps even to France. It was while we were at Cossey that we heard the good news of the fall of the Directorate and the revolution of 18 Brumaire.* Shortly afterwards, M. de Brouquens and our brother-in-law, the Marquis de Lameth, wrote telling us to return to France with German passports, travelling by way of Holland.

Lady Jerningham suggested that my husband should go alone. It would perhaps have been wiser, for I was more than six months' pregnant and could have remained at Cossey until my baby was born. But nothing would persuade me to be separated indefinitely from my husband. While the war lasted, there was always danger that communications between England and France would be completely cut. As it was, the news we received through Hamburg was often taking a month to reach us. In short, I rejected Lady Jerningham's advice. One of the principal reasons for holding so firmly to my decision was an unfortunate remark made one day by my aunt. She said that when the baby was born, it would be hers and she would keep it. I would never have consented to this. On the other hand, I had little confidence in this return to France. I reasoned thus: 'My husband may be banished yet again. If it should be while he is at Le Bouilh, he will go to Spain. How, if it were impossible to travel through France, could I ever rejoin him there on my own, with three children? Also, I have a house in Paris and it cannot be sold if I am not there.' In short, I did not want to leave my husband and refused to listen to reason.

A Danish passport for my husband, myself and my children was sent to us from London and we left for Yarmouth to board a packet belonging to the Royal Navy.† In those days, there were no steamships. Our wait in Yarmouth dragged on through the whole of December. We did not dare return to Cossey, though it was only eighteen miles away, for the captain had said that as soon as the wind became favourable, in other words, blew from the south-west, he would set sail immediately. He was so anxious to leave the very minute it became possible that he was scarcely willing for us

* 9/10 November 1799.
† At the time, warships were used for commercial purposes when not otherwise employed. (Tr.)

to live ashore. Never have days seemed drearier than during that month. We were poorly lodged in two small rooms where our meals were brought to us and which we could not leave because of the terrible weather. Contrary winds blew at gale force and every day we heard of ships that had run aground or foundered. You cannot imagine how such stories depress people who may be called on to set sail at any minute. I was terrified as the days slipped by and the date of my baby's birth drew nearer. I could not rid myself of the fear that it might be born on the journey, which is just what did eventually happen. Ten times a day my son, Humbert, would go down to the harbour to inspect the weather-vane. But the wind continued to blow from the north-east – quite the wrong direction for us. At last, one fine morning, we were summoned on board. Our luggage had been there for some time already and, scarcely had we set foot on deck, than the anchor was weighed.

I straight away took refuge in a bed. As there were many passengers, it would have been unwise to delay finding and staking a sure claim to some place of shelter. In any case, in my state, the rolling of the boat, which was a mere cockleshell, might have been fatal to me. I lay down fully dressed. My bunk was in the room which served all the passengers. They numbered fourteen and included men of every nationality and every degree of social standing: Frenchmen, Russians, Germans, messengers and so on, some stricken with seasickness and all it entails, others drinking punch, brandy or wine. We were all in that small room where the only fresh air was that which came through the door. The seas were so high that the port-hole had been battened down. By day and night, the only light was that from a foul-smelling lamp which did but add to the horrors of every kind which oppressed us in that dreadful hole. I do not think I have ever suffered so greatly as during the forty-eight hours of that crossing.

My husband and my maid were both overcome by seasickness and lay inert on their bunks. My daughter, Alix, lay beside me, terrified by the sight of the men around us. My son, by virtue of his ten years, remained up and looked after everything. He had scraped acquaintance with the passengers, spoke English to the crew and was known to the captain as 'My brave little fellow'. Towards the middle of the second night, we had for a few hours the additional cruel anxiety of knowing that if the river were not free from ice, it might be necessary to set us ashore on Heligoland, a small island in the estuary of the Elbe. Next, the captain told us that if the wind should veer the slightest degree to the north, the heavy weather would force him to return to England without trying to land anyone, as the danger of running aground would be too great. Fortunately, neither possibility came to pass. We sailed past Heligoland without stopping, entered the Elbe and anchored off the small port of Cuxhaven, which we did not enter.

The captain was anxious to be rid of his passengers. Our baggage was bundled out into a long-boat. My husband and my maid took my son with them. Out of regard for my state, the captain sent me and my daughter off in a private boat and ordered the two sailors manning it to put me ashore as close as possible to the town. This order nearly proved fatal to me. As the tide was low when we came alongside the jetty, I had great difficulty in climbing on to it. The two sailors therefore caught hold of my wrists and, despite the rocking of the boat, did not let me go – fortunately, for I should certainly have fallen into the sea – and then hauled me up on to the jetty in such a way that for a few moments I was suspended by the arms. Then they left me there alone with my small Charlotte. I realised I had hurt myself badly but had nonetheless to set out to find my husband, whom I could see in the distance on a waggon with the maid and all our belongings. With great difficulty, I reached them. There was a violent pain in my right side and I have always been convinced that there was some internal injury in the region of my liver. The doctors have never been willing to admit this damage, but it is nevertheless true that since that day I have never ceased to suffer from it and today, at seventy-three, I still feel it.

We knocked at two or three inns without being able to find a lodging, for there were so many émigrés travelling to and from England. Finally, when the people at one of the inns saw that I was unwell, they took pity on me and brought a straw mattress and some blankets and made me up a bed on the floor. Marguérite undressed me – it was the first time in three days that this had been possible – and I was able to lie down. A few minutes later, I was seized with a violent fever and delirium which lasted all through the night. M. de La Tour du Pin feared a miscarriage or some serious illness and was so worried that he sent for a doctor. After a long search, one was found, but he could not speak a word of French. With the help of an interpreter, I managed to make him understand that I thought the pain in my side was due to having been suspended by the arms when the sailors were lifting me from the boat to the jetty. He applied a great plaster of barley boiled in red wine to the place which hurt and prescribed a drug so soporific that I slept for twenty-four hours. When I awoke, I was quite well again.

While I rested, my husband had bought an old barouche for two hundred francs. It was small, but with room enough for us all. After a second day's rest, we set out in this open carriage. It was January and we were in northern Germany. Fortunately, the weather was good during the first days of the journey. On the fourth day, rain fell in torrents without stopping. Marguérite and I were more or less protected in the depths of the carriage, but M. de La Tour du Pin and Humbert were soaked to the skin, despite an umbrella. We stayed two days at Bremen to dry their suits and overcoats beside one of those wonderful great stoves found in German houses, and also to rest. Then, the weather having cleared, we set out again. Much snow had fallen and on the heaths over which we were travelling it was difficult to distinguish the road. Although we never went at more than a foot pace, we had no less than three spills that day. However, none of us was hurt, or at least, was not aware of anything at the time.

Towards evening, we arrived in a small town called Wildeshausen where we were to spend the night. It was in the Electorate of Hanover and had, therefore, a Hanoverian garrison. The officers were giving a great ball that night for another regiment passing through the town and every room in the one and only inn was taken. We had taken refuge in the hall beside the stove and were feeling very low at the thought of spending the night on wooden benches when a dapper little officer, elegantly dressed for the ball, came over to tell me gallantly, in English, that as he expected to dance all night, his room was at my disposal. We asked for our supper to be served there but my husband, noticing that I was not eating, asked if I felt ill. I could no longer hide from him that I felt quite unable to go any further and that the baby's birth was imminent. It is impossible to describe his dismay at hearing this. It was my turn then to comfort him, telling him that babies were born in all kinds of places and that everything would be all right. However, we could not stay in the captain's room.

By signs, we managed to convey the difficulty to the host of the inn who sent to the other end of the town to fetch an old French barber who had deserted during the Seven Years' War and lived in Wildeshausen ever since. The barber came at once, for he had been kept so busy getting people ready for the ball that he had not yet gone to bed. His first care was to find the local doctor, who turned out to be an elegant young man in white gloves, straight from the ball and still breathless from a waltz. His knowledge of French was limited to a few grammar book phrases, all concerned with medicine. As I was lying on the bed wrapped in my cloak, he could not see the fullness of the figure and began asking me what was the matter: 'Fever?' – 'No' – 'What then?' Luckily, Denis, the barber, returned just then and was able to explain. He also asked if I could be safely taken to two rooms on the edge of the little town which he knew were to let. The doctor agreed to this and returned to his ball. Denis hurried off to rouse the owner of the two rooms and before dawn I was settled there.

The house, like all those belonging to substantial farmers in that part of Germany, had a great carriage entrance opening into a roomy coach-house which occupied the whole depth of the house. In front, to the left and right of this coach-house, on the ground floor, were two good bedrooms, very clean and passably well furnished. Marguérite and my two children took possession of one of them, the larger one was given to me and my husband installed himself in a small room adjoining it.

Fortunately, we had with us all the linen and everything necessary for the new baby. As I was not yet in much pain, I had time to attend to all our arrangements and it was not until the following morning, 13 February 1800, that I gave birth to a small and very frail baby girl,* who had completed only a seven and a half months' term. She was so thin and delicate that I scarcely dared hope she would live. Alas, I kept her with me for seventeen years, only to see her die blessed with every gift of beauty, character, intelligence and charm. God took her from me – may His will be done.

We named her Cécile, a dear name borne later by one who took her place and will perhaps glance through these pages.† May she also read in them my gratitude for all the happiness she gave me in my old age.

On the day after my daughter's birth, the local magistrate, who had already sent once for our passports, sent one of his town guards to bring M. de La Tour du Pin before him. In good French, he told my husband: 'Monsieur, your Danish passport is in a false name. You are French and an émigré and, in the Electorate of Hanover where you now are, such persons are forbidden to remain longer than forty-eight hours.' M. de La Tour du Pin was horrified

* Cécile-Elisabeth-Charlotte de La Tour du Pin de Gouvernet, betrothed in September 1816 to Charles, Comte de Mercy-Argenteau, died in Nice on 20 March 1817, before her marriage.
† Cécile de Liedekerke-Beaufort, daughter of Charlotte de La Tour du Pin and Auguste de Liedekerke-Beaufort. Born in 1818, married Baron Ferdinand-Joseph-Ghislain de Beeckman and died in 1893.

to hear this. He said I could not be moved as I had given birth to a baby only a few hours before. But the magistrate was adamant so far as my husband was concerned and told him he must leave for Hanover by the end of the day or return to Bremen, whichever he preferred. Then he added: 'Monsieur, since you admit your French nationality, tell me your true name.' My husband did so and the magistrate exclaimed: 'Good Heavens. Were you once French Minister at The Hague?' My husband said that he had been. 'Well, Monsieur, since that is so, stay as long as you wish. My nephew, M. Hinuber, a very young man, was Hanoverian Minister at The Hague. He visited you often and you were very kind to him . . .' and that good man went on to list the many suppers, cups of tea and glasses of punch which his nephew had enjoyed at our house, as well as the quadrilles he had danced in our salons. From that moment he put himself at our service with an enthusiasm that never flagged. Truly, I would not have been surprised to learn that he had issued a decree that all the inhabitants should place themselves at our disposal! Never has there been a more generous hospitality, or a more thoughtful care than that which surrounded us in that small town from then on. The Lutheran pastor had children and resident pupils the same age as my son and they all spoke English. He came to collect Humbert every day at recreation time, which was spent in the snow which still lay two feet deep. Sportsmen brought me game. Good ladies, whose names I never knew, sent me sweetmeats, cakes and books in English and French. As for the doctor, he called on me every day . . . but so that I could give him a lesson in French.

After a fortnight, I was well again and on the twenty-first day after our arrival, we set out, though not before we had taken tea at the houses of the magistrate, the burgomaster, the parish priest and a number of other local notables. Wildeshausen had a Catholic church and my very small daughter was baptised there. Her sponsors were Denis, the old barber, and his wife who, after forty years of marriage, had never learned a single word of French. I was also churched there.

We took the Lingen road to Holland. A number of young men accompanied us on the first leagues of our journey, staying with us until we reached the inn where we stopped to give the children their lunch. Before leaving, they insisted that I should drink a cup of some German brew which they had mixed themselves. I expected it to taste horrid, but found it, on the contrary, excellent. It was warm Bordeaux wine, into which had been mixed spices and the yolks of eggs. The doctor was among those who accompanied us and it was by his advice that I took this drink, which made me slightly light-headed.

Our kind escort left us with fervent good wishes for our journey. Their wishes must have been effective, for nothing untoward happened and my small daughter bore the journey amazingly well for a child of less than a month. It is true that she did not leave my arms by day or by night and I took the greatest care that she should not breathe, even once, the icy air of those northern plains. If it had not been for the infinite care with which Marguérite and I surrounded her, she would hardly have survived such a long, difficult journey in the month of March.

We arrived at last in Utrecht and my husband went immediately to The Hague to get a proper passport from M. de Sémonville, the Ambassador of the Republic of France to the Batavian Republic. M. de Sémonville trimmed his sails to every wind and had found means to ingratiate himself with the new government headed by Bonaparte. M. de La Tour du Pin had known him well for many years, so that he was received with open arms, and a magnificent passport was drawn up showing that he had not left Utrecht since 18 Fructidor.

During M. de La Tour du Pin's short absence, Mme d'Hénin arrived in Utrecht. It was an extraordinary coincidence and my husband was greatly astonished to see his aunt when he returned from The Hague. So far as I remember, she was on her way to visit M. de La Fayette who had been living at Vianen, near Utrecht, ever since he had been freed after the Treaty of Campo-Formio. I cannot remember if Mme d'Hénin was coming from France or England. She always had two or three different passports and was for ever changing her name and her routes. We spent two days with her and then left for Paris, taking advantage of a carriage that was being sent back, and which we undertook to see safely returned.

On arriving in Paris, we went to the Hôtel Grange-Batelière. My brother-in-law, the Marquis de Lameth, and our friend, Brouquens, were already both in Paris. M. de Lameth had found lodgings for us in a charming, well-furnished small house in the Rue de Miromesnil. Until then, it had been occupied by two of his friends who had recently left to spend the entire summer in the country. We were fated to live in houses belonging to favourites! Our house at Richmond had belonged to an actress and this one had been furnished for Mlle Michelot, a former mistress of the Duc de Bourbon. The walls were covered with mirrors, so many of them that I was obliged to drape muslin over most of them for I found it most irritating to see a full-length reflection of myself every time I moved.

In Paris, I found many of my acquaintance already returned from abroad. All the young men were beginning to turn to the rising sun – Mme Bonaparte – who was living at the Tuileries in apartments that had been entirely re-decorated, as if at the wave of a wand. She already bore herself like a queen, but a very gracious, amiable and kindly one. Although not particularly clever, she fully understood her husband's plans. He was counting on her to win for him the allegiance of the upper ranks of society. Josephine had, in fact, given him to understand that she herself had belonged in those circles, which was not quite true. I do not know if she had been presented at Court or had had the entrée at Versailles – though the name of her first husband, M. de Beauharnais, certainly made it a possibility. However, even if she had been presented, she would have belonged to that class of lady who, after their first presentation, returned to Court only on New Year's Day.

I saw M. de Talleyrand again and found him unchanged towards me: amiable, but not really helpful. During the two previous years, he had steered his fortunes with such skill that I found him established in a fine house of his own in the Rue d'Anjou, laughing quietly to himself at the eagerness of all those who returned to France to secure a Government post. He asked me what my husband was doing and if he needed anything. I told him that he did not and that we intended settling at Le Bouilh. 'So much the worse for you', he replied, 'it is folly.' I told him we were not in a position to remain in Paris but he merely answered that there was always money to be found when one needed it. Such was his philosophy.

As soon as Mme Bonaparte learned from Mme de Valence and Mme de Montesson that I was back in Paris, she asked me to call on her. She longed to be able to boast to the First Consul that she had secured the allegiance of a woman who was still young and very fashionable, and a former member of the royal Household. It would have been a victory indeed, if I may be forgiven for saying so. But I determined to increase the value of my condescension by keeping her waiting a little. Then, one morning, I did go with Mme de Valence to call on her. In the salon I found a group of women and young men, all of whom I knew. Mme Bonaparte came towards me exclaiming: 'Ah, here she is,' seated me beside her and paid me a thousand pretty compliments, repeating more than once: 'How English she looks,' a remark which was soon to imply the very opposite of praise. She studied me from head to foot and was particularly intrigued by the thick braid of fair hair which circled my head and from which she did not take her eyes. When we rose to leave, she could not help asking Mme de Valence in a whisper if the braid was really of my own hair.

Mme Bonaparte spoke to me with much kindness of Mme Dillon, my stepmother, and expressed a keen desire to meet my sister, Fanny, who was also her niece since Mme Dillon's mother and Josephine's were sisters. She went on to say that all the émigrés would return, that this delighted her, that there had been enough suffering, that General Bonaparte wanted, above all else, to set a term to the ills of the Revolution, and so on. A litany of reassurances. She also enquired after M. de La Tour du Pin and said she would like to see him. She was leaving for Malmaison and invited me to visit her there. All in all, she was extremely pleasant and I saw clearly that the First Consul had left her to deal with the feminine side of the Court, trusting her to win it to his cause whenever opportunity arose. It was not a difficult task, for everyone was hastening to gather about the rising star and I know of no one besides myself who refused to become a lady-in-waiting to the Empress Josephine.

In Paris, I met my cousin, General Sheldon, again. He had had many misfortunes since his triumphant return from Grenada with the captured standards.* Eventually, he accepted the invitation of the famous Colonel St Leger, a close friend of the Prince of Wales, and went to live in England. There, he stayed with the prince who showed him much kindness, and it was he, as an English Catholic, who acted as witness at the marriage of the Prince of Wales with Mrs FitzHerbert. This marriage has been widely denied,† but as Mrs FitzHerbert was a Catholic and it was a Catholic priest who blessed the marriage, it is very probable that the necessary dispensations had been granted. This explains why even the strictest Catholic ladies, including my aunt, Lady Jerningham, continued to visit her, despite the publicity of her marriage to the Prince of Wales.

* In 1781, Dominic Sheldon so distinguished himself in the French capture of Grenada that he was chosen to carry the captured English standard to Louis XVI. But, etiquette not permitting the wearing of military uniforms at Court, he had to change into civilian dress before presenting them. This rankled in the mind of Mme de La Tour du Pin as an example of short-sighted policy. (Tr.)
† Shortly before these memoirs were originally published, Edward VII released certain documents authenticating the marriage, but the details of the ceremony are not quite as Mme de La Tour du Pin describes them.

M. de La Tour du Pin and I had never been put on the list of émigrés, though I do not know why. We therefore had to obtain a certificate of residence in France signed by nine witnesses, a necessary formality which deceived no one. For this purpose, I presented myself at the municipal offices of the district with my cloud of witnesses. When the certificate was signed and inscribed with all the necessary lies, the mayor politely handed me a copy, whispering: 'But that doesn't alter the fact that every stitch of your clothing comes from London!' and roared with laughter. What a farce!

During that summer of 1800, the best company in Paris was to be found beneath the arch of a house in the Place Vendôme. Looking towards the Rue St Honoré, it is on the right, at the corner of the Place Vendôme and the Rue St Honoré. It was there that the Commission des Émigrés* held its sessions. This commission could be conciliated fairly easily if one took care not to arrive empty-handed. The crowd that gathered there included everyone, from the highest in the land to tradesmen of every kind. Two phrases dominated all conversations, no matter what the topic: 'Have you been struck off?' and 'Are you going to be struck off?' A man who could produce the most respectable and complete series of certificates of residence in France as proof of how unjust it had been to include his name on the fatal list, would be heard talking openly, on the very doorstep of the building, of what he had done and said in Coblentz, or Hamburg, or London.

The French can find amusement in anything. The Commission des Émigrés had become a centre. People arranged to meet there, went there to find old friends, to talk over their plans, their choice of a residence and so on. Many of those who had come back from abroad looked on it as an employment agency. Fathers began to wonder if their sons might enter the army. People began to talk of 'the country', that country which had bothered them so little a few years ago. In the entrance to this establishment, the bearers of the greatest names in France rubbed shoulders with members of the provincial nobility. What a pity there was not some kind of scale at that door, a weighbridge like those used to weigh carriages on the railway! Many a good and loyal gentleman from the provinces, returned from exile to find nothing but the four bare walls of his home, often without even a roof to shelter him and his family, would have weighed far heavier than many a duke with some famous name.

* The Board charged with carrying out Napoleon's order of 18 Brumaire (November 1799) that many persons should be deleted from the famous list of émigrés. (Tr.)

We ourselves had no dealings with the commission as we had not been on the list, but it was necessary to have my mother-in-law's name removed from it. Despite the fact that she had lived for thirty years in the Convent of the Dames Anglaises in the Rue des Fossés-Saint-Victor, without once leaving it, her name had been included in the list and the consequence of this error was the sale of all the furnishings of her château at Tesson and on two of her farms.

Before his departure for the famous crossing of the Great St Bernard, Bonaparte had decided to create a regiment of hussars manned by young volunteers. Soon all the youngest scions of great families were enrolled in this corps, among them our eighteen-year-old nephew, Alfred de Lameth. Their uniform was a light yellow, so inevitably they became known in Paris as the 'Canaries'. The excuse to buy fine horses and make a splash would quickly have attracted young men, but when they saw that people were making fun of the corps, they gradually merged themselves into the rest of the Army.

I went one morning to Malmaison. It was after the Battle of Marengo. Mme Bonaparte received me extraordinarily well and, after luncheon, which was set in a charming dining room, she took me to visit her gallery. We were alone and she took advantage of this to give me the most boring accounts of the origins of the masterpieces and also of the collection of very fine small pictures standing on easels: it was the Pope who had insisted that she should accept that fine painting of the Albanian woman; Canova had given her 'La Danseuse' and 'Hebe'; the City of Milan had presented her with this and that. I was careful not to take these tales literally, but as I had a great admiration for the victor of Marengo, I should have preferred Mme Bonaparte to tell me the truth – that they had all been taken at the point of the sword. The good woman was an inveterate liar. Even when the plain truth would have been more interesting, or more striking than an invention, she preferred to invent.

Poor Adrien de Mun, then a brilliant young man, accompanied me on that visit. At Malmaison, I found the families of de l'Aigle and La Grange, Juste de Noailles and everyone else, all dreaming of the chamberlains' uniforms I have since seen them wearing.

One thing struck my husband and me very forcibly: the apathy with which the usually enthusiastic people of Paris heard the news of the Battle of Marengo. On the anniversary of 14 July, we went with M. de Poix to walk on the Champ de Mars. After the review

of the Garde Nationale and the garrison, a small formation of one
hundred men marched into the enclosure, all in torn, dirty uniforms,
some with an arm in a sling, others with their head bandaged, but
carrying the standards and Austrian flags captured at Marengo.
I expected wild and very well merited cheering, but there was not a
single shout and scarcely any sign of rejoicing. We were both
surprised and indignant and, thinking it over at leisure afterwards,
could find no explanation for this apathy. Those brave soldiers
had travelled post, we were told, in order to take part in the public
review that day.

❧❧❧❧❧❧❧❧❧❧❧❧ XXVI ❧❧❧❧❧❧❧❧❧❧❧❧

Towards September, we decided to leave for Le Bouilh. We had
sold our house in Paris, though for very little as it stood in a shabby
quarter, the Rue du Bac. I can no longer remember what my
husband did with the money from this sale. On his return to France,
he had found his father's affairs and his own in such great disorder
and so much ill luck had dogged everything he undertook that,
despite his intelligence and ability, everything turned out badly
for him. You may be quite certain that everything he did was
animated by one sole purpose: to improve his children's fortunes.
He is to be remembered with love and respect.

We took with us from Paris a tutor for my son. My husband
went off alone by way of Tesson and I hired a coachman to take us
by easy stages in a great carriage.

The roads were terrible, almost impassable, and near Le Bouilh
the carriage overturned in a rut. Marguérite was hurt protecting
the baby, and the maidservant dislocated her arm but at last we
arrived safely and I was very happy to be back. I greatly needed
rest. An excellent woman whom I had left in charge had taken
care of everything, despite the nominal sequestration which had
been re-imposed on the château. My husband arrived a few days
later and we were at last all united in our home.

M. de La Tour du Pin devoted himself to farming and the education of his son. To the latter task, I also contributed my share,
making sure that he did not forget his knowledge of English.
Humbert was then ten and a half, Charlotte nearly four and Cécile

six months old. My good Marguérite devoted herself to the dear children with even greater care and tenderness than I did myself.

Shortly after our return, Mme de Maurville, a cousin of my husband, came to live with us. She had been dispossessed of everything she had owned in France and her principal income was a pension of £40 paid to her by the English government. This was a widow's pension, granted to her because her husband, a French admiral, had ended in the service of England – not a very honourable thing to have done. All that remained to her in France was an income of 500 to 600 francs. We offered her a roof and she accepted it with the simplicity which characterises the true nobility. She was four years older than M. de La Tour du Pin, to whom she was devoted. Her only son, Alexandre, had been educated at the school founded by the famous Burke for the children of émigrés. When he returned to France, he was eighteen and, having no fortune whatsoever, enlisted as a trooper in the light cavalry under the aegis of the colonel, M. de La Tour Maubourg. It was Mme d'Hénin who secured this patronage for him through the good offices of M. de La Fayette.

Mme d'Hénin came to Le Bouilh several times during the eight years we lived there. On her first visit, which lasted several months, she brought with her M. de Lally's daughter, who had just left Mme Campan,* and asked me to complete her education. Mlle de Lally was nearly fifteen. I welcomed her gladly. She was a gentle, biddable child, fairly proficient in spelling, music and dancing. The education of her mind, however, had been completely neglected. I looked on the task entrusted to me as a very important and rather heavy responsibility. My husband made me promise to undertake it nonetheless and, to me, his wishes were law. I would not even have considered questioning them. As we were too poor to undertake extra expense without inconvenience, my aunt wanted M. de Lally to pay for his daughter's keep and send us the same sum that he had formerly paid Mme Campan. To accept such an arrangement seemed to me to lower us a little socially, but we ended by agreeing to it. M. de Lally also remained responsible for his daughter's personal expenses. She had no reason for complaint in these arrangements and I, for my part, can say that we never found reason to regret them. What I did for Mlle de Lally was a preparation for the education I later gave my own daughters. My husband undertook to teach her history and geography. My part

* A former waiting-woman to Marie-Antoinette. She opened a school for young ladies at Saint-Cyr, much patronised by the Bonapartist elect.

was to teach her English, of which she already had a slight knowledge, and my son's tutor was to give her lessons in Italian. She was also to benefit from our custom of reading aloud to one another. She was much attached to my children, especially to Cécile, and it was she who gave Cécile her first lessons. She was a good-natured, dependable child, rather secretive, and got on very well with Mme de Maurville. They were equally lacking in intelligence and I suspect that their feelings towards me were closer to respect and awe than to affection. But whatever the general opinion of me may have been, I am not a dominating woman. I have never asked of those with whom I have lived more than they were capable of giving.

My husband and I were much preoccupied with our children's future, not the least of the anxieties arising from the low state of our fortunes. The Le Bouilh estate, so far as the value of the land was concerned, was worth very little. The war with England had brought the price of wines down to rock bottom, especially white wines which had never been very profitable in our area. They could be bought for four to five francs a cask. My husband installed a brandy distillery and spent considerable sums of money to ensure that it worked properly, but the profit from this innovation was only just enough to cover our current living expenses and soon it would be necessary to think about my son's future. This problem occupied our minds to such a degree that other anxieties paled before it.

My aunt and M. de Lally wrote us from Paris that all the people we used to know were rallying to the Government. The Concordat had just been published and the re-establishment of religion had had a tremendous effect in our provinces.* Until then, Mass had had to be celebrated in private rooms, not perhaps in total secrecy, but certainly quietly enough not to compromise the priest, who was nearly always a returned émigré. Therefore, when M. d'Aviau de Sanzai, a regularly-consecrated archbishop, was known to have arrived in Bordeaux, and when the irregularly appointed usurper disappeared, the gratitude of the people went out to the great man who held the reins of government and when he declared himself consul for life, this gratitude found expression in the almost unanimous approval of those who had to vote on the matter.

* The treaty of peace of 1802 between France and the Papacy. The people of France had never accepted the revolutionary attempt of 1791 to separate the Catholic Church in France from Rome and attach it to the State, still less the later extravagances of deism, rationalism, etc. Under this Concordat, the Church in France entered again into communion with Rome, was accepted as the established religion of France. Napoleon, like the kings of France before him, reserved the right to nominate the highest Church dignitaries. (Tr.)

Not long afterwards, lists were posted up in the communes and people were summoned to enter their name and reply 'yes' or 'no' to the question whether the consul for life should proclaim himself emperor. M. de La Tour du Pin was extraordinarily exercised over the problem before finally deciding to put 'yes' on the Saint-André-de Cubzac list. I used to see him pacing the garden, but would not permit myself to intrude upon his uncertainties. Eventually, I learned with pleasure when he returned to the house one evening, that the result of his deliberations had been 'yes'.

You will have noticed that I am inclined to confuse the order of events. I have certainly not kept in their proper sequence the happenings which filled the eight years we spent at Le Bouilh. There were six particularly happy months when Mme de Duras and her children stayed with us. My aunt was away at the time, which caused us no grief at all. Despite her intelligence, her kindness and her devotion to her nephew – me, she had never loved, except as a reflection of him – life with her was very fatiguing. Mme de Duras came to Le Bouilh to wait for her husband. He was to meet her there and take her to Duras, his family seat, which lay between Bordeaux and Agen. They had just bought Ussé* and Mme de Kersaint, Mme de Duras' mother, had put into this purchase all the money she had received from the sale of her house in Martinique. The Duchesse de Duras, Amédée's mother, had added 400,000 francs from her personal fortune. This house cost them altogether 800,000 francs and was an excellent bargain.

I had last seen Claire Duras at Teddington, at a time when she was enduring all the wretchedness of knowing that her love for her husband was not returned. I found her quite changed. She had become one of the leaders of the anti-Bonapartist circles of the Faubourg Saint-Germain. Realising that she could never hope to be outstanding in looks, she had been sensible enough to renounce all pretensions in that field. She aimed instead at dazzling by her wit, which was not difficult as she had an abundance of it, and by her ability, an indispensable attribute for anyone aspiring to a leading role in the circles in which she moved. In Paris, it is essential to be definite in one's views, otherwise one is eclipsed: to use a naval term, one must mount a heavier broadside than one's neighbour.

In 1805, I went with Elisa – Mlle de Lally – to spend a while in Bordeaux. At Mass one day, Elisa attracted the notice of M. Henri d'Aux who, by birth, appearance and fortune, was the most

* One of the finest châteaux in the valley of the Loire. (Tr.)

distinguished young man in the town. Elisa was very small, with masses of fine black hair, a dazzling complexion, the bloom of a rose and the loveliest eyes in the world. Our friend Brouquens had returned to Bordeaux indefinitely, his fortune disastrously reduced by the collapse of the army's food supply company. He learned from friends that M. Henri d'Aux had spoken in glowing terms of the young person staying with Mme de La Tour du Pin. None of the young ladies of Bordeaux, he had declared, could equal her in propriety and modesty of bearing. He had made enquiries about us, our way of life, our habits and so on.

My husband had been appointed President of the Canton,* an office he had done nothing to seek, and had gone to Paris for the Coronation. I wrote to tell him what I had heard and he spoke of it to M. de Lally. At the time, the latter was busy trying to secure payment from the State of a fairly large sum which he had been promised would be reimbursed. It had been owing to him ever since his father's honour had been posthumously restored and his death sentence annulled – that is to say, since three months before the beginning of the Revolution. The Council of State (Conseil d'Etat)† had recognised the validity of the debt but since, like all State funds, it had been reduced to one-third of its original value, it amounted by then to only one hundred thousand francs. Napoleon was anxious to persuade M. de Lally to join his Government and therefore wanted the claim met in full. When my husband told M. de Lally what I had written, he declared at once that if he obtained payment of the debt, he would give the money to his daughter on the day she married. He kept his word. We arranged to be in Bordeaux for the carnival so that M. d'Aux might have occasion to meet Elisa at the select balls given in the salons of the former Intendance.

It was at this time that I suffered a very cruel loss. My dear maid, Marguérite, died. My love for her had been that of a daughter and my grief was deep. She remained conscious until the end and bade me the tenderest of farewells. Humbert and Charlotte were also deeply grieved and I was touched by their feeling. That excellent woman had always given them every possible care.

In Paris, my husband saw many of his former acquaintances, all of them attached to the Government. Among them was M. Maret,

* An area, usually comprising several communes, which forms the administrative region of a Justice of the Peace. (Tr.)
† One of the four legislative bodies. Its members were appointed by Napoleon himself and were responsible for drafting bills and for legislation. (Tr.)

later to be created Duc de Bassano.* They urged my husband to take steps to obtain an appointment. He did not exactly refuse, but said that if the emperor desired his services, he knew where to find him, that the role of petitioner was distasteful to him and so on. M. de Talleyrand could not understand any form of reluctance but he did nevertheless perceive, with his mind rather than his heart, that there was a certain distinction in standing a little apart from the mob of petitioners. He contented himself with saying, with a shrug of the shoulders, 'You will come to it' and thought no more about it.

M. de La Tour du Pin returned to Le Bouilh. He had seen M. Malouet, who had just been appointed Préfet Maritime† at Antwerp, charged with establishing there the great shipbuilding yard to which he was to give such tremendous impetus. They arranged between them that when Humbert was seventeen, he should enter the offices of M. Malouet. There were no Auditeurs‡ at the Conseil d'Etat in those days, but there was talk of recruiting them and we thought it would be useful for a young man destined for the public service to work for a while under the aegis of a man as enlightened and able as M. de Malouet. Since he was a good friend, we could entrust our son to him without anxiety. But the thought of the separation weighed heavily on my heart.

My husband returned from Paris and shortly afterwards I realised that I was to have another child. It was to be you, my dear son.§ I had had a miscarriage the previous year and to avoid any fresh mishap, resolved not to take any violent exercise during my pregnancy. But I was unwell nearly all the time. Mme de Maurville, Elisa, my aunt and M. de Lally all went to Tesson and I remained at Le Bouilh with my daughters.

On the morning of 18 October 1806, as I was dressing, I saw my good Doctor Dupouy, who had been staying at Le Bouilh for several days, passing along the terrace. I asked him laughingly where he was coming from at that early hour. He replied that he

* Hughes-Bernard Maret, 1763–1839. A lawyer in the Parlement of Burgundy, he came to Paris early in the Revolution and published summaries of Constituent Assembly Debates. Bonaparte appointed him his Secretary-General and, in 1809, created him Duke of Bassano. In 1811, he became Foreign Minister and, after a period of exile between 1814 and 1820, returned to public service under the Orléanists. (Tr.)
† An admiral charged with the administration of a coastal area. (Tr.)
‡ Highly-qualified professional civil servants – Auditors – just starting their career. The first rank in the hierarchy of the Conseil d'Etat and the Cour des Comptes (Audit Office). (Tr.)
§ Aymar.

had been called out to sign a death certificate for one of our neighbours who had died suddenly as she got out of bed. I knew this person well and had had a long talk with her the evening before. I was so upset that I was seized there and then with the pains which brought you into the world to be the happiness of my old age. I recovered but slowly from the after-effects of your birth, for I developed a double tertian fever. It did not, however, prevent me from continuing to nurse you myself.

We had not lost sight of the important matter of Elisa's marriage. On the excuse of having the baby vaccinated, we went to Bordeaux for six weeks during the Christmas season, staying with our good Brouquens. This incomparable friend had managed to enlist for us the support of M. Marbotin de Couteneuil, a former Councillor to the Parlement and an uncle of M. d'Aux. M. de Couteneuil wanted to return to the magistracy and the fact that M. de Lally was thought to have some influence was an additional help in securing his support for his nephew's marriage. In any case, and I say it without conceit, we were of sufficient standing in Bordeaux to ensure esteem for anyone who had been allowed to share our family life for five years.

The young people met at a number of balls. Elisa danced enchantingly – in those days, people did not waltz and dancing was an art – and was at her best on these occasions. They met again out walking and at Church, where one was certain to meet M. d'Aux. Eventually, Mme de Couteneuil called on me one day formally to request the hand of my protégée for her nephew. Like a good and seasoned diplomat, I replied that I did not know what plans M. de Lally had for his daughter, but that M. de La Tour du Pin would go to Le Bouilh, where M. de Lally was staying, to tell him the proposal she had just made me. He did indeed go the following day, returning before it was over with M. de Lally himself. Everything was soon arranged and then came the congratulations, the dinners and the parties. We received a visit from the father of M. d'Aux, a gentleman of the old school, without a vestige of intelligence or learning. It used to be said of him that he had, quite literally, bored his wife to death. Nonetheless, he enjoyed an income of sixty-thousand francs or more a year.

When the marriage contract was signed, M. de Lally kept his word and counted out to M. d'Aux the dowry he had promised his daughter: one hundred bags, each containing a thousand francs. It was the only time in my life that I have seen so much money at one time.

The wedding took place at Le Bouilh on 1 April 1807. Mme de Maurville, Charlotte and I used the only flowers in season – small red and white double daisies – to make a centre-piece for the dinner. We contrived a charming effect, using the flowers to form the names of Henri and Elisa against a background of moss.

All these preliminaries and the marriage itself had given me much to do and disturbed the tranquillity and order of my days. I was very happy to return to my usual habits and to be able to enjoy Humbert's last remaining months at home.

XXVII

Towards the end of the summer or, by the country calendar, immediately after the vintage, I had to part for the first time with my dear Humbert. I felt the separation most cruelly and had need of all my commonsense and submission to the will of God to enable me to bear it. His father went with him as far as Paris. It was heartbreaking to embrace him when he left, not knowing how long it would be before we saw him again. His elder sister also felt the separation very deeply. Charlotte was then eleven and so forward for her years and so sensible that her brother no longer thought of her as a child. To her, it meant the loss of a companion in her studies and her games, a real comrade. The gaiety of our home went with him.

Le Bouilh was much plagued with demands for military billets. All the troops sent to Spain had to pass through Saint-André-en-Cubzac and we often had to lodge the officers. This was most tiresome, especially when I was alone, for they had to be received at dinner and in the drawing-room. During one of my husband's absences, this gave rise to a small incident which I was able to turn to account. It gave me an excuse to ask that in future I should be asked to lodge twice as many soldiers or troopers, but no officers. Two officers had been sent to Le Bouilh, one of them no longer young. When he saw our fine house and the pretty room set aside for him, he launched into a demagogic tirade worthy of the Convention at its worst. He was so carried away that, when he met me in a corridor, he let fly torrents of abuse, saying that he knew they had cut off the head of the previous owner of the house, but that he wished they would do the same to all nobles who owned such fine houses and that it would give him the greatest pleasure to see the house set on fire. He looked as if he might be accustomed to carrying out his threats so I said calmly: 'Sir, I warn you that I shall lodge a complaint.' I immediately wrote a very civil letter to the colonel, who was staying in Saint-André, telling him of the threats made by this captain. Half an hour later, the colonel ordered the firebrand to return and place himself under arrest. After this incident, no more officers were sent to us. True, we still had to receive a number of uncouth characters, but their noisy gatherings were confined to the butler's pantry.

On one of the great feasts, I was at Mass in Bordeaux when I suddenly noticed that the attention of the whole congregation was focussed on the back of the chapel where I was. Rising to leave, I saw there a magnificent officer, elegantly wrapped in a great white cloak which, being thrown back to leave his sabre arm free, allowed glimpses of deep purple baggy trousers. He left the Church with everyone else and took the road leading to M. de Brouquens' house. He went in and when I followed him into the courtyard, he turned round, exclaiming: 'Ah, so it is my aunt!' and embraced me warmly.

It was my nephew, Alfred de Lameth. How fine he was! An Apollo of Belvedere in the uniform of an aide-de-camp to Murat! The poor boy had a foreboding that all would not go well with him and, after talking to me for two hours about his youthful follies, of which he was beginning to weary, and of the war in which he had not yet, he said, received a single scratch, he said he would like to leave me something by which to remember him. So saying, he opened his escritoire and gave me this knife with a mother-of-pearl handle which you have always seen on my table. Then he embraced me affectionately many times and, as my eyes filled with tears, said: 'Yes, dear aunt, it is for the last time.' The poor boy was wickedly murdered while crossing a small Spanish village on his way to lunch with Maréchal Soult, right in the midst of the marshal's headquarters. The murderer was never discovered but, in reprisal, the village was given over to the fury of the soldiers, who left it a bloody and burning hecatomb.

There was much concern in Bordeaux over events in Spain. A few Spanish refugees had already arrived in the town. Mme d'Hénin wrote from Paris that the emperor was to go to Spain, accompanied, perhaps, by the Empress Josephine, and that M. Maret* would be in their suite. She advised her nephew to pay his

* See footnote, p. 285.

Napoleon, Emperor of the French. By Delaroche.

Louis XVIII.

homage to the emperor and to call on M. Maret who took an interest in him. M. de La Tour du Pin received this letter just as he was setting out to ride to Tesson, where a matter concerning some bill of exchange urgently needed his presence. He was to be away only two days and was certain he would be back before the emperor arrived. But the very next day, orders reached the posting house for horses to be ready for the emperor. I was greatly upset that my husband should be away, but quite determined not to let it prevent me seeing this remarkable man.

Mme de Maurville, Charlotte and I went to Cubzac, resolved to stay there until we had seen Napoleon. We knew the Chief Transport commissioner and asked him to take us in. We settled ourselves in a room overlooking the port. The brigantine which was to carry them across the Dordogne lay ready, with the crew at their posts. The entire population of the region gathered along the route. The peasants might curse the man who had taken their children and sent them off to the war, but they were nonetheless eager to see him. A madness, a kind of frenzy descended on everyone. The first courier arrived and people tried to question him. General Drouot d'Erlon, the commander of the Department, asked him when the emperor would arrive. The man was too weary to reply and could only repeat over and over again: 'Let us cross.' He led his horse, still saddled, into the boat and then dropped to the deck and lay like one dead. When they reached the opposite bank, he was hauled to his feet and set back on his horse.

After seeing the courier, our impatience reached fever point. As for me, I could think of nothing but the ill chance which had taken my husband so far from the place where he should have been carrying out his official duties. The municipal authorities of Cubzac were all there and he, the president of the Canton was absent. An opportunity had been lost which would not occur again. I was exceedingly annoyed. We waited all day and at last, towards evening, the first carriage appeared. It was soon followed by a berline drawn by eight horses with a detachment of Chasseurs* as escort. It drew up under the window where we were and the emperor got out. He was in the uniform of a chasseur of the Guard and accompanied by two chamberlains and an aide-de-camp. The mayor read an address of welcome, to which the emperor listened with an air of great boredom and then went on board the brigantine, which cast off at once.

* Lightly armed troops, both infantry and cavalry. (Tr.)

And that was all we saw of the great man. We returned to Le Bouilh, all three of us tired and very out of temper.

My husband returned the next day. I allowed him only time enough to eat lunch and then insisted on his leaving for Bordeaux where the empress was expected the following day. As soon as he arrived in town, he called on M. Maret, who professed much friendship and good will for him. My husband found him amiable and obliging but was greatly astonished when M. Maret said to him: 'You must indeed have been very upset at having to go to Tesson just when the emperor was to pass through, and you have certainly hurried back.'

'Have you seen Brouquens, then?' asked M. de La Tour du Pin.

'No.'

'Then, how do you know?'

'The emperor told me.'

You can imagine my husband's amazement. 'Mme de La Tour du Pin is to come to Bordeaux,' added M. Maret 'and she will remain here while the empress is in residence. There will be a Drawing Room tomorrow and the emperor wishes her to attend.'

My husband immediately sent a carriage for me, hesitation being unthinkable. I had a few gowns in Bordeaux, made when I was accompanying Elisa to the balls and parties given at the time of her marriage. But none of them was black, and the Court was in mourning. The Drawing Room was at eight o'clock and it was already five. Fortunately, I found a pretty gown of grey satin. I added a few black ornaments and a good coiffeur arranged black ribbons in my hair, a fashion which seemed to me admirably becoming to a woman of thirty-eight who, I say it without vanity, looked less than thirty. We gathered in the great dining room of the palace. I knew hardly anyone in Bordeaux except Mme de Couteneuil and Mme de Saluces, the very two people who were not there. Between sixty and eighty ladies were present, placed according to a list read aloud by a chamberlain, M. de Béarn. He told us that on no account must any of us move, otherwise he would never be able to match people to their names. He also told us to straighten our line, and hardly had we completed this almost military manoeuvre when a loud voice announced the emperor. My heart beat fast with excitement. He began at the end of the line and spoke to every lady. As he drew near where I was standing, the chamberlain said something in his ear. He looked at me, smiling most graciously, and when my turn came, said laughingly to me, in a friendly manner, but looking me up and down: 'I see you are not all affected by the death of the King of Denmark.'

To which I replied: 'Not sufficiently, Sire, to renounce the happiness of being presented to Your Majesty. I had no black gown.' 'Ah, that is an excellent reason,' he replied, 'and in any case, you were out of town.' He spoke next to the lady beside me: 'Your name, Madame?' She stammered something and as he did not catch what she said, I told him her name was Montesquieu. 'Indeed,' he remarked, 'that is a fine name to hear. I went to La Brède this morning to see Montesquieu's study.'* The poor woman, thinking to please him, went on: 'He was a good citizen.' At the word 'citizen', the emperor winced. His eagle eyes gave Mme de Montesquieu a look that would have terrified her had she realised its meaning, and said brusquely: 'No, he was a great man.' Then, shrugging his shoulders, he looked at me as if to say: 'What a stupid woman!'

The empress followed a little behind the emperor and the ladies were presented to her in the same order. But before she reached me, a footman came to ask me to go to the salon to await Her Majesty there. The poor chamberlain, finding Mme de La Tour du Pin no longer in her appointed place, got into a muddle which became the source of many jokes for the remainder of the evening.

When the empress came into the salon, she was extremely amiable, both to me and to my husband, whom she had also had summoned. She expressed a wish to see me every evening during her stay in Bordeaux and began a game of backgammon with M. de La Tour du Pin. Tea and ices were brought in. I still hoped to see the emperor again and was most disappointed to learn that, a courier having arrived from Bayonne, he had left at once for that city.

The empress was accompanied by two Ladies of the Household, Mme Maret and another whose name I cannot remember, by her charming reader, as well as by old General Ordener, M. de Béarn and others. Although the emperor had, to use a common expression, all Spain and Europe on his hands, he found time to dictate meticulously detailed orders of the day for the empress, even indicating the gowns she was to wear. Unless she were ill in bed, she would not have dreamed of changing the smallest detail, nor would it have been possible to do so. I learned from Mme Maret that the emperor had commanded that my husband and I should spend every evening with her, which we did.

But the poor empress was beginning to be cruelly anxious

* The Château de La Brède, near Bordeaux, the home of the Montesquieu family and it was there, in retirement, that the great Montesquieu did most of his writing.

about the rumours of divorce which were already circulating. She spoke of it to M. de La Tour du Pin, who reassured her as best he could. But, having done that, he tried to silence the confidences which the imprudent, irresponsible Josephine seemed disposed to make to him, thinking it would be wiser not to hear them. She was very bitter against M. de Talleyrand, whom she accused of urging the emperor towards divorce. No one was more convinced than my husband that her accusations were well-founded for, on his last visit to Paris, M. de Talleyrand had often spoken to him about it. But he was very careful not to reveal this to Josephine. Accustomed as she was to the adulation of some and the treachery of others, she found it very comforting to talk to M. de La Tour du Pin and to open her heart to him on a subject she had not dared discuss with anyone in her entourage. She longed desperately to leave for Bayonne and every day asked Ordener when they would be leaving. And he would reply in his heavy German accent: 'Truly, I do not know yet.'

One evening, when I was sitting next to the empress beside the tea table, she received a note from the emperor. It was only a few lines and, leaning towards me, she said in a low voice: 'His writing is impossible. I cannot read this last sentence.' And she held out the note to me, putting a furtive finger to her lips to enjoin secrecy. I had only time to see that he used the familiar 'thou' and to read the last sentence, which read thus: 'I have here the father and the son;* it is causing me much embarrassment.' Since that day, this note has been quoted in a document, but much amplified. The original consisted of only five or six lines and was written across a sheet of paper torn and folded into two. I would recognise it if I saw it again.

After tea, General Ordener came up to the empress and said: 'Your Majesty leaves tomorrow at midday.' The oracle had spoken and everyone was delighted. The visit to Bordeaux had involved me in considerable expense, because for ten days I had had to attend every evening in full Court dress. I longed to see my children again. Elisa was nursing her son herself and therefore, to her very great regret, had not been in attendance on the empress. She had

* Charles IV of Spain and his eldest son, Ferdinand. Embroiled in Napoleon's very unsavoury diplomacy and military measures to secure the thrones of Spain and Portugal for his dynasty, Charles IV abdicated in March 1808 in favour of Ferdinand. The specious promises of Napoleon lured Ferdinand to Bayonne. Charles followed to reclaim his throne. Both were held captive. Napoleon's embarrassment sprang from the delay to his plans caused by Ferdinand's obstinate refusal to agree to his terms.

come only to a Drawing Room, where she had been made most flatteringly welcome. Her husband had worn the uniform of the mounted Garde d'Honneur to which all the young men of good family in Bordeaux belonged.

So we returned to Le Bouilh and, despite the warmth with which we had been received by the exalted personages in Bordeaux, we had little or no hope of future preferment. Indeed, how could one expect the eagle eye of the man who controlled the destinies of France to single out someone so entirely aloof from all intrigue as my husband, a man, so to speak, unknown to those in power since he had taken no part in the events of the past few years, one whom an almost total lack of fortune had compelled to live in the greatest retirement.

M. de La Tour du Pin remained behind in Bordeaux to complete some matters of business and I was sitting beside the lamp one evening with Mme Joseph de La Tour du Pin, a penniless cousin to whom we had offered hospitality, when, just as it was striking nine, a peasant arrived in haste from Bordeaux with a note from my husband. It said only: 'I am Prefect of Brussels . . . of Brussels, which is only ten leagues from Antwerp!' I admit that my heart filled with a tremendous joy, most of all at the thought of seeing my son again.

M. Maret had not known that this Prefecture was vacant. Working papers arrived in Bayonne from the Minister of the Interior just as they arrived at the Tuileries or Saint-Cloud, for nothing was allowed to change the emperor's routine. He might be overturning the Spanish monarchy, banishing two Spanish kings – father and son – to prison and exile, and all this might be causing him 'much embarrassment' but when working papers arrived from a minister, he read them, corrected them and changed the appointments. 'Prefecture de la Dyle':* beside it was a suggested name for the post. The emperor took his pen, crossed it out and wrote instead 'de La Tour du Pin'. We learned this later from M. Maret, a man who never raised objections but who, by the same token, never made suggestions. He was an effective machine.

My son was in Antwerp, in the office he occupied as secretary to M. Malouet, when he saw the latter running across the court-yard. Now M. Malouet was the most dignified of men and never had he been known to hasten his step for anything whatsoever. He

* The Department of the Dyle, named after the River Dyle, was an administrative area comprising Brussels, Louvain and Nivelle. It existed only between 1794 and 1814. The Prefecture was in Brussels. (Tr.)

hurried in, calling as he came: 'Your father is Prefect of Brussels.'
Dear Humbert, how happy he was.

A few days before M. de La Tour du Pin was due to leave
Le Bouilh for Brussels, I received an express courier from our
friend Brouquens, telling me a carriage had been sent to Cubzac,
that Charles IV of Spain and his unworthy queen were arriving at
the Palace of Bordeaux and that the emperor had commanded
me to act as lady-in-waiting to the queen during her stay there, a
matter of some three or four days. Fortunately all my court gowns
were still at Brouquens' house. My packing was quickly done and
my husband and I set out together. As soon as we reached Bordeaux, I dressed hurriedly and went to the palace, where their
Majesties of Spain had just arrived.

The king and queen had gone to their private apartments, with
the Prince de La Paix.* In the Household salon I found people
I knew and their greeting: 'Come along, dinner is ready and we
were waiting for you,' was welcome indeed as I had taken only a
cup of tea before leaving Le Bouilh. The company included M.
d'Audenarde and M. Dumanoir, the first an equerry and the second
a chamberlain to the emperor; also Général Reille, M. Iyequerdo,
a chaplain and two or three other Spaniards whose names I never
knew and who spoke no French. These gentlemen told me that two
other ladies-in-waiting had been appointed – Mme d'Aux (Elisa)
and Mme de Piis – and I was charged with telling them that they
were to be at the Palace at noon the following day. I was also told
that Their Majesties would receive official callers in the morning
and the ladies in the evening. M. Dumanoir added that I myself
was to be at the palace at eleven o'clock in order to be presented
to the queen and that I, in turn, would have to present the two other
ladies-in-waiting appointed to serve her.

During the meal, these gentlemen were most attentive to their
new companion. They said over and over again that they would
take me with them to Fontainebleau itself. I was much afraid they
meant it and when I protested, they invariably replied: 'But when
the emperor wishes something, it has to be done.' After dinner, we
tried to think of some form of entertainment for the king during the
two evenings he was to spend in Bordeaux. The problem was
complicated by the fact that he either could not or would not go to
the theatre, fearing the reception that might await him. I remem-

* Charles IV was completely dominated by his wife, Marie-Louise of Parma, and
her powerful favourite, Don Manuel Godoy, whom he created Prince de La
Paix. (Tr.)

bered hearing in Spain that he was passionately fond of music and that every evening he formed a quartet in which he played, or thought he played, the alto violin part. We therefore decided to organise a small concert and the prefect was put in charge of the arrangements.

After returning home, I remembered that it was also said in Madrid that when the king played, there was always a musician beside him familiar with the king's part. It was, in fact, the musician who played but in such a manner as to allow the king to think he was doing it all by himself. I determined to employ the same ruse, but without telling anyone, out of respect for such a sorely tried royal majesty.

I was at the palace at eleven o'clock the next morning and M. Dumanoir begged admittance to the queen's apartments in order to present me. Before opening the door, he turned to me saying: 'You must not laugh.' Naturally, I immediately wanted to, and with some excuse, for I beheld the most amazing and unexpected sight. The Queen of Spain stood in the middle of the room before a great cheval mirror. She was being laced. Her only garment was a little cambric skirt, very narrow and very short, and upon her bosom – the driest, leanest and darkest bosom you can imagine – lay a muslin handkerchief. Her grey hair was dressed with a garland of red and yellow roses. She came towards me, the maid still lacing her, making those movements which a woman uses to ease herself out of her corset. Beside her was the king, accompanied by several gentlemen whom I did not know. The queen asked M. Dumanoir 'Who is she?' He told her. The queen then asked 'What is her name?' He told her that, too, and the queen said something to the king in Spanish to which he replied that I, or rather, my name, was very noble. Then she finished her toilette, telling while she did so how the empress had given her several of her own gowns as she had brought nothing from Madrid. I found such deep degradation very distressing. I did indeed remember having seen the empress in the gown of yellow crepe lined with satin of the same colour which was at that moment being passed to the queen. At the sight, I suddenly lost every desire to laugh and felt far more inclined to weep.

When the queen was dressed, she dismissed me. I went to the salon, where I found Elisa and Mme de Piis and we waited together for the arrival of the official visitors whom I was to present to Her Majesty. While we waited, a large man with a black plaster on his forehead crossed the room. I recognised him as the famous

Prince de La Paix. He walked rudely in front of us, without a word, and we all agreed that neither his face nor his figure justified the favours credited to him by the gossip of the day.

By then, the salons were full and the queen was informed. I presented to her, one by one, the heads of the various municipal bodies and of the administration, beginning with the archbishop, the only person to whom she spoke. M. Dumanoir performed the same office for the king, who was far more gracious. The presentations over, we went back to the small salon where the queen spoke to me in carrying tones of her anxiety at being without news of the arrival of La Tudo, the mistress of the Prince de La Paix. She went on to say, equally loudly, that she knew her two sons* were prisoners, that she was very glad of it, that their sufferings would never match their true deserts, that they were both monsters and the cause of all her misfortunes. The king, poor man, made no attempt to silence her. It made me shudder. At last, she dismissed us with the words '*À ce soir*'.

In the evening, there was a Drawing Room and many ladies to present whom I did not know. Mme de Piis would tell me their names and I repeated them to the queen. Afterwards, we went to the small salon where the musicians were waiting, the king shouting at the top of his voice for 'Manuelito' – the Prince de La Paix. The king was handed his violin; he tuned it himself and the quartet began. But he continually lost his notes and his part was really played by someone else, as I had secretly arranged. Later, there were ices and chocolate and then we went to bed.

The following day, there was a visit lasting a quarter of an hour in the morning and the same music in the evening. The next day, I heard to my great joy that the members of the Spanish royal family were shortly to continue their journey. The prefect and the archbishop came to take leave of them. Then we climbed into the carriages which were to take us to the river crossing, for in those days there was no bridge. We found the brigantine lying ready and, at the end of the crossing, I bade farewell to these unhappy sovereigns. The unfortunate king never, for a single moment, seemed to realise the wretchedness of his position.

And that is the tale of my short time at the Court of King Charles IV, in attendance on the queen, his dreadful wife.

* Ferdinand, Prince of the Asturias, later Ferdinand VII of Spain, and Don Carlos, who later took the title Charles V, refusing to recognise the accession of his niece, Isabella, to the Spanish throne.

XXVIII

Now began a new life. My kitchen garden, my hens, my cows, my flowers, the calm routine which suited my taste, all was to be abandoned for an entirely different existence. It was, as I have said, about nine o'clock in the evening when the messenger brought me the note from M. de La Tour du Pin announcing that he had been appointed Prefect of Brussels. It meant a lot of planning and the idle chatter of my cousin, Mme Joseph de La Tour du Pin, was so distracting that I suggested we should go to bed.

But first I had to write to Mme de Maurville to tell her that my husband's new appointment would change nothing between us and that I hoped she would come with us to Brussels. She was staying with friends about two leagues away and I gave instructions for my note to be given to her at break of day so that she would not have time to ask herself the sad question: 'What is to become of me?' I could have left her at Le Bouilh, which would not have meant any extra expense for us. But why should she not share our good fortune since she had shared the bad? Besides, her affectionate loyalty would help us in many ways. She was without learning, and had little natural intelligence, but she did have the gift of observation and a very penetrating understanding of people. Her devotion to my husband was total and the furtherance of his interests her constant concern. She cared for my children as if they had been her own. I have, thank God, never had to have a governess for my children, but I knew that I could leave them with Mme de Maurville without any anxiety whenever social duties – which I tried to limit as much as possible – took me away from them for a while.

In those few hours alone in my room, I thought more than I would normally have done in half a year. In the important moments of life, any thought which has not occurred in the first twenty-four hours is either pointless, or idle repetition. By the time my husband arrived next morning for lunch. I was ready to talk over this change in our lives and tell him the plans and arrangements which I considered necessary.

Charlotte was then eleven and a half years old, very forward for her age and longing to know all about everything. She pored over every available gazetteer and map of Belgium so that when her father returned and, knowing her well, questioned her about the

Department of the Dyle, she was ready with all the facts and figures. As for little Cécile, at eight years of age she was already a good musician and proficient in Italian, so that her first question was to know if she would have a singing master in Brussels.

My husband immediately made all the necessary arrangements at Le Bouilh, and unfortunately put everything into the hands of a man on whom he thought he could rely as on himself. I was to deal with all the household arrangements and the packing.

M. de La Tour du Pin had been told to travel to Paris without delay, his predecessor, M. de Chaban, having already left to or-ganise the departments in Tuscany, which had just been annexed to the Empire. Our friend Brouquens, whose pleasure in our good fortune was almost greater than my husband's, came for him a few days later and they left together for Paris.

The news of this appointment astounded all those who had for a long time been vainly seeking favours. No one would believe that M. de La Tour du Pin, like Cincinnatus, had been summoned from his plough and given the finest Prefecture in France. But the choice was one of the wisest that the prodigious foresight of Napoleon could have made and for this reason: Brussels was a conquered capital and until then no effort had been made to create any ties which would bind her to her new fatherland. It was a city with a Court and an aristocracy, yet it had until then been governed by people of obscure and even doubtful origin.

M. de Pontécoulant, the first prefect, was admittedly a man of good family and aristocratic courtesy. He had been an officer in the Gardes Françaises and his youth had been spent at Versailles and in Paris, so he might, perhaps, have been a success in Brussels if it had not been for his wife. She was said to have saved his life during the Terror. She had once been the mistress of Mirabeau whose librarian, Lejai, had been her husband. M. de Pontécoulant, surrounded by scheming compatriots who had fallen upon Belgium as upon a prey, had never concerned himself with administrative matters. The emperor recalled him, nominating him to the Senate, and sent M. de Chaban in his stead.

M. de Chaban was worthy, enlightened, firm and an excellent administrator. He abolished many abuses and punished those who had misappropriated property, confiscating it. All his measures had been just and enlightened and to govern the country well, one had only to follow the path he had marked out. But he had made no attempt to overcome the aloofness of the upper classes towards the French domination, and it was this task which fell to us, to my husband and, I dare to claim, to me as well. For the source of any influence of this kind must perforce be in the salons. It is true that M. de Chaban was married, but his wife was ailing and of an obscure family. She did not receive and, as a result, no one ever saw her.

A sort of romantic legend had preceded me to Brussels, based on my adventures in America. These had been mentioned in a note to Delille's poem 'La Pitié'.* This lady from the Court of Marie-Antoinette, the queen whose sister was so well loved throughout Belgium, this lady who, in those distant lands, had milked cows and lived amid forests, was sufficiently intriguing to arouse curiosity.

After I had made all my arrangements at Le Bouilh and sent off by waggon everything I thought might be useful in Brussels and lessen the very great expense of equipping a large house, I set off with Mme de Maurville, my daughters and my small Aymar. M. Meyer of Bordeaux had lent me a carriage, which I sold for him in Brussels, and we travelled post. We stayed two or three days at Ussé to see Mme de Duras, to the great joy of her daughters and mine, and then went on to Paris where I stayed for three or four weeks with my aunt. She was living then with M. de Lally in a pretty house in the Rue de Miromesnil.

Mme Dillon had returned from England long before and I called on her, for she had given M. de La Tour du Pin a warm welcome the previous year when he has passed through Paris with Humbert. My half-sister, Fanny, had grown up. She was then twenty-three and, although not pretty, of very distinguished appearance. She had had many suitors, but the one she preferred and would have married was Prince Alphonse Pignatelli, a pleasant young man, who died of a chest illness. He wanted to marry Fanny before he died so that he could leave her his fortune, but despite his insistence, she refused. The unfortunate young man's days were numbered and she thought it would have shown a lack of delicacy towards his family to have married him then, though she loved him dearly and would have been happy, even in her grief, to bear his name. I myself was very disappointed at her decision, for I would have much preferred my sister's name to be Pignatelli rather than Bertrand.

Since this very ordinary name has now been mentioned, I must tell you something that happened during my husband's previous visit to Paris. The emperor had repeatedly made it known to the

* Jacques Delille (1738–1813), one of the first poets of the romantic school. He was very highly considered in his day and had a great influence on later romantic poets. (Tr.)

empress and to Fanny herself that he very much wished her to
marry Général Bertrand, who had long been in love with her. My
sister would not consent and the emperor was annoyed. When
he knew of her feelings for Alphonse Pignatelli, he ceased to
plague her, but, after the prince's death, he re-opened his campaign.
M. de La Tour du Pin happened to arrive in Paris just at the time
when Mme Dillon had promised a final answer and she asked him
to see the empress on her behalf and tell her of my sister's definite
refusal. It was a somewhat difficult commission, but my husband
undertook it.

The empress received him in her bedroom, where the deep
alcove was curtained off during the day by thick, heavy material,
almost a wall of embroidered damask, its folds held in place by an
edging of heavy gold fringe. She told him to sit beside her on a sofa
placed against this curtain. As they were alone, M. de La Tour du
Pin went straight to the point, delivered his message and apologised
for bringing a decision contrary to the emperor's wishes. The
empress was most persistent. In the course of a long conversation,
M. de La Tour du Pin expressed certain very aristocratic sentiments which did not displease her. Finally, after talking to him
about himself, about me, our children, his fortune and his plans,
the empress dismissed him.

My husband went immediately to Mme Dillon to give her an
account of the interview. The same evening, he called on M. de
Talleyrand who took him by the arm, as was his custom when he
wanted to talk privately in a corner: 'What on earth have you been
doing, refusing Général Bertrand's offer for your sister-in-law?
Is it any concern of yours?' 'But that is what Fanny wished,' replied
M. de La Tour du Pin, 'and my age puts me in a position to act for
her in the place of her father.' 'Well,' continued the wily old fox,
'fortunately your fine aristocratic airs have not ruined your chances.
They happen to be the fashion at the Tuileries just now.' 'Who
told you all this', asked my husband, 'have you seen the empress?'
'No,' replied the other, 'but I have seen the emperor, who was
listening.' So it was perhaps to this conversation, overheard from
behind a curtain, that M. de La Tour du Pin owed his appointment
as Prefect of Brussels.

I was received in Brussels with the greatest kindness. It is a city
which appreciates good society and people were delighted to
know that the salons of the Prefecture were to be presided over by
someone of the aristocracy. The behaviour of the wives of various
officials sent to the town had not made a good impression for they

had thought – mistakenly – to please the Government by not bothering to make themselves agreeable to the Belgian ladies. Two of these Frenchwomen were senior to me, by reason of their husband's position. One was Mme de Chambarlhac, wife of the general commanding the division stationed in Brussels. She was a good-looking Savoyarde and a member of the de Coucy family. It was said that she had once been a nun or a novice and that her husband had carried her off during one of the Italian campaigns and married her. She was forty, but still quite beautiful. Living so long among military men of all kinds had ruined her manners, though a few traces of her original breeding remained. Naturally, I could not consider any connection with such a person. As for Général de Chambarlhac, he was a fool, jealous of my husband and therefore hostile from the very beginning.

The second was the wife of the first president, M. Betz, a learned German who was both intelligent and able. Mme Betz came from the very bottom of the social ladder. She was fifty when I knew her and quite ugly, though it was not impossible to believe that she might once have been beautiful. Her jewels, low-cut dresses and the style in which she dressed her hair were all far more suited to a young girl than to someone of her age. I received her on important occasions but do not remember ever having entered her house, though I did not omit to call on her from time to time, at long intervals.

The bitter jealousy of these two ladies was due to the fact that they were not invited to the Dowager's suppers. These marked the dividing line in Brussels society and an invitation was a coveted honour. The Dowager, as the Dowager Duchesse d'Arenberg was always known, was by birth the Comtesse de la Marck and the last descendant of the Sanglier des Ardennes.* She was, as the Archbishop of Malines remarked, the perfect Queen Mother. She had retired to the house set aside for the widows of the House of Arenberg and there lived simply, but in a manner befitting her rank, daily inviting to supper a company of people of all ages, both men and women. She always dined alone, used an open carriage no matter what the weather and saw her children every day, especially her blind son, whom she loved most tenderly. Whenever a slight attack of gout prevented him from going out, she never omitted to visit him at his home. She received from seven o'clock until

* Guillaume de la Marck (1446–1485), known as the Boar of the Ardennes, who ravaged Brabant and Liège and was eventually defeated and executed by Maximilian of Austria. (Tr.)

nine. The supper guests arrived at nine and so great was the respect in which the Duchesse was held that there was no one in Brussels who would have dreamed of arriving at half-past. After supper, the guests played lotto until midnight. When her son was there, he would organise a game of whist or backgammon with M. de La Tour du Pin, if he happened to be among the guests. There were never more than fifteen or eighteen people present, all from the most distinguished families in town, or visitors of note. But foreigners were rare, for France was at war with the whole of Europe and people could not come as they have done since.

In the days before the Revolution, I had often met Mme la Duchesse d'Arenberg in Paris at the Hôtel de Beauvau, where I had always been received with the greatest kindness. Also, Mme de Poix and Mme la Maréchale de Beauvau had, I knew, both written to the Duchesse to tell her that I would be coming. On the day following our arrival in Brussels, I went, therefore, with my husband to call on this venerable lady. We were particularly kindly received and invited to supper on the following day. The Duchesse also wanted me to present my son, Humbert, who had come to Brussels to meet us. Her kindness set the standard for the attentions we were to receive. The whole town signed our book. They came in person to do so and I took the greatest care to return each call. I forgot none of them. I made lists of all the people who had called, putting after their names a summary of any family details I had been able to gather in the course of conversation or from the peerage books I had borrowed from the Bibliothèque de Bourgogne which was – and still is – very rich in works of that kind. I had two helpers in my task: for contemporary matters, M. de Verseyden de Warech, Secretary-General of the Prefecture, and for the past, the Commandeur de Nieuport, a former Commander of the Order of Malta, who came to see me every evening. After a month, I was as familiar with Brussels society as if I had known it all my life. I knew about all the different liaisons, the animosities, the bickerings and so on. It was a considerable task and I applied myself to it with the same zeal I have always put into any job that had to be done.

Our establishment cost us a great deal of money. I seem to remember that my husband received an allowance for this purpose, but am not certain. The staff included two liveried servants and a liveried office-boy, a porter, butler-valet, an office footman who helped the house staff when we entertained, and two stable boys. We lived in the palace where the King of Holland* later lived. My

* King William I of the Netherlands.

private apartment consisted of a pretty salon and a billiards room. I let it be known at once that I never, for any reason whatsoever, received visitors in the morning. All my mornings were devoted to the education of my daughters, to being present at their lessons or to taking them out, either for a walk or a drive.

Before long, we could count many close friends, including M. and Mme de Trazégnies, Prince Auguste d'Arenberg, the Commandeur de Nieuport and others. My husband was delighted to meet again the Comte de Liedekerke* for in the days before the Revolution, they had been companions in arms in the Regiment de Royal-Comtois when M. de La Tour du Pin was second-in-command. The Comte de Liedekerke had married Mlle Désandrouin, who would eventually inherit an immense fortune, much of which was already in her possession. They had only one son and two daughters. The young man was then twenty-two and an auditeur at the Conseil d'État. There was talk of attaching one of these young men to the personal staff of each Prefect, to act as secretary and gain experience in administration. M. de Liedekerke therefore asked M. de La Tour du Pin, his former Colonel, to request that his son be appointed to his staff in that capacity.

Our own son, Humbert, left Antwerp, where M. Malouet had been a second father to him, and returned to Brussels to study for the entrance examination to the Conseil d'Etat which was to be held a few months later.

In September 1808, I received a letter from my stepmother, Mme Dillon, telling me that my sister had at last decided, after many hesitations and much uncertainty, to marry Général Bertrand. She had yielded in part to his constancy and in part to the renewed persuasions of the emperor to whom one could refuse nothing, so gracefully and so winningly did he set about obtaining what he wanted. My sister was in those days extremely frivolous, a Creole quality she shared with her mother. Napoleon had wanted her to accompany the Empress Josephine on a journey to Fontainebleau and to enable her to appear there to her best advantage, sent her 30,000 francs to provide a wardrobe for the eight days of her stay. It was during that period that he obtained her consent to the general's proposal which, until then, she had so obstinately refused.

The emperor decided that the marriage should take place immediately, despite my sister's protests that her mother had recently lost her other daughter, poor Mme de Fitz-James. Faced with a long

* Marie-Ferdinand-Hilarion, Comte de Liedekerke-Beaufort (1762–1841). In 1813, his only son married Mme de La Tour du Pin's daughter, Alix. (See p. 323.)

delay and certain that the two women, left to themselves, would never be free from one impediment or another, the emperor said to Fanny: 'Tell your sister to come; she will arrange everything . . . I am leaving for Erfurt in eight days' time. You must be married by then.'

I learned all this in a letter from the Duc de Bassano,* for neither Mme Dillon nor Fanny thought to write to me. Although the letter was a very friendly one, it was so clearly a command that I did not even consider refusing. Two hours after receiving it, I left for Paris and reached Mme d'Hénin's house at dawn. She was amazed to find me at her bedside when she awoke. She still kept a room at our disposal in her pretty house in the Rue de Miromesnil. I stayed only long anough to change my dress and send for a livery carriage. Then, after drinking a cup of tea, I was driven to Mme Dillon's house in the Rue Joubert. There I learned that she had left some days before for the country, not far from Saint-Cloud, to stay with Mme de Boigne. She had left no messages for me, so I asked the name of the house and how to find it and, as soon as I had written a note to the Duc de Bassano to tell him of my arrival, set out for the country.

It took me an hour and a half to reach Mme de Boigne's house, Beaurégard, above Malmaison. It was striking half-past-eleven as I arrived and Mme Dillon was still in bed. Fanny exclaimed 'Ah, we are saved. Here is my sister!' Her mother, on the other hand, was alarmed at the thought of the bustle which my energy was about to force upon her. Nothing had been arranged. I began by advising her to get up, dress, eat luncheon and return to Paris with my sister and me. Just at that moment, Général Bertrand arrived. I had never met him before and he probably knew that it was my husband whom Mme Dillon had charged with refusing his proposal of marriage two years before. Being by nature extremely shy, he was much embarrassed. To put him at ease, I suggested a walk in the park until Mme Dillon was dressed. We walked for more than an hour and came to understand one another so well that by the time we returned to the house, we had settled everything.

In the salon, we found Mme de Boigne, whom I had not seen since she was a child, and her mother, Mme d'Osmond, a sister of all the Dillons of Bordeaux.† Neither of these ladies could abide me but when luncheon was announced, could hardly do otherwise

* M. Maret had recently been created Duc de Bassano.
† See p. 37. The Comtesse de Boigne, 1781–1866, was a lady of liberal ideas and Orléanist sympathies. Her memoirs were published in 1907 and show a sharp pen. (Tr.)

than suggest I share it with them. I was very happy to do so because I had eaten nothing since taking that cup of tea with Mme d'Hénin at seven o'clock. The poor general, delighted to find that someone was at last going to put an end to the dilatoriness of his future mother-in-law, watched contentedly as we climbed into the carriage to return to Paris and promised to rejoin us there during the evening.

The following morning, everything was ready and the signing of the contract had been arranged for the evening of the next day. A notice was posted up at the Mairie. By special order, the tribunal met in extraordinary session. Grand-Juge Régnier* was awakened at five o'clock in the morning to send off some document to serve as my sister's certificate of baptism, for Mme Dillon had lost the original, or perhaps had never had one.

Napoleon had also decided that the ceremony should take place at Saint-Leu, the home of Queen Hortense.† He said he might be present, so the queen paid great attention to the instructions he had given for the ceremony and saw that every single detail was carried out. At a moment when he was about to meet all the sovereigns he had conquered, the great man had found time to arrange the smallest details of his favourite aide-de-camp's marriage.

I was presented to the emperor at Saint-Cloud by Mme de Bassano. I had to be at her house at eight o'clock in the morning, in Court dress and plumes. The emperor greeted me most graciously, questioned me about Brussels and Brussels society – 'high society,' he added with a smile that implied 'the only kind that interests you.' Then he laughed at having made me rise so early and teased Mme de Bassano a little about the same thing, a teasing she accepted with a slight air of sulkiness which became her exceedingly well. She has since told me he was most attentive to her at that time.

I can see you smile, my son, as you read that when I was arranging the salon for the signing of the contract and wanted to set an escritoire with paper and pens on the table, I could find no such objects anywhere in the apartment of my stepmother and her daughter. It was fortunate that I had thought of it and, as d'Expilly, the best stationer of the day, lived quite near, I was able to send my servant to fetch everything necessary for the occasion. My stepmother was agreeably surprised at my forethought.

* Claude-Ambroise Régnier, 1746–1814. In 1802, Napoleon appointed him to the Conseil d'Etat, made him a Grand-Juge and then Minister of Justice. (Tr.)
† Hortense-Eugénie de Beauharnais, daughter of the Empress Josephine, wife of Napoleon's brother, Louis, King of Holland.

The great of the earth arrived with the bridegroom and the terms of the contract were read. The evening before the wedding was spent in rather insipid fashion, listening to music. Luncheon the following day was little better. The wedding ceremony was to take place at half-past three. All the mighty arrived: marshals, generals and the like, and we walked in procession to the Chapel. The nuptial blessing was given by the Abbé d'Osmond, Bishop of Nancy, who later became Archbishop of Florence. After the ceremony there was dinner, followed by dancing. A number of young people had come from Paris but Queen Hortense, who loved dancing and excelled at it, was rather out of temper on account of a somewhat amusing incident. The emperor had not come, but he had made it known to Queen Hortense that he had seen the parure of emeralds set in diamonds which the empress had given Fanny and did not consider it sufficient. He knew she had a similar set, he said, and asked her to add it to that which her mother had given in order to complete it. Queen Hortense was extremely angry, but had to do as she was told.

⚜⚜⚜⚜⚜⚜⚜⚜⚜ XXIX ⚜⚜⚜⚜⚜⚜⚜⚜⚜

I returned to Brussels after attending some of the formal dinners given in honour of the marriage, particularly those given by the four witnesses: M. de Talleyrand, the Duc de Bassano, M. Lebrun and another whose name I cannot recall. The dinners were all very tedious and I was delighted to set out to rejoin my husband and my children. We spent a very pleasant autumn and winter in Brussels. I gave two or three fine balls and Mme de Duras came to spend a fortnight with us, bringing her daughters. I arranged dances for them and took them to the theatre where an excellent box was reserved for the Prefecture. They thoroughly enjoyed themselves.

Queen Hortense also passed through Brussels. It was the last time she made the journey to join her husband and spend a few days with him in Amsterdam. I saw her while she was in the city. She pretended to be unutterably bored at having to fulfil her duties as queen.

I do not pretend to be writing history so I shall say nothing of the marriage of the Emperor Napoleon to the Archduchess Marie-Louise.* I shall only record my sister's account of the arrival of this princess at Compiègne. Not only was she herself there, but she also knew from her husband details unknown to others.

The emperor was at Compiègne with the new ladies-in-waiting appointed to serve the empress, and vastly impatient to see his new wife. A small calèche stood ready in the courtyard of the château, the horses put to, waiting to take him to meet her. When the first courier arrived, Napoleon jumped into the calèche and set off to meet the berline bringing this wife whom he so ardently desired. The carriages drew up. The door of the berline was opened and Marie-Louise prepared to get out. But her husband did not give her time. He climbed into the carriage, embraced her and, having unceremoniously bundled out his sister, the Queen of Naples, telling her to ride in front, seated himself beside Marie-Louise. When they arrived at the château, he left the carriage first, offered his arm to his bride and led her into the Household Salon where all the people who had been invited were assembled. It was already dark. The emperor presented all the Ladies of the Household in turn, and then the Gentlemen. When the presentations were over, he took the empress by the hand and led her to her apartment. Everyone expected her to make a change of toilette and then reappear. They waited for an hour and were beginning to think longingly of supper when the Grand Chamberlain† came to announce that Their Majesties had retired. Bertrand whispered in his wife's ear: 'They've gone to bed.' Everyone was greatly surprised, but no one allowed it to appear and they all went in to supper.

The following day, my sister learned from her husband that Marie-Louise had given the emperor a permit or statement signed by the Archbishop of Vienna, declaring that the marriage could be consummated without further ceremony, the proxy marriage being sufficient. As my brother-in-law was a most truthful man, I have no doubt at all that this detail is authentic.

In Brussels there were great rejoicings over this marriage with an archduchess, for memories of Austrian rule were far from forgotten. So far, the nobility of Brussels had remained aloof from the new government, but now, attracted by the courteous ways of a prefect of aristocratic family, they felt the time had come to

* In 1808, in his anxiety for an heir, Napoleon asked Francis 1st of Austria, whom he had just defeated at Wagram, for his daughter Marie-Louise in marriage. (Tr.)
† Général Bertrand.

renounce their old prejudices, which were becoming rather irksome.

When M. de La Tour du Pin learned that the emperor intended to bring his young empress to the capital of her father's former Belgian possessions, he formed a Garde d'Honneur for duty at the Château de Laeken. It was formed exclusively of Belgians and did not include anyone engaged in the service of France. It was put under the command of the Marquis de Trazégnies, who had as his second-in-command the Marquis d'Assche. Many members of the leading families of Brussels were enrolled in its ranks and young men who intended to make a career in either the administration or the army, took this occasion to come forward. Among them was young Auguste de Liedekerke and our own poor son, Humbert. The uniform was very plain: a green coat and maroon-coloured trousers. It was a mounted corps and very well mounted. too. My sister came to Brussels and stayed at the Prefecture. She was present at a big dinner we gave in honour of the Garde, at which all the ladies wore favours of the same colours as their uniform.

The emperor reached Laeken in time for dinner. The next day, he received the Garde d'Honneur and all the officials of the administration. The mayor, the Duc d'Ursel, presented the town officials. In the evening, there was a Drawing Room and I presented the ladies, nearly all of whom I knew. Marie-Louise spoke to none of them personally. Even the most illustrious names – that of the Duchesse d'Arenberg, for instance, or the Comtesse de Mérode who was by birth a Princesse de Grimberghe – made no more impression on her than that of Mme P., the wife of the Réceveur-Général.*

After the Drawing Room, I had the honour of being summoned to play cards with Her Majesty. I think we played whist. The Duc d'Ursel told me which cards to put down and when it was my turn to play. This farce lasted half an hour. Afterwards, the emperor having gone to his study, we separated and, to my great delight, I was able to go home.

The following day there was to be a great ball at the Hôtel de Ville. I was therefore rather annoyed to be asked to dine at Laeken, for I did not see how it would be possible to change my toilette, or at least my gown, between dinner and the ball. However, the pleasure of seeing and listening to the emperor for two whole hours was too great for me not to appreciate such an invitation to the full. The Duc d'Ursel escorted me and as he had to be at the

* An official appointed to receive domaine produce and taxes in a given area on behalf of the Treasury. They were, in effect, the Government's bankers. (Tr.)

Hôtel de Ville in time to receive the emperor, I told my maid to be waiting for me there with another toilette in readiness.

That dinner is one of my most pleasurable memories. We were eight, sitting in this order: the emperor, with the Queen of Westphalia on his right, then Maréchal Berthier, the King of Westphalia, the empress, the Duc d'Ursel, Mme de Bouillé and finally, myself, on the emperor's left. He spoke to me nearly all the time of materials, laces, wages, the lives of lace-makers, and then of monuments, antiquities, charitable organisations, the convents of the Béguines* and the customs of the people. Fortunately, I knew something about them all. 'How much does a lace-maker earn?' he asked the Duc d'Ursel. The poor man was somewhat bothered as he tried to work out the amount in centimes. The emperor saw his hesitation and, turning to me, asked what the local currency was called. I told him it was the 'escalin', worth 63 centimes.

We were at table less than three-quarters of an hour and when we returned to the salon, the emperor took a large cup of coffee and continued the conversation. He talked first of the toilette the empress was wearing, which he liked, and then, breaking off, asked me if I was comfortably housed. 'Not too badly,' I told him, 'we are in Your Majesty's apartment.' 'Ah, indeed,' he replied, 'it certainly cost enough. It was that rascally secretary of M. de Pontécoulant who saw to its furnishing. But half the money found its way into his own pockets – if my brother', he went on, turning towards the King of Westphalia, 'will forgive me for saying so. He has taken him into his service, for he likes rascals,' and he shrugged his shoulders. Jérome was about to reply when he realised the emperor was already launched on a quite different topic. He had gone back to the Duke of Burgundy† and Louis XI and from them he suddenly passed to Louis XIV, saying he had been truly great only during his last years. After commenting on the shameful events of the reign of Louis XV, he mentioned Louis XVI and there stopped, saying sadly and with respect 'That unfortunate prince!'

He went on to speak of other things and teased his brother about gathering into Westphalia all the dregs of France. Heaven knows how many barbed jests Jérome might not have had to endure if someone had not remarked that it was time to leave for the ball.

M. d'Ursel and I fled to his carriage and were driven at a gallop

---

* Women living in communities, principally in Belgium, and vowed to poverty, chastity and obedience. Their vows are not permanent. They occupy themselves with prayer, good works, lace-making and embroidery. (Tr.)
† Charles the Bold, 1433–1477.

to the Hôtel de Ville. I rushed up the stairs as fast as I could. A fresh toilette lay ready for me and I was able to make a complete change of dress and reach the ballroom before the emperor arrived. He complimented me on my speed and asked if I intended to dance. I told him I did not, being a woman of forty. He laughed and said there were, indeed, many of that age who danced and did not reveal their years so frankly. The ball was very fine. It continued after supper, at which we drank to the health of the empress and hoped, though we did not say so, that she might have a very good reason for not dancing.

The emperor and his young wife left the following morning. A very richly decorated yacht took them to the end of the Brussels Canal, where carriages were waiting to take them on to Antwerp. As M. de La Tour du Pin went on board the yacht, he saw the Marquis de Trazégnies, the commander of the *Garde*. Fearing the emperor might not invite the marquis to accompany him in the yacht as space was very limited, M. de La Tour du Pin mentioned his name to the emperor and added that one of his ancestors had been Constable of France during the reign of St Louis. This information worked like a charm. The emperor immediately summoned the Marquis de Trazégnies and had a long talk with him. Shortly afterwards, his wife was appointed a lady-in-waiting. She pretended to be rather bored at the appointment, but secretly she was delighted.

After the emperor's visit, our life in Brussels returned to its normal routine. The summer passed in a series of visits to different country houses, where we were invited to dine. We went to Antwerp for the launching of a large seventy-four,* one of nine on the stocks at that time. Our good friend, M. Malouet, was in charge of the work.

Humbert went to Paris for his examination. It was an ordeal for a young man of twenty to answer the long list of questions but it was infinitely worse when it meant standing before the emperor while he, from his armchair, took over the examination and asked the most unexpected things. Humbert heard the examiner, who was pointing towards him as he spoke, whisper to Napoleon: 'That is one of the most outstanding . . .' and felt encouraged. The emperor asked him if he knew any foreign languages and he replied that he spoke English and Italian as fluently as French. It was his knowledge of Italian which decided his appointment to the sub-Prefecture of Florence. To increase the number of

* A ship of the line, armed with 74 guns. (Tr.)

vacancies for 'auditeurs', some were sent as sub-prefects to the chief towns of Departments where, until then, all the duties had fallen upon the prefect.

M. de La Tour du Pin was recovering from a painful operation on his ankle and still unable to walk when an express arrived one night from M. Malouet with the news that the English fleet had entered the Escaut. It consisted of several large warships and a great number of transports. At dawn, the news was telegraphed to Paris. Napoleon was away, but Arch-Chancellor Cambacérès busily set about collecting troops. All the detachments were sent post, which meant tremendous activity and movement. The English, instead of taking Antwerp and destroying our arsenals and dockyards, as they could easily have done, spent their time laying siege to Flushing. This gave Bernadotte time to assemble an army of Gardes Nationales and troops from several garrisons. The details of this ridiculous English attack may be read in all the memoirs of the day. Although M. de La Tour du Pin had no responsibility in military matters, he assembled the entire Garde Nationale of the Department of the Dyle. This did not prevent him from being accused later of having been slow to do so.

I will tell you here a small personal incident which was rather strange:

We shared to the full the interest aroused by this expedition and drove to Antwerp nearly every day. We stabled three carriage horses at intervals along the route and used them in relays. One was at Malines. We used to leave Brussels at five o'clock in the morning and reach Antwerp by eight o'clock. There, we would breakfast with M. Malouet and by midday be back in Brussels in time for the courier. On one of these journeys we stopped to drink a cup of coffee at the house of Monseigneur de Pradt, Archbishop of Malines. The conversation was entirely about this notorious English expedition and the archbishop told us: 'This Lord Chatham* is a fool. Instead of entering the Escaut, from which he is now unable to withdraw, he should have gone to Breskens and landed his troops there, where we would not have had a single man to oppose them. He would have been able to impose levies on a considerable part of Belgium—on Bruges, Ghent, Brussels, etc.' M. de Pradt had worked out every detail. He traced the route they should have followed, calculated the money and silver that might have been seized, churches and strongrooms that could have been pillaged

* Elder son of William Pitt, 1st Earl of Chatham and brother of William Pitt the younger.

and concluded 'And what could he not have done over there, in the depths of Germany!' I found all this, said with a cold calculation very out of keeping with his cloth, so amusing that, on our return to Brussels, I included an account of it in a letter to my aunt. My letter never reached her, and I will tell you later what became of it.*

The Gardes Nationales from the Vosges and the Departments in the east, who had travelled post from their mountains, were sent to the Island of Walcheren, where they were soon suffering far more severely from the ravages of fever than from the attacks of the English. Within a week, all the hospitals of Antwerp, Malines and Brussels were overflowing. M. de La Tour du Pin organised another in the workhouse recently opened in the Abbaye de La Cambre, near Brussels. The generous response to his appeal for gifts to equip this hospital showed clearly the esteem in which he was held by all classes. In the first twenty-four hours, three hundred mattresses, four hundred pairs of sheets and much else had been handed in at the Prefecture and sent on from there to La Cambre. I visited this improvised hospital a few days later. All the patients were young conscripts. In a ward of one hundred beds, not a single face had seen more than twenty summers. It was a distressing sight.

When the emperor returned, my husband's enemies, led by Général de Chambarlhac, did everything in their power to discredit him, declaring it was the prefect's fault that the Garde Nationale of Brussels had not marched on Antwerp. M. Malouet had recently been appointed a Conseiller d'Etat and he warned my husband of the intrigues being fomented against him.

The emperor made a tour of Belgium, but spent only a few hours at Laeken. My husband went to the palace and asked for a private audience, but before it could take place, the town authorities and staff officers of the Garde Nationale were announced. Acting on reports he had already received, Napoleon dealt with them severely. The commander of the Garde Nationale tried to justify himself by attacking the prefect. At this, a young sub-lieutenant stepped forward and declared courageously: 'With Your Majesty's permission I deny all that this gentleman has just said.' Then he launched into a detailed explanation of what had passed. The emperor was delighted with his self-confident manner and clear account. He heard him to the end without interrupting and when he had finished, clapped him on the shoulder, saying: 'You are a courageous young man. Who are you?' 'I am in charge of the

* See p. 320. (Tr.)

Garde Nationale office at the Prefecture,' replied the young man. 'Your name?'

'Loiseau.'

The emperor turned then towards the accusers and told them: 'All that he has told me is true'. Returning to his study, he summoned M. de La Tour du Pin and listened good humouredly to what he had to say, his previous annoyance quite gone.

That same evening, Loiseau was commissioned as a sub-lieutenant in a regiment and the following day set out to join his new unit. The poor boy fought in all the campaigns and towards the end received a wound which shattered his face and from which, I believe, he died.

Towards the end of the winter of 1810 or 1811, M. de La Tour du Pin and I went to Paris for two months to accompany our son, Humbert, who was leaving for Florence. This departure was the beginning of a long separation and exceedingly painful to me. You, my dear Aymar, have the three hundred and fifty letters he wrote to me during the course of his very short life.* I was as much his friend as his mother and his absence caused me an anguish which each of his letters renewed. I was anxious, therefore, to return immediately to Brussels, but my husband thought it proper to remain in Paris until the birth of the empress's baby, which was expected hourly.

One evening, I was invited to a play given at the Tuileries in a small gallery which had been turned into a theatre. We met in the empress's salon. The emperor came over to me and spoke with the greatest kindness of Humbert and then admired the simplicity of my gown, my good taste, my very distinguished appearance – all this to the great astonishment of certain ladies covered in diamonds, who wondered who the newcomer could possibly be. When we entered the gallery, I was given a place not far from the emperor. The actors were excellent and the play – L'Avocat Patelin† – very funny. Napoleon was extraordinarily amused and roared with laughter. The great man's presence did not prevent me from doing likewise, and that pleased him, as he told me afterwards, mocking a little those ladies who thought it proper to keep a solemn face. It was considered a great favour to be invited to the play, and there were not more than fifty ladies present.

The empress was finally brought to bed on the evening of 19 March. Mme de Trazégnies, who was in Paris at the time, went

* Humbert de La Tour du Pin was killed in a duel in 1816. (Tr.)
† An early eighteenth-century play by Brueys and Palaprat.

to the Tuileries and spent the night there with all the other members of the Household, the principal officers of state and many others. The next morning, at about eight or nine o'clock, I hurried to her house in the Rue de Grenelle, only four doors away. As M. de La Tour du Pin and I were talking to M. de Trazégnies, who had been to the Tuileries for the latest news, his wife returned. We immediately bombarded her with questions. She was herself pregnant, and utterly exhausted. She told us that the emperor had come to the Household salon, where she was waiting with her companions, and had told them: 'Ladies, you may go home for two or three hours. There is a pause in the labour. The empress is asleep and Dubois* says the baby will not be born until about midday.' So they dispersed. Mme de Trazégnies had already removed her mantle, for they had all been wearing full court dress, when we heard the first maroon fired from the Invalides. She hurried downstairs as fast as she could and climbed back into her carriage. We went out into the street. Carriages had stopped, shopkeepers stood in the doorways of their shops and people came to their windows. Everyone was counting the salute. On every side could be heard a murmur ' ... three ... four ... five ...' There was almost a minute between each round. After the twentieth. there was a hushed silence. But at the twenty-first, there were spontaneous, excited shouts of *'Vive l'Empereur!'*

That evening, I dined at my sister's and people came to tell us that the new-born baby† would be given provisional baptism at nine o'clock that evening and that ladies who had been presented might attend the ceremony.

We all went – Mme Dillon, my sister and I. We had to enter by the Pavillon de Flore and walk through all the apartments to the Salle des Maréchaux. The salons were filled with the men and women who constituted Empire society. People crowded together, all trying to be near the passage which the ushers were keeping free for the procession down to the Chapel. We manoeuvred very cleverly so that we stood at the head of the staircase and so were able to follow the new-born baby. From our vantage point, we had a wonderful view of the veterans of the Old Guard,‡ one of them posted on each step, their chests covered in medals. They were not allowed to make the slightest movement, but deep emotion was plainly visible on their rugged faces and I saw tears of joy on their

* The surgeon, Antoine Dubois.
† François-Charles-Joseph-Napoléon, King of Rome (1811–1832).
‡ The original Imperial Guard formed in 1804. (Tr.)

cheeks. The emperor appeared, walking beside Mme de Montes-quiou who was carrying the baby, its face uncovered, on a cushion of white satin covered with lace. I had time to look well at the baby and to this day remain convinced that that child had not been born that morning. It would be pointless now to try to throw light on the mystery, for the child it concerns had such a short career. But, at the time, I was worried and troubled, although I naturally told no one of my doubts, except perhaps my husband.

⚜⚜⚜⚜⚜⚜⚜⚜⚜⚜⚜ XXX ⚜⚜⚜⚜⚜⚜⚜⚜⚜⚜⚜

A few days later, we returned to Brussels, which the emperor had announced his intention of visiting in the spring. His brother, Louis, prevented by Napoleon's iron grip from doing the good he intended, had abandoned the throne of Holland. King William* has told me himself that Louis is remembered by the Dutch with great respect.

It was, so far as I can remember, towards the spring of that year – 1811 – that we sustained an official visit of inspection from a Counseiller d'Etat. In other words, the visit of a superior kind of spy determined to find fault even in those he cannot but esteem, and for that reason always dreaded by Prefects. M. Réal fell to the lot of M. de La Tour du Pin who realised, on his very first visit, that he would try to do him all the harm he could. While he was staying with us, we gave a dinner in his honour, followed by a reception. I had told those ladies whom I knew were well disposed towards me that I hoped they would spend the evening with us, and on returning to the big salon after dinner, we found a gathering that included some of the most distinguished men and women in Brussels society. M. Réal was astounded at the illustrious names, the nobility of their bearing and their elegance. He was quite unable to keep his feelings to himself and told M. de La Tour du Pin he was horrified to see such a salon. My husband replied that he regretted it but that, fortunately, it did not have the same effect on the emperor.

Napoleon came to Belgium towards the end of summer, accom-panied by the empress. He did not stop in Brussels, but as Marie-Louise was still in very low health after her son's birth, he left

* William I, King of the Netherlands after 1814.

her at the Château de Laeken.* We were invited to spend the evening there every day and play lotto. This went on for about a week and was very tedious. The empress continued to be as dull as ever. Each day, she gave me her pulse to count and asked the same question: 'Do you think I have a fever?' and each day I would reply that I was not competent to tell. A few gentlemen would be there to converse during tea. As mayor, the Duc d'Ursel was responsible for suggesting morning outings suited to the weather. One day, Marie-Louise visited the museum and as she seemed to be paying particular attention to a fine portrait of her illustrious grandmother, Maria-Theresa, the Duc d'Ursel offered to have it hung in her salon at Laeken. But she replied: 'Ah that, no. The frame is too old-fashioned.' On another occasion, he suggested it would be interesting to visit part of the Forest of Soignes known as the Archduchess Isabella's Pilgrimage. The holiness and goodness of that archduchess were still warmly remembered. But Marie-Louis replied that she did not like forests. In short, this insignificant woman, so utterly unworthy of the man whose destiny she shared, seemed to make a point of being discourteous in every possible way to the people of Belgium, so ready to give her their affection. I did not see her again until after she had lost her throne. She was still just as stupid.

In the summer of 1811, Talleyrand came to preside over the election of a senator and two deputies. He arrived with a great train of servants and gave several dinners in the fine apartment of the Hôtel d'Arenberg which the Duc d'Arenberg, the blind one, had put at his disposal. Once again, he had reverted to his grandest and most charming manner. It was in comic contrast to that of the Archbishop of Malines, who looked like Scapin in a purple cassock.

On his previous journey through Malines, the emperor had pointedly questioned the archbishop, in front of everyone, about the plan of campaign he would have followed had he been Lord Chatham.† This confirmed his suspicion that it was I who had betrayed the conversation at his house in Malines after my husband and I had lunched with him one morning during the English attack on the Island of Walcheren, for it was then that he had developed this plan in some detail.

* This is not quite accurate. The emperor left on 19 September 1811, to visit the camp at Boulogne, the French fleet and the northern part of the Empire. After his departure, the empress went to Laeken arriving there during the night of 21/22 September. There she was to await the emperor's instructions. She rejoined him at Antwerp on 30 September.
† See pp. 311–12 and p. 320. (Tr.)

The emperor liked people to keep to their own professions and his comments on the archiepiscopal invasion plan were therefore ruthlessly scathing. M. de Pradt took a strong dislike to me. He spoke of it to M. de Talleyrand, who laughed both at him and his suspicion that I was a spy. The joke lasted the four days of the official visit of the Prince Vice-Grand-Elector, for such, I believe, was the title of M. de Talleyrand's office. That angered the archbishop still more and embittered him not only against me, which I could have borne with equanimity, but also against my husband. He became relentless in his efforts to undermine my husband and I do not think I am mistaken in attributing M. de La Tour du Pin's eventual dismissal to him and to a neighbouring Commissioner-General of Police.

In 1812, towards mid-spring, we began to see troops moving towards Germany. Several regiments of the Young Guard* came to Brussels and remained there a while. Others posted through. Instructions came for the requisitioning of farm waggons drawn by four horses. Sometimes an order would arrive in the morning for eighty to a hundred carts to be ready by evening, each provided with two days' forage. Police would gallop out in every direction to warn the farmers. The latter, obliged to leave their ploughing and other farm work, were very angry about it. But who dared resist? From Bayonne to Hamburg, no one would have even thought of doing so. We gave many good meals to groups of officers who arrived at ten o'clock in the evening and had to be off again by midnight. It is certain that very few of those fine men ever returned from that ill-starred campaign.

It was difficult to accustom oneself to the idea that French armies should go as far as Moscow, and when M. de La Tour du Pin returned from a short visit to Paris with a fine map of Germany, Poland and Russia, it surprised us that Lapie should have added at the edge a small square of paper to show Moscow. The map itself did not stretch as far as that city and when it was hung on the wall of the salon, people never failed to comment that the geographer seemed to have taken a quite unnecessary precaution. It was an omen!

During the last months of that year, young de Liedekerke paid assiduous court to my elder daughter, Charlotte. She was

* When it was formed in 1804, the Imperial Guard numbered 10,000 men and included all arms. As its numbers increased, a 'Young Guard' was formed and the original corps became known as the 'Old Guard'. By 1814, the Imperial Guard numbered 120,000 men. (Tr.)

sixteen and very tall. She was not pretty, but most distinguished: a noble 'demoiselle' in the full meaning of the word. She was quick of wit and sensible, and her understanding and memory were all that my motherly concern with her education could desire. Although very well informed, her passion for learning was such that her books had to be taken from her and, at night, every form of lighting had to be removed to prevent her reading or writing until dawn. But she could not have been accused of pedantry or pretension. She was gay, independent in her thinking, but never intolerant of others. Her qualities of heart surpassed even those of her mind. Charity was a matter of conscience with her and in her willingness to be of service to others, she neglected no opportunity of helping people. Her amiability and charm of manner were such that her outstanding qualities evoked no envy.

Young de Liedekerke, carried away by his feelings, but by no means unaware of the worldly advantages, realised that Mlle de La Tour du Pin, with her personal charm, her name and her connections would, despite her lack of fortune, be more helpful to his advancement than some good Belgian girl of wealth but undistinguished birth. He told his parents that he would have no other wife than my daughter. His father raised several objections but his mother, hoping that her son's political career would be furthered by a marriage which would take him outside his own country, managed to obtain her husband's consent. On New Year's Day, 1813, at ten o'clock in the morning, Mme de Liedekerke called on me to ask my daughter's hand in marriage to her son. I was prepared for the request, which I received and agreed to with pleasure. Mme de Liedekerke wished to see my daughter, whom she embraced, and it was agreed that the marriage should take place six weeks later. We settled an income of only 2,000 francs on Charlotte and my aunt, Mme d'Hénin, gave her her trousseau.

My other daughter, Cécile, had been for six months at the Convent of the Ladies of Berlaimont, preparing for her First Communion. I promised her that she should come home on the day her sister was married. At the same time, we heard that Humbert, then sub-Prefect in Florence, had been appointed sub-Prefect of Sens, in the Department of the Yonne. The news set the seal on our content. We were far from suspecting the catastrophe which hovered so close.

M. de La Tour du Pin had gone to Nivelles to be present at the conscription ballot or, more exactly, the new levy of men made necessary by the continuation of the war the emperor was waging. One day, I was at home alone when, before lunch, I saw the Secretary-General of the Prefecture arrive, looking very distressed. He told me that the courier from Paris had just brought the news that my husband had been dismissed and replaced by M. d'Houdetot, Prefect of Ghent.

This news hit me with the force of a thunderbolt, for in that first moment I saw in it a reason for the breaking off of my daughter's marriage. However, I determined not to give in without a struggle and, without waiting for the return of M. de La Tour du Pin, to whom I sent a special messenger, I decided to leave immediately for Paris. In justice to M. de Liedekerke, I must say that he came to see me with a speed and a warmth which would surprise him today, if he remembers the occasion, and begged me not to change our plans.

I left my aunt and Mme de Maurville to pack everything in the Prefecture that belonged to us and set out at four o'clock for Paris. In the two hours before I left, there had been so much to do and to decide that I was already tired when I set out. A night in an uncomfortable postchaise and anxiety about our new circumstances brought on quite a high fever which was still with me when I arrived in Paris at ten o'clock next evening. I went to Mme de Duras' house, but she was out. Her daughters had just gone to bed. They got up and sent someone to fetch their mother. When she came in, she found me lying on her sofa, prostrated with fatigue. There was no room in the house to put me up, but she had the keys to the apartment of the Chevalier de Thuisy, a mutual friend. My maid and the servant who had followed me, went to prepare a bed for me there. I took refuge in it as soon as I could, but was unable to find the rest I so greatly needed. Mme de Duras came early the next morning with Dr Auvity, for whom she had sent. He found me still very feverish but I told him he must, at any cost, put me on my feet as I had to be in a fit state to present myself at Versailles before evening. He gave me a calming potion which made me sleep until five o'clock. I do not remember if I felt recovered or not. In any case, that was the least of my worries.

I ordered a livery carriage and, wearing a very elegant toilette, went to call for Mme de Duras. We left together for Versailles. The emperor was at Trianon. We went to an inn in the Rue de l'Orangerie and engaged an apartment for us both. I immediately got out my escritoire. All I had told Mme de Duras was that I wished for an audience with His Majesty and when she saw me take out a large sheet of fine paper and copy out a draft I had taken from my letter-case, she asked me to whom I was writing. 'To whom?' I replied, 'to the emperor of course. I do not like half-measures.'

When the letter was written and sealed, we returned to our carriage to take it to Trianon. There, I asked for the chamberlain on duty. I had taken the precaution of preparing a short note for him. By good fortune, it was Adrien de Mun, a very good friend of mine. He came over to the carriage and promised me that at ten o'clock, when the emperor came to see the empress at tea time, he would hand him my letter. He kept his word and was as pleased as he was surprised when Napoleon, looking at the direction, said to himself: 'Mme de La Tour du Pin writes an excellent hand. It is not the first time I have seen her writing.' These words confirmed my suspicion that the letter to Mme d'Hénin which never reached her,* in which I had given a rather light-hearted account of the plan of campaign which the Archbishop of Malines would have followed had he been Lord Chatham, had been seized before reaching its destination.

After our drive to Trianon, we returned to our hotel. At about ten o'clock that evening, as Claire and I were discussing my chances of being granted the audience I sought, an inn servant who, until then, had looked on us as ordinary mortals, opened the door and announced in an awe-stricken voice: 'From the emperor.' As he spoke, a man wearing quantities of gold lace came in and informed me: 'His Majesty will see Mme de La Tour du Pin tomorrow morning at ten o'clock.'

This good news did not trouble my sleep and the following morning, after drinking a large bowl of coffee made by Claire herself – to make sure, she explained, that I should be properly awake – I left for Trianon. I had to wait ten minutes in the salon immediately next to that in which Napoleon was receiving. There was no one there, for which I was very glad as I needed that moment of solitude to arrange my thoughts. A tête-à-tête conversation with that extraordinary man was certainly one of the more important occasions of a lifetime, yet I can assure you, in all truth and perhaps with a certain pride, that I felt not the slightest embarrassment.

The door opened, the footman signed to me to enter, and closed both halves of the door behind me. I was in the presence of Napoleon. He came forward to meet me, saying quite amiably, 'Madame, I fear you are very displeased with me.'

I bowed in assent, and the conversation began. I have lost

* See pp. 311–12 and p. 316. (Tr.)

Château du Bouilh, near St André-de-Cubzac, Gironde.

Comte Auguste de Liedekerke-Beaufort.

the account I wrote of this long audience, which lasted fifty-nine minutes by the clock, and now, after so many years, cannot remember all the details. The sum of it was that the emperor tried to prove to me that he had been compelled to act as he had. I then briefly described to him the general attitude of Brussels society, the esteem which my husband, unlike all his predecessors, had succeeded in acquiring, the visit of Réal, the stupidity of Général de Chambarlhac and his wife, and so on. I told him all this very rapidly and, encouraged by signs of approval, ended by telling him that my daughter was about to marry a member of one of the noblest families in Brussels. At this, he interrupted, placed his beautifully-shaped hand on my arm and said: 'I hope that this will not prevent the marriage, but if it should, then you would have nothing to regret.'

Then, as he walked to and fro in that great salon, with me trying to keep pace beside him, he spoke these amazing words: 'I was wrong. But what can be done about it?' It was, perhaps, the only time in his life that he made such an admission and it was I who was privileged to hear it.

I replied that it lay in his power to set matters right and, passing a hand across his brow, he said: 'Yes, there is a report on the Prefectures. The Minister of the Interior is coming this evening.' He went on to name four or five Departments and added: 'There is Amiens. Would that suit you?'

'Perfectly, sir,' I replied without hesitation.

'In that case, it is settled. You may go and tell Montalivet.' And, with that charming smile which has so often been described, he added: 'And now, am I forgiven?' I replied politely that I also needed forgiveness for having been so outspoken. 'Oh, you were quite right to be so,' was the answer. I curtsied, and he walked to the door to open it for me himself.

On my way out, I met Adrien de Mun and Juste de Noailles, who asked me if I had managed to set things right. I told them only that the emperor had been very amiable. Without wasting a moment, I climbed back into the carriage and, with Mme de Duras who, in her impatience, had come to wait for me in the Allée de Trianon, returned to Paris.

After taking Mme de Duras home, I went to see M. de Montalivet, arriving at his house at about half-past two. He gave me a friendly but rueful welcome, saying: 'I could do nothing to prevent it. The emperor has been told a thousand tales against your husband and is very annoyed with him. It is said that people go to your house as if to Court.' To amuse myself a little at his expense, I asked: 'But would it not be possible to give my husband another appointment?' 'Oh,' he replied, 'I would never dare to suggest it to the emperor. When he is angry with someone, whether justly or unjustly, it is difficult to bring him round.' 'Well,' I went on, with a slightly sanctimonious air, 'we must bow to his will. But when you go this evening to ask him to sign the four Prefectoral appointments . . .' – 'How do you know about that?' he asked sharply. Pretending not to hear, I went calmly on ' . . . you will propose M. de La Tour du Pin for the Prefecture of Amiens.' He looked at me in amazement, and I added simply: 'The emperor told me to tell you.' M. de Montalivet exclaimed, took my hands in warm friendship and good will and, at the same time looking me up and down, said he might have guessed that such a charming toilette at that early hour was not intended for him.

The appointment of M. de La Tour du Pin appeared that same evening in the *Moniteur* and I was congratulated by people of my acquaintance who had been concerned at the news of his fall from favour. As you will see, it turned out that this transfer was a piece of good fortune for my husband.

I stayed in Paris for several days, awaiting the arrival of the Comte de Liedekerke and M. de La Tour du Pin, who came to join me for the signing of our children's marriage contract. During this time, there was a Drawing Room at Court and I attended with Mme de Mun. I was very simply dressed, without a single jewel, unlike the ladies of the Empire who were always laden with them, and found myself placed in the last row in the Throne Room, standing a head taller than two small women who, without so much as a by-your-leave, had stationed themselves in front of me. The emperor came in and took in the three rows of ladies at a glance. He made a few rather absent-minded remarks to some of them and then, seeing me, smiled that smile which all historians have tried to describe and which was truly remarkable because it contrasted so strikingly with his usually serious and sometimes hard expression. But the surprise of the ladies near me was very great when Napoleon, smiling broadly, asked me: 'Are you pleased with me, madame?' The people about me withdrew to right and left and, without knowing how it happened, I found myself in the front row. I thanked the emperor most sincerely. After a few amiable words, he continued on his way. It was the last time I was to see that great man.

I left again for Brussels, where I longed to rejoin my children and where a thousand and one things awaited my attention. M. de La Tour du Pin travelled by way of Amiens to prepare accommodation for us there. He then rejoined me, accompanied by my dear Humbert, who had returned from Florence and who, while in Paris, had received his appointment to the Sub-Prefecture of Sens. Who could have foreseen then that only ten months later he would be driven from the city by the Wurtemburgers?*

When M. de La Tour du Pin arrived in Brussels at the end of March, he found me and my children living in the house of the Marquis de Trazégnies who, with great generosity, had offered us warm and liberal hospitality. With a total lack of delicacy, M. d'Houdetot had announced that he would take over the Prefecture the very day after my return to Brussels. I did not wish him to find any trace of our five years' residence there. Everything belonging to us was packed and sent away. As to the furnishings, each article was put back in the place assigned to it in the inventory. Nothing was missing. M. d'Houdetot was annoyed by this scrupulousness and it made him the more sensitive to the regret openly expressed by all classes at the transfer of M. de La Tour du Pin. He found a pretext to return to Ghent and stayed there until our departure, which was fixed for 2 April. My daughter was to be married on 1 April.†

My husband could say with Guzman:‡ 'I was master in these places and I alone command here still.' He therefore summoned M. Malaise, the Chief of Police, and asked him to prevent any too open expression of popular feeling on the occasion of our daughter's marriage. For the same reason, the mayor, the Duc d'Ursel, arranged to conduct the civil marriage at a very late hour – at 10 o'clock in the evening. That did not prevent people from crowding into all the streets through which we had to pass and outside the Town Hall, which was brilliantly lit. On all sides one heard expressions of regret and goodwill towards M. de La Tour du Pin. When, after the ceremony in the Town Hall, we returned to Mme de Trazégnies' house, we found all the ground floor reception rooms brilliantly lit and in the street, beneath the windows, all the city musicians had gathered to serenade us. My husband was naturally very touched by these manifestations of public goodwill.

* From 1802 until 1813, the King of Wurtemburg's army fought for Napoleon but after the battle of Leipzig, the king transferred his support to the Allies and his troops marched with them into France. (Tr.)

† An error of memory by the writer: the civil marriage took place on 20 April 1813.

‡ A character in Voltaire's tragedy *Alzise ou les Americains*. (Tr.)

The following day, my daughter was married in the private chapel of the Duc d'Ursel. After a fine luncheon for relatives and friends, she and her husband left for Noisy,* whither her father-in-law had preceded them by a few hours. I went with them as far as Tirlemont. The parting was cruel, but I had to appear happy. Not long before, my son-in-law had been appointed sub-prefect at Amiens so Charlotte and I were, thank God, not to be separated for very long.

But I must tell you about M. de Chambeau. He had gained possession of a part of the fortune belonging to him and had spent much time in Brussels despite the fact that affairs forced him to spend long periods in the south of France. For the past year he had held a post in Antwerp, a temporary one, it is true, but one which gave promise of advancement. When he heard of the disaster which was causing us to leave Brussels so suddenly, knowing the perilous state of our finances, he came immediately to see M. de La Tour du Pin and told him: 'You are marrying your daughter and you are losing your post. I have 60,000 francs in bonds and will bring them to you. Use them as if they were your own.' He was present at the marriage of Charlotte, who was his god-daughter.

As I write these lines in Pisa in 1845, I am without news of this excellent man. I saw him ten years ago in Paris. At that time, he was living in a small country house at Épinay, entirely dominated by two young serving-maids, who had won a dangerous influence over him in his old age. They were careful to prevent him moving nearer to us. It is unlikely that our poor old friend is still alive.

❧❧❧❧❧❧❧❧❧❧ XXXI ❧❧❧❧❧❧❧❧❧❧

It was April 1813 when we moved to Amiens, where we were to witness the most unexpected events. Our brother-in-law, the Marquis de Lameth, was there when we arrived and his friendly offices had already ensured us a favourable reception from the nobility and leading citizens who, until then, had been far from satisfied with their prefects.

The officials were ill-assorted. In the departmental town itself,

* The Château de Noisy, near Dinant, still the home of the Liedekerke-Beaufort family. (Tr.)

one of the important officials, the Réceveur-Général,* a regicide, has just committed suicide. He had been replaced by his son-in-law, M. d'Haubersaert. A magistrate, the Procureur-Général† was an ex-officer of an hussar regiment and behaved as if he were still in the army. The presidents were all utterly vulgar. Their wives were conspicuous by reason of their grotesque appearance and ridiculous behaviour. They addressed their husbands in public as 'ma poule' or 'mon rat'.‡ The general commanding the division was M. d'Aigremont, whose wife was pretty and quite good-natured. Such society was entirely unacceptable to Charlotte and me and I was careful to ensure from the very beginning that my circle of acquaintance should include only local families of importance. Amiens was the regimental depot of the Chasseurs de La Garde whose commander was a major, M. Le Termelier, a very agreeable, well-bred man. The de Bray family, highly esteemed merchants of Amiens, were also among those we knew, together with a number of others whose names I have unfortunately forgotten.

The house used as the Prefecture was charming. It had just been refurnished and everything was new, elegant and very comfortable. On the ground floor was a self-contained apartment and it was there that my husband and I lived. Next to it, was the Prefect's office, which communicated directly with the other offices. All the rooms opened on to a magnificent and well-stocked garden of seven or eight acres. It was almost as pleasant as living in the country.

The first part of the summer passed very agreeably. We often dined at country houses where our neighbours were spending the summer. My daughter, Cécile, then about thirteen, was already a very talented musician and had a charming voice with a good range. During our five years in Brussels, I had had an excellent Italian master for her. He came from Rome, and since he spoke no French, my daughter had become accustomed to speaking to him in the fine Roman dialect which, by then, she spoke fluently. Charlotte and she not only read in Italian, but also in English. We were living there very comfortably when we heard the first rumbling of the approaching storm. Confidence in the fortunes of Napoleon was so great that no one conceived he had any enemy to fear except the frost and snow which had been so fatal to the Russian campaign.

* A collector of taxes. (Tr.)
† Public Prosecutor.
‡ Roughly equivalent to 'ducks' and 'my pet'. (Tr.)

Yet, after the battle of Leipzig,* there began the first requisitionings and levies of men, the formation of the Gardes d'Honneur.† This last measure brought dismay to many a family.

In the face of such circumstances, M. de La Tour du Pin had need of all the firmness of which he was capable. He served the Government loyally and the possibility of a restoration had not yet occurred to him. He neither expected nor desired it. All the errors and vices which had been at the root of the first revolution were still too vivid in his memory for him to consider a return of the exiled royal family with anything but misgiving. He feared their weakness would bring in its train abuses of every kind. The remark which was to be so well justified – 'They have forgotten nothing, neither have they learned anything' – was often in his mind. But he did try, in so far as it lay in his power, to soften the hardship caused by the formation of the Gardes d'Honneur. In a wool manufacturing town like Amiens, the levies were very heavy and my husband dreaded most of all the greed and dishonesty of those charged with implementing them. It was among the wealthy that resistance to some of the new measures was strongest and I often heard him say: 'They give their children more readily than they give their money.'

It was not until we heard, in Amiens, the booming of the cannon at Laon that we began to realise our territory was being invaded. A few days later, M. d'Houdetot, the Prefect of Brussels, fleeing before the invasion, entered our salon just as the Réceveur-Général, optimistic M. d'Haubersaert, was telling us that he had received a letter from Brussels and that Belgium was secure against any sudden attack.

Soon afterwards came the news that a Cossack formation commanded by General Geismar had appeared in the plains around Amiens. They came so close that we could watch them from the bell tower of the cathedral. The squadron of Chasseurs stationed in the town under the command of our amiable major, rode out to meet them and so impressed them that they were not seen again.

My daughter, Charlotte, was awaiting the birth of her baby. We did not dare to leave her at the Prefecture, fearing that if the town were captured, it would be among the first houses to be

* In October 1813, Russia, Prussia, Sweden and Austria defeated Napoleon and destroyed what remained of the Grande Armée. (Tr.)
† This Corps, consisting of four regiments, was a part of the Imperial Guard. It was recruited among the upper classes and disbanded in 1814 at the Restoration. (Tr.)

pillaged. We moved her to an apartment most generously put at our disposal, together with her sister, Cécile, and yourself, my dear son. We also transferred to it most of our personal belongings. My husband and I remained at the Prefecture.

One evening, a stranger arrived from Paris saying he had been instructed to form a 'corps franc'.* He was Merlin de Thionville and he carried an order from the Minister of Police, Rovigo, which empowered him to enrol any prisoner except those held for capital crimes. He marched off all his ne'er-do-wells who were never heard of again.

My aunt, Mme d'Hénin, was spending the autumn with the Princesse de Poix at the Château de Mouchy, near Beauvais. Mme de Duras and her daughters were also there and I was invited to join them for a few days. M. de La Tour du Pin told me to accept and asked me to return by way of Paris in order to see M. de Talleyrand and hear the latest news. M. de Talleyrand had sent him a note by M. de Thionville but it was so mysterious and the bearer's reputation so bad that my husband, a stranger to all intrigue, feared he was being involved despite himself in some scheme of M. de Talleyrand, who would stop at nothing and had no scruple whatsoever in leading people into danger and then abandoning them in order to save himself.

So I left for Mouchy, and spent three days there. I arrived two hours before dinner and, after paying my respects to the good Princesse de Poix and to my aunt, went up to see Mme de Duras. I found her in a very bad humour indeed. She had already quarrelled with her son-in-law, Léopold de Talmond,† after a series of ridiculous scenes and they had reached the point of writing their arguments to one another in letters four pages long, headed 'From my own apartment' – just like the *Spectator*. She poured out all her woes to me and then showed me a letter from Léopold. It had been written that very morning, and its contents convinced me that he was in the right from beginning to end. I told her so, with the frankness of affectionate and sincere friendship. Her anger was then turned on me and I spent the two days of my stay at Mouchy trying to persuade her to listen to reason. But, to no avail. Mme de Poix was very annoyed at the scenes Mme de Duras made in the salon, at table and before the servants, but lost all hope of their ceasing when I admitted that my influence, too, had failed.

I left one morning after breakfast to return to Amiens by way

* Any volunteer unit raised in time of war. (Tr.)
† Prince Léopold de Talmond, who had married Mlle Félicie de Duras.

of Paris. Since I did not intend staying overnight, I went to the
apartment of M. de Lally, who was at Mouchy. Stopping only
long enough to make myself tidy, I went straight to the house of
M. de Talleyrand. He was alone in his room and received me, as
always, with the amiable courtesy he never failed to show me.
Much ill has been spoken of him – less, perhaps, than he deserved,
though some of the criticisms were, in fact, ill-founded – and it
might have been said of him, as Montesquieu wrote of Caesar:
'This man without a fault, but with many imperfections.' And yet,
despite it all, he possessed greater charm than I have known in any
other man. Attempts to arm oneself against his immorality, his
conduct, his way of life, against all the faults attributed to him, were
vain. His charm always penetrated the armour and left one like
some bird fascinated by a serpent's gaze.

There was nothing particularly remarkable in our conversation
that day. I noticed merely that he repeated rather pointedly that
M. de La Tour du Pin was 'well, very well placed' in Amiens. I
told him that I intended leaving the following morning and he told
me not to do so. The emperor was expected to arrive that very day,
he would be seeing him and would call on me afterwards and let me
know for what hour I should order my post horses. It would certainly not be before ten o'clock in the evening.

I went home feeling very annoyed at being kept a further twenty-
four hours in Paris. After writing to my husband to tell him of this
delay, I tried to occupy my time next day by lunching with my
good friend, Mme de Maurville, and by making various calls. Paris
seemed very dull, but before nightfall I heard salvos announcing
the emperor's arrival. The great man was returning to his capital,
but the enemy was close behind.

At ten o'clock, my horses were put to and waiting at the door.
The postilion was growing impatient, and so was I when, at eleven
o'clock, M. de Talleyrand arrived.

'What madness to set out in this cold, and in a barouche, too!
Whose house is this?' I told him it belonged to Lally. Taking a
candle from the table, he began to study the engravings in their fine
frames hanging on the walls: 'Ah, Charles II, James II, just so.' And
he put the candlestick back on the table. 'Heavens,' I exclaimed,
'what is all this talk of Charles II and James II? You have seen
the emperor. How is he? What is he doing? What does he say
after a defeat?' 'Oh, do not talk to me about your emperor. He is
finished.'

I asked him what he meant and was told: 'He is the sort of man who will go to ground.'* At the time, this description did not shock me so greatly as it did after the remainder of our conversation. I was, indeed, aware of M. de Talleyrand's hatred of Napoleon and his rancour against him, but had never heard him express it so bitterly. I asked him many questions, but he only replied: 'He has lost all his stores and equipment. He has shot his bolt. It is all over.' Then he felt in his pocket and drew out a paper printed in English. As he threw two logs on the fire, he added: 'Let's burn a little more of poor Lally's wood. Here, since you understand English, read this passage,' and he pointed to a fairly long article marked in pencil in the margin. I took the paper and read: 'Dinner given by the Prince Regent for Mme la Duchesse d'Angoulême.'

I stopped and looked up at him. But his face was inscrutable and he only said: 'Well, go on. Your postilion is growing impatient.' I went on reading. The article described the dining-room hung with sky-blue satin decorated with bunches of lilies, the centre-piece on the table decorated with the same royal flower, the Sèvres service with its views of Paris and so on. When I came to the end, I stopped and stared at him in amazement. He took the paper, folded it slowly and put it back into his enormous pocket, saying with that shrewd, malicious smile so characteristic of him: 'Ah, how stupid you are. Now, away with you, but don't catch cold.' And, ringing the bell, he told my servant to call my carriage to the door. He left me then, calling out as he put on his coat: 'Give Gouvernet my very good wishes. I am sending him this news for lunch. You will arrive in time.'

I reached Amiens so quickly that M. de La Tour du Pin was still in bed. Losing not a minute, I told him of the conversation I have just described. It had been puzzling me all through the night and I had been unable to sleep. My husband saw in it an explanation of certain embarrassed remarks made by Merlin de Thionville and told me not to say a word about it for, he said, if it was by such means that the Bourbons meant to regain the throne, they would not remain on it long.

A few days earlier, a special envoy had arrived in Amiens to speed up, so he said, the recruitment for the Gardes d'Honneur. He was a young 'auditeur' of the Conseil d'État, a young man of most charming appearance and very elegant manners: M. de Beaumont. Gradually, his excessive pretensions became apparent. There was nothing in his behaviour to justify reproach or open censure, but M. de La Tour du Pin had him very closely watched

* Lit. '... hide under his bed'. (Tr.)

and soon learned that he was in touch with all the riff-raff of the town. My husband decided to get rid of him. He called him to his office and told him his conduct was known and that it was endangering the peace of the town, for which he, as Prefect, was responsible. He therefore required M. de Beaumont to leave Amiens within an hour and the Department within two hours. My husband added that if he did not comply willingly with this order, two policemen waiting in the ante-room would take him into custody. The man was so surprised by this ultimatum that he did not dare resist.

At the same time, my husband sent Humbert to Paris to discover what was going on there. My son had been in Amiens for two weeks, driven from his sub-prefecture by the Wurtembergers. He had taken refuge with us to recover his health, for he had been ill in Sens with a pleurisy. The illness was at its height when the enemy advanced on the town and, wanting at all costs to avoid being taken prisoner, he left Sens at the last minute, in the middle of the night, taking with him two sick soldiers he had been sheltering and caring for at the Prefecture. He had himself put on a horse, with one of the soldiers riding postilion to hold him in the saddle. In that fashion, they set out for Melun where he arrived half-dead. The two soldiers looked after him so well that two days later they were able to put him into a carriage and take him to Paris, to Mme d'Hénin, where he completed his recovery. From there, he came to Amiens to join us. To reward the two men who saved him, he had them enrolled in the Garde.

Humbert reached M. de Talleyrand's house in Paris while he was entertaining the Emperor Alexander.* He spent the night on a bench indicated to him by M. de Talleyrand, who charged him not to move from it, as he wanted to be able to lay hands on him the moment he judged it right for him to return to Amiens. At six o'clock in the morning, M. de Talleyrand tapped him on the shoulder. Humbert saw that he was fully dressed and wearing his wig. 'Go now', M. de Talleyrand told him, 'wear a white cockade and shout: "Long Live the King!"'.

For a moment, Humbert wondered if he was dreaming. Then, rousing himself, he set out for Amiens where the news of these

* Alexander I, Emperor of Russia (1777–1825), autocrat, Jacobin and mystic. An open admirer of French institutions, he at first admired and then mistrusted Napoleon. After the destruction of Moscow, he hated him bitterly and felt he had a divine mission to become the peacemaker of Europe. After the fall of Napoleon, he was the most powerful monarch in Europe. (Tr.)

events had already begun to filter through and M. de La Tour du Pin was wondering whether to confirm the rumours or deny them. But public opinion soon made itself heard. All classes had been exasperated by the requisitions, the Gardes d'Honneur and the rest. Fear of foreigners was the spark which set off the smouldering unrest. In a moment, as if touched off by an electric shock, there arose on all sides shouts of 'Long Live the King!' People rushed into the courtyard of the Prefecture, clamouring for the white cockades with which Humbert had filled the lockers of the barouche before leaving Paris. The supply was soon exhausted, but I managed to save enough for the officers who led by good Major Le Termelier, came to receive them from me. But the expression on their faces belied the sincerity of their action. It was clearly against their inclination. Only one of them, an elderly man with white moustaches, said to me quietly: 'I wear it again with pleasure.' The youngest looked gloomy and sad. Glory seemed to be receding beyond their reach.

During the day, as rumours of the arrival of Louis XVIII became more widespread, people grew increasingly attentive to M. de La Tour du Pin and me. A few days later, when it was learned that the prefect was going to Boulogne to meet the king and that His Majesty would stop at Amiens and spend the night at the Prefecture, many people came to offer me articles of all kinds with which to embellish the house: clocks, vases, paintings, flowers, orange shrubs and so on.

M. de Duras, who was about to begin his year of attendance on the king, had passed through the town on his way to meet him at Boulogne. Despite the upheavals, he retained all the prejudice, hatred, pettiness and bitterness of a past age. There might never have been a revolution and there is no doubt that in his heart he was still convinced that 'the mob must sweat' – a conviction we ourselves had heard him voice in his younger days, though he denied it later.

M. de Poix also set out for Boulogne but went no further than Amiens. He was very anxious about the reception he would get from the king, for his son, Juste de Noailles, was an imperial chamberlain and his daughter-in-law a lady-in-waiting to the empress. In vain did I tell him that, like so many other families, he had paid a terrible toll to the Revolution, in which both his father and his mother had perished. He was not reassured. However, I had not time to reason with him in an attempt to bolster his courage. This task I entrusted to my daughter and busied myself with the arrangement of the table for twenty-five persons which the king was to honour with his presence. While I was in the dining-room, a gentleman came in and spoke to my servant in a manner I found displeasing. I went over to him and asked him straightly what concern it was of his. He thought to awe me by saying he was a member of the king's suite and was greatly surprised to realise that I was fully determined to remain mistress in my own house and little disposed to allow him to give orders there. He went off grumbling. It was M. de Blacas.*

M. de La Tour du Pin had sent me word that the king had received him with much kindness and that he and Mme la Duchesse d'Angoulême† would stay at the Prefecture. Everything was ready by the agreed time. Twelve young ladies of the town, led by my daughter, Cécile, whose fourteen-year-old charm was delightful, waited to present bouquets to Madame.

The carriage containing the king and Madame was drawn by the company of millers of Amiens, who had claimed their ancient privilege. These good men, fifty to sixty strong, all wearing new suits of light grey cloth and wide hats of white felt provided at their own expense, drew the royal carriage first to the cathedral, where the bishop sang a *Te Deum*. The doors of the cathedral had been kept shut and not until the king was seated in his chair at the altar steps were they flung open. Then came a roar as of a flood breaking its banks, and in less than a minute that huge church was so closely packed with people that not even a grain of dust could have fallen to the floor.

When I think now of the multitude of stupidities which cost his brother, Charles X, his throne, I feel almost ashamed of the emotion I felt then, at the sight of that old man‡ thanking God for restoring him to the throne of his fathers. Madame, who was in tears, prostrated herself at the foot of the altar and I shared with all

* Favourite of Louis XVIII. A rigid reactionary who had to be dismissed in 1814. (Tr.)
† Daughter of Louis XVI and Marie-Antoinette. She was married in exile to the Duc d'Angoulême, elder son of the Comte d'Artois, and is referred to later as 'Madame'.
‡ When Louis XVIII returned to France in May 1814 after an absence of 23 years, he was nearly sixty, gouty and obese. He was plagued, as during his exile, by ultras like the Comte d'Artois (later, Charles X), the Duchesse d'Angoulême and his favourite, the Comte de Blacas. But he remained clear-sighted and a diplomat. He had led the royalist movement inside and outside France since 1791, when he set out for exile at the same time as Louis XVI, who was captured. The last seven years of Louis XVIII's exile were spent in England. (Tr.)

my heart the feelings she was experiencing. Alas! My illusions were to last less than twenty-four hours.

Next, the millers drew the king's carriage to the Prefecture where, before dinner, the king received the municipality and the entire city, both men and women. He did so with the courtesy and ready interest, as well as the wit and charm with which he had been so generously blessed. At seven o'clock we sat down to dinner. It was excellent and the wines were perfect, a fact which the king particularly appreciated and which brought me many kind compliments. Only then did M. de Blacas realise that this prefect's wife whom he, a plain gentleman from Provence, had thought he could address in such cavalier fashion, was in fact a lady of the former Court. He was overcome with confusion at his blunder and tried – without success – to cajole me into forgetting the incident.

My cousin, Edward Jerningham, and his charming wife had crossed with the king from England. The king very graciously declared that Edward had served his cause by the articles he had written in the English papers. They had had a great success. Both Edward and his wife feared that Madame's wholly English style of dress would displease the members of Napoleon's Court who had gathered at Compiègne to await their new sovereign. They both realised it was essential that the first impression should not arouse antagonism. At their urging, I spoke of this to Mlle de Choisy, lady-in-waiting to Madame, and also to M. de Blacas, who mentioned it to the king. But the obstinacy of the princess was not to be moved.

Alas, it was not to be the only reproach she earned during her short stay in Amiens. On the morning of her departure, she received several ladies whom I presented to her. One was Mme de Maussion, wife of the Rector of Amiens University, a woman of noble virtue and conduct, worthy of the greatest respect. Respect is indeed not too strong a word, as you will see from the following incident, which I related to Mlle de Choisy: Mme de Maussion was a prisoner in the Conciergerie at the same time as the queen. She was given an opportunity to escape and found means to suggest to that unfortunate princess that they should exchange clothes, and that she should lie in the queen's bed while the queen left the prison. Mme de Maussion was only eighteen at the time and such devotion on the part of such a very young woman surely merited at least a courteous acknowledgement. This she was not given. Madame did not even speak to her. I do not know which was stronger in me, amazement or indignation. I have never forgotten the incident and, looking back on it after thirty years, feel that everything which has happened since was, after all, merited.

My son-in-law relinquished his French nationality to become a subject of the new king of the Netherlands, that same Prince of Orange whom I had met in England at a time when his fortunes were very low, and returned to Brussels with my daughter in order to re-join his family. I missed them terribly. I returned to Paris and my husband and I settled in a pretty apartment at No. 6 rue de Varenne. Our son, Humbert, came to live with us.

On the very evening of my arrival. I went with Mme de Duras to a fête given by Prince Schwarzenberg, Generalissimo of the Austrian forces. There I saw all the victors and also all the petty meannesses which surrounded and, indeed, almost overwhelmed them. It was the oddest spectacle, if one thought about it. Everything recalled Napoleon: the furnishings, the supper, the people. I could not help thinking that not one of all the people there – some of whom had trembled in defeat before him, others of whom had courted his favour, even so small a favour as a smile – was, in my view, worthy to be his conqueror. The situation was undeniably fascinating but profoundly sad. Mme de Duras was aware of nothing beyond her own good fortune in being the wife of the First Gentleman of the Bedchamber for that year. The fall of the great man, the invasion of the country, the humiliation of being a guest of the victor did not seem to trouble her. I myself felt a shame probably shared by none in the whole of that gathering.

M. de La Tour du Pin realised that a career in administration, though greatly to his taste, would place him in a lower social category than that which was rightfully his. He therefore decided to resume his diplomatic career at the point where the Revolution had interrupted it. M. de Talleyrand, Minister for Foreign Affairs, offered him The Hague. The new King of Holland favoured his appointment and M. de La Tour du Pin accepted it willingly, though he might have claimed a more senior post. But a remark of M. de Talleyrand: 'Take that post for the time being' led him to suppose he intended employing him in some other capacity.

My son, Humbert, unfortunately succumbed to the attraction of becoming a member of the king's military Household and was appointed a lieutenant in The Black Musketeers, so called from the colour of their mounts. This gave him the rank of major in the army.

At the time it was decided to hold a Congress in Vienna, I was in M. de Talleyrand's office one morning. M. de La Tour du Pin had gone to Brussels to attend the coronation of the new king, William I, and to present his letters of credence. He was to return within a day or two. I was just leaving the Foreign Minister's office and already had my hand on the door knob to open it when, looking at M. de Talleyrand, I saw that expression on his face that I knew meant he wanted to play one of the trump cards of his trade. He asked me when my husband would be back. I said I expected him the following day.

'Well, hurry his return as he must leave for Vienna.'

'For Vienna?' I asked. 'Why?'

'So you have not understood. He is to go as minister to Vienna until the Congress, at which he is to be one of the ambassadors.' I exclaimed in surprise, but he added: 'It is a secret. Don't speak of it and send him to me the minute he is out of his carriage.' I waited impatiently for my husband to come, keeping my good news secret from everyone except my son, Humbert.

This appointment was the source of much jealousy. Mme de Duras was furious. She had wanted the post for M. de Chateaubriand, her passionate attachment for him being just then at its height. Adrien de Laval refused to be consoled, even by the promise of the embassy in Madrid, and on all sides there were accusations of corruption because my husband was also to retain his post at The Hague.

We held a family council and decided, to my intense disappointment, that M. de La Tour du Pin should go to Vienna alone and that I would remain in Paris to arrange a marriage for Humbert. M. de La Tour du Pin wrote to Auguste, our son-in-law, who was already thinking of entering on a diplomatic career in his own country, to invite him to join him in Vienna as his private secretary, or even as an ordinary traveller, since he was no longer French, but once again a citizen of the Netherlands. We thought that if M. de La Tour du Pin were to remain in Vienna after the Congress, it would not be difficult to persuade the King of the Netherlands to have Auguste attached to the staff of the Netherlands Legation there. Charlotte and I would then travel to Vienna to join our husbands. These plans like so many others, were overtaken by events, both personal and national. It was agreed, however, that I would accompany my husband as far as Brussels. There he would be joined by his son-in-law and I would bring my daughter and her child back to Paris. This we did.

Before leaving Paris, where Humbert was to remain, I put Aymar to board with a tutor in the Rue Nôtre-Dâme-des-Champs. It was an establishment which had been very highly recommended to me.

Our return journey from Brussels to Paris passed most pleasantly, though I was very sad and put out not to be going with M. de La Tour du Pin to Vienna. But there was nothing to suggest that his absence would last as long as it eventually did. Also, I had been assured that there would be two special couriers every week from the Ministry of Foreign Affairs so that I could expect to receive regular and up-to-date news of my husband.

We travelled by way of Tournai, where we paid long visits to two factories, one producing fine carpets and the other porcelain. We also visited the cathedral where we saw the magnificent chalice of St Eleuthera, which had been dug up not long before in a garden where it must have lain hidden since the days of the very first Frankish invasion. We stayed two days in Amiens and when we reached Paris, news of our travellers was waiting for us. I settled into my own apartment and Charlotte took over her father's.

I took her to meet people of my acquaintance. We went every day to call on the daughters of Mme de Duras – this was always the objective of our morning walks – or spent our evenings with them. Félicie had married young Léopold de Talmond and Clara lived at the Tuileries with her mother. My daughter, Cécile, was still too young, being not yet fifteen, to go into society. Her mornings were devoted to lessons and she only went out in the evening to come with us on a visit to our aunt, Mme d'Hénin, or to Mme de Duras when there was no company.

When M. de La Tour du Pin went to Boulogne to welcome the king on his return from England, he passed through Abbeville, a Sub-Prefecture of his Department, where he had felt it his duty to tell the sub-prefect, André Dumont, that he considered his rôle at the Convention and his conduct when on special missions as the people's representative, an insuperable barrier to presentation to the news overeign. M. de La Tour du Pin had asked him, therefore—and if he refused to comply willingly, the request would have to be considered an order—to find some reason for being absent from Abbeville at the time the king was expected to pass through the town. André Dumont, of bloody memory, accepted this decision which, by mutual agreement, was to remain a secret between him and M. de La Tour du Pin. The king himself was unaware of what had passed.

However, the regicide harboured a very bitter resentment against his prefect and immediately after M. de La Tour du Pin left for Vienna, he had a pamphlet printed in which he pointed out the forbearance shown to other regicides and represented himself as the victim of ill-will on the part of my husband, whom he accused of injustice, abuse of power and even of fraud. I heard from Amiens that this libellous pamphlet had been sent to Paris to be distributed there by M. Benoît, Chief Secretary of the Ministry of the Interior and a friend of Dumont. My son, Humbert, went to see M. Benoît, who received him none too warmly. He did not try to justify Dumont, for that would have been impossible, but set out to show that my husband's severity had been excessive.

I, myself, went to see M. Beugnot, Minister of Police, to tell him of the publication, which he might be able to stop. That would have been the best solution, for its contents were such as to prejudice M. de La Tour du Pin in his new appointment. It was certain that those who wished him ill would seek to use it.

M. Beugnot was very amiable and helpful, as always. The conversation turned to other matters, particularly the plottings of the Bonapartists. At Court and in royalist drawing-rooms it was the fashion to deny their existence, but to the Minister of Police they were a constant anxiety. After a long chat alone with M. Beugnot, he finished by asking me if I saw my stepmother, Mme Dillon. I told him that of course I did, whereupon he said: 'Well, then, do her a service. Tell her that Mme Bertrand has no need of "embroidered bonnets".' I longed to know what it was all about, but he insisted that was enough, so I took my leave.

The next day, I went with my daughters to call on my stepmother. She was already suffering from the illness which was to cause her death three years later. After talking for a while of this and that, I said quietly to her as I rose to leave: 'My sister has no need of "embroidered bonnets".' After a startled exclamation, she cried: 'Lucy, in Heaven's name, who told you that?' I told her it was M. Beugnot, whereupon she collapsed into her armchair muttering 'All is lost!'

Unfortunately, all was not lost so far as the conspirators were concerned, for everyone obstinately refused to believe in the conspiracy. At the Tuileries, in the ministries, at the house of Mme de Duras or the Duchesse d'Escars, everywhere, the royalists vied with one another in ridiculing the fearful who saw Napoleon around every corner. They made music, danced and amused themselves like school children on holiday. One evening at this time, Mme de Duras' guests included two or three generals and their wives, the latter very much be-jewelled. Among them were Maréchal Soult and his wife. M. de Caraman leaned from behind me and murmured: 'The eyes of Notre Dame del Pilar are upon you.' There was, indeed, a rumour that the two enormous diamonds gracing the ears of the Maréchale Soult had been taken from the miraculous statue of that name which was so greatly venerated throughout Spain. But not even such glittering jewels could prevent that extremely plain woman from looking like a *vivandière*.*

It was about now that my poor Charlotte's daughter died from a teething fever which carried her off within two days. She expired on my knee and I wept for her as if she had been my own child, though with the added grief of realising her mother's suffering. I tried to distract my poor Charlotte by taking her to spend the next day with Mme d'Hénin while Humbert attended to the sad duty of burying the poor, pretty child whom we all mourned.

No sooner had Humbert joined us at Mme d'Hénin's house than my maid came hurrying in to ask him to return home as some-one was waiting for him. It was our son-in-law, Auguste, who happened to be the courier for that week and had arrived with dispatches. Since he could not stay more than two days, he had hurried to find his wife. Charlotte's distress at the loss of her baby was so intense that I thought it best to send her to Vienna with her husband. Her father loved her dearly and it would be a great happiness to him, too, to have her there. I had an excellent travelling barouche and undertook to buy and pack everything necessary for the elegant toilettes she would need at the functions held during the Congress. I also gave her my own maid, a very clever woman.

I was left with my little Cécile, who was then fifteen, and my two sons, Humbert and Aymar. Not long afterwards, Aymar almost died from a pleurisy caused by his tutor's negligence. It was my custom to visit him twice a week and on one of these visits, towards the end of November, I was told on my arrival that he had a cold. When they took me to the infirmary, I began to feel anxious. It was a gloomy room on the ground floor, facing north, and opening on to

* Women cooks who travelled with the armies. (Tr.)

the courtyard. I was horrified to see that the window and doors were open, the excuse being that the chimney was smoking. I found my son with a high temperature and symptoms which filled me with alarm. I asked to see the doctor of the establishment. He was not expected until the following day. Hearing this, I did not hesitate, but climbed back into my carriage and went to fetch my own doctor, Auvity. Luckily, he was in. By the time we reached the school, more than two hours had elapsed and Aymar was worse. Auvity, shocked at finding him in such a miserable room, told me: 'Madame, if you wish to save your child's life, you must take him away from here.' He rolled him up in the bed covers, carried him to the carriage and took us home. For several days, the illness continued to grow worse. Auvity came three times a day. On the sixth day, he asked to call in his father* and M. Hallé,† the leading doctor of the day, for a consultation. They told Humbert he must prepare me for the loss of his brother, saying he would not last out the night. Then, having each pocketed a napoleon for pronouncing sentence, they departed, never to return.

Auvity himself refused to be discouraged. He sent for a cantharidine waistcoat‡ from the only chemist in Paris who prepared them. It was applied to Aymar's poor little eight-year-old body, already so wasted, and covered it entirely, except for the arms. Mustard poultices were applied to his feet and renewed every quarter of an hour. Every two minutes, he was given a teaspoonful of some refreshing, nourishing drink. The following day, his body was one large sore, but the fever had gone and Auvity pronounced the words so sweet to a mother's ear: 'He is safe now.'

Once relieved of anxiety for my son's health, I went out a great deal into society that winter. I collected every possible scrap of news, all the gossip and even mere tattle to put into the letters I wrote regularly twice a week to M. de La Tour du Pin.

How did I spend my days after the restoration of the monarchy? Firstly, I went to the Tuileries when the king received the ladies, which was once or twice a week. As a former lady-in-waiting to the queen, I had certain privileges. Instead of mingling with the crowd of ladies in the first salon, that of Diana, to wait for the king to be wheeled into the Throne Room – he could not walk – I went with the other ladies who enjoyed the same privileges straight to my place on the Throne Room benches. There, we always found

* The Chévalier Auvity, Surgeon to the Children of France during the Empire.
† A former Physician-in-Ordinary to the emperor's Household.
‡ A plaster jacket impregnated with cantharidin, used for raising blisters. (Tr.)

a number of gentlemen who also had the 'entrée' and would sit very comfortably, chatting together until the time-honoured formula 'The king' brought us to our feet and compelled us to assume a reasonably correct and respectful attitude. Then, we would pass in turn before the royal chair.

The king always had something amusing or amiable to say to me. For instance, on the feast of St Louis there was a 'grand couvert'* in the Gallery of Diana. A barrier was set along almost the entire length of the room to form a passage for all those who wanted to see the horse-shoe shaped table at which the royal family sat. The king sat alone at the head of the table, facing the stares of the curious. On one side of the table sat the Duc d'Angou-lême and his wife and, facing them, the Duc de Berry and, perhaps, the Duc d'Orléans. Behind the king stood the great officers of his Household and, behind them, the ladies stood on the tiers of benches. On that particular day, I chose to remain with the crowd in order to walk past with my daughters. The king saw me among the people and called out: 'It's just like Amiens!' That brought me considerable respect from the good people around me.

During that winter, the Duc de Berry gave two balls to which he invited all the leaders of Bonapartist society: the Duchesses de Rovigo, de Bassano and so on. They did not dance and appeared to be in exceedingly bad tempers, despite the conciliatory efforts and attentions of the prince and his aides-de-camp. Mme de Duras and I took Albertine de Staël to these balls. We had achieved a metamorphosis in her appearance, managing at last to persuade her mother – herself always dressed like some tight-rope walker, despite her fifty years – to allow us to dress her according to our own taste. It was not an easy task, for it meant remaking everything she wore, even to her chemises. But everyone found her so greatly changed for the better that she renounced there and then all her former attachment to English styles. The Duc de Broglie was much in love with her and I think I am right in believing that it was at one of these balls that he decided to ask her mother for her hand in marriage.

Since I have mentioned Mme de Staël, this is the place to tell you that when she returned to Paris shortly after the Restoration, I had resumed my old acquaintance with her. I had met her in the meantime: in 1800, when I returned from England shortly before Napoleon obliged her to leave Paris, and again at various other times. On 18 Fructidor, when more than intimately linked with

* A formal dinner which the king and the royal family ate in public. (Tr.)

Benjamin Constant, she had been very revolutionary. But during her stay in England her ideas changed for the last time and she returned a royalist. She entertained brilliantly, and with much kindness, all the notables from European countries who flocked to Paris during the winter of 1814–1815. I happened to be in her drawing-room on the evening the Duke of Wellington arrived in Paris. A hundred other persons were gathered there, all as eager as I to see this already famous man. My own acquaintance with him went back to childhood: we were of much the same age and his mother, Lady Mornington, had been a very great friend of my grandmother, Mme de Rothe. The young Arthur Wellesley, his sister, Lady Anne and I had spent many an evening together. I had seen Lady Anne in England, at Hampton Court, when I went to visit the Prince of Orange, the old Stadtholder. The duke greeted me as an old friend, delighted to find someone in that large salon who could understand and answer his questions, for although he was the cynosure of every eye, he knew no one.

One day, Humbert came in looking very worried. On his way back from the headquarters of the Mousquetaires, he had met two generals whom he had known quite well at Sens. They had invited him to lunch with them at the Jardin Turc and after oysters and champagne, had begun to sound him on the state of the government, the general discontent, their regret at being no longer in the emperor's service. They made some very indiscreet remarks which startled Humbert. He was far from suspecting Napoleon's daring landing on the French coast but it was clear from the conversation that a summons to the emperor's standard was preparing. The two generals were by no means prominent men but it was easy for Humbert to guess the identity of the real leaders of the conspiracy – Queen Hortense in particular, at whose house the Bonapartist Committee of Direction held its meetings. When he told Mme de Duras about this luncheon and what he had heard, she too thought it very disquieting and told her husband. He in turn told the king, but M. de Blacas was there to soften the anxiety and ridicule those who believed the emperor would return. M. de Blacas lived in considerable state. His overweening complacency did not allow him to admit the least possibility of a plot. He shrugged his shoulders and laughed contemptuously at those who were inclined to think that Napoleon might not be far away.

One evening in early March, I was in the apartment of Mme de Duras at the Tuileries, at a large gathering which included Général Dulauloy and his wife. My curiosity was sharply aroused by two or three almost imperceptible signs I saw pass between the general and his wife. They seemed to mean: 'No, they know nothing.' Mme Dulauloy looked fearful and seemed anxious to take her leave, especially when M. de Duras crossed the salon on his way back from the king's 'coucher.' Her colour rose and she got up to leave, taking her husband with her. I stayed until the last, waiting for Mme de Duras to return from her husband's room, for she had followed him there. When she reappeared, I saw that she was very troubled and she told me: 'Something terrible has happened, but Amédée will not say what it is.' I returned home with Humbert and, as is always the case, we guessed at every possible cause except the right one. Next morning, news of the landing in the Golfe Juan spread through Paris, brought by Lord Lucan. He had set out the previous evening for Italy and, several stages distant from Paris, had met the courier arriving from Lyons with the news. He had turned back at once and returned to Paris where he made the news known.

The consequences of that landing belong to history, so I will tell you only how it affected me, personally.

I had too thorough a knowledge of the Court on the one hand and the strength of Napoleon's supporters on the other to doubt, for even a moment, the efficacy of the measures which would be taken. Although M. de La Tour du Pin was one of the four ambassadors of France to the Congress of Vienna and was dealing for the moment with the diplomatic affairs of France in Austria, he was still French minister in Holland. I decided that I could not remain in Paris when Napoleon might arrive at any moment and thought it best to go to Brussels or The Hague. My plans were submitted to the king by M. de Jaucourt, Deputy Minister for Foreign Affairs. The king approved my decision so I began making my preparations.

From the moment it was decided that the king would leave, Humbert had to remain on duty at the headquarters of the Mousquetaires. I therefore had to make all the arrangements for the journey entirely on my own and would be accompanied only by my daughter, who was sixteen, and Aymar, who was eight. I remember that there were many minor difficulties but there is one incident about which I must tell you. I called on the Minister of Finance during the evening to collect my husband's salary, wishing to take it with me. The king was to leave that same evening at midnight. I had known the minister, M. Louis, fairly well for a long time and when I reached his office, I found him in a terrible rage: 'Look,' he said, showing me a hundred or so small casks similar to those in which anchovies are packed. 'I have had these casks made and they each contain ten to fifteen thousand francs in gold. I intended giving one to each member of the bodyguard accompanying the king, but these fine gentlemen refuse to take them, declaring that their duties do not include such tasks.' While he was telling me this, he signed my receipt and I went immediately to collect the money. I took it to my man of business to have it changed into gold. I had asked M. Louis to give me one of the casks of gold in his office, but he had absolutely refused. It was after nine o'clock when I left my man of business and he told me to come back at eleven o'clock, when he would give me the gold he would meantime have procured. I went to say goodbye to Mme d'Hénin, who had also decided to leave. I found her with M. de Lally, in a state of indescribable confusion: packing, gesticulating, urging on her portly friend who left everything half done. Seeing me, she cried: 'Are you not leaving then that you look so calm?'

I went to take my leave of M. de Jaucourt, 'my' minister and to ask him to countersign my passport and provide me with an order for post horses, a necessary precaution for by midnight there might be none available. At last, on the stroke of eleven, I returned to my man of business in the Rue Saint-Anne and he gave me twelve thousand francs in rolls of 'napoleons'. I had hired a cabriolet and, as I got back into the carriage, told the driver to take me home. I was living at No. 6 rue de Varenne. We wanted to take the road through the Carrousel, but on account of the king's departure, it was shut. The coachman therefore drove me along the Rue de Rivoli and just as he was about to cross the Pont Louis XVI, he heard midnight strike. He stopped dead and told me that nothing in the world would persuade him to go one step further. He said he lived at Chaillot, that the gates had to be shut at midnight, asked for his fare and suggested I should continue my journey on foot.

In vain did I use all the eloquence I could muster, promising a magnificent tip if he would take me even as far as a fiacre. He refused. I had to get out, and was terribly afraid. Fortunately, just at that moment, I heard the sound of a carriage. It was a fiacre and, thank Heaven, empty. I rushed towards it, offering the coachman a generous sum to take me home...

I sent immediately for the post horses, but although the journey was official and the permit bore the minister's signature, I had to wait until six o'clock for the two miserable animals to be harnessed to the small barouche which was to carry me, Aymar, my beloved

Cécile and a small Belgian maid whom I had brought up and kept in my service. I spent the long hours of waiting at the window listening for the horses. Never have I been more impatient. Men passed ceaselessly beneath the window, all going in the same direction. Most of them were soldiers, recognisable under the street lamps by the gleam on the waxed cloth covers of their shakos. The weather was fine but the covers hid the white cockade and on them they had pinned small bunches of violets as a rallying sign.

Our journey passed without incident. All we saw was a regiment of cuirassiers cantering in disorderly fashion across the highway near Péronne or Ham. They shouted 'Long Live the Emperor' as they passed. We arrived safe and sound in Brussels, where I took a very small lodging in the Rue de Namur. In Brussels I found all my friends, both Belgian and French. Everyone welcomed me warmly, except such Bonapartists as the families of Trazégnies and Mercy.

I called on the King of Holland, who was in Brussels, and he received me with every courtesy. As we sat on a sofa in what had once been M. de La Tour du Pin's office, he turned to me and said: 'In this salon, I try to discover means to be as well loved as your husband was'. Alas, the poor prince has not succeeded. I spoke to him with some insistence about the future of my son-in-law, who had become one of his subjects and I think it may have been this conversation which paved the way for his diplomatic career. I should like him to remember that.

Mme de Duras, too, had come to Brussels with her daughter, Clara, and her mother, Mme de Kersaint. Mme de Duras and I were spending an evening together when we were told that a 'gentleman' of our acquaintance wished to speak to us. It was added that he did not dare to present himself in our salon as he was not correctly dressed. In those days, strange happenings were no surprise, so we went out on to the landing of the Hôtel de France. There, we found a servant, bespattered with mud, whom Mme de Duras recognised immediately. He opened the door of one of the rooms for us and, on entering, we found ourselves in the presence of the Duc de Berry. He told us that the colonel of a *corps franc,* in other words, of a band of brigands, had stolen his baggage, pillaged his carriage and taken everything, even his shirts. As I knew Brussels very well, he asked me to find him a new wardrobe. I immediately put him in touch with good Mme Brunelle, and was delighted to be able to put such a profitable occasion in her way.

Shortly afterwards, my dear daughter, Charlotte, arrived from

Vienna, travelling alone with her maid and her father's servant. She told me that the Congress had dissolved on learning of Napoleon's landing at Cannes. Everyone had hurried off with all possible speed and the allies, who had been on the verge of becoming enemies, had buried their differences in the face of the common danger. They had only one idea: to make France pay dearly for her welcome to the hero who, by making her so powerful and so glorious, had roused so many enemies against her.

PRINCIPAL MEMBERS OF
MME DE LA TOUR DU PIN'S
FAMILY AND CONNECTIONS
AND THE
IMMEDIATE FAMILY OF THE
MARQUIS DE LA TOUR DU PIN

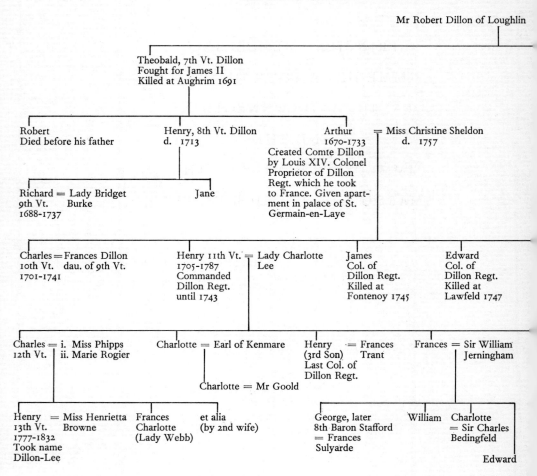

Mr Robert Dillon of Loughlin

Theobald, 7th Vt. Dillon
Fought for James II
Killed at Aughrim 1691

Robert
Died before his father

Henry, 8th Vt. Dillon
d. 1713

Arthur = Miss Christine Sheldon
1670-1733   d. 1757
Created Comte Dillon
by Louis XIV. Colonel
Proprietor of Dillon
Regt. which he took
to France. Given apart-
ment in palace of St.
Germain-en-Laye

Richard = Lady Bridget   Jane
9th Vt.   Burke
1688-1737

Charles = Frances Dillon   Henry 11th Vt. = Lady Charlotte   James   Edward
10th Vt.   dau. of 9th Vt.   1705-1787   Lee   Col. of   Col. of
1701-1741   Commanded   Dillon Regt.   Dillon Regt.
                                Dillon Regt.   Killed at   Killed at
                                until 1743   Fontenoy 1745   Lawfeld 1747

Charles = i. Miss Phipps   Charlotte = Earl of Kenmare   Henry   = Frances   Frances = Sir William
12th Vt. ii. Marie Rogier   (3rd Son) Trant   Jerningham
                                                           Last Col. of
                                                           Dillon Regt.
                                Charlotte = Mr Goold

Henry = Miss Henrietta   Frances   et alia   George, later   William   Charlotte
13th Vt. Browne   Charlotte   (by 2nd wife)   8th Baron Stafford   = Sir Charles
1777-1832   (Lady Webb)   = Frances   Bedingfeld
Took name   Sulyarde
Dillon-Lee   Edward

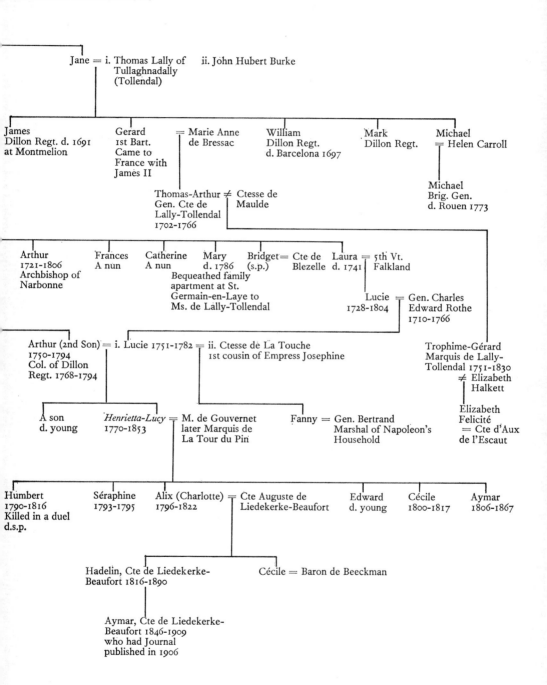

IMMEDIATE FAMILY OF THE MARQUIS DE LA TOUR DU PIN

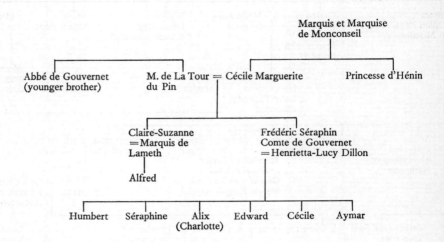

SET IN 12 POINT BARBOU TYPE
AND PRINTED BY W & J MACKAY LTD,
THE TEXT BY LETTERPRESS
AND THE ILLUSTRATIONS BY LITHO
ON GUARD BRIDGE SMOOTH LAID PAPER
BOUND BY W & J MACKAY LTD
USING REDBRIDGE BUCKRAM CLOTH
BLOCKED WITH A DESIGN
BASED UPON A BINDING BY RONDEAU
OF ABOUT 1800–3 WITH THE
FAMILY ARMS ADDED